# THE KIBBUTZ:
# AN ANTHROPOLOGICAL STUDY

# KIBBUTZ, COMMUNAL SOCIETY, AND ALTERNATIVE SOCIAL POLICY SERIES

JEROME S. WEIMAN, *Publisher*

## EDITORIAL ADVISORY BOARD

# THE KIBBUTZ:
# AN ANTHROPOLOGICAL STUDY

**by Israel Shepher**

**FOREWORD**

**by Uri Leviatan**

**Joseph Blasi, Editor-In-Chief**

**VOLUME VIII**
**KIBBUTZ STUDIES BOOK SERIES**
NORWOOD EDITIONS
Norwood, Pennsylvania
1984

**Library of Congress Cataloging in Publication Data**

Shepher, Israel.
  The kibbutz.

  (Kibbutz studies book series ; v. 8)
  Bibliography: p.
  1. Collective settlements--Israel--Case studies.
2. Quality of work life--Israel--Case studies.
I. Title.  II. Series: Kibbutz, communal society, and
alternative social policy series ; v. 8.
HX742.2.A3S52  1983     307.7'76'095694      83-13161
ISBN 0-8482-6464-9 (lib. bdg.)

Manufactured in the United States of America
NORWOOD EDITIONS
Norwood, Pennsylvania 19074

# ACKNOWLEDGMENTS

The study I present in this book was carried out under the auspices of the Bernstein Israeli Research Trust. I am most grateful to the Trustees for giving me the opportunity to undertake my research and for their generous financial support. I am grateful to the Victoria University of Manchester in many ways but in particular for my appointment to a lectureship post which enabled me to continue working on this study while teaching in its Department of Social Anthropology.

I am deeply indebted to the late Professor Max Gluckman for including me in the research scheme. Without his initiative and help I could not have done the research. I was also fortunate in being personally supervised by him during my PhD studies. I owe him a great deal for all the help, theoretical and otherwise, that he gave me.

My thanks go to Professor Emrys L. Peters who as an anthropologist has influenced my thinking, an influence which is probably reflected in my analysis.

I thank Dr. P.T.W. Baxter, Senior Lecturer in Social Anthropology in the University of Manchester, for help which exceeded that which is customary between colleagues.

I express personal gratitude to Professor Emanuel Marx of Tel-Aviv University for the encouragement he has given me throughout my studies, research and work. I am indebted to him for his major part in 'converting' me to social anthropology.

My thanks also go to Dr. Joseph R. Blasi, Director, the Project for Kibbutz Studies, the Center for Jewish Studies, Harvard University, to Mr. M. Topel of Kibbutz Mefalsim, to Mrs. R. Parnass, and to Mr. A. Grunberg, for helping me, in various ways, in preparing this manuscript for publication.

I want to express my thanks to the Social Science Research Committee at Tel-Aviv University and to the Fund for Scientific Publications on Settlement for the financial grants which helped me to extend and elaborate my analysis. My thanks go, in particular, to the members and the authorities of my own home-community of Ayeleth-Hashahar for the moral as well as the material encouragement given to me.

I owe both gratitude and apologies to the people of Hofra.
I owe them gratitude for the friendly manner in which they
accepted me and tolerated my research work.  People were well
aware of the purpose of my long stay yet they exposed the community for research with trust.  It is my return, for their trust,
for which I offer my apologies.  I hope and believe that in
presenting this study, and the material from which it derives,
in which I have been directed only by the conscience residing
in research itself, that I have not betrayed any of their trust.

# C O N T E N T S

The Project for Kibbutz Studies at Harvard University's Center for Jewish Studies is pleased to present Volume 8 of the Kibbutz Studies Book Series. This volume represents the continuation of our cooperation with the Institute for the Study of the Kibbutz and the Cooperative Idea at the University of Haifa, in creating a comprehensive English library on the Israeli kibbutz, and its significance for various fields of research and inquiry.

This current study by anthropologist Israel Shepher, who is a member of the research staff of the University of Haifa Institute, will have a combined interest to historians of the Israeli labor movement, social scientists interested in the kibbutz, and researchers with an interest in the quality of working life and worker control.

## ETHNOGRAPHIC STUDIES OF THE KIBBUTZ

Past ethnographies on the kibbutz have stressed a general description of kibbutz life (Spiro, 1956), an evaluation of the quality of life in the kibbutz with special emphasis on value conflicts and stratification (Blasi, 1979, 1980); more recently, Rayman (1982) has used an ethnographic approach to examine the kibbutz's relationship to the upbuilding of the Jewish State in Israel and the influence of this relationship on internal developments in the kibbutz, and Lieblich (1982) has examined community history and the life history of individuals in another study of one community. The particular strength of Shepher's research is a detailed focus on the sphere of work in the kibbutz. The handful of in-depth ethnographic studies available, and the introductory descriptions that often accompany many research articles on the kibbutz (see Shur, Beit-Hallahmi, Blasi, and Rabin, 1981 for examples) have definitely not succeeded in accurately representing the tremendous diversity between individual kibbutzim. In light of this limitation in the research literature, Israel Shepher's approach represents a significant step forward.

This book comprises a highly specific ethnography of the kibbutz workplace. This includes the most detailed social history yet available in English on a kibbutz, an important discussion of the mutual interactions between this specific kibbutz and its immediate natural and social environments, a series of detailed individual worker case histories in kibbutz agricultural branches, and a careful discussion of the conflicts between the individual and his community in his work branch. This approach of integrating social history with ethnography, and case studies with articulate analyses of social conflicts in the workplace, creates eye-opening continuities in understanding the kibbutz. The connection between unique developments in the early Israeli labor movement and the work behavior of the member today become clearly evident. Under the anthropologist's microscope, this community and its workplaces appear as a comprehensible whole, and not as a detached, arcane description of an isolated sector of social life. While the kibbutz is organized as a collective, there is a complex network of expectations, obligations, conflicts, and conflict resolution between individuals and the community, and among individuals in their individual workplaces.

This is the first time (in my knowledge of the literature) that a detailed description of non-cooperative, and conflictual behavior in a collective, has been presented. Shepher is not, after all, exploring the social position of the worker who is deviant, who has left, or who was thrown out of the kibbutz; but rather, the delicate exchanges which must occur to make a cooperative workplace function on a day-to-day basis.

In this sense, the study responds to a persistent weakness of research on intentional communities and utopian experiments. Often, the general description of egalitarian, democratic, and communitarian structures--in short, the picture of a whole Gemeinschaft--wallpapers over the fact that a community is essentially a collection of small groups, and that a network of conflict and cooperation exists both between every small group and the community, between every individual and the community, and among individuals in small groups themselves. These facts do not deny the importance of structural innovation in communities and workplaces. Rather, they focus our attention on the true story of such cooperative social inventions: namely, individuals can never be homogenized, even with the loftiest ideological goals, the most supportive infrastructural institutions, and the most non-competitive social structures. In fact, inside the new social invention, individuals still identify the strengths and weaknesses of their own social position, and try to negotiate with each other about both maintaining their individual autonomy and accomplishing group goals. If there is any uniqueness in the kibbutz as a social invention, it is not in the fact that these conflicts and negotiations are eliminated. They may be reduced in quantity, but even that is not certain. Their nature and quality are certainly different, because they occur in the context of preserving (or at least attempting to preserve)

egalitarian and democratic rules of the game. It is for social
scientists to help us determine whether these new social arrangements are simply innovative admixtures of the same old social
problems, or whether they really do amount to a step forward
for humanity--not in eliminating individual autonomy, but in
defining it in the context of the human community that both
respects persons and strives for certain definite human values.
The answer to this riddle can only be contained in the kind of
intimate understanding of the kibbutz which Shepher's work
achieves. It is thus fascinating to see that when the market
of competitive capitalism is eliminated, a different type of
labor market still exists; when the control of a faceless
hierarchy or managerial team is avoided, a larger community
must control the worker-managed branches. When "resources
are allocated consciously on an equal basis" (see page 187),
public opinion still maintains itself as a significant determinant in the social organization.

Just as the social historical background of Shepher's work
opposes the notion of social inventions being created "on the
spot" by people who whip up a few ideas, organize a group of
people, and expect to create a social invention as easily as
they might bake a cake, his ethnography refutes the notion
that the kibbutz is a utopian society. The conclusion is
clear: human beings must still struggle for position, even
though their obligations and bonds to each other are transmuted, the reward system is based on cooperation not competition, basic equality of material rights governs their economic
life, and democracy is a concrete norm throughout the community,
not an exercise reserved for textbooks and occasional elections.
The community is not without its problems.

## WORKERS' CONTROL AND THE QUALITY OF WORKING LIFE

If any sphere of the kibbutz has wider outside application, it is the sphere of work. This is because the kibbutz
work branches are organized almost as if they were small sub-
sidiaries of a larger firm, or departments of one company.
Shepher's ethnographic study of the workplace highlights some
significant problems in the study of worker control: 1) What
is the relationship between the democratic context--the commu-
nity--and the democratic workplace? In other words, does an
alternative form of power distribution, if it exists in the
kibbutz workplace, exist because of the larger support of
the kibbutz community? 2) How is individual autonomy
balanced with group control in a situation of workers' con-
trol--that is, where emphasis can be either on the individual
working life of the worker, or democratic autonomy of the

iii

working group? One of the complex issues of worker management that needs to be resolved is that the step towards worker management now constitutes opening the Pandora's box of the individual versus the community conflict in the work organization, whereby the social position of each worker as an individual becomes part of the work agenda. In a certain sense, it may be easier to have someone else work through these issues and conflicts with his or her hierarchical authority, to give to the workers an escape from this type of freedom. This is the usual approach in most work organizations.

Shepher's book points out that when hierarchy is done away with formally, informal hierarchy does <u>not</u> disappear, and workers are faced with an ongoing problem of determining their position in the work organization, distributing the assets of that social position, and strengthening their position, while at the same time preserving a spirit of cooperation. In short, Shepher's analysis of the kibbutz is a poignant response to the plethora of worker-control literature which emphasizes the macro-level of society, and claims that political democracy requires economic democracy. These large-scale claims may be justified, but without further research on the micro-setting to determine just what worker control is, there can be little understanding of what this transition really means. The diffusion of power that occurs in a worker-controlled organization does not automatically translate itself into an harmonious blending of individual and group needs. The challenges to individual development, management, and communication required to resolve this conflict still remain. The particular strength of Shepher's methodology is that he reproduces, with great specificity, how workers in the kibbutz workplace go about resolving these dilemmas. To the extent that such dilemmas have been glossed over in the ideological literature and the social surveys of worker control is the extent to which the findings of this study represent an important resource for practitioners and theoreticians alike.

In 1982, the United Food and Commercial Workers' Union, A & P stores, and the Philadelphia Association for Cooperative Enterprise made history by setting up a Philadelphia-based worker owned grocery store chain to save the jobs of the workers in stores that A & P had earlier closed down. A & P also decided that approximately twenty of the closed grocery stories would be re-opened under a new management decision-making structure, known as a quality of working life program. In addition, for the first time in U.S. history, a union established an investment fund which was set up jointly with A & P, whereby substantial tax deductible contributions totalling 1 percent of gross annual sales per store of the twenty stores to be re-opened under a quality of work life program (without worker ownership) will create a permanent investment fund. Forty percent of the monies generated in this fund would be distributed as an employee benefit program to workers as annual wage bonuses, but the remaining sixty percent would capitalize a perpetual employee ownership investment fund to support future worker buyouts and start-ups of employee-owned and managed enterprises.

What is the relationship between this unexpected social inventiveness in Philadelphia and the kibbutz in Israel? Indeed, the issues we have raised above will become real determinants of success of such initiatives, and the experience of over seventy-five years of the kibbutz movement can be an important resource for these and future ventures in the U.S. and around the world. Shepher's study is an important step in this direction.

Joseph Raphael Blasi
Director, Project for Kibbutz
   Studies, Center for Jewish
   Studies, Harvard University
Editor-in-Chief, Kibbutz Studies
Book Series

## References for Introduction

Blasi, J.R.
   (1979)    "The Quality of Life in a Kibbutz Cooperative Community." Project for Kibbutz Studies Monograph, Cambridge, MA: Harvard University.

Blasi, J.R.
   (1980)    The Communal Future: The Kibbutz and the Utopian Dilemma. Norwood, PA: Norwood Editions.

Lieblich, A.
   (1982)    Kibbutz Makom. New York: Pantheon Books.

Rayman, P.
   (1982)    The Kibbutz Community and Nation-Building. Princeton, NJ: Princeton University Press.

Shur, S., B. Beit-Hallahmi, J.R. Blasi, and A. Rabin
   (1981)    The Kibbutz Bibliography. Norwood, PA: Norwood.

References for Introduction, continued...

Spiro, M.
   (1956)    Kibbutz:  Venture in Utopia.  Cambridge, MA:
                 Harvard University Press (reprinted in 1963
                 in New York:  Schocken Books).

# FOREWORD

## by Uri Leviatan

When outsiders to kibbutz society are asked about drawbacks of kibbutz life, the two most cited problems are:
"restriction on personal autonomy and freedom" and "problems in satisfying unique, personal needs." These two
possible problems of kibbutz life are to a great extent independent from each other but they also share a common denominator. They both focus upon assumed inherent and in-
soluable conflicts between society and its individual members and both are nourished from the assumption that social
organizations which have external, political goals to be
realized--goals which are not directly derived from the immediate expresssions of needs and states of their individual
members--must harness their members' need-satisfaction and
compromise on their members' freedom in order to have them
contribute all their resources for the common goals of the
community.

The assumption about an inherent conflict between individual members and their organizations as concerns their
personal autonomy and freedom, touches also a theoretical
debate among students of organizations and political sociology:  namely, whether or not it is the case that when one
component of a social system gains more control and power,
the other components must have less control and power and
that they must have less autonomy and freedom. This view
has been labeled as the "fixed-pie" view of power in organizations. The alternative case is that it is possible that
all components of a social system may have more or less
power and autonomy at the same time--the "ever-expanding
(or ever shrinking) pie."

An actual empirical investigation of the assumed conflicts and of the theoretical debate is possible in the
kibbutz society, but first I present the ideological organizational principles that the kibbutz society planned to use
in regards to these questions.

The view from inside the kibbutz society is a little
different than from outside. Not that the above two dilemmas
are not central or not relevant, on the contrary they are on
the kibbutz agenda and have been so since the establishment
of the first kibbutzim. But it seems that some of the basic
principles of kibbutz life which were, perhaps, aimed at other

vii

domains of life, are in fact very relevant in handling these problems.

Indeed, the kibbutz society seems to attack these two dilemmas head-on by stating (regarding need satisfaction) that the kibbutz principle of conduct is "to each member according to his or her needs..." which means an emphasis upon the satisfaction of individual needs, and at the same time stating that "from each according to his or her capabilities" (for the furthering of collective goals), which means an emphasis upon the realization of collective goals. The dilemma of power and control seems also to be handled by the establishment of very strong means of public control and authority (by way of public opinion, social cohesiveness, and value internalization) and at the same time by involving consciously, as many members as possible in taking responsibility and authority. This is done by means of the mechanisms of direct democracy and rotation in office-holding and the distribution of offices from different domains of life among as many members as possible (rather than concentrate them in only a few hands).

From the point of view of the principles applied, one may conclude that the uniqueness of the solutions of the kibbutz society to the two possible conflicts between individuals and society (in the domain of need satisfaction and the domain of control, power, and autonomy) is expressed on three fronts:

First, no unsolved conflict is assumed but rather questions are stated regarding possible solutions.

Second, the possible solutions are not in directions of preferring the individual over society nor vice-versa, nor are they solutions of compromise where both individual and society are requested to give in each a little so that the system continues to exist. Rather, the solutions sought after are of the creative kind whereby both parties are satisfied to a maximum and whereby more satisfaction of individual needs contributes to more satisfaction of society's needs and vice-versa, and whereby more power in the hands of individual members would mean more power and authority for the society at large.

Third, the kibbutz society strives to adapt the concrete solutions to changing circumstances and changing historical conditions and demands, while standing by the afore-mentioned principles.

Thus far I stated possible problems and principles that are aimed at their solutions, but do these principles indeed bring about the desired solutions?

Research should tell us whether or not the kibbutz carries out the creative and integrative solutions to the dilemmas posed and also what the nature is of the adaptations the kibbutz makes in its solutions when the situations and conditions change.

Indeed some research into these questions is available, and it corroborates the statements of previous paragraphs about the ways kibbutz society handles these two dilemmas. This had been demonstrated in studies of industry in the kibbutz, in studies of the absorption of the second genera- tion and in studies of consumer behavior and reactions (Tannenbaum, et al., 1974; Leviatan and Rosner, 1980: Leviatan, et al., 1977; and Rosner, et al., 1980). All these studies have shown that conflicts between the individual and the community are minimal because of individual identification with community goals, but also because the solutions are integrative for individual and society alike. The studies have also shown that the "ever-expanding pie" of power is a truer description of reality: the greater the authority the individuals have, the greater the power the community realized in many instances.

Most of these studies were of the survey research type, and did not always give enough insight into the mechanisms and processes through which the desired solutions were achieved. Neither did they describe the actual reality where and how those processes occured. Therefore, their readers who are unfamiliar with kibbutz life missed out on the reality feeling.

Shepher's book touches on the theoretical questions de- scribed here and is therefore another addition to the accumu- lating pile of research that corroborates the major findings of previous research, noted above. Its further contribution to our understanding of how the kibbutz society solves the seemingly conflicting situations between individuals and society in changing environments, is in its ability, being an anthropological study, to describe processes and changes through time. This is a point of view which is lacking in cross-sectional or even longitudinal survey research method- ologies.

As an anthropological study, it vividly brings out the

ix

complete story of the relevant events it describes. It in-
forms uninformed readers of the flavor of reality of kibbutz
life with real instances and real human actors rather than
scores or categories of variables. This work is enriched
tremendously by the fact that Shepher is not only an anthropologist, but also a kibbutz member for many years.
The deep familiarity of Shepher with the social milieu in
which he had worked has produced a study that is quite authen-
tic in its descriptions, insightful in its interpretations,
and above all, a work that gives the reader a grasp of kibbutz
life with an uncanny portrayal of its components in just
the correct proportions. This has been found lacking in
some previous publications on the kibbutz, carried out by
researchers not having the same intimate familiarity of kibbutz life that Shepher has.

## References for Foreword

Leviatan, U.
    (1980)    "What Do Israelis Think of Kibbutz Life and Why."
                Haifa: Institute for the Study of the Kibbutz and
                the Cooperative Idea, University of Haifa.

Leviatan, U., E. Orchan, and A. Avnat
    (1977)    "Increasing Retention Among Kibbutz Born Members."
                Haifa: Institute for the Study of the Kibbutz and
                the Cooperative Idea, University of Haifa.

Leviatan, U., and M. Rosner
    (1980)    Work and Organization in Kibbutz Industry.
                Norwood, PA: Norwood Editions.

Rosner, M., Y. Gluck, and A. Avnat
    (1980)    "Satisfaction with Consumption in the Kibbutz as
                Affected by Economic, Social, and Value Factors."
                Haifa: Institute for the Study of the Kibbutz and
                the Cooperative Idea, University of Haifa.

Tannenbaum, A., B. Kavcic, M. Rosner, M. Vianello, and G. Wieser
    (1974)    Hierarchy in Organizations. San Francisco:
                Jossey-Bass.

# CHAPTER I

## The Problem

This study is an enquiry into the relative independence of
the individual in a society committed to collectivism. Collectivism, or a degree thereof, whether as an ideal or theory or
whether in practice, may vary from one such society (or organization, or association) to another. Collective and collectivist
social units may thus be posited on a continuum which represents
degrees of collectivity. The commitment of the Israeli kibbutz
to collectivism is to an all-pervasive conception of it and the
degree of collectivism practiced in the kibbutz is large, by any
standard.

In any social reality, where human beings interact, communicate and maintain relationships, the distinction, or separation, or indeed - the autonomy of the individual from the 'social
whole' is relative. Even Simmel's ideal-type of the 'isolated
individual' presupposes relationships with a 'society' without
which the very meaning and the very analysis of 'isolation' and
'freedom' cannot be considered (Simmel, 1950: 118-122). Such
relationships imply in principle only a relative degree of isolation or freedom. Social relationships imply that there is some
control.

The kibbutz society poses the problem of the individual's
autonomy in an acute perspective. The kibbutz is defined (by the
Collective Association Bill, Chapter 13, par. 174, 1971; see
Daniel, 1975: 89) as "an association for settlement which is [at
the same time] a separate village; that maintains a collective
society of its members; that is organized on the tenets of public
ownership of property, of self-labor [i.e., avoidance of the use
of other people's labour] and of equality and collectivism in all
areas of production, consumption and education... The kibbutz is
also entitled to have, in addition to the said tenets... [tenets
of] way-of-life" (1971, par. 175). The perspective is acute
because the kibbutz is, according to this definition, a corporate
organization, which applies the collective tenets within one social
unit to a variety of areas as property, productive economy, consumption and education, it is imbued with, and committed to, a
collectivist-communal ideology. These features are anchored,
though incompletely, in State law (CAB, 1971).

It is hoped that a study of the relative autonomy of the
individual in a collectivist community which embraces a 'total way

1

of life' (Martindale, 1964: 61-87) may help in clarifying issues
pertaining to similar theoretical problems in societies whose
degrees of collectivity and communality (or: collectivism and
communalism) may be similar and/or different.

Whether one takes as a point of departure the professed
values of the kibbutz, or looks at the institutional structure
to which the former is related and which claims to express it,
or examines individual and societal relations to means of production and to allocation of resources, one is bound to realize
that the kibbutz puts public-collective considerations before
considerations pertaining to the individual.  There is a commitment to the primacy of society/community.

The problem can now be defined thus:  How is the autonomy
of the individual assured in a social unit which virtually controls all property, means of production, and access to consumable
goods; which gives rise to powerful mechanisms of social control,
and which elevates the primacy of collectivity and collective
considerations into an ideal?  Is it assured by the very set of
values which publicly extols collectivism?  Is autonomy accepted
(normatively and/or de facto) and recognized in the realm of
economics and production?  Is it established in law?

This question admits the existence of tensions between individual and society as distinct entities (see Daniel, 1975: 88).
That is to say, in addition to the study of relations and relationships between social actors, relations between the individual
member of a social unit and the unit per se can be examined.  The
social unit itself is perceived both as an entity distinct from
any member thereof and from the sum of its members, and as the
aggregate collectivity of all its members.  In principle, recognition of the distinction between an individual and his/her social
unit does not imply that the two are necessarily, and permanently,
in conflict.  Harmony may prevail as well.  Harmony and voluntary
mutual adjustment are to be found in practice and are emphasized
in the kibbutz literature.  Nevertheless, being distinct entities,
tension between the two exists potentially and is present in the
background of their relations.  Incidentally, I would suggest here
that harmonious relations, tensions or conflict, can co-exist in
social realities.  In analyzing one such relation one should not
overlook the existence of others.

The sociologist looks for a relation between two or more
variables, actors, phenomena, institutions, processes or the like.
Talmon-Garber (1956, 1964, 1965), for example, posited the kibbutz and the family within the kibbutz community as two distinct
institutions, and examined the changing relations between the two.
Cohen (1966) suggests a model in which two inherent principles of

2

kibbutz culture, namely, progress and communality, determine the development and the changes of this society.[1] The present work examines how an actor, an individual with his sociological pro erties, encounters a corporate 'social whole' to which he belongs as a full member. Specifically, I study an aspect of relations between the two, the aspect of autonomy. An observer of kibbutz life must reach the conclusion that the individual member posses- ses a considerable degree of autonomy within the kibbutz. In the negative sense of the notion, the individual is able to resist control and pressures which are considered in the kibbutz culture and by his fellow members as excessive encroachments on his social rights or status. Stated positively, autonomy permits the indi- vidual to make choices, within the limits of collective life and economy, as to type of work, occupation, specialized skills, job, company, leisure activities, social and communal activities, and to pursue intellectual and cultural interests. In short: the individual member of the kibbutz does achieve considerable auton- omy in his society.

My point of departure is the individual. It is possible, of course, to approach this problem from another point of view, that of the group, the community, the 'whole.' Thus Bowes (1975), who analyses material sometimes similar to that presented in this book, often chooses to do so in terms of the 'whole,' of the 'society.' For instance, while I try to locate resources which serve the individual in establishing his social position in the sphere of labor, Bowes pays attention to the distribution of the same resources throughout the community thus affecting the struc- ture of power in the entire kibbutz-community.

Indeed, the individual's autonomy affects both the individ- ual and the community. It affects the kibbutz itself and its functioning with this approach, so autonomy can be analyzed in func- tional terms: it can be regarded as functional or dysfunctional, or it can be examined as to what the aspects and situations are in which autonomy may prove functional or dysfunctional. This approach is manifestly one which takes as point of departure the 'whole' - the kibbutz, the organization. The problem of the individual's auton- omy would thus appear to be that of its "functional contribution to... [the] system" (Katz, 1968: 34).

Such an approach is of course plausible. Katz's analysis of autonomy in complex organizations (Katz, 1968) offers a pene- trating insight into the theoretical problem of the individual's autonomy in organizations in general and also deals with the impact of this autonomy on the organization. Many of Katz's theoretical suggestions are relevant and applicable to the analysis of the kibbutz, though the kibbutz, according to the above definition, is of course more complex even than the organizations discussed by him.

3

Katz's main argument is that in order for an organization to function properly it must leave a degree of indeterminance within its prescribed rules of behavior, that is, a degree of autonomy for the individual. Thus autonomy is not only tolerated, but is structured, though differentially (according to categories and echelons of actors and to other criteria) into the social arrangement, the organization. He deals with the relative independence in the organization.

Adopting Katz's point of departure would have led me to concentrate on a problem somewhat different from the one I have set for the present analysis. I have no space to go on into the course, or dimension, suggested by Katz, fruitful as it would have been. I do think, however, that not only the member's accommodation, commitment and devotion to, or even compliance and conformity with, the kibbutz should be studied systematically, but also the effect of the member's autonomy on the kibbutz.

As for the 'contribution' of autonomy to the kibbutz, I do not doubt that the individual's autonomy does 'contribute' to the functioning of the kibbutz: assuming that the kibbutz is a unified, single system, the contribution is sometimes functional, sometimes dysfunctional. Autonomy can also be regarded as both when it is examined contextually and situationally. My distinction between the kibbutz as an entity apart from its constituent members and the kibbutz as a joint aggregate of individuals, offers some insight into this problem (contribution to the 'whole') as well. Autonomy of the individual member within his own commune may indeed be conceived in different terms when each of the above facets of the kibbutz serves as the point of departure for the analysis. Furthermore, not only autonomy in general, but each autonomous act may elicit different responses from a member in his different roles of (1) a person committed to the primacy of the kibbutz as a distinct entity and (2) of a member of a community of individuals. For the analyst too, the definition of the 'functional contribution' to one of these facets does not require the same definition for the other.

When the 'whole' (the organization, the system, the community) is the focus of the discussion, autonomy of the constituent member can be analyzed in terms of 'necessity' for this 'whole.' Therefore autonomy is defined as basically functional. Even if the individual uses his autonomy not strictly in accordance with what seems to be the immediate interests of his particular organization, autonomy is an inseparable part of the organization's functioning. However, when the focus is on the member, autonomy is analyzed in terms of strategy of the individual. In Katz's terms (1968: 31), the member 'achieves' autonomy vis-a-vis his relevant whole, be it the kibbutz, the branch team, or his fellow workers. His community

4

of fellows 'ascribes' the right to this autonomy to him and to every member of the kibbutz. This 'ascribed autonomy' (Katz, 1968) gives substance to the realization of the community of equals. The individual's autonomy may indeed be as integral to the kibbutz structure as the kibbutz's authority over and claim to allegiance of the individual (this problem, as stated, falls outside the scope of this book), but it must be achieved. My analysis focuses on how the individual achieves relative independence in one of the spheres of kibbutz life.

The individual derives his resources for independence from various institutional spheres and from various relationships. It would be far too much to cover even a few of these in one book. I choose then to focus my analysis on phenomena of relative independence in one sphere, the sphere of labor in the kibbutz.

I shall identify the sociological properties, within the sphere of labor, which provide the individual with a degree of independence from the fellow-members and from the collective as such. These properties are distributed among the entire membership (in the relevant sector of the kibbutz economy). I shall discuss them without going into the hierarchical and managerial differentiation. I do so because the latter does not apply to all the individual members.

My interest in the constituent elements of social position in the sphere of work is hardly accidental. It is probably an outcome of my studies in the Department of Social Anthropology in the University of Manchester which often stressed the importance of economic and political variables in social-anthropological analysis. As a student, I was impressed by Professor E.L. Peters' re-analysis of his own study of a Lebanese village (Peters, 1963) in which he searched for sociological components of power in the community (Peters, 1972). I was impressed both on the theoretical and methodological level. This theoretical interest may have influenced my study, both while in the field and in the present work. It probably lies behind the choice of the central problem.

In the tradition of many social-anthropological studies, the analysis of behavior and social relationships in economic and other fields, follows the presentation of ecological conditions. My training in the tradition has probably influenced my choice of the central problem, the weight given in the analysis to certain variables and spheres (at the expense of others), the general theoretical approach and the structure of the presentation of material and argument.

The analysis seeks to identify the sociological variables which help the individual become autonomous in the spheres of labor

5

and production. These are to be found mainly in processes of
settling on the land, in the development of the kibbutz economy,
and in structural characteristics of the kibbutz itself. These
elements are treated as independent variables. I am aware that
I could have chosen othe: independent variables. Spiro, to whom
I often refer in this book, states that

> to have begun this monograph in the usual fashion, with
> a description of the natural environment or of the sub-
> sistence economy of Kiryat Yedidim [the kibbutz he studied]
> would do violence to the inner meaning of its culture...
> Kiryat Yedidim, to be sure, is an agricultural village con-
> sisting of men and women who inhabit a common geographic
> area and who make their living by tilling the soil in a
> cooperative fashion. But Kiryat Yedidim is also - and
> primarily - a fellowship of those who share a common
> faith and who have banded together to implement that
> faith. To live in Kiryat Yedidim means to become a
> member of a kibbutz... that is, a person who is dedicated
> to the social, economic, and national ideals for which
> the kibbutz stands. (Spiro 1956: 10-11)

Spiro thus suggests that one analyzes events and patterns
of events, processes and social relationships in the kibbutz primarily in terms of their relations to the values of the kibbutz
common faith. The researcher of the kibbutz is called upon to
study behavior in the kibbutz primarily as a reflection of the
kibbutz's professed ideology. Social actions in the kibbutz,
patterns of relationships, and perhaps the individual's conduct,
not to mention the behavior of the kibbutz as a whole, thus appear
to express in concrete terms ideals and meanings rooted in the
kibbutz ideology and culture. In aiming to comprehend kibbutz
life, the task of the researcher would then be to disclose and
unveil the meaning of action and relationships as these are related to the kibbutz's ideological tenets, and to study the degree
of congruence of the former with the latter.

Values indeed play an important part in social action and
are important in forming and changing social relationships. That
is, values everywhere are components, or ingredients of behavior.
In the kibbutz, values - particularly as related to its institutional organization - ostensibly have a significant role. But
by granting this, one should not overlook other inputs which together make social action and relationships. Ea . of these inputs
can serve as a pivot around which the discussion is developed.
Ideology and faith are important such inputs. A student of the
kibbutz, of its history, the various movements and their mergers
and splits, of various youth movements affiliated to the kibbutz,
of the arguments over size of community, over the relative impor-

6

tance of agriculture and industry, and over education, and the like - would realize the significance of the ideological input. The uniqueness of the kibbutz probably influences the student so as to attach paramountcy to ideology. But surely no one input can determine exclusively behavior and reality. A variety of inputs go into behavior and relationships and their relative importance as well as the interplay between them, is open for assessment. The assessment of the weight of inputs undetermined in advance is one of the subject's fascinations and premises. Any given 'social reality' can be better understood when viewed from various angles.

I believe that the problem I have chosen to discuss in this book, congruent as it is with my theoretical interest at the time of the analysis, will be presented and analyzed in an approach appropriate for its formulation and study.

Incidentally, (a) I assume in this book that the basic ideological and moral postulates of the kibbutz are known and need no particular discussion; (b) I make references to these postulates throughout the analysis when this is necessary; and (c) the problem of contrasting official ideological postulates with social realities or of measuring discrepancies between them, a problem the choice of which would indeed necessitate the discussion of these postulates as the background for the analysis, falls outside my chosen subject-matter.

## The scope of the discussion

Because of lack of space I concentrate on the sphere of labor only. I further reduce the scope by concentrating on economic enterprises in the kibbutz. By doing so I exclude from the discussion those members who work outside the kibbutz (in cooperative regional enterprises and organizations of which the kibbutz is a constituent member, in or on behalf of the national kibbutz movement, in other jobs away from home with the consent of the kibbutz). I also omit from the discussion the following categories of work within the kibbutz, or refer to them only where necessary: services to the agricultural sector (such as garage, repairs, maintenance jobs, stores, etc.), services to members (the communal kitchen and dining hall, clothing store, laundry, shoe-store, infirmary, etc.), and services to children and education. As industry in the kibbutz I studied was only just beginning, I omit non-agricultural economic activities. Thus, this study deals mainly with the agricultural sector of the kibbutz. This prevents me from making comparisons with other sectors, an undertaking which could be of considerable benefit to the present analysis and to the understanding of the position of the individual in the sphere of labor in the kibbutz in general.

I also usually refrain from discussing agricultural workers who are not members of the kibbutz. These are teenage children of the kibbutz, occasional groups of teenagers from city schools or from Israeli or overseas youth movements, temporary residents in the kibbutz, and hired workers. This exclusion limits my ability to contrast the position of the member-worker with that of each of these categories of workers in the agricultural sector itself. I am left, then, with the member of the kibbutz who works in the agricultural-produce sector of the kibbutz. I therefore consider this work to be only a partial study of the sphere of labor in the kibbutz.

## 'Extreme' cases

For the great majority of members, in most situations, the properties which determine social position discussed in this book are obvious and are not usually discussed. Their presence (or absence) is usually recognized by the people concerned whenever an issue arises. In order to expound their full significance, it will sometimes be necessary to view these properties from a negative angle, i.e., to analyze the rare situations where a given property is absent from, or is undeveloped in, a member's position. By using this method I should be able to expound the significance of the presence of a given sociological property for the position of a member. I present a few such unusual cases in order to sharpen the argument.

## Attitudes and norms

This study is not based on research into attitudes, but on material accumulated through 'participant observation.' I worked daily in various agricultural (as well as other) branches of the kibbutz with members and other workers. I focused my observation on behavior and practice in agricultural work which obviously included verbal attitudes of people. Those attitudes were expressed in a variety of situations, which were markedly different from those that could have occurred during structured research. I shall incorporate some of the attitudes, unstructured as they are and sometimes situational as they are, into the analysis. Given that the expressed attitudes, or norms, are neither the main tool of analysis nor its point of departure, they are an important aspect of the behavior studied. Again, due to limitations of space, I cannot describe fully, let alone analyze, the wealth of material on attitudes and values and norms (which sometimes conflicted with one another) that I have studied in the field. Nor can I devote much space to the study of the relation of these norms to actual behavior in varying situations. However, as they constitute an aspect of actors' behavior, I shall refer to them without studying their inner structure, logic or consistency.

My use of the term 'norm' requires some clarification. I am aware of a tendency to identify 'norms' with abstract, detached, constructs, the relevance of which to actual behavior is at best partial. I cannot be concerned here with theoretical discussion of norms, their meaning, and effects on behavior nor of the interrelationships there may be between them. Influenced by early studies (see Bierstedt, 1963: 220-224; Chinoy, 1961: 22-25) I follow the definition of a 'norm' as a guidance to specific behavior in specific circumstances.

## Use of Hebrew terms

Two notes on the use of Hebrew and kibbutz terms: (i) I use Hebrew terms mainly when I feel that they have a special meaning, which would be lost in translation. Whenever I first use a Hebrew term a translation and a brief explanation are given.

I try to transliterate Hebrew words as closely as possible to accord both with actual pronunciation by the present-day Israelis and with the Hebrew spelling as scientifically transliterated into the English. These two practices do not always coincide, there are some inconsistencies.

(ii) I translate a few kibbutz idiomatic terms, which mostly relate to public offices and roles, in order to avoid conveying misleading notions about the social nature of the office and its holder. The closer the term to the 'vernacular,' the closer I hope to bring to the reader its meaning. But there is also another consideration. The kibbutz-commune has some unique features. Its social and organizational systems affect the range and complexity of the communal agencies and the distribution of power and authority in the community. Thus the public offices are endowed with meanings which differ from the equivalent offices in extra-kibbutz communities and economic enterprises. Rather than using terms such as 'managers' or 'directors' and then qualify them, I use English translation of the kibbutz terms.

I call the group of founders of the kibbutz which I studied The Kvutza. The members of the kibbutz still refer to their kibbutz as 'The Kvutza.' I call the national kibbutz movement with which The Kvutza is affiliated 'The Movement.' Similarly the youth movement within which many members were recruited to The Kvutza is called the 'Youth Movement.'

9

Finally, my statements and conclusions apply specifically to the kibbutz I studied. Kibbutz settlements vary in location, in history, in affiliation to national movements and political bodies, in size of the community, in magnitude of the economy, and in demographic structure; some have introduced industry while others have not, some employ more outside workers (in absolute numbers or in percentage of their own labor force) than others, and so forth. However, having knowledge of other kibbutz settlements, I suggest that given similar conditions to those of the community I studied, this analysis, as a guiding idea, would be applicable beyond the boundaries of this specific community. Indeed, I do sometimes use material from another kibbutz when I am satisfied that I am able to trace similar patterns of problems or processes.

NOTES

1. Two well-known anthropological studies take this approach:
   Leach (1954) and Turner (1957).  Both construct a dynamic
   model of the societies they studied, in which relations
   between two inherent principles of social organization are
   examined.

# CHAPTER II

## ENVIRONMENTAL AND HISTORICAL BACKGROUND

### a. The Valley

The content of this book consists of a theoretical analysis
of ethnographical data, the bulk of which was collected in a kibbutz which I shall call Hofra. It is generally expected in social-
anthropology that when the 'end product' of field-research is presented to the reader a detailed report of ecological data be introduced. The intimate relations between the 'society,' a section
thereof, or the community studied and its ecological environment
need no elaboration; the relevance of the latter to the social
anthropological analysis of the former is evident. If I do not
follow this rule to the letter it is because the detailed presentation and analysis of the ecological data is not essential to the
argument. I shall therefore introduce here only data relevant to
and necessary for the analyses of both individual cases and of the
general argument. For a more detailed description of the field
the reader is referred to the relevant chapter in my PhD. thesis
(1972) which is also based on a study of Kibbutz Hofra.

Hofra is located in an area which might well be termed the
Citrus Belt of Israel (for further specification, see Orni and
Efrat, 1966: 44). It is a valley which stretches from Mount Carmel
in the north to the Gaza Strip in the south, and forms an extension
of the Mediterranean sea-shore. Baldwin (1972) and Abarbanel (1974)
describe the area as a developed agricultural region and the center
of citrus farming. The communities they studied (also under the
auspices of the Bernstein Israeli Research Trust) are in the same
valley (which I shall call The Valley) and the reader is advised to
consult their monographs for ecological details.

Climate. The climate of The Valley, being moderate throughout most of the year, is suited to citrus farming and to other
crops such as subtropical and deciduous plants and vines.

Soil. The soil varies according to location. Several dunes
have thrust inland from the sea-shore through the ravines made by
rivers near their mouths. Three crests of another soil-composition,
known as kurkar stretch from north to south. This perforated but
solid rock is composed basically of particles of lime in the chains
of dunes. The average width of a chain of the kurkar hills is some
5 kilometers. The columns of these hills determine the wavy shape
of the general view of The Valley.

The eastern crest is covered by a layer of red sand called
hamra (Arabic: red). The hamra's most important attribute is its

12

retention of water as compared to the capillacious white sand and the absorbent kurkar. Water thus remains in the upper layer of the ground and is available for plant growth. It is particularly suitable for citrus farming.

The kurkar crests determine the morphological structure of The Valley: two longish narrow valleys lie between the central and the eastern crests and between the eastern crest and the mountains. These valleys resemble gutter-spouts and in fact are called 'spouts.' Each spout is covered by the rich soil eroded from the mountains. This humus alluvium is 'heavier' in composition than the white sand and is composed of rough particles and organic substances. Hofra's land is concentrated mostly on the hilly areas of the eastern, hamra-covered, kurkar crest and extends towards and into the Eastern Spout. Another important plot of land is situated at the edge of the Central Spout. Thus, Hofra benefits from some of each of the different categories of soil in the Valley. During various stages of its development it has been able to grow wheat and barley, fodder, vegetables, flowers and flower-bulbs, deciduous crops, citrus, sub-tropical trees, vines, cotton, and bananas. Indeed there is hardly an agricultural crop in Israel which the settlers of Hofra have not been able to plant. Some crops, to be sure, yield better harvests in other regions and have been abandoned, but the Valley is undoubtedly a fertile region.

Water. Sources of water are not limited to the local rain. The region uses its own underground sources, particularly those in deep wells in the Eastern Spout (excessive use of wells in the western Valley, near the sea-shore, has led to infiltration of sea-water into wells in this area). Pipes have been laid westward so that clear water can be pumped into over-used wells. The National Water Carrier Galilee-Negev, which runs along the Eastern Spout, is also utilized. Hofra itself uses its own wells and purchases water from the national company, Mekoroth.

According to Hofra's Economic Plan for 1969/70, the sources of water (in annual quantities) are:

| | |
|---|---|
| Own pumping | 1,051,000 cu. meters |
| Mekoroth | 538,000 cu. meters |
| Surface water[1] | 700,000 cu. meters |
| Total | 2,289,000 cu. meters |

Advantages of having water close to the surface, however, are counterbalanced by excessive accumulation of water during heavy rains in the Valley itself or in the mountains. Since the river-beds are both narrow and shallow, they cannot channel the

13

large quantities of water which flow into them from the tributaries, and flooding inevitably ensues. In the past the spouts
were flooded. Dunes which moved into the mouths of the rivers
and filled them with sand coalesced with soil composed largely
of clay to create, together with alluvial soil carried from the
mountains, floods and swamps. Consequently, during periods of
unstable or underdeveloped governments large areas of the Valley
were covered by swamps. The latter, in turn, in addition to
being incompatible with systematic agricultural development, constituted sources of malaria and misery. Patches of land near the
tributaries of the nearby rivers into which swamp water used to
infiltrate have, in the course of time, undergone changes in their
composition. Plots of 'heavy soil' are scattered in the Valley
thereby enabling the farmers to vary the range of crops. Hofra
has exploited these plots (one of which is called 'Heavy Soil')
to grow vegetables, artichokes, bananas, grain crops, vines and,
recently, cotton.

Flora. These crops (and those mentioned above) have not
always been abundant in the region. Toren (1955: 31) presents a
concise list of some hundred plants, some of them groups of plants,
in his study of the natural flora, but the natural, original flora
has been in retreat and has diminished as a result of the introduction of modern cultivation into the region during the last few
decades. Modern human settlement has disrupted the previous equi-
librium in nature by introducing new species and by changing conditions for both flora and fauna.

History. The Valley has witnessed, so to speak, the lengthy
history of Palestine and Israel and even the most concise historical review of the region would prove to be too lengthy for the
study.[2] Although the history and development of Hofra cannot be
divorced from the conditions and history of the entire region,
only the essentials of the Valley's history can be introduced here.

The Valley may be historically characterized as a region of
transit: roads led via the Valley to Syria and Mesopotamia in the
north and to Egypt in the south, to the sea on the west and the
Arabian Desert in the east. Successive armies moved along these
roads, two of which (running parallel to each other) were known as
Via Maris. Nowadays two main roads run south to north, one alongside the sea-shore and the other crossing the central hilly area
of the Valley. Less important are the 'woof' west to east roads,
some of which run across the middle of Palestine.

As far as the ethnic and political history of the Valley is
concerned, suffice it to note that successive peoples have settled
in the region and successive nations have dominated it.

Evidence collected from documents of the 19th century[3] portrays a picture of neglect, swamps, poverty, and under-population. This state of affairs followed a long period of virtual desolation initially brought about deliberately by the Mameluke sultan and his Turkish horsemen centuries earlier. Two Bedouin tribes roamed the region where Hofra is now located. Traditional sources of livelihood (wages paid by the Pasha) having been discontinued in the 19th century, the Bedouin resorted to banditry.

The Valley, in the strict sense of the word (Hofra's region) was owned by three family groups, all of whom lived abroad, when they sold the land to the Jews in the late 1920's. The local tenants were squatters. Most of them lived in tents or in mud-huts. In 1929 the Bedouin numbered some 850 people and they cultivated approximately one-tenth of the land which was sold to the Jews. Another part of the land was cultivated by fallaheen from a large village to the east. During the last decade of their residence in the Valley, the Bedouin earned their living by herding sheep and cattle, selling manure to Jewish farmers, and working for the latter.

The Eastern Spout has a different history. Parallel to the Jewish settlement, which began in the Valley in the 1880's, Arab settlers descended from the mountains into the Valley. Old villages abandoned for generations were re-settled, and scores of small villages were established. The eastern part of the Valley was gradually populated while the swamps and the sandy areas were left to the Bedouin groups.

The Zionist settlement. Zionist efforts to purchase the land of the region were protracted. The procedure of the transaction was long and complex.[4] Although the transaction was made in 1929, it was not completed until 1933 and negotiations with one of the family groups continued until 1940.

The purchase of the land of the Valley near Hofra coincided with a recession in other Zionist activities. The Jewish agricultural settlements as a whole, based on mixed farming, suffered setbacks owing to inexperience, successive droughts and livestock diseases. Owing to the world economic depression, Zionist funds fell behind commitments. The economic crisis of the time resulted in large-scale emigration from the country and a virtual cessation of immigration. The new 'wave of immigration' (Aliya),[5] commencing in 1929, was followed by political unrest and bloody rioting by Arabs. The general attitude and policy of the Mandatory Government towards Zionist activities and policies changed for the worse. The Zionist Movement, suffering from the combination of all these factors, felt an urgent necessity to renew immigration and further settlement. It was hoped that citrus farm-

15

ing and a new settlement project would afford a partial solution to the difficulties encountered.

Palestinian citrus had sold well in overseas markets. New citrus-groves were planted, mainly in the Judean Lowland and the Valley. Jewish workers in the agricultural 'colonies,'[6] employed mainly in citrus farming at the time, were attracted by the idea of 'self settlement.' The idea, controversial as it was at its outset, was endorsed and even encouraged by the Labor Movement. Workers were prepared to establish their own enterprises, cultivate the plots allotted to them on land provided by the Jewish National Fund (JNF) and invest savings in the project. Groups of workers settled in the vicinity of the big 'colonies.'

The purchase of the Valley provided the Jewish Agency with an area ideal for intensive farming with a plentiful supply of water and soil suitable for citrus cultivation. The settlement plan in the Valley was designed for settlers of different economic categories: workers, middle-class people, and a wealthier section. A plantation company allotted portions of land to the middle-class settlers and, like the JNF in its project for draining the swamps, employed worker-settlers and the newly-planted citrus groves. The founders of Hofra as well as of other kibbutz and moshav[7] settlements, were employed in these jobs.

Of the 30,800 dunams purchased in the Valley, 27,500 were suitable for farming. They were allocated to 1,920 families, i.e., approximately 20.8 dunams per unit. The variety of soil in the area affected the distribution of plots of land to the constituent farming units. An effort was made to allocate a variety of soil to each unit so that each farming unit would obtain an equal share of the different types of soil (Halperin, 1957: 18). Kibbutz settlements such as Hofra were allotted plots in different parts of the Valley.

Altogether, the land was allotted to 11 'middle-class' settlements, 8 Histadrut (General Federation of Labor) affiliated (4 moshav and 4 kibbutz) settlements, and 4 settlements affiliated to other workers' organizations. The purchase of a neighboring area, the Wadi, enabled Zionist agencies to complement land quotas and allocate land to new groups. Prior to the establishment of the State of Israel 27 villages were founded, mostly in the western and the central areas of the Valley.

The Arab-Israeli war in 1948-49 left large areas of the region abandoned, mostly in the Eastern Spout. The Israelis pushed the front line eastwards, away from their villages in the Valley. This front line became the Israel-Jordan Armistice Line, later to be regarded as the de facto border between Israel and

16

the Hashemite Kingdom of Jordan until 1967.  Very few Arab inhabitants remained in a handful of villages.  A new process of
settlement followed.  Most of the new villages are moshav settlements.  Three transitory camps for new immigrants were established,
later to become permanent residential quarters.  Farmers of the
Valley, kibbutz and moshav members alike, as well as near-by
urban enterprises, have employed workers of the one-time transitory camps.

At the time of the research (1970) there were 48 communities
(or settlements) in the Valley.  Hofra is one of them.  They are
constituent members of the Regional Council, the municipal authority of the Valley.  Four Arab villages joined the Regional Council
in 1969.

b.  The Kvutza: historical background

The Kvutza

The history of Kibbutz Hofra can best be understood against
the broader background of contemporary Jewish settlement[8] in
Palestine.  However, as in the discussion of the ecological conditions, I must condense my review as there is no space for
lengthy description and/or comment.  Therefore I shall have to
refrain from discussing subjects, relevant though I consider
them to be, which have no direct bearing on Hofra's specific
history.

Zionist historiography numbers six 'waves of immigration'
which have successively contributed to the modern emergence and
growth of the Jewish community of Palestine (later Israel) since
the 1880's.  The founders of Hofra emigrated from Europe with
the Third (1919-1922) and the Fourth Aliya (1923-1927).[9]  They
had personally experienced as had many of their fellow immigrants,
the First World War and the Russian Revolution; they had witnessed
the pogroms against the Jews which took place during the civil
war in Russia and warfare between the states of Eastern Europe;
they had been familiar with and influenced by the social and
political ideologies of the time, particularly those of socialism, though they did not believe in the messianic destiny of
socialism for the Jews and for Judaism unless it were related
to Zionism.  They had also been acquainted with Zionist organizations and some of them belonged to the youth movements which
were a new phenomenon in Jewish public life.  The Zionist World
Organization, having secured the recognition of Palestine as a
National Home for Jews from the new Mandatory Government, and
the Labor-affiliated 'Hehalutz' (the Pioneer), organized and
channelled immigration of individuals and of groups.

17

In Palestine, the founders of Hofra joined the newly-established Histadrut (General Federation of Labor), itself founded jointly by members of the Second and Third Aliya. This organization has combined activities in the fields of trade unionism, ownership and management of economic and financial corporations, health services, education, mutual aid and community work, and politics. Within the framework of the Histadrut, of most importance of the time were the institutions of the Agricultural Centre (Central Executive) under whose authority all settlement (Hityashvut), hired agricultural labor and the search for agricultural employment were organized, and the Department of Public Works, which dealt mainly with the construction and paving of roads.

Harsh conditions, difficulties in adapting to physical labor and to a new environment and different climate, frequent unemployment, the transition to different culture and language, loneliness and other hardships, all gave rise to the need for co-operation or some sort of collectivity. This need, in part a consequence of the youth of the people concerned, was further stimulated by contemporary ideas favoring collectivism, and collective ideologies, to produce the organization both of the kvutza (later to be more commonly known as kibbutz) and the moshav,[10] and also the conception of the Histadrut as an 'Incipient Workers' Society.'

The degree of collective organization varied. Members of some groups undertook certain work collectively but did not share income. In others, members did not necessarily work together, but shared their earnings. Some groups were temporary in nature, their members dispersing once the specific undertaking had been accomplished. On the other hand, there were groups which strove to remain intact throughout their peregrinations across the country, and there were those which emphatically wished eventually to become a kvutza. And lastly, there were established kvutza-communities scattered across the country. One may perhaps define the group that wished to become a kvutza, i.e., (in contemporary terms) to settle on the land, establish its own economy and develop a permanent collective organization as an incipient kvutza. The incipient kvutza usually had to wait for the purchase of its land (mainly by the Zionist agencies, such as the JNF) and in the meantime its members made a living by working as hired laborers (when work was available) in towns and 'colonies.'

Whereas the Third Aliya witnessed the Zionist drive in Palestine set in motion at a hitherto unknown pace and scale in hityashvut (settlement), immigration, purchase of land, and establishment of new institutions and organizations (among them

18

the Labor Histadrut and its agencies), the Fourth Aliya was beset
by numerous crises.  Shortage of jobs resulted in mounting unemployment.  Public works by the government either came to an end
or were reduced.  The Jewish agricultural economy could not support the thousands of new immigrant workers and central Zionist
funds were insufficient to finance further economic expansion
and particularly expansion of agricultural settlement.

In 1924, in an effort to curb the growing unemployment,
the Agricultural Centre initiated cultivation of tobacco as a
new project in Lower Galilee.  Several hundred workers were due
to be employed and, in contrast to the public works, the project
was to be the workers' own.  Descriptions in Hofra's local bulletin 15 years later (in 1939) portray, in picturesque style, the
enthusiasm of the people concerned and the attraction of the project, which, however, was eventually discontinued, having proved
a failure in economic terms.  Most of the workers left the Galilee and the few who remained in a small colony were assisted by
the Histadrut to secure employment in various jobs.  Amongst this
small aggregate, or community, of workers (most of whom lived on
the same site, in tents, their organizational and social center
being the workers' wooden hut which served as the Histadrut
office, employment bureau, cultural centre, etc.), a group of 8
to 10 people formed The Kvutza.

A member, who is said to have been the organizer of the
group and the unofficial leader of all the workers in the region,
reflects 15 years later (in a conversation cited in the bulletin
of 1939):

"When we, 8 or 10 people, got organized, we had no knowledge of what we were.  We were gathered together with one goal
only: the conquest of labor in the colony.[11]  That was the
limited aim of these 10 people, but even then the end was [in
fact] not so limited.  [It was] only at the end of the year,
when we realized that the will of these people could serve more
important goals, that they were able to delineate their way
henceforth as well.  We concluded that we all wished to constitute a kvutza."

So it was through the collective Conquest of Labor that
The Kvutza emerged.  Interpersonal relationships, developed
within the larger aggregate of workers in the 'colony,' and
strengthened by common, almost identical, personal experiences
in the circumstances described above, resulted in the emergence
of The Kvutza.

There was, moreover, the living 'reference group' - Degania,
the first kvutza.  A reference group need not necessarily exist
in reality in order to affect hopes, expectations, criteria for
behavior and actual modes of conduct.  It can affect people's

19

behavior, choices and decisions while being a mere image (see Shibutani, 1955: 563; also Kuhn, 1964: 27). But Degania, the first Kvutza was real, and not far away, just 'beyond the mountain,' although it did assume some legendary features in the not-so-old Labor movement. It provided an example not only of collective responsibility for an economic project, but also of collective ownership of the enterprise, in addition to observance of the other tenets of kvutza, which many groups motivated by the ideal of Conquest-of-Labor, practiced de facto. There was also Kinnereth, the 'large kvutza' with some three score members. For years the Labor Movement together with its youth movements affiliated to kibbutzim (pl. of kibbutz) was engaged in an argument over how large the kvutza ought to be (see Luz, 1962: 133 on; and Z. Shepher, 1960: 28-32). The model for the founding members of The Kvutza remained Degania, not the 'large kvutza.' This choice may have been influenced by the members' political affiliation, the origins of which went back to pre-immigration days. In broad and general terms we may say that Degania, and later settlements of the 'small kvutza' type were mostly affiliated to one of the Labor parties of the time, whereas most of the members of the kvutzoth (pl. of kvutza) committed to the theory of the 'large kvutza' were affiliated to a different party. The Labor parties at the time were much more than political parties; they were felt to constitute the core of ideological commitment, crystallizing as they did the various approaches towards the realization of Zionist and Socialist hopes; they provided actual support for, and in turn gained support from, affiliated groups in the process of development, either through their representatives and affiliated bodies or directly. The parties also constituted a sort of 'reservoir' from which potential membership of kvutzoth could be recruited.

During the period spent in the Galilee, The Kvutza initiated a new project: an association of all the kvutzoth in the region with the aim of meeting present difficulties and future challenges as one large body. In their terms, "We were contemplating [the establishment of] the kibbutz [ingathering] of kvutzoth for the Conquest of Labor." The Kibbutz of Kvutzoth failed: other kvutzoth in the Lower Galilee moved out of the region. New members joined the only remaining kvutza on the basis of former acquaintance or political connections until it numbered 20 to 30 men and women. The Kvutza attempted to recruit new members, in particular young women. A nearby working women's group, employed on farms and a plant nursery, was the main target of recruitment, but these efforts too met with little success.

After two years in the small colony, The Kvutza moved to a Galileean town. "In the town," reminisced an old-timer, "we were quite well off, by the standards of these days, but we were always troubled by the question: Where is the future? Where is the kibbutz?" So after a year the Kvutza moved again, to another nearby 'colony.' The Histadrut had just (in 1926) formed the Yakhin Company, an agricultural contracting company. Old members of The Kvutza are still proud of their being the first group in Palestine to work with Yakhin, in that colony. They were engaged in planting banana, grapefruit and citron trees. The members lived in one large building and in tents, but found satisfaction in three aspects of their new circumstances: they earned well; they were engaged in agricultural work, a prestigious occupation in the Labor and 'pioneering' movement whose highest recognized ideals were embodied in the kibbutz (at the time based almost solely on agriculture); and they lived in the Galilee, a region imbued with an aura of prestige by some mysterious romanticism about the 'far north,' cereal farming (falha) and guard duties, a romanticism which may be traced back to a previous (the Second) Aliya.

Here, however, they were confronted by a difficulty they could not surmount, namely malaria. The high ideals of living in the Galilee gave way to harsh reality: after one year in the new colony it was decided to leave. Yakhin Company, whose relationship with The Kvutza was a close one, stepped in, and offered a limited contractual job in a large colony in the Judean Plains.

From this colony The Kvutza moved again to a colony in the Sharon Valley (henceforth: The Colony). Yakhin Company offered The Kvutza a project of planting a 200-dunam[12] citrus grove "with a possible extension to 600." The period of work on RaShal Garden (the name given to the grove) is still nostalgically mentioned in Hofra, by veterans[13] and treated with indulgent humor by the young generation.

The Colony was "the last station," as old-timers say. The camp[14] consisted of 7-8 tents which provided accommodation, and a dining room.

Five years (1928-1933) were spent by The Kvutza in The Colony. These five years of 'consolidation' witnessed three major changes: the emergence of families through marriage,[15] the establishment of an auxiliary farmstead and a union with other kvutzoth.

The small-scale incipient 'independent economy' established on a modest plot purchased by The Kvutza in The Colony benefited its members in four ways: Firstly, it provided some income in addition to that earned as hired laborers, and secondly, it sup-

21

plied them with food. The latent benefits were no less important; experience was gained in future branches of Hofra's economy,
and lastly, a new entity developed, on the basis of which there
emerged a cohesion of a different kind from that which had hitherto prevailed. Not only did the members share earned income and
develop a collective pattern of consumption, but they now also
began to share ownership of a farmstead. They owned it collectively, and some of them worked on it together. A new kind of
relationship was burgeoning.

The Kvutza had by now gained experience in different kinds
of agricultural work and crops. It had succeeded in the Conquest
of Labor and had realized the twin tenet of Conquest of Man to
Labor,[16] but it had not given up its central goal, that of hityashvut, becoming an independent settlement. It was with this
in mind that efforts were made to merge with other kvutzoth. To
be sure, The Kvutza had lost members and had experienced difficulty in filling the gaps left by defections, but the policy of
uniting with other kvutzoth rather than concentrating on bringing in new individuals had several advantages, and was considered
by all kvutzoth as a means of ensuring future settlement. Three
small kvutzoth came from a town in which several Labor kibbutzim
had disintegrated in 1929-30 in the wake of the depression, unemployment and growing disappointment during that critical period
in Zionist history. The Kvutza, thus enlarged, merged with a
relatively large kvutza stemming from the Youth Movement[17] affiliated with The Movement,[18] with which The Kvutza, too, was affiliated.

The Youth Movement came into being in East Europe, mainly
in Poland and Galicia. It was mainly a movement of young students,
in their teens, who were influenced by the early German Youth
movement on European youth associations. This stamp was marked
by an emphasis on simplicity, nature, immediate and frank interpersonal relationships, loyalty to the people, and respect for and
joy in work. This direction of youthful idealism developed into
a collective drive to found, and become the super-structure of,
the intense framework of 'youth culture' embodied in The Movement.
The groups scattered in the 'nests' (local branches) of The Movement constituted social frameworks for experience in youth culture,
while crystallizing a collective ideology coincident with the
contemporaneous image of kvutza. National and social tenets crystallized as Zionist and socialist, with a demanding moral commitment. The ultimate framework within which the values implied in
the 'youth culture' would materialize was to be the kvutza. The
kvutza presumably embodied values of national as well as social
redemption, ideals voluntarily materialized by people who joined
it. On the individual level, it constituted a living example of
the predominance of idealistic values of personal redemption

through physical labor, return to nature, simplicity, and close
and intense interpersonal relationships.[19]  Thus, intense and
close interpersonal relationships developed among networks of
young people, despairing of future hope at home, and moved by a
Zionist ideology pointing to what was felt to be a way out of an
impasse in Jewish life.

In conclusion, a combination of various factors led the
Youth Movement to the kibbutz: the prospects of immigration in
Palestine, conditions in Palestine, the process of Zionist expansion in the country, the existence of kibbutzim and kvutzoth
and the roles the latter played on the national level in relation to immigration, settlement and patterns of work and mutual
aid.  The combination of these factors was fed by the youth
culture experienced in the Youth Movement and by its ideological
tenets.  The approach developed in the Youth Movement towards
group-life and kvutza, led it to take a stand in the argument
within the Kibbutz Movement between the 'small kvutza' and the
'large kvutza'[20] in clear favor of the 'organic' as against the
'economic-mechanic' conception   (Z. Shepher, 1960: 28-32; Luz,
1962: 135-139).[21]  That brought the Youth Movement to The Movement.

When they came to Palestine, the early kvutzoth of the
Youth Movement had to make a living.  Like other kvutzoth not
settled on their own land, they set up their 'camps' in 'colonies,'
sought for employment and looked forward to hityashvut. One such
kvutza, whose members were employed mainly in citrus groves in
'colonies' was approached by The Movement to merge with The
Kvutza.  The prospect of hityashvut seems to have played a significant role in the decision made by both groups.  Now, wrote an
old-timer, "we were in such a [satisfactory] social state, so as
also to be able to go on hityashvut."

## Hityashvut (settlement)

The history of The Kvutza has been presented against the
background of the Zionist process of the twenties and the early
thirties.  A brief examination of the Zionist strategy shows
that settlement (hityashvut) was conditional on immigration
(aliya).  It also involved, by necessity, (1)  acquisition of
land wherever possible (though efforts were not made equally
throughout the country), and (2)  national inalienable ownership of the land, leased to the settler.  That last principle was
not, however, implemented throughout the country because of
chronic poverty and because control over land ultimately lay
with the Mandatory Government.  Yet the Jewish National Fund,
the land-purchasing agency of the World Zionist Organization,

23

set out to accomplish those targets with the means it possessed.
In subsequent years the strategy of land acquisition developed
a politico-geographical aspect and emphasized the purchase of
areas extending in between areas already settled with Jews.
Demanding security problems and political long-run assessment of
prospects became involved. The acquisition of The Valley may be
viewed in these terms. The Valley extended, at the time, between
two Jewish-populated regions. National land was invariably associated with settlement. The hityashvut signified expansion of
the Jewish economy, with more employment and more settlements on
the newly acquired land, thereby strengthening the Jewish hold
in various parts of the country both physically and politically.

All forms of hityashvut were zealously ideologized: the
small kvutza (later usually identified as kvutza), the large
kvutza (later known as kibbutz) and the moshav.[22] Hityashvut
became a sort of cornerstone in the recognized ideology of the
Labor Movement of Palestine, and its stable stronghold. It was,
and had always been, a focus of high evaluation (and center of
efforts) for the majority in the Zionist Movement (for reasons
set out above); and it became the ideal model set as the ultimate educational goal for youth movements.

## The establishment of an independent economy

Throughout this chapter attention has been drawn to the
ideal of hityashvut, the desire of The Kvutza to settle on the
land, under the hope of emulating Degania. To this end kvutzoth
living for years in the 'colonies' exerted pressure on Zionist
agencies to help them settle, and to fulfil hopes and strengthen
the prospects of hityashvut they selected other groups to unite
with them. The term hityashvut itself, as intimated above, had
had manifold connotations for different people and circles. But
above all these, one hope was dominant: The Kvutza, upon settlement, was to establish a meshek[23] - an economy of its own.

That The Kvutza had always looked forward to hityashvut
through establishing a meshek - economy of its own - is obvious
from the above historical sketch. Like other kvutzoth it had
to wait its turn, that is, to wait for land to be allotted to
it, to wait presumably for loans from the central Zionist agencies (within the settlement-appropriation of the Zionist Organization) for initial investments, and to wait its turn as one
group amongst others in The Movement and in the entire hityashvut movement (kibbutz and moshav groups). In the end this involved the recognition by The Movement and the Agricultural
Centre that The Kvutza was able to undertake the task.

24

Every kibbutz is a meshek. It must seem, even to the reader
who is not familiar with the Israeli kibbutz, quite obvious. On
further thought, if one seeks understanding of the kibbutz as a
commune, it is not so obvious. A commune is not necessarily a
meshek. The history of The Kvutza itself would justify this
statement. Ten years of communal experience (1924-1933) preceded
the foundation of its meshek. Through changes of places, changes
of employment, increase in age and even change of membership
(through defection of old members and absorption of new ones),
The Kvutza remained a commune. Historical evidence, outlines of
which have been sketched above, show that the emergence of commune preceded the pattern of the kibbutz as a meshek. In other
words, a commune can presumably consist of people who would share
incomes earned in the labor market, share all or most of their
property, develop a system of communal consumption and services
and perhaps also education, and live in the same locality. That
is, it can be, in broad terms, a communal organization of the
consumption of its members and of basic property without having
a productive economy of its own. Such communes are to be found
in Great Britain at present (Saunders, 1970: 78-83) and there
has been a mushrooming of communes in the USA. Not only did the
commune (in this sense), as has been noted, precede the settled
kibbutz (with a meshek of its own), but alongside the expansion
and growth of hityashvut, communes continued to exist in towns
and in 'colonies.' In 1924, 13 communes with 417 members worked
and lived in the three large towns (Tel-Aviv, Jerusalem, Haifa),
and in 1926 there were communes with 435 members (Executive
Committee of the Histadrut, Report to the Third Convention, 1927).
One may consider this against the background of harsh conditions
in Palestine, economic difficulties, unemployment, and difficulties in adaptation to the new environment. Co-operative and collective groups (some called 'Kibbutzim'), in large numbers,
existed at the same time. But it should be emphasized that those
communes, like others disintegrating in the colonies (remnants
of which joined The Kvutza in The Colony), did not survive. In
retrospect one may state that the commune in Palestine faced a
dilemma: in order to survive it had either to become a kibbutz
(in the present sense of the term) and have a meshek, or to disintegrate and let its members disperse.

Those communes which did not embark on the Zionist expanding process of settlement have disappeared, many as they may have
been. The pattern that emerged to prevail has been that of the
'Full Co-operative' in Buber's terms,[24] i.e., a society in which
production and consumption are communally organized. This is
the kibbutz. Historians of, and commentators on, the kibbutz
who take note of this inescapable fact tend to analyze it in
terms of ideological Zionist identification and commitment:[25]
the kibbutz succeeded because it embarked on the essence of

25

Zionism, hityashvut. In this connection, I would rather suggest that, in historical perspective, we can see that tendencies to form collective associations were encouraged by factors both in the local situation in the country and in the background of the young immigrants before migration, but they were successful only when they could co-operate in production, given the specific conditions provided by Zionist settlement at that period. Once settled on the land, the foundation or establishment of a meshek makes relationships between the members of the commune more binding. The meshek economy, since it is an independent, self-owned, economy, makes the relationships between members qualitatively (and quantitatively) different from earlier relationships. Collectivity based on a productive economy, above all on one single communally-owned meshek, is effectively binding. Essentially voluntary relationships set up among members of a commune are affected by, in addition to giving rise to, institutions that develop within the commune of consumption. The tacit recognition of the presence of alternatives to the very system itself helps the relationships grow stronger. Quantitatively, the frequency of interaction amongst members is increased by growth of, and responsibility for, matters pertaining to the common economy, since the number of relationships which emerge in the 'Full Co-operative' embracing production and consumption (including services) in the one united combination of 'meshek and community,' are much more numerous. By their very contents, they produce binding ties. The relevance of the Zionist process here is in the spur it gave to the process of development from commune to kibbutz,[26] in the pre-immigration period by driving home the impasse in which Jews dwelt, and converting their aspirations into a drive to move to and settle in the Land of Israel.

The State has basically endorsed this conception of the kibbutz. The Co-operative Association Bill, 1968 (Reshumot, the official gazette of Israel, 778, June 5th, 1968), aims to provide the kibbutz with a legal standing and defines the kibbutz as "an association for hityashvut being a distinct settlement which maintains a collective society of its members, organized on tenets of public ownership of property, self labor and equality and collectivity in all spheres of production, consumption and education" (Reshumot, 1968:174). (See also Appendix I.)

## The establishment and development of Kibbutz Hofra

I return to The Kvutza. The Kvutza elected to become a kibbutz, i.e., to settle and to have a meshek. Collective experience in the Galilee, together with the high prestige conferred on this region (and probably also the concentration of diverse kibbutz-type projects in the North in general), served to keep

alive the old hope of eventually settling in the north, throughout
the period spent in the Sharon colony.  But no further settlement
in the North was planned at the time.  A new project of hityashvut,
in the Valley, was initiated.  As it was to be a concerted project
of all settlement organizations affiliated to the Zionist Organization, The Kvutza was given the opportunity to settle by virtue of
its membership in The Movement and received priority owing to its
senior position amongst all the groups which were waiting their
turn.  The Kvutza, which had previously rejected an offer by the
Agricultural Centre to settle in the Sharon Valley, now reconsidered its policy.  The decision to join the project of hityashvut
in the Valley was adopted and The Kvutza sent its first group of
5 members to the Valley.  The new settlement was given the name
of Hofra.

The first tract of land allotted to Hofra measured 620 dunams, including the area for residential quarters.  It consisted
of two plots, the one known as 'the Camp [site]' and the other
as the 'Heavy Soil [plot];' the latter name, in fact, indicating
the nature of the soil in that plot.  The first crops grown in
the 'Camp' were vegetables, and later gladioli, and field crops
(falha) in 'Heavy Soil.'  Newly-purchased tractors worked with
Yakhin, first in The Colony and later in the Valley, outside the
meshek.  The plant-nursery in The Colony, besides growing plants
for the market, now supplied seedlings for a citrus grove in Hofra.
The small herd of dairy cows and chicken run were transferred from
The Colony to Hofra.  Hofra began to become a meshek.

Constant economic and financial difficulties marked the
early years of Kibbutz Hofra.  Some economic branches, such as
the citrus grove, yielded sufficient income to support a community only after several years.  The 'Budget' (a term used to
denote loans given by the Jewish Agency to settlers as part of
its settlement appropriation) was made available in small sums
intermittently over a period of 12 years.  The meshek was "sub-
merged in debts," as Ohad, the treasurer at the time, described
it.  "Only in 1942 did we somehow get over this crisis."

In 1941 another union took place.  A kvutza of the Youth
Movement, living and working in a town, was approached.  Its
members' personal and collective experience was essentially
similar to that of their predecessors who had merged with The
Kvutza in The Colony:  encompassing unemployment or occasional
employment; agricultural labor in groves associated with the
necessity and ideal of Conquest of [manual] Labor; adaptation
to a new environment, scarcity, and the like.  This union gave a
further impetus to Hofra's development.

27

The 1940's found Hofra with a __meshek__ of 1,623 __dunams__ of land in four tracts, amongst which were the camp site and sur-roundings, the Heavy Soil Area, and the Wadi. The local bulletin (16.1.1945) gives the following list of economic branches: cereal crops, fodder crops, vegetable garden, vegetables grown for home consumption, flower bulbs, bananas, vineyard, orchard, sub-tropical plantation, citrus grove, dairy, bee-hive. The following also are listed: work outside the kibbutz with trac-tors and lorries, cobbler's workshop, tinsmithy, smithy, bakery, and 'outside labor.'

Following the 1948/49 War of Independence, an additional large area of 1,517 __dunam__ was allocated to Hofra, known as Gderoth, which extended from the hills eastward into the Eastern Spout. Citrus crops, apples and plums, were planted there as well as sub-tropical ones, such as pecan-nuts. Later, cotton was introduced into the area.

Yet Hofra, notwithstanding its fairly developed __meshek__ and its careful, and cautious, yet ambitious, economic policy, has never become a big kibbutz. It endorsed the course, at one time prevalent in The Movement, of the 'small __kvutza__.' Let me state immediately that this notion of the 'small __kvutza__' itself under-went significant changes. From the original idea of 8-10 indi-viduals (see Luz, 1962: 135-136) it developed into a framework of 25-30 (and later even 60, as in the case of Hofra) units recog-nized by the settlement agencies (Luz, 1962: 140). The conception[27] of the 'intimate __kvutza__' has developed into the 'organic __kvutza__.' That last concept connotes the idea that communal life involves mutual selection of the group members by one another, mutual suitability of the people concerned to the group and to kibbutz life as conceived according to the demanding values of the group, and the primacy of these considerations. This selection aims at the development of a harmonious social network of relationships, as even more important than economic interests. The __kvutza__ can grow, and may grow, to be sure, but that growth shall be 'organic,' and the pace must, by implication, be cautious and slow. The Movement defined this idea as follows:

> The size of the __kvutza__ is determined by the __kvutza__,[28] with the authorized institutions of the movement taking part, in accordance with its economic and social capabil-ity while maintaining the tie man has with the __kvutza__ and with the possibilities of the revelation of the individual and his development. The [final] decision on the size of the __kvutza__ rests with the __kvutza__ itself.[29]

Let is be understood again, that The Kvutza endorsed this policy. I believe that previous social and ideological experience within

the Youth Movement played a significant role in this policy.
When the meshek developed and grew and Gderoth Area was obtained,
economic realities (and the logic of further development implicit
in economic enterprise where this is potentially possible), combined with demographic variables, helped to change the policy of
the 'small kvutza.' This change coincided with a similar nationwide change in The Movement (Luz, 1962). The whole kibbutz movement
suffered (as it still does) from shortage of members. But when
economic horizons widened throughout Israel, only a minor flow
of immigrants joined the kibbutz movement. Of these who did, a
very small percentage have remained.

Hofra was not an exception to the rule. In 1948 the last
organized group of members coming from a youth movement joined
Hofra. This was not The Movement. In practical terms, The
Movement, as well as the vast majority of Jews, and Jewish youth
who might have joined youth movements and become the 'natural
reservoir' for kibbutz membership and Jewish organization, were
largely exterminated in Europe by the Nazis. Its survivors were
co-founders of another youth movement formed in the concentration
camps in Europe liberated by the Allies, and in the British holding camps in Cyprus. Members of this movement comprised that
group which joined Hofra. Only a few of them have remained.
Since then no organized group has joined Hofra, even though individuals have. Thus Hofra in 1970 is a well-developed agricultural meshek for its size, a kibbutz composed of people who
came in organized groups at different stages of its history
with different background and experience, of people who joined
individually, and, lastly, of their grown-up children who have
joined as members.

Conclusions

In this chapter I have focussed on the emergence of The
Kvutza and on the subsequent emergence of Kibbutz Hofra against
the wider historical background. I have approached the problem
from several points: the successive 'waves' of immigration;
changing physical, economic and political conditions in Palestine (and later in Israel); the growth of the Labor Movement
(with which the kibbutz is affiliated); the youth movement and
its role in recruiting prospective members to the kibbutz; the
process of Zionist colonization; and the emergence of the kibbutz as an economic corporation. Each aspect has been touched
upon in relation to the successive historical stages of The
Kvutza. From necessity this discussion has been condensed.
Although I confine the discussion in the subsequent chapters
to a limited subject, the various aspects of kibbutz life
touched upon in this chapter help, I believe, to set the discussion in some perspective.

Two main points emerge from the discussion above. Firstly, the kibbutz is a commune founded on an economy: i.e., it is an economic enterprise as well as being a residential community. The transformation of the <u>kvutza</u> from a commune based on the sharing of consumption and consumable property to the <u>meshek</u>-based kibbutz is a decisive one. A new entity emerged thereby.

This is not to argue that the economic-productive kibbutz represents a total departure from its pre-settlement predecessor. Important aspects of kibbutz life, though still under continual change, were crystallized in that period. Some institutions, more often than not in the sphere of consumption, were developed in the pre-settlement period, which itself was also marked by change. People, by sharing together common experiences, difficulties and gratifications, developed standards which eventually developed into a normative system. The latter, in turn, together with other variables, affected the members' subsequent conduct and actions. Furthermore, it may be noteworthy that people took steps to involve themselves in group life of a certain kind which, under given conditions, made further demands on them. The grouping of people itself gave rise to a social entity. Nonetheless, the transformation of this commune into the kibbutz in its present sense is decisive because through embarking on the course of <u>hityashvut</u> the commune had acquired the properties of an economic corporation. It is the behavior of members as members of an economic corporation which I propose to study in the following chapters.

Secondly, the size of the <u>meshek</u>, the economic corporation, has been mainly determined not by economic considerations but by the members' concern, at a certain point of time, to remain an intimate community. The connection of this wish with the affiliation of The Kvutza to a national kibbutz movement (and a political party) and a youth movement has been shown. The policy of The Movement in relation to the problem of the size of its constituent <u>kvutzoth</u> and the wish of The Kvutza itself were taken into account when quotas of land and other resources were determined. The size of the <u>meshek</u> was thus determined by non-economic considerations. Two, or more, such different considerations may be reconcilable, but they may also clash. Evidently, the members of The Kvutza in the pre-State period, placed a higher value on so-called 'social' (in the kibbutz idiom) considerations than on the economic considerations of growth and further development. The kibbutz as a <u>meshek</u> obviously has economic considerations and depends on the logic of economic development. Yet other considerations have proved to have been given the greater weight, though they have influenced the economy itself. When The Kvutza, or rather Kibbutz Hofra, was prepared to revise its policy of the

'intimate kvutza,' by possibly increasing its membership, it was
faced by a sharp decline in the influx of new members into the
kibbutz movement. The meshek, as described above, has grown
whereas the population of Hofra has only increased slightly. The
resulting situation is what is called in the kibbutz movement,
'lack of members' to meet the demand of labor brought about by
economic growth. The implications of this situation are the
subject of the following chapters.

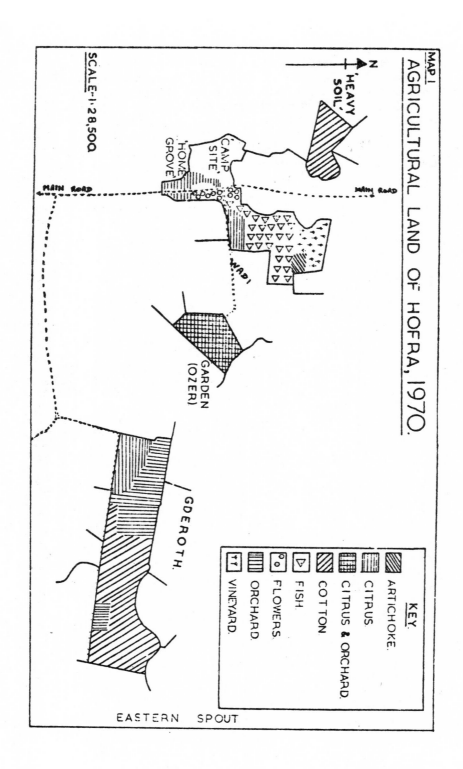

MAP 1

AGRICULTURAL LAND OF HOFRA, 1970.

N

'HEAVY SOIL'

SCALE 1:28,500

'HOME GROVE'

'CAMP SITE'

MAIN ROAD

MAIN ROAD

'WADI'

GARDEN (OZER)

GDEROTH

KEY

| | ARTICHOKE. |
| | CITRUS. |
| | CITRUS & ORCHARD. |
| | COTTON. |
| | FISH. |
| | FLOWERS. |
| | ORCHARD. |
| | VINEYARD. |

EASTERN SPOUT

32

NOTES

1. Mainly from springs and a tributary of a nearby river, used
   for the local fish ponds situated on what had previously been
   swamp land.

2. The reader is advised to consult Avi-Yonah (1964).

3. To mention only (a) a map drawn in 1808 (following Napoleon's
   journey through the area in 1799), (b) Lady Montefiore's
   diary in 1839 and (c) the PEF map in 1878.

4. For details the reader may again consult the relevant chapter
   in my PhD thesis.

5. See discussion of the term below, footnote 9.

6. 'Colony,' a village or a small town originally based on an
   agricultural economy, Hebrew: moshava.  The first colonies were
   established in the 1880's, thus pioneering modern Jewish agriculture in Palestine.  Unlike the Kibbutz or moshav, its
   farmers and inhabitants have no commitment to co-operative
   principles of organization.

7. Moshav, a smallholders' co-operative settlement, based mainly
   on farming.  For studies of moshav villages in the Valley,
   see Abarbanel (1974) and Baldwin (1972).

8. There are two meanings to the term 'settlement' as used here,
   and elsewhere.  The two meanings are used in two contexts of
   discussion: first, the individual 'settlement,' namely a village or any other group of people settling on land in a specific location; and secondly, 'settlement' as a sequence of
   activities, a process, of settling in the country (Hebrew:
   'Hityashvut').  The latter bears the connotation of 'colonization,' a term not used in modern Zionist vocabulary.

9. 'Aliya,' literally ascendancy (or 'going up'), is the term
   used in Zionist terminology (adapted from Ezra 1, 2 and
   2 Chronicles, 36, 23) to denote Jewish immigration to
   Palestine (and Israel).  In the present context it means a
   'wave' of immigration.  On the aliya 'waves' see Eisenstadt
   (1967, particularly pp. 9-12; 13-31).

10. Moshav.  See footnote (7) above.  For references to the
    origins, tenets and organization of the moshav and the Moshav
    Movement see:  Eisenstadt (1967: 29, 144, 169-175), Dayan
    (1974), Labes (1962), and Orni (1963).  These references do

not include detailed analyses of moshav communities founded after the establishment of the State of Israel in 1948. On the kibbutz and the moshav see also Ben David (1964).

11. See footnote 6 above. The speaker refers to 'colony' as a national category connoting mainly the idea of the Jewish agricultural economy in Palestine.

12. 1 dunam = 1,000 square meters, 0.247 acres.

13. 'Veteran' - term used in defining old-timer, usually in relation to a newer member. This is a relative notion, seniority being measured according to the length of time the person has been in the unit under discussion.

14. The "camp" included both the dwellings and the farmyard. The use of this term stems from the early days of settlement when people lived in tents or huts crowded together. See footnote 8 above.

15. Old-timers, in retrospect, often claim that this process gave rise to "a real kvutza." A kvutza is thus perceived as being 'real' only once the family emerges as its structural core. Compare with Talmon-Garber (1965).

16. 'Conquest of Man to Labor' is the expression used to denote the idea of change from traditional occupations (mostly conceived as middle-class occupations) pursued by Jewish people, to labor, particularly physical labor, in Palestine. This change is promoted to the level of an ideal. The ideal seeks the redemption of man and the realization of his creative and spiritual potential through work. As a means for achieving this end, man should be 'conquered' by this ideal: he should elect to become a laborer. The noted promoter of the value of labor as a means toward individual and national redemption was A.D. Gordon. His name is associated with the exaltation of the ideal of labor to a 'Religion of Labor' (Gordon, 1952; also on Gordon and his ideology, see Schweid, 1970).

17. The Youth Movement, in capital letters: the young movement affiliated with the Kibbutz Movement (see next footnote) of which The Kvutza was a constituent member.

18. The Movement in the 1920's was the remnant of the national League of Kvutzoth and Kibbutzim established formally at the Kvutzoth and kibbutzim's convention in the autumn of 1925. The first national convention took place in 1920. National kibbutz movements refused to accept the League's authority and eventually walked out altogether. In the autumn of 1932

34

the Youth Movement affiliated itself with The Movement.  In
July 1933 the association of the Youth Movement's kyutzoth
decided on a full union with The Movement which formally
came into being in 1934 (Z. Shepher, 1960: 212-228; Luz, 1962:
302-206, 308-209.  On the history of The Movement see also
Ben Avram, 1976).

19. (a)  I am aware of limitations inherent in such an attempt to
    summarize briefly the development of a youth association,
    itself related to many social, historical and political fac-
    tors, and to a youth movement, committed to a specific goal
    and, more significantly deeds.  But the subject under dis-
    cussion here is not the Youth Movement itself, which is
    touched upon only in so far as it is relevant to The Kvutza.
    On the other hand, one cannot totally ignore the background
    of, or the agency through which, an organized group came to
    accept the kibbutz way of life and, in particular, to join
    The Kvutza.

    (b)  One might suggest, even for a brief sketch, an alter-
    native sociological approach which would draw attention to
    the role played by youth movements in conveying frustrated
    Jewish youth from deteriorating economic and political con-
    ditions by providing them with a framework for adaptation to
    new conditions in a foreign, harsh, environment, and in re-
    sponding to their need for justification and interpretation
    in ideological terms.  Again, that would require embarking
    on the analysis of a different subject.  Also, see, in par-
    ticular, footnote 1 on p. 33 above.  Its argument, in essence,
    becomes even stronger in the case of this particular Youth
    Movement.

20. Those interested in the terminology used here, whose concep-
    tion of the terms 'organic' and 'mechanical' is rather differ-
    ent from Durkheim's (1893) might read Shatz (1929); and
    Spiro (1956: 53-55).

21. See p. 20 above.

22. All these terms have changed meaning over time.  Reading
    literature written in different historical periods may con-
    fuse the unfamiliar reader - particularly since all of the
    terms are still in use.

23. Meshek, in the modern Hebrew use of th. word, is the term
    referred to when an economic unit is discussed.  More
    accurately, it is the economic aspect of that unit.  Thus,
    the meshek of a kibbutz is the kibbutz as an economic unit.
    (In Biblical Hebrew the term means household.)

24. For Buber's own analysis, see Buber (1949).

25. Related, in turn, to that aspect of the kibbutz movement ideology known as 'the kibbutz as an instrument.'

26. Again (referring to the previous footnote), it may be considered in ideological terms as the relationship between the conception of 'the kibbutz as an instrument' and 'the kibbutz as an end in itself.'

27. For illuminating presentation of this subject, in the context of the growth and enlargement of the kvutza, see 'The Growth of the Kvutza and the Social Changes' in Luz (1960: 133-153, written in 1944).

28. Kvutza, in this context, is the term for the constituent kibbutz of The Movement, the individual kibbutz.

29. Having stated the considerations the kvutza is expected to take in regard to its size, the final decision is to be made by the individual kvutza. In another kibbutz movement (HaKibbutz HaMeuhad) whose proclaimed policy was that of the 'big and growing kibbutz,' the ultimate authority was with the national movement which could overcome local hesitation in regard to the size of the community by sending new and more candidates for membership into the constituent kibbutzim, thereby determining their development in accordance with movement principles.

CHAPTER III

PERMANENCE IN WORK

## Annual cycles of labor

In terms of income Hofra is mainly an agricultural farm.
The primacy of agriculture in its use of labor can be seen from
the following data. Of the total estimate of 47,000 return-
yielding[1] labor days for 1968/69, 25,700 were required to meet
the demands made by the agricultural branches. That is to say,
some 53.9% of return-yielding labor was to be invested in agriculture (Economic Plan for 1968/69). The balance sheet for
1967/68, approved by the Audit Union, states that IL 2,974,110.65
out of IL 4,033,697.37 (i.e., 73.7%) of the annual income of the
kibbutz, was obtained from agriculture. No marked change has
taken place in the last year. The importance of agriculture in
the economy of Hofra affects demand for, and supply of, labor,
and the composition and structure of the labor force; and these,
in turn, influence the social relationships.

Two main features of Hofra's agricultural economy are
relevant to a discussion of its working population. The first
is that it has mixed farming, some implications of which will
be discussed later, and the second is that, as in most agriculture, work has an annual cycle - i.e., it varies with the seasons.
A few examples will elucidate this last statement. One very
important branch of Hofra's farming is cotton, which extends
over 980 dunam out of a total of 2661 dunam of agricultural land.
In December 1968 and in January and February 1969, two, three
and four labor-days respectively are reported to have been
employed in that branch, while 182, 223 and 173 labor-days
respectively were invested in May, July and September, 1969.
These figures demonstrate graphically the seasonal variation
in labor requirements. Or take the vineyard: in November and
December 1968, eight and three labor-days respectively are reported to have been invested in the branch. In March and April
1969, 203 and 273 respectively; in August and September, 885
and 581 respectively. Each crop determines the cycle of labor
it requires. Cotton requires cultivation, spraying, sometimes
re-cultivation, irrigating, and finally harvesting. Vines require cultivating, pruning, thinning and interlacing of new
twigs, fertilizing spraying and irrigating, and finally the
grapes have to be picked. This kind of cyclical pattern runs
through the cultivation of all crops, and there is a never-ending
cycle of work which follows the seasonal nature of the various
plants. Methods of cultivation and harvesting change, and they

37

do so quite rapidly (and the technological changes  affect the
human realm which we are considering), but basically they are
responses to the cycles.  In raising animals (in Hofra - chickens
and fish) one must respond to changes in each type of animal's
life-cycle in relation to variation of demand in markets.  In
short, the seasonal nature of farming entails a cyclical organization of labor.

That would have been simple (though of course other problems
would have arisen) if Hofra's agricultural economy were monocultural.  Its mixed farming is organized through a small number of
branches, each of which is autonomously controlled by the cycle.
As each branch with its team faces the demands made upon it by the
nature of the crop, the meshek as a unit has to organize its labor
on a diversified pattern.  Table 3.1 illustrates the nature of the
work demanded.

Obviously, not all types of work require equal amounts of
labor, as is shown by the observations on cotton and vines in the
table below.  The maximum of labor is demanded for the harvesting,
which, owing to climatic factors, must be accomplished within a
very short period for each crop.  Unequal amounts of labor are
required for each seasonal phase of each type of crop.

The people who work in a given branch must meet the demands
imposed on them by the changing requirements of the different
seasons.  They, both as individuals and as a group, participate
in the various and different tasks throughout the annual cycle.
With experience accumulated through years of work, most of the
members of a branch-team have gained a fair measure of understanding of basic labor problems, knowledge of different tasks,
methods by which certain problems were solved in past years both
technically and organizationally, and some scientific knowledge.
In the orchard, for example, practically everyone would know how
to prune varieties of deciduous trees in the winter, to irrigate,
to thin unripe fruit, to pick fruit and to organize picking, and
to cultivate.  They will also know the immediate and long-run considerations, even if they do not engage in it themselves, of the
factors which govern decisions about spraying against summer pests.
Almost everyone can distinguish between different varieties of a
crop, spot their location in different areas, guide strangers to
the various plots, sort and pack fruits, and plant and replant.
This is not to say that everybody does in fact do all these jobs.
There is division of labor and responsibilities within the group,
but all the members in a group operate as a team and most of them
are capable of carrying out any of the various tasks required in
the branch.

Table 3.1: Nature of Work in Selected Branches Throughout
The Agricultural Year[1]

| | Cotton | Artichoke | Vineyard |
|---|---|---|---|
| October | HARVESTING | harvesting | harvesting, IRRIGATING |
| November | harvesting, cultivating, fertilizing | harvesting | - |
| December | fertilizing, cultivating | harvesting | - |
| January | - | harvesting | PRUNING |
| February | fertilizing | harvesting | PRUNING |
| March | SOWING, cultivating, fertilizing | harvesting | PRUNING |
| April | SOWING | cutting off | tying, thinning, irrigating |
| May | checking (insects) cultivating | cutting off | tying, spraying, irrigating |
| June | IRRIGATING, cultivating, checking (insects) | - | tying, spraying, irrigating |
| July | IRRIGATING, checking (ins.) | PLANTING, irrigating | IRRIGATING |
| August | checking (insects) | irrigating | HARVESTING, irrigating |
| September | HARVESTING | irrigating | HARVESTING, irrigating |

KEY: Capital letters signify that the item is either a
main task at a given period, or pressure is brought
on the branch team at that time.

[1] Minor jobs are not included.

Table 3.1 continued...

| | Fish-Ponds | Orchard | Citrus |
|---|---|---|---|
| October | CLEARING, TRANS-FERING (to ponds) | HARVESTING, (apple, sub.tr., pecan, persim-mon) IRRIGATING | harvesting, irrigating, care |
| November | CLEARING, TRANS-FERING (to ponds) | harvesting, (sub.tr., pecan, persimmon) irrigating | HARVESTING, irrigating |
| December | shipping (market), working on equip. | harvesting (sub.tr., pecan, persimmon), pruning (plums) | HARVESTING |
| January | working on equip. | pruning (apple), harvesting (sub.tr.) | HARVESTING |
| February | stocking (ponds) | PRUNING (apple) | HARVESTING |
| March | stocking (ponds) | PRUNING (apple) | harvesting, cultivating, spraying |
| April | STOCKING (ponds) culling (fish) | pruning, irrigating | HARVESTING, cultivating, spraying |
| May | culling (fish) | care, IRRIGATING | harvesting, cultivating, spraying |
| June | CLEARING, SHIP-PING, culling | harvesting (plum apple), IRRIGATING | care, IRRIGA-TING |
| July | CLEARING, SHIP-PING, culling | harvesting, IRRIGATING | care, IRRIGA-TING, pruning |
| August | culling | HARVESTING, IRRIGATING | care, IRRIGA-TING, pruning |
| September | transferring (fish to pond) | HARVESTING, irrigating | care, irri-gating, pruning |

Similar skills and adaptability are shown by members of other agricultural branches once they have gained personal and group experience in their respective branches. In other words, it is through working in a branch for a long time, even if not permanently, that the member gets experience. Long service places a member in a social group (a branch-team), and his membership endows him with obligations to the team and to the assignments of the branch. This point will be dealt with fully below. For the present, I only want to stress that a team is engaged in the different tasks of the seasonal cycle. At harvest time, a team cannot possibly cope with all the tasks included in the large-scale operation of gathering the crop (which in some branches coincides with other vital tasks, such as irrigation, spraying of pests, or cultivation); and other workers are drawn in. But even then the permanent team operates as the nucleus around which the non-members concentrate. When a peak season, whether of gathering the crop, pruning, or anything else, is over and the temporary workers leave the branch, the permanent team is proved conspicuously to be the residual group of the branch. This can be illustrated by the distribution of labor-days in Table 3.2. It would be advisable to study Table 3.2 as against the background presented in Table 3.1, which shows seasonal fluctuations in the agricultural branches in Hofra. In Table 3.2 I have not included children's labor. In 'others' I have included all categories of workers who are non-members. To be sure, not all labor-days of members in the Table are those of the permanent workers in the branches; some are mobilized for the season (or part thereof), but in the large branches there are very few of these. The vast majority of labor-days of members reported in the Table are those of permanent members of the branch-team.

The number of 'permanent' members varies from branch to branch. Assuming that there are 25 labor-days in a month, the difference between branch members and 'others' in relation to long-term or transitional position in the branch is quite conspicuous. As well as fish ponds and cotton, branches which employ children and altogether do not employ relatively large numbers of workers, there is the vineyard whose 'permanent' team consists of two men only. For the pruning period (late winter and spring) experienced pruners who work in other branches are asked to join, and during the vintage season young members who are students at the Technion in Haifa (past members of the branch-team) return to the branch while on vacation. Similar accretions of labor take place in other branches, but these are less conspicuous numerically in the large branches. In the orchard, the minimum number of labor-days worked by members in one month (the kibbutz unit of calculation) is reported as 171, but the average is 227.8 per month, which divided by 25 would indicate some 8.9 to 9 permanent members per day. 'Others'

Table 3.2: Labor-Days of Members and Non-Members in Agricultural Branches (Children Excluded) in 1968/69

| Branch | Gladioli | | Artichoke | | Cotton | | Fish-Pond | | Vineyard | | Orchard | | Citrus | |
|---|---|---|---|---|---|---|---|---|---|---|---|---|---|---|
| Category of Workers | Mem-ber | Other | Mem-ber | Other | Mem-ber | Other | Mem-ber | Other | Mem-ber | Other | Mem-ber | Other | Mem-ber | Other |
| **1968** | | | | | | | | | | | | | | |
| October | 74 | 60 | 40 | 50 | 123 | 9 | 70 | 16 | 32 | - | 220 | 262 | 241 | 206 |
| November | 52 | 34 | 53 | 93 | 63 | - | 48 | - | 8 | - | 236 | 366 | 318 | 379 |
| December | 53 | 30 | 102 | 78 | 2 | - | 74 | 1 | 3 | - | 251 | 171 | 320 | 424 |
| **1969** | | | | | | | | | | | | | | |
| January | 51 | 3 | 84 | 64 | 3 | - | 45 | - | 64 | - | 245 | 90 | 341 | 374 |
| February | 31 | 3 | 98 | 89 | 4 | - | 17 | - | 125 | - | 171 | 137 | 374 | 305 |
| March | 72 | 60 | 84 | 66 | 61 | - | 28 | - | 105 | 70 | 197 | 171 | 331 | 363 |
| April | 41 | 42 | 42 | - | 75 | 2 | 84 | 20 | 109 | 95 | 191 | 38 | 353 | 461 |
| May | 56 | 44 | 15 | 40 | 108 | 72 | 55 | - | 104 | 69 | 215 | 134 | 232 | 168 |
| June | 63 | 70 | 16 | - | 114 | 18 | 50 | 1 | 98 | 81 | 234 | 278 | 247 | 157 |
| July | 73 | 98 | 52 | 33 | 141 | 32 | 72 | 2 | 90 | 49 | 232 | 221 | 255 | 91 |
| August | 70 | 89 | 52 | 2 | 118 | - | 45 | 5 | 132 | 661 | 251 | 510 | 219 | 153 |
| September | 81 | 36 | 35 | - | 135 | 21 | 52 | 6 | 146 | 385 | 255 | 551 | 208 | 125 |

Source: Labor Registration, Hofra, 1969.

41

totalled 38 labor-days (in April), which is less than 2 workers per day, up to 551 labor-days (in September) which gives a figure of some 22 workers per day, as compared to 10 members. Or, as in the citrus grove, if we take as an index of 100 the lowest figure of members' labor (208 in September), the highest will be some 179.8 (374 actual labor-days in February). With the lowest figure for 'others' (91 in July) as an index of 100, the highest will be 506.5 (461 in April).

The fluctuations in the temporary labor-force in the branch are thus much bigger than are those in the permanent membership. This reflects the difference between the two annual cycles of labor of these two categories of workers. The members of the team respond to the seasonal requirements within the branch (unless there is absolutely nothing to do in a slack season) whereas the 'others,' the temporary labor-force, are assigned to tasks which arise from seasonal changes when the agricultural economy of Hofra is considered as a whole. The nature of the cyclical employment of a branch's requirements reinforces permanence.

Permanence, in turn, further develops scientific and technological knowledge concerning the tasks required in the branch as well as close acquaintance with, and experience in, all other aspects of its work, while temporary employment does not lead to increasing knowledge but concentrates on periodical, limited assignments which are related to a wider context (or cycle of events) with which the temporary worker is unfamiliar. His chance of getting access to, and experience with, mechanical equipment is scanty; he is most likely to be assigned to tasks where many unskilled work together, as is inevitable in some branches at certain seasons. The difference between the position of permanents and that of transients, who are usually not members of The Kvutza, is related to the different scales of the agricultural cycle of each 'branch' and the cycle of the whole meshek respectively, and covers the distinction between categories of people working in the same branch. The division of labor, in broad terms, is such that temporary laborers, better called 'others' (for reasons given below), are peripheral to the central team.

## Permanence of the branch-team

Several considerations contribute to increasing permanence of the branch-team as such. Firstly, it is advantageous to keep the inventory, tools and especially the mechanical equipment in a good state of repair so that shifts in personnel are largely undesirable. It is in the interest of the meshek as a whole that a maximum measure of responsibility be taken by the personnel involved in the management and the running of any branch, including care of equipment, the latter including soil, water-pipe networks, stores, tractors and other vehicles, various machines and the like. The more experienced the team is and the more familiar it is with inventory and equipment, the more conscientious and responsible the meshek may expect it to be.

Then there is the professional interest of the meshek. Obviously, the longer a group of workers is engaged in the same labor and responds collectively to recurrent patterns of changes in given assignments, the more skilled it may be expected to become. As various agricultural crops in different agricultural branches are diversified, it is in the interest of the overall economic unit that skill should further develop within the group working in a given branch whilst the group operates as a team. A highly developed, skilled team is inevitably beneficial to efficiency and development, and ultimately to production.

Thirdly, this last aim ties in with economic considerations. The kibbutz is obviously a running business enterprise. It supports itself by the various branches of its production. It is in its interest that its agriculture be as productive and efficient as possible, so that it tries to encourage the improvement of crops, increased production and reduction of expenditure. Permanent membership in the branch teams help to achieve these aims, though it does not guarantee success. With the tendency of farmers everywhere to increase those crops which are profitable at a particular period, eventually good profits on any crop must fall, and the margin of profitability becomes crucial. Hence there are economic pressures to reduce changes in branch personnel as far as possible. In short, the establishing and the running of the agriculture, and particularly its expansion and further development, demand permanent teams of workers, each of which both works in and takes responsibility for one agricultural branch. The expansion and development of each branch (and therefore of the meshek as a whole) brings about a further discrepancy between demands for labor and supply, a development which facilitates permanence of membership in each branch.

## Attachment of the individual to a branch

The striking phenomenon which immediately presents itself even to the casual observer is the fact of the permanent attachment of members to particular branches. It appears in the personal records of members working in agricultural branches. Records of labor engagements of nearly all members are available since 1952, or for some since 1954. (Records of earlier years have been destroyed.) The figures are shown in Table 3.3. I have recorded in this table the percentage of labor invested by every member working in his (or her) permanent branch compared

with the percentage of labor invested in other branches of the
meshek and other assignments during the economic year 1969/70.
By presenting the figures in percentages, this fact presents
itself strikingly. (Absolute numbers are not given in order not
to confuse the reader with information which is irrelevant to
the subject discussed here. The Table does not aim to show all
details of labor distribution and therefore the figures do not
add up to 100 per cent. The main issue is the difference between
'labor in permanent branch' and 'labor in other branches.') The
members are listed first in two categories: (1) those who have
worked in the meshek as a whole for five years and more and
(2) those who have worked for less than five years; and within
each category, according to seniority in a branch as recorded in
the Labor Records. In most cases this coincides with the actual
order of seniority in the branch even before 1952 or 1954.

Comparing the figures in the first two columns, one realizes that in all the branches, without exception, there is an
overwhelming difference between labor of any individual in his
permanent branch and that in other branches. This fact is even
more striking when one bears in mind that here I am considering
only agricultural branches, which are inevitably affected by
seasonal cycles. In other words, even though the growth of the
crops worked by the various branches entails seasonal fluctuations in the demands for labor, permanent attachment to one
branch is little disturbed by demands from other branches. Members remain in their respective branches for as long as possible.
If a member does work outside his branch, it is the 'service
duties' presented in the Table that suggest themselves first.
These are duties required from all members, men and women alike,
to work in the dining-hall (or kitchen) and (for men) on night-
guard, on a rota (see Talmon-Garber, 1964).

But it is possible to discern three main differences among
members in regard to the ratio between amount of labor in the
permanent branch and other assignments. Firstly, there are two
branches, the vineyard and the artichoke garden, which conspicuously employ much less labor (in percentage) of members throughout the year than do others. The seasonal nature of work in the
vineyard is so pronounced that the small team cannot escape the
need to find some complementary employment elsewhere during the
slack season. Two members in the vineyard (V2 and V5) are
assigned to other branches during seasonal peaks when they are
available, but even these two men spend most of their yearly
working-time in their own branch. I venture to suggest that had
the vineyard been larger than it is, they too would have shown
a bigger percentage of time worked in the branch. For a complex
set of reasons the artichoke garden in Hofra was not replanted in
the following year, so that in addition to the problem of season-

Table 3.3: Labor Distribution of Members in Agricultural Branches, 1969/70

(In percentage)

| Branch | Code name of member | In permanent branch % | In other branches % | In Service duties % | Community Activities % | Management % | Movement % | Notes |
|--------|------|------|------|------|------|------|------|------|
| **Citrus grove** | | | | | | | | |
| 5 year in the branch & over | G1 | 81.25 | - | - | | | | 18.75 - care of ill wife |
| | G2 | 97.37 | 1.75 | - | | | | |
| | G3 | - | - | - | | | | ill |
| | G4 | 98.09 | - | 1.10 | | | | |
| | G5 | 99.21 | - | 0.79 | | | | |
| | G6 | 98.84 | - | 0.77 | | | | |
| | G7 | 94.41 | 2.54 | - | 2.54 | | | |
| | G8 | 93.42 | 0.47 | 0.70 | | | | |
| | G9 | 64.10 | - | 4.39 | | 7.69 | 23.80 | |
| | G10 | 89.74 | 3.00 | 1.80 | 5.46 | | | |
| Less than 5 years | G11 | 96.07 | 0.58 | 2.36 | | | | |
| | G12 | 95.67 | 4.33 | - | | | | |
| | G13 | 97.65 | - | - | 1.40 | | | |
| | G14 | 53.58 | 0.75 | 0.35 | 9.05 | | 35.47 | |
| **Orchard** | | | | | | | | |
| 5 years and over | O1 | 97.01 | 0.33 | 2.65 | | | | including employment in national orchard board |
| | O2 | 91.34 | 3.90 | 3.90 | | | | |
| | O3 | 95.71 | 1.04 | 2.40 | | | | |
| | O4 | 90.40 | 2.21 | 6.64 | | | | |
| | O5 | 90.90 | 2.16 | 3.89 | | | | |
| | O6 | 87.61 | 6.53 | 4.08 | | | | |
| | O7 | 94.28 | 0.99 | 3.94 | | | | |
| Less than 5 years | O8 | 86.63 | 3.20 | 2.94 | | | 7.22 | |
| | O9 | 84.90 | 3.28 | 2.62 | 5.69 | 3.28 | | |
| | O10 | 64.31 | 4.22 | 1.40 | 3.75 | | 22.53 | |
| | O11 | 90.39 | 3.39 | 2.82 | | | | |
| **Vineyard** | | | | | | | | |
| 5 years and over | V1 | - | - | | | | | ill |
| | V2 | 72.06 | 14.82 | 9.99 | | | | |
| | V3 | 6.86 | - | 2.26 | | | 90.52 | |
| Less than 5 years | V4 | 55.74 | 16.75 | 2.05 | 3.68 | | 22.95 | |
| | V5 | 72.46 | 27.12 | 0.40 | | | | |
| **Cotton** | | | | | | | | |
| 5 years and over | C1 | 88.68 | 5.84 | 2.19 | 3.28 | | | |
| | C2 | 85.11 | 5.34 | - | | 9.54 | | |
| Less than 5 years | C3 | 97.11 | 1.91 | 0.48 | | | | |
| **Artichoke** | | | | | | | | |
| Over 5 years | A1 | 64.82 | - | 35.18 | | | | |
| | A2 | 77.20 | 5.44 | 17.34 | | | | |
| | A3 | - | - | - | | | | away for studies |
| **Flowers** | | | | | | | | |
| Over 5 years | F1 | 90.47 | 3.56 | 4.36 | | | | |
| | F2 | 91.17 | - | 8.40 | | | | |
| **Fish-ponds** | | | | | | | | |
| Over 5 years | P1 | 92.76 | - | 4.52 | | | | |
| | P2 | 94.79 | - | 2.60 | | | | |
| **Chicken-coop** | | | | | | | | |
| 5 years and over | R1 | 95.63 | - | 4.36 | | | | |
| | R2 | 68.83 | - | 12.41 | | | | 17.66 care of ill mother |
| | R3 | 100.00 | - | - | | | | |
| | R4 | 98.00 | - | - | | | | |
| | R5 | 89.86 | - | 7.43 | | | | |
| | R6 | 96.40 | - | 3.20 | | | | |
| | R7 | 96.72 | - | 3.28 | | | | |
| | R8 | 90.32 | - | 9.14 | | | | |
| | R9 | 99.67 | - | 0.33 | | | | |
| | R10 | 96.98 | - | 3.02 | | | | |
| | R11 | 98.81 | - | 1.08 | | | | |
| | R12 | 97.80 | - | 2.20 | | | | |
| | R13 | 93.80 | 1.38 | 2.77 | | | | |
| | R14 | 81.01 | 6.48 | 3.70 | 8.80 | | | permanent work includes part-time teaching |
| | R15 | 84.43 | - | 1.98 | | 13.24 | | retiring secretary |
| | R16 | 53.07 | 1.53 | 0.77 | | | 44.63 | returning from movement job |
| Less than 5 years | R17 | 98.84 | 0.30 | | | | | |

Source: Labor Records for 1969/70, Hofra.

ality, the two remaining men have been looking for alternative future employment. Working in the kitchen has always been a temporary berth for people who are moving from one branch to another.

Secondly, the Table shows that there is some tendency for the junior, and mostly younger, male members to be assigned to branches other than their own. The average percentage of a member of over five years standing in the branch working in other branches is only 1.69, whereas that of members of less than five years standing is 5.32. Obviously, those members who have worked in the meshek for less than five years are, in general, younger than the others. But, even if we add those in Hofra considered 'young' to this category and subtract them from the 'veteran' category, the difference would be 1.54 (for the 'veterans') as against 3.59 (for the young). One important reason for this difference is the recurring mobilization of young men into hard physical work such as that required in the fish ponds, loading lorries in the busy season, and the like. As this kind of work cannot possibly be done regularly by older men of the community, it becomes selective and is highly admired. To belong to the club of the temporary, seasonal, hard workers gives one some prestige. Thirdly, the female members (R1, R2, R5, R7, R8, R10) take their share in 'service duties,' namely in the kitchen or the dining-hall, but none of them work, even part-time, in other agricultural branches. Yet all members, including those working in highly seasonal branches, whether older in age or senior in tenure in the branch, or whether younger, male or female, tend to show permanent attachment to a branch throughout the year.

This tendency is not new and has evolved in practice over many years. The more the meshek develops, the more deeply its people become rooted in their respective branches. From the point of view of the meshek this movement towards permanence can continue, not only because it is congruent with its interests, but also because larger branches have more work which needs to be done throughout the year than have the small branches, and the larger demand more labor. From the individual's point of view, this tendency assists his efforts to become permanently attached to a branch. The demand for workers helps him to establish himself in a branch. Mixed-farming allows him some sort of choice among branches. Most of the members have, in fact, changed their branches since they began working in the meshek of Hofra. Yet notwithstanding the change, it seems that everyone, even while changing his branch, has sought permanence in a branch, whether in the previous branch or in the new, alternative one. No-one has willingly 'floated' with the purpose of being a 'cork' (the term used by Hofraites, though

46

scarcely applicable in practice as there are really no members without a permanent branch). An examination of the records of the present-day branch members in previous years gives us a fair description of this growing permanence. It shows that those in the kibbutz engaged in agriculture have not been, as is sometimes popularly believed, members of some 'labor corps,' subjected to frequent, if not daily, shifts from one type of work to another, or from one branch to another.

Table 3.4 presents the labor records of the members who worked in 1970 in the agricultural branches, and who had been working in the meshek for over five years. There are, of course, differences among members. But a comparison between the first two columns clearly shows that members do not tend to float among branches. Some do occasionally change branches, though most of them have not repeated this pattern more than once or twice, and they tend to seek permanence in the branch they are in.

A few qualifications should be stated:

(1) It is obvious that sheer quantity (i.e., length of time, number of years working in Hofra) affects the internal distribution of employment. A given percentage of permanent work in a branch during a period of, say, six years in that branch is quite different from the same percentage of permanence when the tenure in the branch is sixteen years. A relatively large percentage of work in 'other branches,' for example, represents quite a different phenomenon for the young and for the 'veteran.'

(2) The difference between branches is discernible again. All members working permanently in the vineyard show a rather low percentage of permanence and the same is true for the vegetable garden (artichoke) and cotton. This phenomenon may again be related to the differences between branches in regard to season-ality and in some cases to size. While other people of those branches (such as V1, V2, A1, A2) tend to work during its slack season in 'service duties,' younger members tend to work in 'other branches' (C1, C2), though, of course, I speak of a ten-dency only. Taking all the members of all the branches together, all the 'veterans' but one (R16 who returned from a long period of work outside Hofra after which he took some time to establish himself in a branch) show records of labor in 'services' greater than in 'other branches.' All those considered 'young' in Hofra (roughly second-generation members and spouses) except for two, show records of work in 'other branches' to exceed those in services (the gap in the case of these two is very small indeed: they are P2 and R13). Two 'young' members (G8 and A3) show equal distribution. Part of this phenomenon has been interpreted above in relation to Table 3.3.

47

Table 3.4: Labor Distribution of Members in the Agricultural Branches, 1952-1970

(in percentage)

| Present Branch | Code name of member | Record for number of years | Branches | Permanent branch | Other branches | Service duties | Children's homes | Community activities | Management | Movement and Public | Notes |
|---|---|---|---|---|---|---|---|---|---|---|---|
| Citrus grove | G1 | 18 | Bee-hive, grove | 93.15 | 0.79 | 2.77 | | | 3.98 | | |
| | G2 | 18 | grove | 92.73 | 0.52 | 2.73 | | | | | 3.26 - care of ill wife |
| | G3 | 15 | grove | 92.65 | - | - | | | | | 7.24 - services ill 1969/70 |
| | G4 | 17 | grove | 91.95 | 0.17 | 4.90 | | | 3.36 | | |
| | G5 | 19 | Vegetables, grove | 90.83 | 0.06 | 7.99 | | | | | kitchen in transition period |
| | G6 | 18 | grove | 43.60 | 0.30 | 2.60 | | | 53.31 | | |
| | G7 | 8 | grove | 85.05 | 4.83 | 2.64 | | 3.85 | | 0.38 | |
| | G8 | 8 | Bee-hive, grove | 83.12 | 2.60 | 2.60 | | 5.49 | | | 5.49 Regular Army |
| | G9 | 18 | Bananas, grove | 29.33 | 0.71 | 3.70 | | 24.52 | 19.04 | 20.75 | |
| | G10 | 6 | Vineyard, grove | 84.14 | 4.76 | 3.27 | | | | 8.13 | |
| Orchard | O1 | 19 | Orchard, Fruits Board | 94.68 | 0.49 | 2.16 | | | | | |
| | O2 | 19 | Vegetables, Orchard | 85.96 | 1.33 | 8.66 | | 2.36 | | | kitchen in transition period |
| | O3 | 18 | Carpentry, Orchard | 71.51 | 2.10 | 2.80 | | | | | |
| | O4 | 19 | Bakery, REO*, Orchard | 92.52 | 1.56 | 5.03 | | | | | kitchen in transition period |
| | O5 | 19 | Bananas, Orchard | 90.80 | 1.71 | 4.61 | | | | | |
| | O6 | 16 | Bananas, Orchard | 52.66 | 2.54 | 14.19 | | | 1.69 | 28.01 | kitchen in transition period, and while in bananas |
| | O7 | 6 | Vegetables, Co-op. Orchard | 88.09 | 7.33 | 3.94 | | | | | |
| Vineyard | V1 | 17 | Orchard, Vineyard | 86.92 | 3.20 | 7.75 | | | | | kitchen in slack seasons |
| | V2 | 18 | Grove, Vineyard | 86.44 | 2.80 | 8.24 | | | | | Seasonality |
| | V3 | 12 | Tractor, Co-op., Vineyard | 65.32 | 15.13 | 8.07 | | | | 9.99 | |
| Cotton | C1 | 14 | Tractor, Cotton | 77.61 | 19.72 | 1.69 | | 0.64 | | | Seasonality |
| | C2 | 9 | Bananas, Cotton | 71.60 | 16.33 | 2.02 | | | | | Seasonality |
| Artichoke | A1 | 18 | Vegetables (Artichoke) | 80.62 | 0.62 | 6.90 | | | | 12.62 | |
| | A2 | 19 | Vegetables, Co-op. | 81.98 | 1.39 | 16.34 | | | | | Seasonality ill health |
| | A3 | 9 | Vegetables, Vineyard | 55.13 | 4.63 | 4.63 | | 2.54 | | 32.09 | |
| Flowers | F1 | 19 | Flowers, Co-op. | 94.69 | 0.64 | 3.51 | | 0.71 | | | |
| | F2 | 19 | Flowers | 95.88 | 0.02 | 2.36 | | | | | |
| Fish-ponds | P1 | 19 | Tractor, vegetables, flowers, fish | 86.86 | 4.04 | 3.56 | | 1.52 | | 2.74 | |
| | P2 | 5 | Fish-ponds | 68.46 | 1.17 | 1.79 | | 2.18 | | | 26.30 - seamanship |
| Chicken-coop | R1 | 19 | Coop | 81.35 | - | 17.02 | 0.34 | 1.04 | | | 1964-66 kitchen |
| | R2 | 17 | Coop | 81.48 | - | 12.15 | 0.18 | 1.17 | | | 3.57 care of ill parent |
| | R3 | 17 | Coop | 98.67 | - | 0.53 | | | | | |
| | R4 | 16 | Coop (incl. REO) | 95.83 | - | 1.25 | | 0.89 | | 0.61 | |
| | R5 | 19 | Flowers, coop | 78.19 | 1.85 | 13.93 | 0.27 | | | - | 2.26 miscellaneous services |
| | R6 | 19 | coop | 97.14 | - | 1.12 | | | | | |
| | R7 | 17 | Orchard, coop | 66.10 | 0.04 | 32.79 | 0.07 | 0.42 | | | 1954-58 kitchen |
| | R8 | 11 | Coop | 67.89 | 0.18 | 13.41 | 15.05 | | | | |
| | R9 | 19 | Flowers, coop | 63.00 | 1.34 | 13.80 | | 1.21 | | 17.34 | kitchen in transition period |
| | R10 | 8 | Coop | 66.38 | 0.17 | 18.08 | 10.36 | | | | 1.84 Post Office |
| | R11 | 7 | Coop | 57.47 | 4.10 | 0.58 | | | | 37.52 | |
| | R12 | 17 | Landscaping, coop | 95.69 | 0.50 | 3.32 | | | | | |
| | R13 | 10 | Orchard, bakery, coop, driving | 92.40 | 3.32 | 3.61 | | | | | |
| | R14 | 7 | Bakery, grove, coop, teaching | 60.10 | 9.00 | 2.80 | | 5.10 | | 23.00 | No records for 1967-8 |
| | R15 | 17 | Falha, fish, orchard, coop | 64.94 | 0.35 | 7.22 | | | 12.18 | 9.14 | 4.62 accounting |
| | R16 | 18 | Bakery, coop | 41.87 | 2.27 | 0.68 | 2.63 | | 2.37 | 50.04 | Children's home maintenance |

Source: Labor Records for 1952-66; 1967-1968; 1969; 1970, Hofra.

*REO - Regional Economic Organization.

48

(3)    All women have for some time been engaged in work in children's homes, the younger ones (R8 and R10) for much of their time (though that does not mean that the others were not engaged in that work in a period previous to 1952 or 1954), whereas only one man was engaged in this work, and his was in a maintenance job, not the care of children.

(4)    There is a tendency to work in the kitchen (or the dining-hall, or in both) during a transitional period, i.e., in a period following departure from a branch and admission to a new one.  That period may extend over a few months to a few years and is reflected in the records as in 'service duties' though it has no relation to the principle of duty, performed in rotation, by all the members who share labor in kitchen (or dining-hall) and nightguard.  It may have happened that members, upon leaving branches, worked for some time in the kitchen, then reconsidered and rejoined their branch-team again rather than seeking a new one.

(5)    There are, of course, people who have found it difficult to adapt to any branch for a long period and although they were 'permanent' in the branch, they have sought permanence somewhere else.

But the overall picture is that the tendency is for the individual member to seek or find permanent affiliation to one branch not only throughout the yearly cycle but also throughout the course of years.

I have stated (in discussing Table 3.3) that young men are frequently 'mobilized' for heavy work, and this is shown by the relatively larger percentage of their labor in branches other than their own, and in another aspect, by the percentage of labor which is invested by young men in other branches as compared with that invested in service duties.  One can also look at the labor of young men from another angle.  For those young men who have just returned from military service, this is the first phase in their adult civilian life.  When a second-generation 'child of the kibbutz,' or his (or her) spouse, returns home, and if he wishes to remain in the kibbutz, he thinks of establishing himself in a branch.  Joining an agricultural branch is not difficult: because of the scarcity of membership and the high demand for labor, a young man can practically choose his branch.  But having once chosen the branch, he is by no means irrevocably bound by his - and the kibbutz's - first decision. He may respond willingly to invitations from other branches or agree cheerfully to requests made by the Labor-Co-ordinator of the kibbutz to work, whenever necessary, somewhere else.  He may like to keep his options open, even though he 'belongs' to a team, or is so considered by his fellow-members. That is to say that new members, who are usually young, tend to be somewhat undecided about their commitment to permanence in a given branch during the first phase of their actual membership (equivalent to the phase of working as an adult in the meshek) in the kibbutz. A new member seeks permanence, but his choice of branch naturally comes first. As the years pass, permanence grows both quantitatively (amount of labor invested in the branch) and qualitatively (through widening access to more and more responsibilities in the branch and through becoming more experienced in the branch's tasks).

Today (1970) this process is discussed in terms of the 'new' and the 'young.' Reports and stories of 'olden days' (before 1952 and possibly in the 1930's and 1940's) disclose that basically the same process took place during the initial periods of working life of practically every member in Hofra. Oldtimers, when talking about the early history of Hofra, have referred to Malakhi (A1) variously as once a 'fallah' (grain-crop agriculturist), as once 'the chicken-coop man,' and on other occasions as 'the vegetable-garden man.' The practice for a new member seems to have been to take any possible assignment and to establish himself in a branch through trial, experience and selection. Again, one could - and still can - change branches; but the point discussed here, is not the change from one branch for another, but the process of move-ment from the initial, somewhat undecided, phase of working life to a more permanent attachment. This phenomenon of seeming indecision reappears if and when a member changes from a branch after attaining 'permanent' affiliation. While he is moving, possibly, to temporary work in the kitchen, he accepts assignments to temporary jobs in other branches.

Permanence in labor in a given branch has been presented here as an immediate fact which I feel should strike even any casual observer. I have stated that a tendency to permanence coincides with the economic and technological (including care of capital equipment) interests of the meshek. It has further been postulated that it is not only in the interests of the collective, but it has also become an aim of the individual, for the individ-ual to seek a position of permanence at work. At this point the question should be asked: with what in the kibbutz's community life is permanence in a job, or position in work, connected?

The essence of the collective aspect of the matter has been explained. Other aspects, related to those already dis-cussed, are referred to in the Conclusions of the Meeting of the Kibbutz in Degania in 1923 (Hakvutza, 1924: 41). The follow-ing statement occurs in the chapter on Arrangements and Change of Personnel in Labor:

1.  The frequent changing of workers in various branches
    of the _meshek_ hinders the development of the branches
    and the specialization of members in them...

4.  On the other hand, permanence of [only] a few members
    in the branches might decrease the adequate interest
    of the rest of the membership in those branches, and,
    also, decrease the interest of those members working
    in another branch of the _meshek_.

The solution to this dilemma was sought in terms of another
kibbutz institution, which is believed to embody communal responsibility and democracy:

5.  As a result of all the above, the Meeting holds that
    a joint [collective] and permanent consultation of
    all the members, in general meetings, is necessary
    [to discuss] even the details of each of the _meshek_
    branches.

It seems that in this early period not all members in the
young kibbutzim could gain permanence in branches, owing to the
relatively small size of the branches and to the small size and
instability of the _meshek_'s agriculture. Nor is it certain that
many of them were interested in permanent attachment, for reasons
given earlier when discussing the mobility of new members, and
for other reasons which have to do with a particular phase in
the historical development of the kibbutzim and the members'
image of the kibbutz. The conference at which the above recommendations were passed does not seem to have envisaged the
growing rate of permanence in branch-labor for all members. It
shifted the attempted resolution of the dilemma into the realm
of community institutions. I must say immediately that there
_is_ a problem in the kibbutz of differential knowledge of, and
interest in, the "details of each of the _meshek_ branches" as
well as the _meshek_ as a whole, some aspects of which will be
discussed below. But the Meeting seems to have been unable to
make up its mind whether the need for permanence in economic
branches (as implied in §1) should be met by encouraging members
to specialize in them (thereby losing interest in other branches
as implied in §4), or by preferring overall communal considerations viz., increasing "adequate interest" in all the branches
and therefore encouraging members to shift from one branch to
another. The latter might leave many members without a permanent branch, thereby causing loss of interest in the branch to
which they would be temporarily assigned and ignoring the economic
and technological need for specialization. As three different
problems were discussed at one time (interest of specialization
in the branch, redundancy of people in seasonal branches at some
stages of economic growth, and maintaining the interest of all

members in the _meshek_ as a whole), the solution was sought at a different level.

But, in the end, members as individuals, despite the kibbutzim's awareness and discussion of the problems as these affect the community's institutions, have, with the process of economic growth, obtained permanent membership in branches.

Nowadays the kibbutz as an economic enterprise recognizes, and stresses, the advantages it has achieved through the process of specialization. This is one explanation of the individual's tendency to permanence. It is based on the economic considerations of the interests of both branch and the _meshek_ as a whole.

## Viewing permanence from the kibbutz's set of values

Another explanation may be sought in the kibbutz's set of values. This is a mode of explanation by implication. The kibbutz places effective labor high amongst those values expected to be achieved by each member. Any work you do is important and it is important that you work. Exalted ideals are achieved, first and foremost, by work: preaching ideals, or 'idle' talk, sublime and gratifying and illuminating as they may be, do not bring those ideals alive unless you work. The individual as well as the commune experiences self-realization first and foremost through work. Spiro (1956)[2] argues that labor is not merely a necessity, it is a calling. When you perform your job, "it becomes a sacred task... in the religious sense of that term" (1956: 89). It is performed with an ethical-ideological consciousness (1956: 88), which has emerged through the internalization of the value system by the individual. "For the chaverim [members]," writes Spiro, "it is... labor which is the highest vocational goal. This goal, it must be stressed, is primarily a spiritual goal - it is a means to self-realization" (1956: 14). "It is little wonder that one of their first goals was 'the conquest of labor'" (1956: 14). The internalization of values has succeeded. It is shown through "What Veblen termed, 'the instinct of workmanship', or what is called 'mode pleasure' - in contrast to 'end pleasure'" (1956: 84).

Thus far I am still discussing the fact that the individual internalizes spiritual values as indoctrinated in both kibbutz and Youth Movement. I stress that it is worth remembering, in this connection, that the majority of the 'veteran' members of Hofra have come from the Youth Movement which exalted the ideals of a "Religion" of Labor, a "religion" that emphasizes self labor as both an ideal and a means to individual self-realization. Working devotedly ideally gives deep satisfaction. Logically, the more you are acquainted with the work you do, the greater your achievement. Agricultural work often necessitates repetitive and dull jobs, but it is hardly an assembly-line type of work. Agricultural work has been placed high in kibbutz values as the essence of the components in the "Religion" of Labor, redemption through work and return to nature. The better acquainted you become with all aspects of agricultural work and its ever-increasing demands, (and this could be extended to other tasks) through permanence and experience, the closer you will get to realizing your potential.

This last idea is not explicitly stated by Spiro, but it follows from his argument. Furthermore, if intrinsic satisfaction (see Spiro, 1956: 84) is derived from work - and I do not dispute that it is - and an acquaintance with a particular branch's cycle of work will probably increase chances for this satisfaction, then we may expect the individual member to seek opportunities to achieve such an aim through attachment to a branch. As Spiro says, "The average chaver [member] is [sic.] a permanent member of a particular economic branch - the orchard, the wheat fields, the dairy, etc. - and his immediate attachment and identification is with his branch, taking pride in its success and becoming depressed by its failures" (Spiro, 1956: 84). Here we ascend, as it were, to the social level proper, as the arena is not only the individual's own disposition, in which he has internalized components of the set of social values, but also, it must be noted, the individual acting within the commune. Spiro continues: "And though he wishes to see the entire kibbutz prosper, he derives great satisfaction from knowing that his branch contributed its share - or more - to this prosperity. Hence, he is motivated to work hard in order for his branch to receive a favorable rating in this informal competition [between branches]" (1956: 84-85). Spiro then moves from the level of psychical motivation (i.e., of internalized values) onto that of conscious reasoning: "... his own standard of living is dependent upon that of the group which, in turn, depends upon the productive capacity of its members... Hence, one important source of work-motivation in Kiryat Yedidim is the motive of personal economic improvement." In other words, both prestige and income are drawn from achievements of the branch, by which an individual has contributed to the benefit of the kibbutz as a whole; the more you improve, invest labor and contribute to the development of the branch, the better are the chances for the kibbutz (the meshek) to prosper. In doing so you prosper yourself. This is achieved by means of identification of self with the kibbutz as a meshek. As we have seen, permanence entailing specialization would contribute to that prosperity.

Lastly, values - if they form a normative system - require and are supported by mechanisms of social control. This problem is also discussed by Spiro, and I will return to it.

## Public opinion and permanence

Spiro, throughout his book, is careful to speak only about
the community he studied and he does not generalize about kibbutzim, but in the light of the issues he discusses there is every
reason to believe that similar, if not identical, processes and
issues occur in this type of kibbutzim established by graduates of
European youth movements at a certain period in Jewish history,
and probably also in other types of kibbutzim.  Spiro writes: "It
will be remembered that labor is one of the paramount values in
the culture of Kiryat Yedidim, and that hard, efficient labor is
a necessary, if not sufficient, determinant of prestige.  In the
absence of the profit motive, the respect of one's fellows has
become an important motive in this society" (1956: 85).  It is
conspicuous now that in addition to belief in values and behaving
according to norms derived from them, and to the intellectual
reasoning about the welfare of the kibbutz community and the
success of its economy, whether in the branch or the meshek as a
whole, there is the control exercised on the individual through
his wish to be respected.  He derives prestige from good work.
As stated earlier, it would be only logical - though again it is
only implied in Spiro's context - that by achieving permanence
(and what one achieves through permanence) the individual member
gains prestige in the community's eyes, for his chances of more
"productive and economic behavior" (1956: 5) are secured by means
of permanence in the branch.  The mechanism typical of the kibbutz is public expression of opinion (1956: 5).  It bestows prestige on, or withdraws it from, an individual in accordance with
the ever-present and ever-changing interplay between individual
and community.  Good laboring is indeed a major variable in this
interplay.

These last three sentences enable me to embark on a different level of argument - namely, one in which I will be protected from slipping, as it were, into psychological or socio-
psychological, and even purely ideological, modes of analysis.
But before doing that, let me say that I do not regard those
modes as irrelevant, wrong or unhelpful.  On the contrary, I do
believe that far from being so, they may even illuminate the
analysis of the sociological anthropologist.  By taking their
findings and statements 'naively' (Devons and Gluckman, 1964:
13-19, 158-261), whether those statements are made within the
discipline of psychology or form part of a systematic ideological
quest, they may be applicable in sociological analysis.  I do
not elaborate further on Spiro's analysis or follow further the
line of argument adopted by him because I am trained in a different discipline and therefore I do not feel competent to discuss scientifically, psychological or socio-psychological views
of the kibbutz and its inhabitants.  The Kibbutz has been dis-

cussed abundantly in a non-scientific manner. It is not worth embarking on a course of analysis, with the formal ideological postulates of the kibbutz as a starting-point, and thus inevitably examining all behavior in terms of its congruence or incongruence with ideological postulates, since so much has been written on this theme that there is hardly anything additional to be said. But, I repeat, I do find all these modes of analysis illuminating and helpful.

What then, is public opinion in the kibbutz about the individual's permanence in the branch? In general, it approves of permanence in a branch and the related aspect of further specialization. It judges by considering facts as positive or negative, and it values those phenomena marked as in different degrees acceptable or reprehensible. Among other things, it develops stereotypes. One such stereotype in the field of employment and labor in the kibbutz is the already-mentioned simile of a "cork." Why does this stereotype appear to be evaluated negatively? That is, is being a "cork" really regarded as reprehensible?

I have already stated that the development of Hofra's economy and its main branches of agriculture increased the demand for labor. The conclusions of the Meeting of the Kvutzot, that there should be a nucleus of permanent members in each branch while "the rest," perhaps even the majority, were mobile, reflected an organizational stage which has given way to the permanence of practically all the staff in each agricultural branch. Now there is hardly a member who is a "cork" except as listed temporarily above, and even then it is "temporary permanence" rather than "floating transience." Fifty-four members are mentioned as members of the branch-teams in 1970 in Table 3.3, and all of them are permanent. However, there are still two members who are considered "corks," though I would hesitate to affirm that they deserve this title. Probing into this phenomenon may help reveal the super-structural nature of this stereotype. The two are young men, 23 and 22 years old. They have been engaged in work for several years. Neither of them had established himself permanently in a particular branch, though their mobility between branches is circulatory, and, for each of them, encompasses only two to three branches - the orchard and the citrus grove in harvest season for both, and cotton or chicken-run respectively for one of them. Even though young men are mobilized into helping branches other than their own, the seasonal shifts of these two young men cannot be regarded as a usual 'mobilization of the young.' Neither of them can point to one particular branch as his 'permanent' branch. Other age-mates of theirs, even though they have been engaged in work in the meshek for a shorter period of time, have managed to establish themselves permanently in branches (given the reservations made earlier in regard to young

people's permanence in and choice of a given branch). In the
light of the gap between supply and demand for labor at the present
stage of the meshek's development, the position of those two seems
odd. It is not even a choice of options left open by the men in
question themselves for subsequent selection of a branch. It is
not they who have decided to remain unattached: the meshek's central
agencies dealing with work as well as the branches themselves regard
these two men as such.

Both Yonah and Yamin tried to volunteer for activities designed
to benefit the Israeli society at large. Many young members of
The Movement spend at least a year in such activities. They were
rejected. Their rejection followed personal histories of difficulties in emotional adjustment to the expectations, claims, and
requirements of Israeli society, and of the kibbutz. They both
began working as adults at a relatively early age. It is difficult
to say whether it was entirely the effect of previous difficulties
which inhibited them from meeting the requirements and claims of
kibbutz society in the field of labor, or whether the failure to
meet these requirements and claims was affected by the low expectations of that society once they were recognized as 'difficult.'
Probably both processes operated. The fact remains that they have
failed to prove themselves able to gain a permanent position in
any branch. No branch has refused either Yonah or Yamin in seasonal
work, mostly of a mass nature, but no branch would employ either
of them in a more elaborate kind of task, and therefore it would
not grant them the position of permanence, which this implies. In
other words, they still move from one branch to another, following
seasonal needs, in the manner of temporary laborers rather than in
the manner followed by kibbutz members who move from one task to
another within a branch.

However, it should be added that neither of them changes
his branch every day, nor is either pressed to do so by the Labor
Distributor.[3] Neither of them changes branches more than a few
times a year and I believe that eventually they will settle in a
branch. And, indeed, their labor records, particularly Yamin's,
show a tendency to less and less frequent changes. For the time
being, however, they are 'corks', even though not in the traditional sense of persons who are at the daily orders of the Labor
Distributor and who do not know in advance where they will be
working the following day or the one following that. They are
'corks' by virtue of their 'not belonging' since they are
'difficult,' and the difficulties are real and not imaginary.
They have become difficult social cases, though the origin of
the problem may not have been on the communal level. The community has to treat the problem in its social context. The
kibbutz granted both of them the status of membership, together
with their age-mates, at the age of eighteen and in the same

ceremony, it granted them all social rights (in housing, vacation, clothing, services, etc.) and security, and it has also provided them with employment within the meshek. Thus, institutionally the kibbutz has done its share, and much more than that, so far as their status of equal membership is concerned. But they are still exceptional in terms which, while not social in origin, have proved relevant in social contexts. One of these contexts is labor in the branch. The problem, obviously, has always been present, and it has been present in this context too. A person who fails to conform to such minimal norms as a reasonable ratio between number of work days and absence from work, adequate assumption of responsibility in various branch-tasks, adequate interest in work and to an extent in the branch, and what is considered reasonable reliability in work, must fail to belong to a team, as a group of people whose basic interrelationships depend on those claims. There does not have to be a formal discussion of the case nor is it necessary that a formal test of the person in question take place. A person who does not, or cannot, fulfil minimal requirements set by the group, requirements which in turn are imposed by the nature of the branch, the state of the meshek, organizational institutions and the like, cannot have a position of permanence in the team. That does not mean that he is prevented from working in the branch; it only hinders his chance 'to belong.' In the contexts of membership of agricultural branches, it is argued that such a person's permanence in the branch is not necessary in the off-season and that therefore, his presence in the branch should not become an argument which the central bodies of the meshek can use to avoid assigning other members to the branch.

Difficulties of this nature, arising from an individual's past, and possibly remaining with him into the present, might be intensified, in this context, by the workings of society itself. Prejudgment by others of the said individual's probable future establishment in a branch and ability to sustain branch responsibilities may affect the central officers of the community (such as the Labor Distributors or the Meshek Organizer) in assigning them to a given branch, or in securing the agreement of a team to accept him or her as permanent members. I emphasize that such attitudes do not imply personal hostility to these particular young men. They are merely not seen as workers in a branch, and members feel for them as human beings, members, members' sons, and so forth. In a community in which so many aspects of life and so many statuses intermingle and overlap, the individual is not judged by a single criterion relevant to one status or role only. But in the context of branch labor, the problem presents itself and can hardly be avoided.

If a central officer of the kibbutz in charge of assigning labor accepts that Yamin or Yonah "are not ripe for permanence in a branch" (as it was said to me) and acts accordingly, and if the team accepts that they "cannot be counted on in more skilled, off-season, work and they might be more helpful in another branch now" and lets it be known that this is their appraisal, the two are likely to conduct themselves accordingly.  The treatment by 'society,' in the form of a few branch-teams and a group of officers, contributes to the crystallization of this emergence of only a minute social category of people 'unripe for permanence.'  Several mechanisms may allow this minute category to emerge: 'understanding' the specific individual circumstances leading to procrastination in reaching a solution; assignment of the individual to a certain kind of work with, or without, explanation that his assignment to another task is extremely difficult if not impossible under the circumstances; relatively frequent transfers from one branch to another by the Labor Distribution; or - in a more delicate manner - by his being kindly asked by the branch foreman in another branch to help in shouldering the task facing the team in the harvest season.  And there are other mechanisms.  All these events contribute to the development of public judgment on those in this category.  Once the social category comes into being, and particularly once its presence is recognized against the background of almost universal permanence, as it were, of membership in the branches, public opinion puts its stamp on the fact.  And it does not do this without passing judgments or labelling.  Impermanence, then, is a product of both individual variables and society's response, or rather the interplay of both in the context of the ratio between demand for and supply of labor.

The approving of permanence by public opinion (and the ensuing negative labelling of impermanence) can be thus regarded: the normal, in the numerical sense, has become the normative. This process has been congruent with the economic development of the kibbutz and its demands, and there is no contradiction of ideological postulates.  There is nothing in the tenets of the Israeli Kibbutz that would regard permanence in a branch as undesirable.  Therefore no ambivalence exists about this development such as there is about the facts of women's labor, or hired labor.  The economic, technological and other interests of the branch and the meshek which encourage permanence, coincide with a Zionist element of kibbutz ideology calling for productive hityashvut (settlement), ensuring permanence for the member's life in his community - his meshek.

As has already been said, permanence does not imply that the member does not, or should not, leave his branch.  The very figures in Tables 3.3 and 3.4 prove that.  All members, unless they are defined as too old or disabled, are required to give their share in services; young men are assigned to temporary,

58

seasonal, heavy work; there are 'mobilizations' of the entire
membership to help in picking oranges in leisure time, on the
Sabbath or in the early hours of ordinary working days. Members
do leave their branches in off-season days if they have no work
to do in the branch. Some members may sometimes leave their
branch for another, permanently. Hofra has now reached the stage
when older people are about to retire from permanent agricultural
labor. All these events do take place, but none leads to the
permanent position of being a 'cork.'

A young member of Kibbutz Hardoof asked for a long period
of leave of absence. This request followed some affair in the
kibbutz in which he was alleged to be involved, which cast some
doubts on his conduct. It had nothing to do with
either work or permanence in a branch. While discussing the
issue informally, before the convention of the General Assembly
of the kibbutz, people tended to agree to grant the leave, but
then recalled his conduct, whether or not it was relevant to the
request or to the affair. Amongst other things frequently mentioned about him was that he had not achieved permanence in any
branch, though he had been in the meshek, back from his military
service, for a few years. This fact was quite easily connected
with the reference to the alleged misconduct. There appeared,
as it were, to be a "halo effect" on social grounds so that recalling one mode of disapproved behavior led to recalling another.
But people were very careful not to raise in the Assembly the
subject of impermanence in a branch. Not only were they aware of
the difference between situations of informal talk in which they
could relate different events one to another, and the formal situation of the General Assembly in which this liberty was hardly
acceptable, but they were also aware of the apparent irrelevance
of impermanence in a branch to a problem regarded as one of moral
conduct. Yet, the young man's father raised the issue. He said
he knew that people, active and central members amongst them, had
used this argument in the affair, that they still used the fact
(which he did not deny) of his son's impermanence as a slandering
label against him. But instead of differentiating the issues, he
asked: "How can you use this fact against a young member? Here
we have a young man who is ready to respond positively to whatever
need arises in any branch and who is ready to forego the position
and the status of permanence; a member who is always ready to co-
operate with the Labor Distributor and has always done so; who
regards the needs of the meshek above his own. It is a deliberate
act of slander." Whether because of this appeal or not, the son
was granted permission to go.

The speaker was aware that impermanence could be a basis for
what he regarded as slander. He knew that it conveyed a critical,
negative meaning in public opinion. He knew, furthermore, that

59

deviation from social standards in one context, as they were,
might be connected in the process of informal judgment with
deviation from social standards in another context. And, of
course, he may have known that members would not relate these
two different issues to one another in the formal context of
the Assembly. His presentation of this issue would hardly have
met with approval had it been done on an informal level; it
would have run counter to standards accepted by the public, i.e.,
the standards of permanence sought, if not immediately achieved,
in a branch. A formal situation is of course different. However,
it is not the difference between situations that is the subject
here, but the role that impermanence or permanence in a branch
can play in establishing a member's social position in the
community as a whole. A member may find himself caught up in an
issue which apparently has no relevance to belonging to a branch,
but this affects his position on that issue: this shows that the
normative demand for permanence far exceeds the limits of a branch
of labor. The failure to respond to this demand, or expectation,
puts one in the category labelled as 'difficult cases' or
'misfits.' While the group, or "society", categorizes the individuals concerned socially and approves this act of categorization
socially, it labels them - as well as interprets their conduct -
in personal and psychologistic terms.

Permanence in a branch is highly valued, but it is not in
itself a proclaimed value, in the formal ideological sense of
the term. It is implicit in approved modes of operating relationships, and also - as I believe I have shown above - in the
'paramount value' of labor in kibbutz culture and in the 'respect'
the working member can derive from successful, efficient labor.
If public opinion approves permanence by encouraging people formally through the kibbutz institutions, as well as informally, and
if there is censure of those who fail to respond, it is in the
social relationships of the 'public' concerned that the 'opinion'
originates. The 'public' (that is, all the members of the community) work unless they are not able to do so. One might say,
the community works. Most of the members work in the collective
economy. Labor is the conspicuous way of making a living. The
meshek, large as it is in some respects, is small enough to make
the actual labor invested in it by individuals quite conspicuous.
There is an ideological demand for equality in the investment of
labor on the part of the individuals (though this demand is
qualified by age, health, and other variables). Collective labor,
even while people work in different branches, is based on collective ownership of the entire meshek and this makes it possible
to have, so to speak, control by all over everything. Clearly, in
other contexts the members are not necessarily equal. Working
is a common enterprise in which members meet, spend time, share
interest, develop expectations, and evaluate one another. It is
also that aspect of a member which primarily presents itself in

60

interpersonal encounters within the communal context. In these relationships there arise differential measures of 'respect.' In other words, the system of relationships which evolves in branch and meshek work confers upon the member a status which has a direct relation to the member's work. Permanence is a prerequisite in most contexts for any positive prestige in the realm of work. But obviously it is not the only context in which prestige is conferred on the individual member, nor is it always the critical or the most important one. This depends on the total set of constellations in which a person operates socially. But undoubtedly work is an exceedingly important constellation. Respect and prestige, and the resulting status, are to a large extent determined by this variable.[4] Since labor is a fundamental value both in the actual maintenance and development of the meshek and in the ideological tenets of the kibbutz, and it always implies moral obligations, it becomes the basis of the effectiveness of much social control in the kibbutz. An important agency or mechanism of this control is the public opinion of all those involved in the community.

## Dependence and permanence

Thus far a few variables influencing the individual's search for permanence in a branch have been discussed: the interest of the meshek, his own personal interest in a particular branch or work, the intrinsic satisfaction he may get from it, implications of the high value attached to good and efficient work, and public opinion as it functions in exercising social control. The problem of social control in this context has yet another aspect, that of the individual's dependence on, and involvement in, the kibbutz's institutions.

The case of the young man above showed that his position in the context of labor affected how members treated him in other contexts in community life; and it is evident that position in work can be regarded as a key to position in other realms of community life. Indeed, it is in this wider context that the problem of dependence, or involvement, in relation to permanence in the branch is considered.

The member of the kibbutz applies to committees, agencies and officers of the community whenever he wants something that is within his rights as a member. When he needs cash, he gets it from the Internal Treasurer; when he gets new clothes, it is the person in charge of clothing to whom he first applies, and who is also bound by communal regulations; in matters affecting the care and education of his children there are nurses, teachers, the educational officer (the Chairman of Educational Committee), and ultimately the plenary meeting of Committee itself; and he applies to other communal agencies over problems of housing, health, personal needs, etc. All these "officials" are supposed to work within the rules of, and decisions taken by, kibbutz institutions. The officials are either elected by the members or hold their offices by virtue of their occupation; and all reside in the same village as co-members of the same commune, and as fellow-shareholders, so to speak, of the same meshek. Of course, a man (below, Ego) may himself be such an officer or a member of a committee which deals with interests and applications of other members, a condition which intensifies joint interpersonal involvement. A person may be an official in one context and a supplicant in another.

But it is the position of Ego as the one who is dependent on communal institutions and officers which is at present under discussion. Ego is personally involved in several sets of relationships in his different roles and capacities. His involvement can be seen as the part played by an individual member, or individual component, in the interplay of all other components of the system. Above all, this reflects the ultimate interdependence of all members of the kibbutz. But, looking at it from the angle of Ego, it is dependence rather than interdependence that first strikes one. Even an office-holder, say a treasurer, has no authority over matters other than those in his particular area of responsibility. He cannot exercise control, let alone govern, in issues in the realm of cultural or health activities, though his influence may be considerable. Ego thus finds himself constantly involved in situations in which he has to abide by the rules of the community and its institutions, as almost all social activity takes place within the small community. It is obvious that in a kibbutz the individual depends on the whole (whether this whole is in the form of meshek, finance, elected bodies, support of peers and members, General Assembly or the like) more than the whole appears to depend on him alone. This does not eliminate the facts of interplay or interdependence.

A man can ease the intensity of external control by securing 'a stronghold' so to speak, in one institutional sphere. Such a sphere is labor. Once he gets this stronghold in the form of permanent position in a given branch, he eases his control, and it is further eased if he can become an equal partner in the 'public' within which public 'opinion' evolves. The institution of labor demands that one should work as devotedly and as efficiently as possible within regulations concerning length of working career, personal ability, age, kind of work, demands of the season, and so forth. Series of demands have, in fact, already been mentioned. They are associated with permanence in the branch. Public opinion sees to it that those demands, many of which are formulated in Regulations for Labor drawn up by the General Assembly in accordance with the Regulations established by The Movement, are fulfilled. If a member belongs to the 'normal' (in the numerical sense) category of members, his chances of fulfilling these demands (or norms) are considerable; if he does not, he is open to further pressures and control. Not only is he labelled lazy or incompetent by 'public opinion' - this is only one aspect of the problem - but also his dependence on officers like Labor Distributor, the Meshek Organizer or branch foreman, becomes increasingly great. Within limits, all members work where they have decided to work, but the range of choice may be restricted as it is determined by the composition of the meshek, and within this range most of the members have changed branches. But the permanent member of a branch gets returns, in independence and in security, from his position. The member without permanence in a branch has no chance to get such 'returns.' Return, or reward, may mean such things as satisfaction with work in a chosen place, some advantage peculiar to a particular branch, appreciation by fellows, and those other advantages which have already been discussed. The impermanent member - and this seems to be more important on sociological grounds - does not have a strong position from which he can bargain with the Labor Distributor or other officers who represent the central interests of the meshek. As he is not 'essential' in the branch he can hardly expect support from the team if he refuses to be transferred to another branch nor does he have grounds to negotiate and his range of choice is very limited. The central interests of the meshek in the field of labor (which require transfers of the labor force) paradoxically press most heavily on those who are most easily compelled to accede to them because they do not have the stronghold of permanence that would make such transfer hard to accomplish. The permanent member can refuse a request to move (again, within limits), can mobilize support in the branch, can bargain, can prove that it is in the branch's and ultimately the meshek's interest that he does not move, or at least he can negotiate the conditions, terms and time-limit of his own. In short, he reduces the intensity of his dependence. Bargaining or negotiating with him is different from bargaining with his impermanent counterpart. And that is known throughout the community. It affects a person's general position in the community as a whole. An argument, such as that used by the father of the young man in Hardoof, just rouses a wry smile, if not a smirk, and at best is considered naive. So, the first step to a fairly reasonable position in the community is to achieve some standing of permanence in a branch (or for that matter, in any department or working place in the kibbutz). Subsequent steps in retaining, consolidating or changing the position acquired are a different matter.

## The labor authorities

Before discussing labor organization and its machinery, it is advisable to ask: When do the communal central agencies enter the picture? This question will be introduced briefly, but without a full analysis that might divert the course of the present discussion. Members of the kibbutz distinguish between contexts when they answer this question.

(1) When a member is considered essential to the branch: "In general, members who incline to work in that branch are assigned to those [branch] teams. But it sometimes happens that it is necessary, to compel a member to work in a branch despite his unwillingness; whether because it is found that he is essential to the branch owing to his expertise or experience, or because no other member has been found more suitable than he... imposition of work on a member according to the view of the whole [kibbutz] cannot be avoided" (Z. Shepher, 1960: 106). Expertise, experience and acquaintance with the branch and its details are indispensable. "In a society which maintains a meshek in mutual responsibility it is inconceivable to abandon one of its branches because an individual is not prepared to work in it, when he is the appropriate man to work in it [that branch]. As said, it is only seldom that the kibbutz is compelled to impose its will on the individual" (1960: 107). Compulsion rarely happens, it is explained, because (a) the man experienced in a branch tends to work in it; (b) he recognizes the needs of the branch and the value of his own work in it; (c) his joining another, new, branch in which he is inexperienced involves difficulties which are not negligible; and (d) the principle of mutual responsibility is his as well (1960: 107; and see also Spiro, 1956: 76). Responsibility, in this context, leads him to respond to what is presented to him as the interest of the kibbutz without the latter's resorting to compulsion.

(2) When several members are equal in experience in a branch and all are unwilling to work in it, the kibbutz cannot dispense with the possibility of returns from the branch. Then, "if the member persists in his refusal, and persuasions have not sufficed, it is decided against his will" (Z. Shepher, 1960: 107).

(3) A refusal to leave the permanent branch for temporary service or an office (such as night-guard, kitchen, central office) may lead to a similar decision, i.e., the imposition of the kibbutz's authority over the individual member.

(4) The central agency is supposed to take responsibility for problems arising from aging or deterioration of health.

And (5)  Compulsion may be requisite when labor needs to
be shifted to help out branches temporarily, in their high ("hot")
seasons (Z. Shepher, 1960; and Spiro, 1956: 75-78).

Formally, all members of the kibbutz are under the authority
of the kibbutz's elected bodies and are subjected to the decisions
made by the General Assembly and the committees and officers to
whom it has delegated authority.  The authority to assign members
to a department or branch of work is vested in the General Assembly
and these bodies.  Consequently, every member is a worker on whose
acquiescence and co-operation the relevant committee or officer is
entitled to count when the need arises to assign workers to different places.  Without this assumption those bodies could hardly work.
The development of the economy, the process of specialization, the
interests of the branches, the gap between labor demands and supplies, and the tendency of the members to achieve permanence in
their working places, and their interest in doing so, have all
contributed to the qualification, in practice, of this formally
undisputed authority.  Thus the two major subjects with which the
central bodies related to labor deal are planning of distribution
and assignment of labor, particularly for crop harvesting in the
various branches (mostly from outside a branch's permanent labor-
force) and settling internal difficulties in a team should these
arise.  Assignment of new members to a branch or department of
work is discussed in appropriate institutions; but as has already
been made clear, with the gap between demand for and supply of
labor, in the end the individual has considerable, if not ultimate,
power in deciding.  The increasing gap between demand and supply
in the field of labor in the kibbutz further strengthens the role
of the individual, vis-a-vis "society," in the selection of work
and occupation.  This selection leads to the choice of branch (or
department of work) and to the individual's establishment in the
branch.  Thus, this gap leads to the consolidation and the
strengthening of the position of the individual member.

The history of the kibbutz movement was marked by the phase
of the "intimate kvutza" (prior to its development into the
"organic kvutza") in which not only was labor organized, or
scheduled, daily, but also this was done by the entire membership.
The motto, "Comrades, let's organize the work," referring to the
entire membership taking part in the organization of work,
originated in the first days of Degania, when in the late evening
all the members used to assemble (around one table, it is said)
to discuss current labor problems and indeed any subject pertaining to the kvutza, and work out together plans to tackle all.
This initial practice of direct and immediate democracy was rooted
in the conception of the commune as an 'intimate kvutza.' Everybody was involved in all the problems of the newly settled kvutza,
its economic and labor aspects included.  This daily get-together

was the institution from which, with the growth of the kvutza, the General Assembly has emerged. The General Assembly still retains its position as the highest authority in kibbutz life, though it has suffered significant setbacks and has undergone changes. While retaining ultimate authority, it has delegated authority over work to elected committees and officers. In the field of labor it does not discuss the daily schedule of work though it does discuss plans of work, which involve the meshek and the membership (such as 'mobilization' of the public to help in spare-time picking of oranges, or at the partial expense of their daily permanent work, or the acceptance of temporary laborers from outside the kibbutz, or the Regulations of Labor). The actual drafting of plans, whether the latter are brought to the Assembly or not, is done by the committees concerned, or more commonly still, by the officers who bring their views for discussion in the committees. Current problems arising in the field of labor are dealt with by the officers and their committees. Such problems are brought before the General Assembly when the officers and the committees to whom authority has been delegated feel that recommendations, motions and resolutions made by them require sanctioning by the community.

In kibbutz literature we find the following description. After stating that "there is a detailed registration of all labor days (as well as of machines and work-tools) according to branches and kinds of labor in the branch and also according to the workers' names," Z. Shepher (1960: 109) goes on to say: "The allocation of the labor force and the co-ordination of tasks are in the hands of the Labor Committee, which is elected by the community annually. The Committee confers on one or two of its members that [task of] labor organization in practice. The Committee itself discusses in its meetings matters of labor in respect of their general co-ordination, according to the needs of branches and seasons and to the suitability of people. The actual organization of labor, on the basis of the Committee's conclusions, is conferred on the Labor Distributor." My own present discussion does not elaborate on the institution of Labor Distribution in all, or even most of its aspects, yet nevertheless it is worthwhile here to get an impression of this general process through the following description by the same writer, a member of a kibbutz: "In large and old meshakim the task of labor distribution requires a full day [of work], inclusive of the evening. The settlements wish the Distributor to remain in office for at least a year. The reason is obvious: continuance means experience and continuity of method. But it is not always possible. As a matter of fact, it is mostly impossible. The office is very difficult. It requires constant debate with the branches whose needs are numerous. It also involves negotiation with people who are required by the needs of the meshek to be transferred from one task to another, either

because the member's turn to take up work which is done in rotation has come, or because another member has fallen ill or left
and it is necessary to find a substitute for him in his work.
The task [of distributing labor] is exhausting. For the most
part the needs of the branch from which the Labor Distributor
has come - the Distributor also belongs permanently to a branch -
do not permit him to be absent from it for a whole year as well.
Therefore the kibbutzim which have managed to retain a permanent
Labor Distributor for the whole year are very few. In those
kibbutzim the Distributor participates in the central management
of the kibbutz. In most of the kibbutzim alternation in the task
of Labor Distribution either every half or quarter of a year is
common [customary], and the members of the Labor Committee fulfil
the task by rotating it internally among themselves" (1960: 109).

The communal body endowed with the responsibility and
authority in the field of labor is, then, the Labor Committee.
The officer who represents its authority is the Labor Distributor.
He, in his daily work, and the Committee--with whose counsel he
acts, to which he brings problems considered to be important and
of a more than temporary nature for discussion, and from which
he gets backing--are supposed to 'cover' all subjects pertaining
to labor.

Given the paramount value attached to labor in the economic
building up of the kibbutz, in its ideology and in general in
communal life and social control, no wonder it has been institutionalized; and furthermore, it is little wonder that this
institutionalization has been marked, among other things, by the
constitution of a community committee designed especially to deal
with all problems pertaining to labor.

"Labor," as such, has been singled out as a unified institution. That is not to say that the members do not realize its
diverse meanings. People, of course, recognize that labor is an
aspect of economic affairs; they view labor as one factor of
economic production; labor is obviously recognized as a physical,
time- and energy-consuming sequence of actions, which demand
certain environmental conditions and physical prerequisites.
That is to say, its physical and biological aspects are taken
into account in relevant contexts and are understood as such.
Labor is a fundamental constituent of the kibbutz set of values
as crystallized in the normative system. It also constitutes a
major component of the social status of the member. This diversity of meanings of the concept, and, not less important, diversity of spheres to which the concept is applied, is fully recognized. The relevance of labor to other aspects, or institutions,
of the kibbutz is obvious and appreciated. In other words, the

members of the kibbutz do discuss subjects and problems pertaining to the different contexts in which those may arise. Yet the institution of labor is conceived as distinctive, having its own merits as a major tenet in the kibbutz culture. Organizationally, the conception of labor as one unified institution has been reflected in the agency appointed to attend to all labor problems, namely the Labor Committee.

The growth in membership has affected the institutionalization, the organization and the functioning of kibbutz democracy and has been affected by a growing division of labor and allocation of responsibility among various and different committees and agencies and by a lesser involvement of the individual in all the activities of the kibbutz. A similar tendency can be discerned in relation to the economic expansion. The kibbutz economy is no longer based on one agricultural branch. Many kibbutzim, probably most, Hofra amongst them, based their economy on mixed farming from the outset. Relatively large, and distinct, branches have developed, calling for specialization and further development. Labor, obviously, is not the same in all agricultural branches. Even greater differentiation has evolved between the farm branches and those agencies of the meshek whose task is to provide services for the agricultural branches when necessary, agencies such as the garage, carpenter's shop, smithy, electrical service, the setting up and supervision of the irrigation system, and the like. Apparently, the skills required and the kind of work vary in these different agencies. Furthermore, an even sharper distinction is made between the above fields of labor and those called "services to man" in the kibbutz, namely departments of work catering for consumption and education. Not only is this growing differentiation understandable in terms of economic growth itself, but it is also further affected by a variable which lies behind the present discussion, namely the growing gap between the demand for labor made by the various branches and services and the strictly limited number of workers available within the kibbutz community. The labor-force of the kibbutz can no longer meet requirements. In the virtual absence of new members, it is the second generation and the temporary labor force (in its various forms and categories) which must be relied upon. With economic growth, problems of labor have grown more and more complex and numerous.

From the point of view of the individual, this trend usually means that he (or she) becomes increasingly involved in the specific work and responsibility he is attached to at the expense of direct involvement in the whole of the meshek. One cannot be directly involved in the running of the whole diversified farmstead and have even a superficial knowledge of the multiple aspects of labor in the economy of the kibbutz unless one occupies

68

a central position in the meshek administration. Obviously, very
few members can be in such a position. The farther an issue (in
the field of labor) is from one's branch or occupation, the vaguer
one's knowledge of, and familiarity with, that issue is likely to
be. Permanence in the branch, division of labor and specialization
within the branch intensify this process.

Variables such as age and sex do, of course, affect the
allocation of work. Thus individual members of the kibbutz do not
necessarily conceive labor in identical terms. Labor may mean different things to different people. One faces problems arising from
work first and foremost through one's own position: one's branch,
occupation, tenure, age, sex, physical capacity, and personal properties. In this sense, labor has become compartmentalized and is
treated by different individual and social categories from different points of vantage. As a result of all this, the position of
the individual vis-a-vis the organized whole and the communal
agencies, has become consolidated. The functioning of the communal
agencies themselves has changed. It is to this change, as against
the background in which labor is still treated as one distinct
institution, that I move now, in discussing these agencies and
agents.

The agency mentioned above is the Labor Committee; the agent
- the Labor Distributor. These institutions were designed to deal
with all problems in the field of labor and particularly with the
allocation of responsibilities and delegation of authority to various agencies within the commune. Obviously, other committees
were designated to look after other activities. (On the organizational structure of the kibbutz and on Committees, see Leon, 1964:
62-64; Z. Shepher, 1960: 182-188; Spiro, 1956: 90-97). One committee, relevant to the present discussion, is the Meshek Committee
(Kanovsky, 1966: "the economic committee" (p. 27); Spiro, 1956:
Committee on Economic Policy (p. 79).) "It deals with over-all
planning, efficiency of the various branches of production, and
allocation of resources" (Kanovsky, 1966: 24). It "initiates
policy on all economic matters affecting the kibbutz, and makes
most of the important long-range economic decisions" (Spiro, 1956:
79). In addition to its responsibility for both general and
annual economic planning, the co-ordination of economic activities
and investments, the committee discusses major changes in plans
and activities within branches. It is also authorized to discuss
the cancellation of such plans. In short, this committee can be
regarded as being directly concerned with the productive aspect of
the kibbutz's economy. Its executive officer is the Meshek
Organizer (Spiro, 1956: "the general economic manager"; Kanovsky,
1966: "economic manager"). In Hofra, the Committee is composed
of the Meshek Organizer, his predecessor in office, the external
treasurer and three to four members who are elected directly each

year during the election period. Their interest, knowledge and
experience in economic affairs and their personal merits are
presumably taken into account when they are nominated and elected.
Theoretically, then, there is a clear division of work and of
authority between this committee and the Labor Committee.

But in practice this division is blurred. The Meshek Committee and the Meshek Organizer have become increasingly involved
in problems of labor. A new division of responsibility has emerged
between the two committees, and the role of Labor Distributor itself is changing. Although the Labor Committee is still formally
responsible for all labor matters, practice has eroded this responsibility and has given rise to changes in the communal allocation of responsibility in these fields.

This process of change in the organizational allocation of
responsibility has its roots in the growing complexity of the
kibbutz economy and the heterogeneity of the composition of the
membership, with their implications for the individual. With the
growing permanent affiliation of each member to a branch, and as
an additional labor-force from outside the kibbutz has become
available, the practice of assigning members frequently to different branches has been decreasing. The Labor Distribution
Officer has functioned less and less on tasks of fundamental value,
such as the permanent assignment of members to branches, and has
dealt more and more with the problem of substituting members
temporarily for others. Practice has now become the norm: the
Labor Committee has followed the pattern of action of its executive officer. While retaining its formal overall authority over
assignment of members to different kinds of work whensoever and
wheresoever necessary, it usually restricts itself to the discussion and working out of plans of an essentially impermanent nature.
It deals with vacancies, whether expected or unexpected, occurring
in various departments of work, with the necessity of substituting
members so as to keep the meshek running, with planning and distributing of tasks which are allocated according to the principle
of rotation, and with settlement of disputes or disagreements
between branches or within a branch.

If the Labor Committee finds it exceedingly difficult to
deal with problems of permanent affiliation of members to branches;
if it finds it difficult, and in many cases undesirable, to take
issue with the individual member who has achieved permanence in
a branch; and if - partly as a result of this - it realizes that
its ability to deal with the productive branches in its own sphere
of responsibility is indeed on the decline, those problems, difficult as they may be, are nevertheless present. The kibbutz, as
a meshek and otherwise, cannot avoid being involved in them.

Planning, co-ordination, and major shifts of or changes within the present labor force are inevitable if the meshek is to run as a whole. Labor, as a component in the economic field, cannot be left to itself. Consequently, in the branches conceived as 'productive' and those directly related to them, the major economic organs of the kibbutz have stepped in. Labor is an inseparable component of the economic system and therefore the growing involvement of these organs in these fields of labor is inevitable. The practice of treating labor as one field dealt with by a specialized community agency could not be maintained. The Meshek Committee and the Meshek Organizer have assumed more authority (and consequently, responsibility) in this realm. This seeming "encroachment" of the Meshek Committee on the authority of the Labor Committee has taken place in just one field of labor: the "productive" branches, including the crafts and the branches' direct services. The Meshek Committee is involved in relation-ships between branches and sometimes in the assignment of members to them. It has not assumed authority or responsibility in the commune over all aspects of labor. The other fields of labor are left to the specialized labor institution (though not exclusively). Although what is left to the Labor Committee and the Labor Dis-tributor is far from being negligible, it is only a residual part of its original role. This trend intensifies, in turn, the weak-ening of the latter institutions vis-a-vis the position of the individual.

The Labor Distributor does not tell the individual member to move from his permanent branch; he begs him to do so. He applies as many means of persuasion as he can muster in negotiat-ing with the member. He explains the problem which has created the vacancy which must be filled; he explains why it is this par-ticular member who is approached; he explains the experience or talent for the ordinarily impermanent job under discussion: in short, he negotiates. Although he represents the authority given by the kibbutz to the Labor Committee on whose behalf he works, he very rarely - if at all - refers, in the course of argument, to this authority. He may, of course, summon the member to the plenary meeting of the Committee, but he does not resort to the sanctions vested in him as an elected officer representing the kibbutz. That is, he does not order the member to comply. Thus, he may be said to have authority while lacking power. Although he is formally authorized to order a member to move from or to a branch, in practice he can only beg him to do so. To present the change more abstractly: initially, the authority delegated to the Labor Committee and its acting officer lay in the power of the kibbutz community and represented a latent power which could be activated should a member not comply. In the course of time this authority has increasingly represented no such power.

71

Power, as it were, has abandoned it and left the authority hollow.

This development raises a theoretical problem. Authority is usually conceived as implying power. The situation in which the Labor Committee and the Labor Distributor in Hofra find themselves clearly shows that in the course of time the authority with which these agencies have been endowed carries less and less power to make it effective. As stated above, the authority of the committee and its officer is virtually powerless. This situation therefore raises doubts whether authority in all situations depends on power.

Power, according to Weber, is "... the chance of [for] a man or of a number of men to realize their own will in a communal action even against the resistance of others who are participating in the action" (Gerth and Wright Mills, 1967: 186). While 'power' is defined from the actor's point of view, 'authority' is defined from the viewpoint of those who are supposed to comply. It is the legitimacy given to 'imperative control,' the latter being "the probability that a command with a given specific content will be obeyed by a given group of persons" (Weber, 1947: 152). Authority, therefore, implies power (through giving a command) and not, necessarily, vice versa. In other words, assuming the presence of power as given, it is its legitimacy that, in the main, denotes authority.

The situation in Hofra (and in other long-established kibbutzim) is that the legitimate entitlement of the Labor Committee and the Labor Distributor is not challenged. Their authority, in other words, is upheld. Power, that is, the chance to realize the Committee's (and the officer's) will "in a communal action even against the resistance of others who are participating in the action" is the element which has gradually been declining, and left formal authority groundless and thereby handicapped in practice.

This is the present situation in relation to members who work in the agricultural branches and the related services. The situation in the early days of the establishment of the meshek was different: then the authority of the Labor Committee and the Distributor did imply power. Before touching on the fundamental difference between these situations in the same economic establishment it seems necessary to draw attention to the theoretical problem which has arisen: the extent to which authority that contains power varies from one situation to another.

Let me clarify the argument. I have stated that there is no effective power to back the authority of a communal agent (in

72

relation to a category of population) in the present situation when the agent is involved in a communal action. Furthermore, he acts on behalf of the community. In relation, again, to a particular category of people in the communal context, power is divorced from authority. Therefore, it is not a measure of degree, nor extent, of power that is contained in the authority which is at the bottom of this situation. It is the absence of power, while authority, as said before, is not challenged. On the other hand, in the 'early days' power was contained in authority. It seems, therefore, reasonable to conclude that we are dealing with two constructs which are interrelated in many situations but which can appear separated from one another in a communal context. In essence, the two are related in that they are both concerned with the realization of "will in a communal action even against the resistance of others who are participating in the action" (Gerth and Mills, 1967 ). But while power concerns the 'chance,' or the probability, to realize the will, authority concerns the right to do so. A communal agent may legitimately possess the right to command while having no 'chance' that his command will be obeyed and carried out. In other words, a communal agent may find himself in a situation in which the area of authority bestowed on him does not overlap with areas in which power may be exerted.

I return to discuss the difference between the situation in the early days of the economy of Hofra and that of the present day. In the initial stage of the economy of Hofra, the newly founded farmstead, was small and not highly diversified. There was a constant flow of people into the kibbutz to fill all vacancies. Consequently, the meshek did not largely depend on the individual. In contrast, the present situation is that of a fairly large farmstead with developed branches and a scarcity of permanent labor. The development of Hofra as described above has entailed a change in the disposition of power. The Labor Distributor cannot exercise the authority bestowed on him as the individual member has grown indispensable, both for the kibbutz as a whole and for the branch, as against the background of shortage of labor. The distributor's tactics, therefore, must accordingly undergo some change if he does not wish to fail in his own task and undermine his personal position. If he wants, as presumably he does, to operate as efficiently as possible in the circumstances, then the chances are that he will get better results if he does not approach the member from the angle of an officer endowed with formal authority to shift members from branch to branch. I repeat, he begs rather than orders.

One qualification is in place here. The suggestion made here that the efficiency of the Labor Distributor and his colleagues in the Committee has consistently been declining, and that this is correlated with an increase in the individual member's power vis-a-vis the meshek; and the further proposition that this development

73

is correlated with the growing gap between supply of and demand for labor, do not mean that the conduct of the Labor Distributor has drastically changed.  It does not imply that previously the Distributor merely gave orders while nowadays he pleads endlessly with every individual.  The Distributor, in wishing to be efficient while retaining good personal relationships with friends and comrades in the egalitarian community (in which his post as Labor Distributor was less relevant) did not, in the early days, refrain from lengthy explanations and negotiations, but as the comparative bargaining position of his counterpart was different, he could more easily exert his implicit authority.  He did not always <u>have</u> to bargain and negotiate.  Nor does the statement imply that nowadays the Distributor <u>always</u> tries to persuade his counterpart and does not resort to his formal authority.  Indeed he does use it with temporary workers who reside in the kibbutz.  They have either not been able, or have had no wish, to build up a position of permanence in the field of work.  The institutional authority of the Distributor does imply power, then, in their case.  Authority can also be applied in such cases as those of Yonah and Yamin described above.  To persons who have not achieved permanence, the formal institutionalized means for distributing labor are still applied.

But, it is only the general membership which concerns us in the present context.  All members but two have achieved permanence and it is in relation to them that the position of the Distributor and his Committee colleagues is discussed.

The Labor Distributor, then, does have power to back his authority in relation to people who have not acquired permanence in a branch.  If "... the power to control or influence the other resides in control over things he values" (Emerson, 1962: 32), then the difference in its application to the two categories of workers in the 'productive' field, permanents and transients, emerges more clearly.  The very task to which the transient is assigned is controlled by the Distributor.  He can change it daily.  In contrast, the permanent's job is controlled by himself. The Distributor controls, of course, the resource of formal authority to assign to various branches and tasks, but if he cannot exercise his authority because the permanent's work is controlled by himself in his branch's control, then his authority is powerless.  His control over this resource (at least) which has a considerable value for the transient worker in the kibbutz vests his authority with some power.  This distinction between the categories of workers in the branches of the <u>meshek</u> helps, in turn, to elucidate further the difference between the degree of power by which the authority of the labor assignment agencies of the kibbutz has been backed in the development of its economy. Some members of Hofra, when discussing the change in the efficacy of the Labor Distribution institutions, refer to the 'good old

74

days' when "The Kvutza was [presumably] based on the goodwill of all its members, mutual understanding and acceptance of authority of its elected bodies." Clearly, it is not simply the dimension of time as such which has operated. The variables which have taken part in the change are touched upon above. They have changed the foci of control through changes in the structure and magnitude of the economy of Hofra and the composition of its labor force.

As stated above, the limited ability of the Labor Committee and its executive officer to tackle the problems arising from the relative immobility of members in the occupational field has called for the intervention of the Meshek Committee and its executive officer (the Meshek Organizer). With the authority bestowed on them by the kibbutz they control the economic resources of the meshek. Economic planning, co-ordination between branches, financial investments, and allocation of water and power are largely in their control as are tractors and central supplies. This does not mean that access to all these resources is chanelled only through the Meshek Organizer, the External Treasurer or their colleagues and that there are no contacts or encounters between persons in different branches or the branches as teams; indeed, there is much of this. What we are concerned with here, is that the control and authority of the Meshek Committee and its officers are more effective than those exercised by the Labor Distributor. This subject will be discussed in due course. Suffice it to say, that the main committee and its members do not derive their efficiency from, nor does the latter depend exclusively on, intracommunity relationships. This agency cannot ignore the labor component of the meshek as an economic enterprise. It sometimes has to step in. The intervention of the Meshek Committee, whether on its own initiative or as an instance of appeal, has further weakened the position in which officers and members of the Labor Committee find themselves.

This process has led to a change in the selection of the social category from which Labor Distributors are recruited. In some kibbutzim a change in the composition of the Committee has also taken place: it has become a committee composed of officers serving their turn in rotation rather than a body of persons elected to organize long-term, as well as current and temporary problems of work distribution. The pattern in those kibbutzim has become to elect only those nominees who are considered suitable for the job of daily work-distribution, leaving the task of overall labor planning, co-ordination and supervision to the Meshek Organizer and his colleagues. In other words, the Labor Committee has become a group of functionaries whose task it is to cope with daily problems rather than also with major problems (i.e., those "encroached" on by the Meshek Committee). In Hofra, the Committee has traditionally been composed of the Meshek

75

Organizer, ex officio, the acting Distributor, and four to five
elected members.  Officially, it is not a group of functionaries
whose members fulfil their turn in rotation, but a unit whose
task is the one traditionally designated to the kibbutz Labor
Committee.  The distributors are elected annually to the limited
job of Labor Distribution and once such an elected officer has
finished his turn, he ceases to be a member of the Committee to
which he has not been elected.  In Hofra, unlike other kibbutzim,
membership in a committee cannot be acquired by virtue of one's
job, unless one is elected to that job, thereby becoming a member
of a committee ex officio.  Once the member resigns the job, he
ceases to be a member of the committee, again, unless he was
personally elected as a member of the committee.  Thus, if a
member is elected a Labor Distributor, he attends all the meetings
of the Committee - indeed the Committee cannot function without
him - but he discontinues his attendance when his successor takes
over.  Thus two sets of persons are elected simultaneously in the
annual elections, members personally elected to the Committee
(four to six) and officers who are ex officio members.  However,
this distinction seems also to be blurred in Hofra.  In 1971 the
candidates for the job of Distributor were nominated as candi—
dates for membership of the Labor Committee.  Members admit that
this distinction, though upheld formally as a matter of democratic
principle, has lost its significance when it is the problems of
labor that need to be solved rather than problems of communal
democracy.  When problems of labor arise they require efficient
solution and members are aware of the fact that both the officers
and the Committee are handicapped in their effectiveness.

But public recognition of the changing position of the
Labor Committee and its officers can be discerned in the selection of the recruits to the job.  There are some data available
on the composition of the Labor Committee since 1951, although
some of them are inconsistent.  It is indeed very difficult to
make a judgment now, in 1972, on the status of those members in
the 1950s and the 1960s in the community, but I can state that
some of those who were members of the Committee in the 1950s were
and have remained influential persons in Hofra until the present
day.  More significant is the emergence into this field of activity
of a category of members clearly distinguished as the second
generation.  This phenomenon can be measured and then discussed
in relation to the proposition under discussion.  The available
data are presented in Table 3.5.

The emergence and numerical growth of the second generation
is obviously a demographic phenomenon, which can be discussed in
relation to various aspects of communal life in Hofra.  What I
wish to draw attention to here, is the fact that with the gradual
decline of power of the Labor Committee and, in particular, of

the Distributor, the proportion of the younger generation in these offices has grown larger. In a reverse order, one might say that the larger the proportion of the younger generation in labor offices, the weaker the power of these offices becomes. This proposition may sound like a paradox when one bears in mind the confidence the community constantly expresses in its second generation and the reputation most of the young activists have achieved in Hofra. But before taking up this issue some comments on the data presented in Table 3.5 must be made.

1956 is the first year in the history of Hofra in which persons of the younger generation were elected to an office in this field. A continuous tendency for a larger proportion of persons of this category to appear in both the Committee and the actual distribution of labor is discerned. Since 1967 only persons of this category have been Labor Distributors. Taken as a category, the position of the second generation (and attached persons) in the community obviously cannot but consolidate and grow in influence owing to internal demographic processes and to the virtual absence of new incoming members. But it is the position of the labor organs and not the subject of the second generation which is under discussion here. Note that (a) labor distribution has become exclusively an office held by the second generation, and (b) that the greater the ascendancy of the new generation, the more the effectiveness of those offices occupied by persons of this category declines.

The background to this development is, as stated, the role the process of permanence of the individual has played in weakening the bargaining power of the communal agent. But I should explain why it is that the job of labor distribution has become an exclusively younger generation job. Members of the older generation have not relinquished other jobs nor have they left the Labor Committee. The answer seems to lie in the realization by many members who have acquired experience in communal life that the authority of the office of the Labor Distributor is less and less backed by power to implement its decisions. The office is judged by its effectiveness and people who have had experience of labor distribution in "better days", or people who looked forward to such an office in those days, would be reluctant, or even not wish, to take the office. Persons who were, or could be, efficient in labor distribution when the economy of the kibbutz was small and less differentiated, and when labor was not scarce and permanence in a branch was not 'entrenched', as it were, would be less efficient now. The idiom of "honor" is used in explaining their withdrawal from this kind of activity, for as one man in his late thirties said

Table 3.5: Second Generation as Members of the Labor Committee and as Labor Distributors

| Year | Membership of Labor Committee | | Labor Distributors | | Comments |
|------|-------|--------------------|-------|--------------------|----------|
|      | Total | Second Generation | Total | Second Generation |          |
| 1951 | 8 | - | no data | no data | |
| 1952 | 7 | - | " " | " " | |
| 1953 | 7 | - | " " | " " | |
| 1954 | 5 | - | " " | " " | |
| 1955 | 6 | - | " " | " " | |
| 1956 | 5 | 1 | 6 | 1 | |
| 1957 | 6 | 1 | 6 | 2 | |
| 1958 | 7 | 1 | no data | no data | |
| 1959 | 7 | - | 6 | 3 | |
| 1960 | 5 | 1 | 5 | 2 | |
| 1961 | 7 | 3 | no data | 1 | |
| 1962 | 7 | 3 | 5 | 1 | |
| 1963 | 6 | 1 | no data | no data | |
| 1964 | no data | no data | 5 | 3 | |
| 1965 | 6 | 2 | 5 | 3 | |
| 1966 | 5 | 1 | no data | no data | |
| 1967 | no data | no data | 5 | 5 | |
| 1968 | 4 | 1 | | | All distributors second generation |
| 1969 | 6 | 3 | | | " " |
| 1970 | 5 | 3 | | | " " |
| 1971 | 7 | 4 | | | " " |

78

to me: "Why should I take such a job? It is beneath my dignity to plead with all those people, usually getting the answer 'No'; then pleading again, mostly in vain. And what do I get for this? - just a good deal of contempt." "This is not a matter for real adults", said another member, "we all have our branches and jobs. Why should I make a nuisance of myself, going about and begging people to leave their jobs in order to substitute for other people? What do I get for this and what, in the end, do I achieve?"

The office, with its present deficient power, is left then to young members: "For them it is not dishonourable to beg older members to move from their permanent jobs." When I speak of the 'young' or the 'second generation,' it is not because they are demographically second-generation (or their spouses, or equivalent to them): this does not constitute their sociological attribute in the present context. It is their belonging to a category of people who stand in a particular relation to the permanent membership in the field of labor that marks them out. The 'young' or the 'second generation' member is: (a) a person whose tenure in adult work is fairly short yet is still promising in this field; (b) a person whose relatively short experience in adult work has not yet affected his status in the community as compared with the status of older members; (c) a person whose short tenure in full-time work is weighed against his life-time residence in the communtiy; (d) a person whose networks of relationships stemming from his family of origin are present, if latent, in the background. Yet, his own active relationships are with peers, and to a lesser extent with fellow branch-members. In other words, the 'young' person is in his initial period as an active member of the community while having an, as yet, inactive life-history in, and a fair knowledge of, community relationships. A person who has returned from military service can be given a post whose doubtful authority seems to match his own somewhat ambivalent position (of a fairly new active member in the field of adult work while having a fairly long tenure of life in the community prior to his having the status of membership). He is given the credit of formal authority, if he takes the post, without foregoing the personal gains in the field of labor which all the members of the community have established. Or, in other words, the kibbutz has given him authority; but the members of the kibbutz, taken together, have left him with inadequate power to carry out plans which may affect the gains they have achieved personally. Oldtimers and experienced members, themselves entrenched in permanent jobs and occupations and themselves emeshed in complex networks of relationships, would tend not to take this office of Labor Distribution. But this office is necessary, so it has become the arena for the members of the 'young' category to practice their first steps in communal public

79

activities as central officers. Upon returning from their
military service they acquire full membership of the kibbutz,
equal to others. The job is limited from the outset, as explained above, but within its limits the credit given to the
new recruit to the office is tested in practice. This is an
avenue available for the 'young,' after returning from military
service, to show skill in communal activity. This skill is
tested by all members, those affected by his management (or
mismanagement) of the job as well as by others. So, while the
manifest function of the office is the distribution and organization of labor, its latent one has become to serve as an arena
of initiation into a central communal field of activities. And
in considering this function, the limits set on the efficiency
of the office have no great importance as they are taken by both
recruits and public as given. It is within these limits that
all the new recruits to the office have to function.

The motives of persons of the 'young' category for accepting this office may vary. Though I concentrate on the sociological analysis, it should be stated that not everybody within
this category is necessarily interested in taking this office.
This issue is a problematic one and an index which shows its
problematic nature is the rota principle which has been established to regulate the holding of the office. This principle
is applied in the commune when a job or a certain task in
services or in the central offices on the one hand is necessary,
while on the other, members are reluctant to do them permanently
or the Kibbutz as a whole would object to let a member hold an
office permanently (Spiro, 1956: 7; Talmon-Garber, 1964).

These last subjects fall outside the scope of the present
argument and should be discussed in relation to other problems,
though they affect the institution of Labor Distribution. But
the argument should not go astray. The argument is that the
community in the sense of the sum total of the members, recruits
persons for this office from a certain category because (in
relation to this subject) the latter would tend to accept more
readily the limited, temporary and palliative nature that the
office has assumed. The motives of persons in accepting the
office, the differential interest people of this category show
in the office, and regulations for holding the office, whether
by rota or otherwise, are matters for a different discussion.
The fact is, however, that since 1967 the office of Labor Distribution has been exclusively manned by 'young' members
(Table 3.5).

The change in the pattern of selection of Labor Distributors, and the confusion in defining the actual tasks of the
Labor Committee as reflected in the uncertainty of its structure

(Distributors' committee or non-officers' committee), mark, on
the organizational level, the decline in their position. As
described above, when problems arise in the income-yielding
branches and their immediately attached services, the meshek
agencies have stepped in. Yet their interventions or 'encroachments' on the task of Labor Distribution, usually called for,
have not filled the gap created by the interest of the meshek
in a planned, organized and co-ordinated allocation of its labor
force on the one hand and the inability on the other hand of the
Labor Distributor and his colleagues to achieve this allocation.
Attempts have been made to fill in this gap by the establishment
of a new office, that of the Labor Organizer.

The Labor Organizer is elected by direct popular vote on
an individual basis. He is not given the office as a result of
being previously elected to membership in the Labor Committee.
In other words, it is not one of the members of the Committee
(who are nominated and elected as a group) who takes this office,
whether by turn (i.e., by the principle of rota) or otherwise.
Rather, it is a person who is elected directly and personally
to this office. By virtue of his office he is the chairman of
the Labor Committee and a member of both the Meshek Committee
and of the Secretariat of the Kibbutz. Thus while the single
institution of Labor Committee is retained, he introduces, by
his very office, an actual differentiation of authority in the
field of labor. He chairs the Labor Committee; he serves as a
second level of appeal in the event of disagreement between a
member and the Labor Distributor; he takes charge of seasonal and
other labor planning; and, with particular relevance to the
present discussion, he is responsible for organizing actual distribution for labor of the members working in the branches of the
meshek. While the institution of organization and distribution
of work remains one (through the presumed authority and activities of the Labor Committee), the differentiation between the
branches and attached services (in regard to the permanent members) and other departments of work, and the temporary labor
force of the branches themselves, is reflected in the division of
labor between the officers of the Committee. The Labor Distributor finds replacements for workers in the non-'productive'
departments of work and in the assignment of temporary workers
to branches and other departments alike, while the Labor Organizer,
in addition to his involvement in long-range planning, is the
actual labor distributor for the permanent branch members as well
as being the authority for the establishment of non-branch members
in permanent occupations, and he is a yet higher court of appeal
for all the members. The growth of this differentiation is
reflected in actual discussion of problems of work which arise
in the branches. The Labor Organizer, having assumed direct
access to and involvement in these problems, does not always see

to it that they are brought to the Labor Committee; in one of the meetings of the <u>Meshek</u> Committee he said, "This Committee cannot ignore problems of labor; these are not detached from economic issues in which this Committee is involved. The Committee cannot overlook problems of labor by simply arguing that they fall outside the field of its authority. If there is an official elected communal body to tackle these problems, it is this Committee." One should perhaps add that the present (1970) Labor Organizer is a zealous defender of the authority delegated to the various committees, the Labor Committee included, and of the principle of election as a pre-condition of their respective authority. The distinctions between the realms of different committees and the authority delegated to the different committees to function within their respective realms as well as an implied premise that all office holders are bestowed with their authority by virtue of their being duly elected, are carefully observed in Hofra, much more than in other kibbutzim known to me. If this distinction is blurred, it is evidence that however careful and zealous the institutionalization may be, and however meticulous the officer in question (the Labor Organizer himself) is, the process described is stronger than the pre-established organizational institutionalization and its underlying assumptions.

In conclusion, the argument is that the agencies the kibbutz community formed in its 'Bund' early days, to borrow Talmon's observation (Talmon-Garber, 1956: following Schmallenbach's suggestion) in order to tackle problems in the field of labor, have undergone a considerable change in their institutional aspects as well as in their effectiveness. The change, as expressed in the formation of posts and communal agencies, in their endowment with authority and in the subsequent emergence of a differential distribution of effectiveness among them, is correlated with economic diversification, the growth of the <u>meshek</u>, the shortage of permanent membership, the consequent gap between demand for and supply of labor, and the subsequent consolidation of the position of the individual attached to a branch. The kibbutz as a communal society and as an economic enterprise, cannot manage without an agency to function in this field on its behalf. It adapts to the changes described, though with some confusion, in various ways, one of which is the organizational structure and the recognition given <u>de facto</u> to the differential effectiveness of its agencies.

## Deterrent power

The individual member, when confronted by an agent of the Labor Committee, needs to be able to refuse the latter's request, whether this request is couched in the form of a request, appeal, demand or order, in the name of the cause of the community. He needs to be able to resist such pressure if he wishes to acquire, or to retain, the status which permanence confers on a member. Having the ability to resist such pressure does not imply that one uses it frequently. Being a nuisance or continuing to refuse appeals made by the labor agents does not contribute to one's position in the community. The community expects a member to give his share in services which are run on the principle of rotation; and it expects him to respond with understanding to appeals made by the labor officers - if they are not made too frequently. But above all it also respects every member's potential ability, and implied right, to resist these demands. There are of course limits to the community's power to insist and apply sanctions - as there are to the individual's ability to resist. The labor officer has to maneuver within these limits.

One cannot, considering the evidence, say that the ability to resist the demands of the labor officer is constantly exhibited in a member's behavior, or that his being equipped with that ability always deters the labor officer from requesting him to change his job. Potential ability does not imply, nor does it necessitate, constant demonstration. But, the ability of the member to withstand pressure is significant and it affects both his own behavior and that of the labor officer. This ability, in turn, provides the member with a bargaining position from which he can negotiate with the labor officer. With this quali- fication in mind, I can recapitulate the statement that virtually all the members seek permanence in a department of work and once satisfied there, would like to retain it. They wish to be in a bargaining position, vis-a-vis the labor officer.

In a sense, this bargaining position, or the ability to resist pressure on which the latter is based, is an aspect of power. Power, in Weber's terms, seems to be defined in terms of the initiating actor's will, and its eventual 'realization in a communal action' (in Gerth and Wright Mill's translation) or 'carrying out [this will] within a social relationship' (in Anderson and Parsons' translation). There is a will, and further- more, a 'chance' or a 'probability' that that will, shall be carried out. There is an active move which might be performed with the intention of realizing the will. In other words, power is lodged with the party which is defined as having (a) a will; (b) a chance, or probability, of realizing it 'even against the resistance of others.'

The meaning of the concept 'power' may be broadened to apply efficiently to both parties concerned, if we first note that they are involved in a social relationship. That is, power resides two-sidedly in the relationship. Secondly, if we do not assume a priori that it is the labor officer who is necessarily, by virtue of his office, the focus of the discussion of power as the initiating actor, but try to study the position of the respondent member, <u>within this relationship</u>, the meaning of the concept will emerge more clearly. The power-relationship between the officer and the respondent is an interplay in which the resources of each are seldom fully used.

While the power which is inherent in the officer's position and official authority is obvious and clearly corresponds to the definition of the term in relation to the initiating actor (realizing his will "in a communal action"), surely the ability to resist this power is also based on the presence of power, though of a somewhat different kind. If the officer has initiated the encounter, then his power can be defined in positive terms, while the member's power, resistance, is negative. It implies the possibility of active resistance to an open pressure, once this is exerted upon the member. It does not imply an active, positive, initiative on the part of the respondent. His is a deterrent power in the context of his relationships with the officer. This power may prove weaker than the power enjoyed by the office-holder, once an open encounter occurs; or it may prove stronger and more effective: but on most occasions it is not openly tested. Certainly the member's power is neither crystallized clearly, nor is it stable and solid throughout the community, as his position there is composed of other elements in addition to his role in labor. Nor is it ossified throughout the member's tenure in the branch, let alone throughout his life-time, even in the field of work. But his power is always present to some degree and when the labor officer wishes (or feels obliged) to 'realize his will' in moving a member against the latter's wish, it is this 'negative' or deterrent power that he has to consider. It is this consideration that makes this deterrent power only potential in its nature, not openly and constantly exercised.

Open disputes between officer and member are rare though strong pressure on the officer is exerted by the gap between demand for and supply of labor in the growing economy of the Kibbutz. This is balanced by the associated result that individuals are freer to select a branch and to acquire a permanent position in it. These conflicting processes might produce many more contentious encounters, were it not that the labor officer can exercise more effective power over the temporary labor-force to plug gaps.

In dealing with members of the kibbutz, he makes requests and applies varying modes of pressure according to their health, age, personal problems, physical disability and the like. There are some members whose very work in their respective branches and

services is considered by the economic activists of the kibbutz,
as well as by the branch foremen, to be detrimental to the productivity of the branch or the efficiency of the service; and
yet those members are very seldom requested to move. Nevertheless, even these members, when considered to be better and able
to carry out the work required, find - or found if they are now
exempted from this request because of age - themselves seeking
this deterrent power.

A dispute between a member and the Labor Distributor is
rarely brought into the open in a meeting of a committee or
otherwise. But one can frequently hear the Labor Distributor
reporting, or complaining: "I have appealed to him/her, but
he/she promptly refuses to listen. There is nothing further
that I can do." Or, "I have tried to explain time and again,
but to no avail. You just cannot do anything to (or with) him/
her." Or, "I have tried to persuade [the member] as much as I
could. There is nothing beyond it which I can efficiently do.
What is the point of going back to him/her?"

Each event is clearly better understood if it is studied
in relation to a particular case or even to a particular situation. By observing the Labor Distributor in his constant
negotiations and bargaining, or watching the Labor Organizer in
his arguments with members, one can distinguish the presence of
elements of power about which the more generalized statements
above are made. Perhaps a presentation of an extreme case will
make the issue clearer than these statements made by harassed
Labor Distributors.

Olya is an old-time member. She joined the Kvutza before
it settled in the present site of Hofra. Upon joining the
Kvutza she became an agricultural worker. Apparently she
derived some prestige from being a long serving woman agriculturist, as oldtimers still praise her agricultural experience
and skill. At one time the kibbutz suffered from a shortage of
qualified and skilled teachers, so it recruited members for this
task from among its untrained members. Thus, Olya was selected
to teach in the local school. One may assume that her selection
for the teaching job demonstrated a fair degree of community
approval as she had not been trained for the job nor had she
even acquired a formal secondary-school education. In the late
1950s she got a newly created job in the Secretariat, and to
follow this case, I have to explain the work of the Secretary
and accountants, which is also necessary as background for the
general theme.

Until 1957, office work in Hofra meant employment in book-
keeping or accountancy which was, and still is, regarded as a

department-of-work on its own, in which members - presumably qualified for the job - are permanently employed. In this sense it is a branch within which there is division of labor. Its tasks include the preparation and issue of the annual balance-sheet, financial follow-up, dealing with traders' and creditors' bills, labor records, control and check of inflowing resources and supplies and outgoing products to markets, and the like. In broad terms, the office deals with the economic or financial aspects of Hofra, and it is not designed to assume responsibility for activities not connected with accounting. These are left to the care and the responsibility of the elected Secretary. In other words, non-economic activities of Hofra, not necessarily of a temporary nature, which required clerical and office work and the daily routine clerical work such as correspondence (save the accountant's or the treasurer's business), telephone communication, postal service and so forth, were carried out by the elected central officer of the kibbutz. In the past these tasks were not recognized as requiring permanent personnel. The role and the activities of the Secretary were not clearly defined and they corresponded, in effect, to the residual tasks left for him by the other officers of the kibbutz's central management. The growth of the kibbutz made these activities more numerous and they took more time. Moreover the Secretary was not a mere member of a com-mittee (the Secretariat): members of committees are expected to carry out their activities in their spare time. He was, in ad-dition to that, a full-time officer in the administration of the kibbutz. It all led to a situation in which the Secretary found himself obliged to do clerical, typing and similar routine work, hardly reconcilable with his communally defined and expected responsibilities.

In 1957 Hofra followed the pattern of other kibbutzim. The growth of the meshek and the community, resulting in the increase and routinization of office work, called for the institution of a new job - the office secretary of the administration. The office secretary (called in most of the kibbutzim the Technical Secretary so as to distinguish this office from that of the elected General Secretary) was, and still is, supposed to receive, open and dis-tribute to the officers all incoming mail; to type letters written or dictated by central officers and to post them; to answer, follow and make telephone calls; to keep books and files which fall out-side the realm of the accountant's office; and to help in adminis-tration, thereby freeing the elected Secretary from this routine and enabling him to perform his communal role. Olya was given this job. In addition, she was given the part-time job of a local post-office clerk.

It was regarded, so I was told, as a very satisfactory sol-ution of a problem of employment for an oldtimer. Here was a woman

who had given up agricultural work, who had been employed as a
teacher when the local school needed her but could not go on
teaching with the development of the school, and who was not considered suitable for child-care, a job which is commonly conceived to be a female task.  Presumably, Olya also considered
the issue in these terms, took over the newly created job, and
settled in it.  Over the years dissatisfaction with her performance of the job mounted to a general state of resentment.  Members complained that she sometimes caused damage to Hofra's
external relationships by slamming down the telephone receiver in
the midst of a conversation if she was angry or upset, regardless
of the importance of the call; that she refused to type letters
for office holders; that she consistently angered members by
treating them impatiently; and that even her post-office job was
mismanaged.  The Postal Agency was a Grade C, which meant that it
was limited to only certain services, which excluded services
such as telegraph, parcel post or the Postal Bank.  There was no
objection on the part of the Post (now: Communication) Office to
upgrading the local agency, which would have meant the provision
of more services to the community and would, incidentally, have
promoted the local clerk in the wage-scale of the Office.  The
promotion was apparently in the interest of Hofra.  The Secretariat advocated accepting this offer, but Olya would not agree.
I was told that her argument was that the acceptance of this
offer would have resulted in more work for her personally.  She
is said to have ignored all complaints and requests to abide by
the rules implied in running the job, whether dealing with members
or outsiders.  Growing resentment, particularly of central officers
such as the Secretary or the Meshek Organizer, did not affect her
conduct, rather, it made her dig in her heels.  As far as she was
concerned it was 'her' job and she had acquired permanence.  The
central officers demanded her resignation from the office, but
she would not listen.  She was entrenched in her position in her
work.  The situation became quite awkward:  people, including
central officers of the community, wanted her removal.  On the
other hand they could not ignore the 'rights' she had acquired
to retain her permanent post.  They also acknowledged a cluster of
misfortunes which, they maintained, had contributed to her
inefficiency in work and her behavior.  Those were her age, her
deteriorating health, and some personal misfortunes.  This cluster
of misfortunes had to be - and was - taken into account when the
problem of the service of this work to the community was considered.  The search, then, was not merely aimed at expelling her
from the job so as to achieve a better discharge of the tasks
contained in it, but also, at the same time, at finding her an
alternative job.  She kept rejecting offers to change her job
and defied the labor officers.

A new incumbent was elected by popular vote to one of the central offices. He had made one condition to his consent, namely, that Olya should be removed from her secretarial work, despite her thirteen years permanent service. He considered that the mode and manner in which she did her work would impede his own. I do not know whether Olya was aware of this condition. Popular dissatisfaction (though coupled with sympathy for her personal state) and the officer's resentment, apparently feeding one another, had now been reinforced by the condition made by the new candidate, the only person who consented to take the vacant central job. This development gave a renewed incentive to the central officers to put pressure on Olya. Again, she would not agree. This time, however, the issue of Olya's position in her job reached a critical stage. It was no longer a matter of mounting dissatisfaction on the part of the public, nor was it associated with particular complaints of officers or members who argued that the interests of the community had been damaged. As against these there had always been, though more by silent consensus than by an open discussion, the realization that the above factors did not equal in importance the factors operating in favor of her continued permanence in the job. This time it seemed that the balance had shifted against her. The conflict over principles, and dispute about her position, seemed to reach a climax so that it could no longer be overlooked. The condition made by the officer-elect had brought the issue into the open. The labor officers were compelled to act once more. Could the labor officers - and others - find a reconciling solution to the dilemma posed by the two apparently conflicting principles, of Olya's right to permanence in "her" job and of the newly elected officer's right to refuse to work with her, on grounds accepted by all? It seemed that they would not be able to reconcile the conflicting demands and that there must be a showdown. But a showdown, in the sense of one winning absolutely at the expense of the other, did not occur. Despite the effort of the officer-elect, supported by branch foremen and other office-holders of the kibbutz (all dependent on the efficient work of the office-secretary including her work in the post office), Olya was not totally ousted. She did vacate the office of the Secretariat of the kibbutz, and relinquished her secretarial job, but she was promptly given another office-room, thus enabling her to retain her job as the local post-office clerk. Olya's position did indeed suffer a setback and she was hurt. ("She treats me like her eternal foe. She will never forgive me. She thinks that it is a personal grudge against her which has motivated me to attack her, undermine her position and remove her from office," said the officer-elect). Nevertheless, she retained her job, although not the whole job, which she used to have. Indeed, it is not quite the same job, as it was stripped of secretarial responsibilities, but it is essentially in the same "branch," so to speak. People, central officers included, had wished her to be totally removed from her work and failed. One may recall that dissatisfaction with her work, felt by office-holders, branch foremen and the public in general, was related to her performance at the post office as well as to her secretarial job. Nevertheless, the combined efforts of central officers and of the labor officers in particular, did not remove her. The solution was, in effect, to create another, new, job with the "branch" as a "sideways move."[5] Only by creating this new job, or - in other words - by the division of the original job into two, could one of them be taken from her by the elected officers of the community.

The division of her job into two has left Olya with only part-time, low-grade, employment in the post office. This so-lution aroused no worries or uncomfortable feelings among the labor officers or even among the general public. Olya had grown old and her health had deteriorated. People were quite content with the fact that she had relinquished part of her services to the community, and yet at the same time her "right" to permanence in her branch was respected. Her retention of the job - even in a curtailed form - which could apparently be accomplished only through the creation of a new job, had proved to be the only solution. The "solution" of this personal, or as the idiom of the kibbutz would call it, this "social" problem, overrode economic considerations, which might have shown that labor of two members was thereby not being efficiently used.

I have stated above that permanence in a branch can be reconciled with the kibbutz's economic interest in productivity, as permanence in a branch is a prerequisite to experience and also to interest in work and success, thus contributing to efficiency and productivity. Thus the member's interest in acquiring a permanent position in the branch coincides to some extent with the interest of the meshek. The meshek therefore supports the tendency of the individual to achieve and to retain permanence. Here, however, we deal with what I have termed an extreme case. The interests of the individual, Olya, and that of the meshek, looking at the latter from purely economic point of view, were not identical. The officers of the meshek acted according to economic consider-ations, provoked by a political move (made by the officer-elect), but the non-economic variables of Olya's 'negative' power could not be totally overridden.[6]

But this was not the end of the affair. Olya had to leave her post-office temporarily, if reluctantly, because of ill health, Her successor as the office secretary, who was admitted to the job on the understanding that it was temporary, took over Olya's post-office responsibilities, thus reinstating the previous practices of the office. An additional desk was fixed in Olya's new office-room, occupied by another member. Olya had not returned to her office by the time I left Hofra, but she claimed that she would eventually do so. She used to come every once in a while to the Secretariat's office, "to inform" her successor that she would soon return, and to warn her that she should be prepared to vacate the office soon. I do not know whether Olya has ever returned to her post-office work. "Not while I am in the office," the officer-elect said to me; then reconsidering, he added, betraying his lack of confidence, "But what can I, in fact, do about it...." It seemed that all the people concerned had seized on the opportunity of Olya's leaving her work - presumably for a short while - to make this temporary arrangement more permanent.

The case of Olya can be approached from various angles, such as discussing it as part of the problem of aging of members, or in relation to the subject of women's employment, or in analyzing the occupational structure of Hofra. I have brought it (a) into my discussion of permanence in work, and (b) into my analysis of the potential confrontation between the member and the labor officers over the member's right to permanence.

I labelled this case as "extreme" for several reasons.

(a)    It is "exceptional" in the sense that it was brought into the open. As has been indicated above, it is very rare for such an issue to break out into an open argument, let alone an argument in which many members are involved. The interplay between officer and member is usually resolved without reaching the stage of an open confrontation.

(b)    The confrontation in this case was direct. The pressure to remove Olya from her permanent place of work reached its climax when it was formulated as a prerequisite before a member elected to office would begin work.

(c)    The "branch" under discussion is a small one, in fact originally a one-person branch. Size and composition of a branch can certainly affect the effectiveness of pressure and resistance.

(d)    The branch concerned is, in essence, a direct and immediate service to the public in general, to all the members individually, and to the administration of the meshek: therefore anything which had any effect on its management and running was widely known throughout the community and, furthermore, evoked people's active reactions.

(e)  The career of the member concerned had certain features
     which, taken together, were not shared by the majority of
     her fellow-members and obviously these had some repercussions
     on the issues.  (Their relevant implications will be dis-
     cussed below.)

     With these qualifications in mind (as any case is likely
to produce qualifications when it is discussed in relation to a
more general problem), I believe that the role played by Olya's
permanent position in the struggle over the secretarial-postal
job emerges quite clearly.  Permanence in work is a cumulative
process.  The longer one stays in one's job, the stronger one's
claims on the job are likely to be.  Although the expansion of
a branch over time created pressures from within or from without,
the permanent worker's claims grew stronger (see previous footnote).
Despite growing dissatisfaction with Olya's performance and conduct, it was increasingly difficult to take active steps to
remove her from her job.  Had she only been in that job for a
short time, it would have probably been easier to remove her.
The longer she held to the job, the harder it grew to dislodge
her from it.  Permanence is cumulative also in another sense: it
should suffer to interruptions.  Olya had occupied the job for
over thirteen consecutive years, broken only by illnesses and
holidays.  No one, as far as i know, had attempted to compete
with Olya for the job, and no one else had claims to holding it
permanently.  Continuity in a task, as absence of competition
for it, contributed to the cumulative nature which is inherent in
the power of permanence, despite inefficiency.

     One may recall that when Olya did relinquish part of the
job, thereby decreasing her productivity in work, people were
quite content.  They were not disturbed by the resultant decrease
in productivity and the apparent waste of working potential.
(See Kanovsky, 1966: 136).  As long as she had performed her job
- even if unsatisfactorily - she was in a position to hold the
job.  Again, she was able to hold the job because she still
worked in her office.  But I add that people appeared to be
satisfied with that solution because Olya's health had deteriorated, since it was recognized, because of recent experience, that
she would frequently be absent from her office owing to ill health
and hence her partial removal would be manageable.  (She had in
any case, to be supported as a member.)  Frequent absence from
work would contribute to weaken her claims on the future continuation of the hitherto permanent job, so that one can conclude
that:

(a)  so long as Olya worked in her office her claim to holding the
office was strengthened by cumulative tenure and it was exceedingly
difficult to succeed in removing her; but

(b) once the element of continuity in the position of permanence had been repeatedly disrupted, a move by officers became feasible.

Olya's accumulated claim to hold her office had contributed to what I have previously called 'deterrent power.' Her ability to resist pressure, an ability which is negative in essence, had its 'positive' counterpart in the accumulation of elements of permanence which constituted an aspect of power. This deterrent power is present potentially between members in negotiations, controversies and disputes when the latter arise in the field of labor, but is better perceived when it is brought into the open in the encounter between member and labor officer. It is tested not as a variable present in relationships between two members, but as a variable contained in one member's position when confronted by an authorized representative of the community. Ultimately, it is vis-a-vis this community, on whose behalf the officer acts, that the deterrent power of the individual may have to be activated.

I discuss Olya's case from two angles, that of continuity in office and its impact on permanence, and that of the position of the labor officer in confronting the defiant member. In dealing with the latter issue, while bearing in mind the 'community' or the 'public' in the background, I shall re-introduce another dimension, which was touched upon in other contexts in the discussion of previous cases.

I am referring to the 'price' which a member may be required, or be prepared, to pay in extreme cases of defiance of community norms. This problem will be discussed, then, on the level of norms. Yamin and Yonah, it will be remembered, had defied, though not intentionally, the norm of establishing permanence in a branch, and this had contributed to their uncomfortable status in the community. The young man of Hardoof failed to conform to a similar norm and his failure was eventually taken into account (though not formally) when he was alleged to have committed an offense, which was apparently irrelevant to the issue concerned. In both cases the 'price', so to speak, took the shape of a public sanction. The sanction is informal as it is made by informal public opinion. (That is not to say that no formal steps are, or were, taken in connection with specific issues, which are related to the general informal public opinion, but these do not enter the present discussion.) It takes the shape of the label "cork" (and others), and the label is defined in terms relevant to the personality of the people concerned. A similar sanction has been imposed on Olya. She has become a 'difficult person'[7] or a 'difficult case.' Disagreeable elements in her behavior in encounters with other people - both outside and within Hofra - have been explained in terms of personality traits. In so far as people have been prepared to associate her alleged total dismissal of resentment and criticism with interpersonal rather than with personal factors, they would suggest that personal misfortunes had resulted in her becoming a "difficult person," or to say the least, "odd." It is not my intention to discuss the phenomenon of informal labelling and its properties in the kibbutz in general. Obviously this phenomenon is present not only in relation to permanence in a branch or even in the wider field of labor. I touch upon it in reference to the limited subject of permanence in work.

In this context, the label conferred on Olya seems to stand in contra-distinction to that which has been attributed to the young men of the above cases. They have been labelled, because they failed to begin with to accept the commitment of permanence. Olya has been labelled in association with her failure to abide by norms contained in the commitment of permanence once permanence is established. It seemed that once she was in office, she held her permanent job and that was that. In crude terms one might say that they had too little of permanence, while she had too much. The labels of a "difficult case," "difficult person," "a problem" and the like, usually applied to the same person, allude to personality, or psychical traits. The persons mentioned above (and others whose cases I have refrained from bringing out here so as not to over-burden the discussion) have all been thus referred to by the com-munity. I do not argue that psychological observation is irrele-vant or is not illuminating, nor do I discuss the validity of the above-mentioned psychologically defined statements. I argue that in discussing these seemingly different cases in connection with the issue of permanent work, their sociological characteristics emerge. These may be defined as the extent of failure or success, in a communal context, to establish permanence in work and to ful-fil the commitments attached to permanence. (I will discuss these commitments at a later stage.) It should have become quite clear by now that there is no clear-cut set of rules with which a member should comply in seeking permanence in work; but if the expecta-tions by the community about permanence are not formally formulated in the normative set, they nevertheless operate informally. If a member does not comply with these mores, then the sanction corre-sponding to the breach of these norms is activated, i.e., public opinion applies a pejorative label.

One possible reaction by the sanctioned person is further stubborn entrenchment in his position. This step is, of course, effective only to a limited extent both in relation to his ends and in time. Olya, for one, evidently did just that. In the context of her job this response proved effective. Being a "difficult case" provided her with considerable defensive power. Labor officers as well as people at large became increasingly cautious. One thinks twice before confronting a "difficult" person. But this very consideration helps, in turn, to amplify the powerful effect of "labelling." The more refractory Olya grew, the more she was regarded as "difficult"; consequently, people grew more cautious; the more cautious they were, the stronger the disapproval of public opinion grew. It was a self-feeding process.

So, one 'price' of Olya's exercise of her deterrent power, like the price of the young men's lack of it, has been their pejorative labelling by public opinion. It is not my intention at present to go into the subject of the functioning of public opinion nor into the analysis of the derived actual effective behavior of the people who comprise the 'public' behind that 'opinion.' It is too complex to discuss this without analyzing it as a subject on its own. But it is possible to state in this connection some characteristics of public opinion:

(a) It operates, or acts, in communal life (in the present discussion by, e.g., labelling).

(b) Public opinion is effective in the young men's cases, in eventual actual actions by the community beyond labelling. But in Olya's case, the reverse happened. She persisted in her course of action. That is, the effectiveness of a perjorative label is limited once the person labelled already has deterring power and is willing to risk exercising it in the face of the public.

(c) Public opinion is not uniform and the primacy of some of its constituent elements changes from one situation to another.

The 'price,' then, paid by the labelled person who risks exercising his deterring power may be conceived as a negative sanction levelled by the community. Limited in effectiveness or not, the sanction cannot but be adverse to his or her reputation in the community. But it is not altogether adverse to his position of power. In fact, being labelled as "difficult" may provide this person with a further deterrent element which is reflected in the cautious approach practiced by the "others." If you are "difficult," then you are likely to be less amenable to influence than others. "Oddity," being "difficult," thus may add another ingredient to the composition of deterrent power. It sets limits, though not formal ones, to the efficacy of the officers of the community who function within the norms of public opinion. I note that the present discussion is about permanence in work, therefore I should further clarify this statement by saying that being so labelled cannot count <u>per se</u> as a contribut-

94

ing variable to the aspect of deterrent power in permanence in work.  Such a label is applied to a person not only when it is relevant to work, let alone position in work, but also when it is associated with this issue:  it is not an inherent quality to be found in the deterrent aspect of permanence as that itself is conceived.  If we discuss those persons who have established this position, being "odd" and so on, is not a necessary component of this aspect.  When it is present, it usually emerges in the course of interplay between the person concerned and the "others," whether the latter are members of the public or office-holders. It is a variable which adds strength to the deterrent aspect of power in permanence but is not an indispensable ingredient in its composition.

Deterrent power relates, of course, to certain others.  In the present discussion these 'others' are the community in general and its officers in particular.  It is the community in which this kind of power emerges and it is here where it is exercised and tolerated.  The labor officers, both the Distributor and the Organizer, work within the community, the ownership of whose meshek and whose membership they share, on an equal footing, with the "difficult" member.  The authority bestowed by the kibbutz on its elected office-holders is given to the incumbents with the understanding that these will function within the limits, often not precisely defined, that are approved by informal public opinion.

If successive labor officers could not remove Olya from her job, so long as she performed her work, it was not because they lacked authority.  It was because they could not exercise that authority against the deterrent power exercised by Olya.  And they could not do so because informal public opinion would have withdrawn the necessary support from them had they done so.  And this was not because the public approved of Olya's conduct.  They obviously did not.  It was because the popular disapproval of Olya's conduct did not equal, let alone overcome, the strength of her position of permanence in her office.  Again, formally, every member of the kibbutz should be prepared to abandon whatever work he is engaged in for the benefit of the kibbutz if he is asked to do so by authorized agents of the kibbutz; and it is the primacy of the interests of the meshek over individual interests that should guide the agents' performance of their job.  But it is the informal code of mores, upheld by public opinion, that permanence in work should be sought by the member, and, furthermore, respected as far as possible by the agents of the community. The latter norm does not necessarily stand in principle in contradiction to the former, as has already been shown; but situations arise in which it does so stand.  Labor officers cannot, consequently, invariably mobilize public support by referring to

the "benefit of the kibbutz" or by resorting to their formal
authority. Without this approval, whether active or acquiescent,
of public opinion, they cannot discharge their duties. As a
result, the element of deterrence which has become welded on to
the position of permanence through the individual's performance
is further crystallized through the limits set on the performance
of labor officers by an informal code of mores.

But there is at least one arena in which public adherence
to, and reconfirmation of, the formal rules of the kibbutz may be
expected. This is the General Assembly. The situation of the
Assembly meeting whose management and proceedings have been formally institutionalized, would be an ideal forum to reconfirm rules
and, if necessary, to apply them to a particular situation. Why,
then, does the Labor Distributor or the Labor Organizer refrain
from bringing his difficulties with defiant members to the plenum
of the Assembly? More specifically, why did labor officers not
bring Olya's case to the Assembly?

As I cannot embark at this point on another course of analysis, namely that of the subject of the General Assembly, I will only
refer to those aspects relevant to the present discussion. Firstly,
not everything is brought to the open meeting of the Assembly. It
will be recalled that with the growth of the kvutza, the direct
democracy expressed in discussing, deciding on and running all its
affairs has given place to the emergence of committees and full-
and part-time officers. As authority has been delegated to them it
is not expected that they should bring all the issues they deal
with to the Assembly. In the field of labor, the elected office-
holders should turn to the Assembly only in the following circumstances:

(a)   When either new regulations, or changes in present regulations,
      are proposed;

(b)   When certain tasks require a break in the routine of work,
      because of the seasonal nature of agricultural work, and
      the labor force has to be mobilized;

(c)   When the issue of a member's place of work gives rise to
      controversy between the Labor Committee and other committees,
      such as the Education Committee and consequently the whole
      issue is transferred to the highest organizational insti-
      tution of Hofra, the General Assembly; and

(d)   When they see no other hope of solving a problem, as when
      a member flatly refuses to co-operate - which happens very
      rarely.

96

Of course, the Assembly, as has already been stated, is a court of appeal for the individual against decisions made by office-holders and committees. A labor officer is likely to resort to the Assembly in those rare cases of a dispute with a member if he estimates that there is a chance that his motion will pass in the Assembly. His assessment usually undergoes two phases of examination by other members before his motion is brought to an open discussion. The first is in the Labor Committee which would discuss the issue and normally make the decision whether to transfer the problem to the higher authority of the Assembly (sometimes the first forum would be the Meshek Committee). The second is the Secretariat which determines the agenda for the weekly General Assembly. If it places the matter on the agenda, its members' opinion on the issue itself, and not only on its urgency, has considerable weight. Thus there is a filtering process through which the labor officer's motion (which may result from anger, conviction or an incorrect assessment of the situation) goes, before it can finally reach the Assembly. It is 'filtered,' as it were, through the combined assessment of other members all of whom, whether in the Labor and Meshek Committees or the Secretariat, hold influential positions in the community. They may support the contents of his motion but may estimate that it should not be brought to the Assembly or that if it is brought, it is unlikely to be adopted by the Assembly's members. Thus the delegation of authority to committees and officers in itself deters the transferring of such an issue to the General Assembly.

Secondly, Hofra with its approximately 240 members and 420 inhabitants is a relatively small community, and of the features of such a small community is widespread and detailed knowledge about its people. The knowledge may be based on distorted information, but it is present, and distorted as it may be, it always has the same weight as truth. Channels of information emerge, multiply and develop in the community, the more stable the membership grows. If one takes into account that the meshek of the village is collective; that most of the members work within the meshek and are exposed to constantly flowing information in the branches; that people meet in the dining hall, in the communal stores, in the collective children's homes, on the village lawns and, as everywhere, in social circles, one will appreciate that there are a myriad of channels of information. Put in another way, there are very numerous occasions and situations in which a member is exposed to basically the same contents of information. Therefore it would not be an exaggeration to state that there is a very detailed store of knowledge of and about people and many of the latter's affairs in the community. I therefore call it, following Frankenberg, 'redundant knowledge' (Frankenberg, 1966: 276-296).[8] One of the norms regulating communal life is that one does not discuss openly, nor communicate openly, all

knowledge about one's fellows. This is, of course, true everywhere, let alone in a small community. If it is true in a small
community, it is likely to be true in a collective organization
of social life such as the kibbutz, in which so many relationships are intricately involved and overlap. And if it holds true
for the kibbutz in general, it certainly does in the formal situation of the General Assembly. The members of the kibbutz, who
comprise the congregation of the Assembly, all have some information or knowledge concerning the person whose problem might be
brought to the meeting. Indeed, they have, as stated above, an
extremely detailed, redundant, knowledge. The information they
share may be unevenly distributed amongst them. It may be inac-
curate or even distorted, but they all _know_. They know more or
less the issue at hand without depending on the formal presentation by the Chairman or the labor officer. Furthermore, they
know the person, and this is what ultimately counts. It is the
total set of his social attributes that is considered, and not
only his standing in relation to the particular case at issue.[9]

This total set is certainly not discussed in the Assembly,
and this for three reasons.[10]

(1)   Adherence to norms which enjoin that one refrain from doing
      so in the open is, as said above, necessary for social
      relationships to endure.[11]

(2)   The meeting is called for discussion of a specific issue,
      and not for discussion or judgment of the respondent's
      personality. Redundant knowledge implies knowledge of
      issues which are not, and indeed cannot, be discussed in
      public and the office-holders as well as the committee
      members are fully aware of this. They know that the people
      present in the congregation have a fair measure of infor-
      mation, both about the person in question and the issue, well
      beyond the information presented formally in the meeting.
      They have to take into account that, in these circumstances,
      the attempt to keep the discussion and the resultant decision
      within only the defined limits of the issue, may not be
      successful. The stage provided by the General Assembly is
      indeed ideal for officers of the kibbutz to carry out their
      plans in the name of the primacy of the kibbutz's interests
      over those of the individual, but they cannot depend on
      automatic support because:

      (a)   People may differ in their assessment from that of the
            officers;

      (b)   they may interpret the "interests of the kibbutz" in
            quite a different manner;

98

(c)    they see not only the officers' side of the question, but also that of the respondent; and

(d)    as stated above, they know too much about kibbutz life to be moved by emotive appeals to the "primacy of the kibbutz's interests."

The General Assembly is indeed committed a priori to this primacy, but the people present in it may refuse, by their votes, to accept without challenge that this general commitment applies to the particular case and the particular person as suggested by the officers. Thus knowledge and norms shared by the public set limits to initiative by its officers, an initiative which is based on responsibility and authority delegated to them, when another member is concerned.

(3)  Thirdly - and this is connected with the preceding suggestion- given the ideological commitment to primacy of collective interests in the situation of the Assembly, it is people who comprise the congregation. Their considerations, though affected by the situation, are not bound to be governed by formal norms only. Informal norms also operate even in formal situations. Sometimes they take on formulas of formal norms by means of adaptation and interpretation. Much as the member attending the meeting is committed to the underlying requirements of the institution of the Assembly, nonetheless he considers other issues as relevant and as bearing on the subject.

I suggest that had officers brought Olya's case to an open discussion in the Assembly, and argued there that the interests of Hofra were being damaged, the issue would inevitably have provoked also considerations other than those they invoked. People would have pointed out her personal and health problems and would have called for tolerance and patience. As against the "interests of the meshek," they would have raised the norms of support for the less fortunate member, the value of mutual aid and, above all, the right of the individual to permanence in work. Some members might have gone as far as to re-interpret the term "interests of the kibbutz" so as to apply these to the interests of the constituent members, without whose personal satisfaction communal life would suffer a setback. But even if those ideas, and their like, were not expressed openly (and I believe that they would have been) they would nevertheless have been thought and felt, and they might have affected the outcome of the meeting. The possibility of such a development may in itself deter offic- ers from resorting to their relatively most promising tool of communal action - viz. calling on the General Assembly.

## Deterrent power - recapitulation

The discussion has reached a stage which permits me to recapitulate my analysis of deterrent power. I will concentrate on those elements of deterrent power which characterize the position of the individual member, the respondent, vis-a-vis the initiating actor, the authorized officer of the community, and the community as a whole.

In relation to the discussion of Olya, it is not her personal traits which can form the point of departure of this analysis (see Devons and Gluckman, 1964: 13-19; 158-261, and also my comment earlier on the psychologistic approach in the community), let alone her 'total identity' (in Garfinkel's meaning; Garfinkel, 1956: 420). Although people in the community do tend to relate difficulties in communicating with her and the difficulties in the attempts to change her job to her personal attributes - as they do in most cases of difficulties with people - discussion by a social anthropologist of these attributes cannot lead to a meaningful analysis of the deterrent power of either officer and community, or of Olya herself. Deterrent power, which has been discussed in relation to the case of Olya, is not an attribute of theirs or hers. Rather, it can be analyzed as a cluster of factors which affect her relative standing in her relationship with the community and the communal authorities in the sphere of work. In the following summary, analysis of the components of this standing will be isolated.

Essentially, power is a relationship between people (Dahl, 1957: 203) and not an attribute of the actor (Emerson, 1962: 32). Looking at it this way, and assuming that the relationship is not static or indeed ossified, the observation can be focused on the respondent as well as on his counterpart, and initiating actor. The respondent's participation in the power-relationship is as essential as the participation of the other actor. Power, therefore, consists not only of 'the realization of will' by one actor, but also of the resistance by the respondent to its being exercised. Resistance determines to a considerable extent the amount of power to be exerted by the initiating actor and the combination of variables (or resources) which make up this power. Similarly, potential resistance to a realization of another actor's will determines the choice of resources the respondent may exploit and their amount - if he has access to them. In other words, potential resistance is also an aspect of power. It is an aspect of power, (a) because the initiating actor must consider it before taking his initiative and must assess the resources at his own command so as to overcome it (or attempt to find a reasonable accommodation with the respondent); and

100

(b)  because it constitutes a factor in the 'chance' that the
party I call 'respondent' will realize his own will in the relationship.  His own will, in this context, is the will to resist
pressure; it is a defensive will aiming to protect things he
values.  I have termed this aspect of the respondent's will,
'negative,' so as to emphasize its defensive, 'responsive' nature.
It is negative in the sense that it rises in opposition to another
actor's initiative and aims to take steps to resist it.[12]

The power relationship between two persons can be described
as a continuum at the one extreme of which there is, ideally, no
resistance (including no potential resistance) at all, and at the
other extreme a total absence of ability (for whatever combination
of reasons) to 'realize will.'  In this last case, assuming that
the relationship is not a dead channel, the respondent is able,
ideally, to change the relationship radically so as to realize his
own will, meeting no resistance from his counterpart.  This is, of
course, a model.  Where there is a relationship between actors the
two extremes are not likely to occur.  But this model helps to
show that even the terms 'initiating actor' and 'respondent' are
relative.  The respondent, in his resistance (again, that would
include potential resistance) can activate as well as neutralize
resources which are at the command of his counterpart, turning
the latter, in a sense, into respondent.  In other words, the two
are both initiating actors and respondents engaged in a relationship.  Nevertheless, for the sake of clarity I will treat the community agent who is endowed with authority as the initiating actor
and the individual member, in this case Olya, as the respondent.
Almost by definition, the power she has at her command is a power
of resistance.  In effect, it is more than that: it contains a
deterrent element.

The initiating actor wishes to 'realize his will'; the
respondent wishes to resist it.  Each attempts to use, and to
acquire, resources which would be effective if conflict breaks
out into the open.  The efficient way for both would be to gain
control over the things that the other party values (Emerson,
1962: 32).  The value, or the importance, of these resources,
and their significance for the actors, are influenced by the
presence in the background of the third factor, the kibbutz.
The kibbutz provides the background for these relationships,
since most of the resources which flow through them are meaningful in the kibbutz.  The kibbutz sets the arenas for the actors
and sets the rules, both formal and informal, for approaching a
conflict, should that arise.  In a word, the power of resistance
as well as that which it intends to resist, acquires its significance from their common background in the kibbutz.  I will return
to these problems after the discussion of the resources which
have been mentioned above.

Dahl (1957: 203) analyses power in reference to its base (or source); its means (or instruments); its amount (or extent); and its scope (or range), all in relation to the respondent. The resources I refer to correspond roughly to what Dahl calls the 'base' of power, i.e., the things the actor "can exploit in order to affect the behavior of another" (1957 ). I have analyzed some of these resources in their relation to the community at large. I have touched upon other components of power relations suggested by Dahl only insofar as they help to elucidate the significance of the resources.

Both the labor officer and the respondent may have similar resources in the kibbutz. These may be networks of relationships based on common experience in The Kvutza or even prior to joining it; they may be relationships based on common interests of members as parents, or neighbors, or peers, and so forth; they may consist of belonging to a branch, of membership in committees, and so forth. They are similar in that such relationships are shared by most of the members of the kibbutz. Nearly every member enjoys at least some of such relationships: he is a neighbor, a parent, a one-time member of a youth group, a branchman, etc. These relationships may be mobilized as resources in events of confrontation between members, in formal as well as informal situations (see Fedida, 1972: 79-82). An important aspect of these resources lies in their wide range of distribution in the community and in members' almost equal access to, and the potential use of them. Because access to these resources tends to be equally shared, this aspect operates so as to maintain equality amongst members. The availability of these resources reduces, to an extent, differences of status which members have in relation to a particular issue[13] - statuses such as labor officer and respondent, and an issue such as holding a job or staying in office.

Similarity of resources, then, and essentially equal access to them, are in themselves an advantage for the respondent. This advantage is, in turn, a further resource to be exploited by the respondent in a possible confrontation. But what emerges in a situation of a conflict between the labor officer as an initiating actor and the other member as a respondent, and particularly so in such a situation, is also the difference in the resources to which they have an access. Of course a variety of resources is exploited by, or is potentially present, so as not to be exploited by adversaries .in various situations, including the work situation. But in the present discussion I am interested only in the work situation, in resources which are particularly significant in this situation and, within them, in those which are particularly relevant to the relationship between officer and respondent. This interest leads to the discussion of the essentially <u>different</u> resources which are at the command of these two actors.

102

The main resource to be used by the labor officer is the authority delegated to him by the kibbutz. He is authorized (and even under pressure) to take initiative when necessary in the field of labor. His authority vests in him because he is representative of the community and is backed by the fact that he is elected according to the democratic principles of the kibbutz. In Hofra, the officers are elected by a popular vote, in secret ballot. I repeat: the labor officer himself, as a member of the kibbutz, does have access to other resources in the community (his own branch affiliation, peer and family relationships, personal achievements, etc.). In the encounter, whether or not these resources are practically used or referred to, they are nevertheless present, for they are encapsulated, so to speak, in his position. But what distinguishes him is the resource which, in this situation, only he has access to, his authority.

The respondent, likewise, has access to many resources and he uses them more frequently than does the labor officer. Events in which relationships such as family, peers etc. have been exploited to exert pressure on the kibbutz authorities have occurred not too infrequently. They are widely known in the community. If I have not discussed them it is because (a) I have not space to discuss the whole variety of situations in the sphere of labor and (b) I wish to draw attention to what I believe are the crucial factors in the member's position in this sphere. So, if I hold the relationships and other resources the bases of which are outside the sphere of labor "proper" constant, the main resource the member enjoys is his attachment to a branch. The prevalence of this attachment is at the bottom of relationships within the branch, the task in the branch, the responsibility delegated to the worker in it, and so forth. This attachment gains in significance the more it becomes permanent. Permanent attachment to a branch can activate relationships within the branch-team which will be discussed in the following chapter. It is the individual member who controls this asset of permanence in his branch. As stated above, although the authority over all labor problems has been bestowed by the kibbutz on the labor officer, the members of the kibbutz have all accepted that control over permanence in work lodges with the individual, and this control is recognized as his right. The underlying background is, of course, the economic conditions, the diversification of the economy, and particularly the gap between the demand for and supply of labor. The consolidation of the position of the individual, understood in these terms, makes him less dependent. The less dependent he is, the greater his power to deter threats to his position.

This analysis becomes meaningful when its relation to the kibbutz community is considered. It is the community in which the resources mentioned here are to be mobilized. It is also the community which provides the arenas for the various relationships to express themselves and for strife to occur. One important factor which lies in the community itself is the interest shared by every member in permanence in work. A threat to an individual's state of permanence in the branch is, albeit indirectly, a threat to everybody's interest. It is essentially a threat to other members' common interests through the importance which the kibbutz attributes to the role of precedent. Once a member can be shifted from one work to another against his own wish, or even his own acquiescence, because the officer considers this necessary for the kibbutz's interests, such a decision may facilitate further moves. (The role of precedent is discussed in the next chapter.) This common interest, conceptualized as a right of every individual member, is a resource of power for both the individual and for all members in the communal context. That is, it is deterrent in nature.

Another important aspect related to the community interests which lie in the background, is the constraints under which a controversy or a dispute can take place. Although the dispute reveals the disparate immediate interests of the persons who are at loggerheads, they have joint interests beyond these immediate ones. They are members of the same kibbutz, the welfare of which determines their own; they both depend on the kibbutz for a practical solution to the present problem; the solution itself must be found within the kibbutz and, most likely within the meshek (and both the community and its economy have access to limited resources); and so forth. In other words, they live, and work in, and appeal to, the same universe of relationships. The maintenance of these relationships is essential for both parties. In addition, in other contexts of communal life, they may find themselves in other, different, roles which provide the basis of co-operation, and mutual aid and possibly even for a show of amity, possibilities which in themselves impose constraints on their behavior. In a word, "... there are common as well as conflicting interests among the participants" (Schelling, 1963: 4). These common interests, although not always in full consciousness, call for mutual accommodation. "Pure conflict," writes Schelling, "...would arise in a war of complete extermination, otherwise not even in war. For this reason, 'winning' in a conflict does not have a strictly competitive meaning; it is not winning relative to one's adversary. It means gaining relative to one's own value system; and this may be done by bargaining, by mutual accommodation... the possibility of mutual accommodation is as important and dramatic as the element of conflict" (Schelling, 1963: 4-5).

For the respondent the retention of his job is the paramount consideration. This is what he values and his interest in beating the officer, if such an interest appears in the course of the argument, is overcome by his awareness (albeit not always immediate and conscious) of the other, joint, interests he shares with the officer. The "value system" of the community essentially supports him. The interests of the community agent are more complex: he is interested in carrying out what he (and others) consider to be his responsibility, but he is open to other pressures because he is an officer of the community at large. In Olya's case, the labor officer could not disengage himself from considerations such as health, age, the possibility of alternative occupation, and the like. Concern in finding a satisfactory solution to Olya's problem could not be ignored in the light of what seemed to be a more pressing problem, the functioning of the office. In this sense his interest, though not identical with Olya's, was, at least, in essentials a joint one. Not less important, perhaps, is his dependence on the community. Even if one ignores Olya's personal story and her position in the job, her very membership in the kibbutz calls for mutual accommodation, or at least for an attempt to find such accommodation.

Both the interest shared by everybody in the community in retaining permanence in work (and its conceptualization as a personal right) and the presence of joint interests (only some of which I have touched upon) can be viewed as 'bases,' in Dahl's terms, for the power of the respondent. And both are deterrent in nature.

This power is deterrent because it is concerned with access to, and control over, resources without which the initiating actor cannot force the respondent to comply with his will. The resources discussed above - permanence in the branch, the interests of all the members in retaining permanence in principle, and constraints imposed by joint interests - are controlled by the respondent more than they are by the communal officer. As long as the respondent can retain this control, he is able to deter a move against his interest.

Control of these resources, in a communal context, implies conduct in work which reconciles with communal expectations. Failure to reconcile actual conduct with the role expected (for a variety of reasons) has two results: (a) it may lead to a loss of control. The deterring power which the respondent enjoys gradually weakens as he is handicapped in rallying support from the community. It may culminate adversely, as it culminated in Olya's case in her partial removal from office; and (b) it may lead, in some situations, to a process of alienation, ostensibly expressed in labelling the respondent as "odd" or otherwise pejoratively. This process, while tending to affect the respond-

105

ent's 'total' standing in the community, may, if the respondent
further alienates himself, reinforce his deterrent power. New
elements enter the scene, elements of his personal conduct. In
Emerson's terms (Emerson, 1962: 35), Olya, by ignoring criticism
and expectations, reduced motivational investment in goals mediated
by the kibbutz (such as personal acceptance and reputation). She
could, therefore, at least for a while, be less vulnerable to
reproach from her fellow kibbutz-members. This, in turn, has
strengthened the deterring elements of her position.

Schelling, in discussing deterrence (particularly in relation to international relations) states that it is "concerned with
the exploitation of potential force" (Schelling, 1963: 9). Indeed,
the essence of deterrent power is its not being in active use.
Its potentiality, its tacit presence, is its significant essence.
Emerson (1962: 32) suggests that this property is inherent in
power in general: "... the power defined here will not be, of
necessity, observable in every interactive episode between A and
B, yet we suggest that it exists nonetheless as a potential, to
be explored, tested, and occasionally employed by the participants."
It is a property of power since "power is," in turn, "a property
of the social relation" as such (1962: 32). In any social relationship there is inherent, then, the property of power; and deterrence
is an ingredient in power. Deterrence lies in its potentiality,
that is, in the constellation of the 'bases' of power, the conditions under which the participants and the 'bases' are set, and
the accessibility of the 'bases.'

This nature of deterrent power explains why it is associated
mainly with what Schelling calls 'tacit bargaining.' In a sense,
the state of potentiality, when power is not explicitly employed
yet the relationship is present, is a state of bargaining, of
mutual assessment. But it is a tacit assessment, not always aimed
at a specific end, nor is it even always conscious. The mutual
tacit assessment may be made consciously and may be associated
with an end, but not necessarily so. In a communal context, where
nearly everybody interacts with everybody else, clusters of resources and assets are established by participants in the social
relationships and those assets and resources are, in turn, present
in the interaction itself. A process of bargaining also takes
place, again not necessarily in a conscious form, in situations
of interaction. The clustering of resources affects not only the
immediate situation of interaction but also future possible situations. The potential, deterrent power, made up of variables
discussed above (and of others to which I have only alluded) is
present in this state of tacit assessment and, I would add, tacit
bargaining.[14] Deterrent power, being essentially potential, is
weighing mainly in situations themselves inherent with the nature

106

of potentiality. Deterrence, after all, is designed to avert an open conflict from a standpoint of power. And, to conclude this argument I quote Schelling again: "The deterrence concept requires that there be both conflict and common interest between parties involved..." (1963: 11). I have referred above to the intricacies of relationships in the community amongst which the relationship between officer and respondent constitutes only one such relationship. The persons involved are not necessarily adversaries. They may be friends. But deterrence, as a property of a relation of power, "is as relevant to relations between friends as between potential enemies" (Schelling, 1963: 11).

An impression which may arise from the present discussion that conflict outweighs co-operation in the kibbutz would be misleading. But the study of the position of the individual in the field of labor leads necessarily to the discussion of a possible confrontation of the member with labor authorities. This discussion, in turn, leads to the analysis of the individual's deterrent power. This last element in the position of the individual, potential as it is in nature, is mostly relevant to a state of disagreement. It is in the terms of this state that it is analyzable. One is not necessarily a potential enemy, or an adversary, in a relationship of deterrence: "deterrence is relevant," as said above, "to relations between friends" (Schelling, 1963: 11) as well.

## When permanence is discussed in public

Before recapitulating the discussion of deterrent power I noted that the General Assembly was not called upon to discuss a problem of transferring a member (Olya) from a permanent position in work.

But a motion to transfer a member from his work which was considered as permanent, was once considered in the General Assembly in 1970. The member, Ohad, had been working outside the meshek in a national economic organization of kibbutzim. He had held a central position in the management of the organization for years. Although the organization is a kibbutz organization whose sole aim is to serve the kibbutzim (through the regional purchase organizations), Ohad's work in it was not regarded as a service to The Movement. Service to The Movement implies, among other things, the notion of a temporary job. Members are "mobilized" from the constituent kibbutzim to work for The Movement and are expected to relinquish their offices and return to work in or for their home-meshakim upon finishing their term of work for The Movement.[15] Ohad had worked in the organization for many years, and whether or not his initial years with the

107

organization had been recognized by The Movement as "mobilized service," by 1970 his office with the organization was regarded as permanent and he was definitely not included in the category of Movement workers ("activists"). In 1969 it was felt that one of the branches required the help of financial and commercial expertise in order to overcome internal organizational difficulties and commercial obstacles in dealing with external markets and clients' situations. It was decided that a member experienced in finance and commerce should join the branch. It was felt that Ohad would fit into the new job as he had experience as external treasurer of Hofra itself,[16] and, he had also accumulated experience in the national economic-financial organization, and thereby had developed a wide range of business and personal ties. If I may make my own estimate, I would suggest that other considerations also operated in choosing Ohad as candidate for the job. One such consideration was the fact that Ohad's office, though regarded as permanent, was "outside work," i.e., outside the meshek. Calling him "back home" would not threaten the permanent position in work of other members, working within the meshek. At the time nobody in the meshek showed interest in taking the office. It seems to have been easier to disrupt a member's "outside work" rather than to threaten the permanence of a member's work within the meshek.

For Ohad, the new suggestion apparently created a dilemma. He had been away from work in the meshek for many years. He had had little to do with Hofra's affairs and had ceased to take an active part in them. Having in mind and in memory his years of active participation in Hofra's social life and leadership in its financial affairs, and recalling earlier years of hard work in agriculture, Ohad was presented with an offer to regain an active position in the communal life. Whether or not he had liked his activities outside Hofra, he was now presented with a chance to renew his active communal life and regain a prestigious position within Hofra. On the other hand, he had been engaged for years in the top management of the national organization one of whose founders he was. Attachment to the office he had virtually created and to the organization was probably associated with satisfaction with the work itself, with its range of authority, and with networks of working and personal relationships which had developed over the years. He was now in his early 60s, nearing his probable retirement. So far as I can tell, he had no competitors for the office and his work there was widely appreciated.

Ohad responded formally to the suggestion presented to him and to the dilemma with which he was confronted by stating that "as a member of The Kvutza, whatever The Kvutza decides, I will carry out," a most irregular response. It is very unusual for

people not to state their personal preferences.  By so doing Ohad
publicly adhered to the principle of primacy of kibbutz over individual considerations and left the officers who discussed the matter
with him in the dark about his personal preference.  The only practical comment was the reasonable request that the organization
should be given time to look for a successor.  Members wondered
what Ohad's real preference was.  This could not be ignored.

Certainly, Ohad's response differed from Olya's since circumstances were different.  Ohad's office was "outside work" whereas
Olya's was in Hofra; Ohad's removal from his present job would have
given him a promising office in Hofra itself, an office which he
would have created; for him removal from his present employment did
not mean alternative work in which he had no interest, or alternatively, one which he had a strong interest not to take; and finally,
his future work would have most likely been appreciated as it was
created by the Meshek Committee in response to economic interests
of the meshek, and therefore would have conferred some power and
prestige on the incumbent.  His would have been a change in office;
hers would have been an unmistakably adverse change in work.  The
different responses may be viewed from this angle.

Months had elapsed and a successor had not been found.  Ohad
continued to work in his office in town.  Delegations came to
Hofra, asking for the kibbutz's consent to the continuation and
indeed the extension of Ohad's work in the organization.  People
wondered again what Ohad's personal standpoint was and, furthermore,
what their own attitude should be.  I was told that the first
statement in the General Assembly concerning the "recall" of Ohad
from his post "back home" was made by the Meshek Organizer, following Ohad's response which had been interpreted as affirmative.  A
second statement was made by the same officer in another meeting
while discussing economic issues.  There was no intention on his
part to raise this subject as an issue for the agenda.  But a few
months had passed between the two meetings; and by this time
hesitation about the right attitude and doubts about the initial
decision, although it had been formally approved by the first
meeting of the Assembly, had cropped up.  Disregarding the fact
that that issue had not been included in the agenda, Ozer, an
old-time member, reacted to the statement which confirmed the
expectation that Ohad should soon leave his office and take the
new office proposed for him.  Ozer raised an objection.  It was
true, he said, that Ohad had agreed to discontinue his present
job at The Kvutza's request; it was also true that Hofra needs
a competent trained person for the newly created job in the
branch; it was further true that Ohad could fit very well in that
job, but the interests of the meshek could not simply override
personal and individual considerations.  As no-one had proposed

109

to remove Ohad from his present job; as Ohad seemed to be satisfied with it; as he - and this is the main argument - was advanced
in age and happy with his virtually permanent work; and as all
these factors have an accumulative nature, these considerations
should have carried more weight.  The kibbutz should endure the
difficulties.  Someone else should and could be found for the job
at home.  (Indeed, the outgoing elected Secretary had volunteered
to take the job temporarily.)

The assembly did not vote on the issue, as it had not been
included in the agenda in advance, but the very reaction in public
proved that that feeling prevailed throughout the community.  The
Meshek Organizer's only comment was that he had only been recalling
a previous statement which, incidentally, he added, had been endorsed by the Assembly.

I draw attention to several points:  (a)  the objection to a
decision to recall Ohad from his office was made in public in the
General Assembly (the first meeting had been held before I came to
Hofra);  (b)  it was made although the initial decision was considered formally valid;  (c)  the underlying argument was that
Ohad had a right to permanence in his work, although other variables, age in particular [associated with the one I have termed
'accumulation'], were stressed; and (d) the nature of the personal,
or individual, considerations, to be weighed by the community as
equal in value to its own collective interests, were not economic
in essence, although economic reasoning could have been used,
such as the importance of holding this central position in an
economic organization for Hofra, for instance.

If the Meshek Organizer felt he should cling to the prear-
ranged agenda in order to resist Ozer's objection, and to reiter-
ate the formal decision, it was, among other considerations,
because of his knowledge that his colleagues in the Secretariat
and in the Meshek Committee were wavering.  Ohad did not defend
his permanent hold on his work, but his reaction gave rise to a
widespread interpretation that he actually preferred his present
job.  Although nobody disputed the economic advantage Hofra would
get from recalling Ohad to the new office, a general opinion
prevailed that if circumstances permitted, this move should not be
carried through.  This opinion was shared by the central officers
(with the exception, perhaps, of the Meshek Organizer) and added
to their hesitancy.  The tactics used by the officers in negotiat-
ing with the visiting delegations is of no interest to this discussion.  Let me just add that Ohad has remained in his office
with the organization (and was elected, after an interval of many
years, to the Meshek Committee).

In relation to the general course of the discussion two
arguments crystallize.  Firstly, the labor officers cannot

invariably count on the support of the General Assembly when they handle an issue which is related to an individual member. It is indeed difficult, but not impossible, to oppose them as they represent the interests of the _Meshek_ and therefore must be given credit for being as well informed as necessary, and qualified to make their calculations, suggestions and decisions. Secondly, non-economic considerations prove to carry significant weight. When an individual's position is threatened, even if it be in the name of the collective and by the latter's officers, public opinion may go out of its way to find ways to protect the individual's "right" in the face of economic and administrative considerations.

From these two arguments a third one emerges. Public opinion is not stable nor is it uniform. Many events, or many issues, give rise to 'public' reaction. The reaction, as stated before, is usually inseparable from moral evaluation. Moral evaluation leads to moral judgment on the part of the people who constitute the 'public.' As events and issues keep cropping up and are numerous, so are the opportunities which call for reaction. As people are many (relatively speaking) and events are numerous, one cannot expect a unanimous response, or reaction, to social events. Various persons who occupy different social positions, which stand in certain relationships to other positions occupied by other persons in the community, are likely to react differently. Also, as situations change, people's reactions are likely to be affected by these changes. So, the different events, or issues, which occur in the community give rise to a variety of opinions within the public, rather than to a unanimous 'public opinion.' For an issue to evoke what one would call 'public opinion' in the sense of an opinion which is likely to be shared and expressed by most people in the community, the issue must be definable in a way which would have the same effect on that majority. It must be defined and conceived in terms sufficiently broad so as to arouse a similar reaction in the majority of people who belong to various social circles. Not only should it be conceived in broad terms so as to cover, under its definition, various and perhaps different phenomena which appeal to wider circles, but it should contain an element of significance for the community so as to be able to subject other (and perhaps contradictory) considerations to its own primacy. And this is not always possible. It should also be sufficiently clear-cut and omit complexities. And, lastly, it should imply a moral standpoint.

Public response, representing the mores prevalent in the community, is thus a mechanism of social control in two different respects. Firstly, it urges officers of the community to take initiatives vis-a-vis the individual member when this is felt necessary, and, alternatively, it is used by the officers when this initiative creates confrontation. This is the angle of the

collective and its agents. Secondly, it raises informal barriers
against those very officers' actions, thereby appearing as something on which the respondent member can lean in that confrontation.
That is to say, 'public opinion' affects considerations and behavior of both parties when an encounter arises, and it can be - and
is - employed by both, in selecting different moves relevant to
the situation which may appeal to the same members of the community.
As public opinion emerges mainly from and is borne by the prevalent
web of social relationships in the community, both the officers
of the kibbutz and their counterparts in a dispute, or any member,
for that matter, in considering steps in the field of labor, take
this informal medium into account. If they do not, or if their
considerations prove to be based on misjudgment, they suffer a
negative, though informal, sanction by the community. Therefore
officers must subject considerations - both personal and collective
- not only to the formally 'recognized' interests of the meshek or
'the kibbutz' but also to this informal medium. They also have
to know whether the issue at hand is of a nature that can arouse
the general 'public opinion' (in association with which they can
act) or not. In that last event, they may expect a variety of
opinions within the public rather than public opinion. This
informal medium sets limits on, or alternatively defines the range
of possible actions for, any member. Withdrawal of support, whether in the form of a silent agreement or even a mere overlooking
of certain modes of behavior, makes life in a commune hard to
endure.

As I do not embark on a separate analysis of public opinion,
I cannot go further than that. But I must make one additional
comment. In sociological studies, informal public opinion is
studied in reference to social control. As one of the mechanisms
of social control, it is placed, as it were, on a continuum whose
one end is signified by the mildest mechanism of folkways and the
other by the law of the State which is supported by the theoretical
monopoly of the State over the use of force. If a breach, or
threat of a breach, occurs in the normative system, these mechanisms
are set into motion, with the selection of the mechanism, or agency,
depending on the nature of the breach and the norm. If informal
action proves to be insufficient and the breach is regarded as
serious, the group in question (community, organization, "society,"
and the like) may resort to its formal agencies. One can find this
approach in the literature of, and about, the kibbutz. Spiro
(1956: 88-104) extends the forms of social control in "Kiryat
Yedidim" from the individual's "hakkara" (or "consciousness,"
p. 88) through informal public opinion, semi-formal public opinion,
and then "when the pressure of public opinion, exerted in informal
and semi-formal ways, is not effective, the kibbutz has recourse
to more formal procedures" (1956: 101). "The first procedure is

to bring the person's dereliction to the official attention of the
kibbutz at a town meeting" (1956: 101) (which I call, following
the terminology of most kibbutzim, 'General Assembly').

While I am not at odds with this typology and its use,[17]
what I try to elucidate is that the official institution of the
General Assembly (and committees to which it has delegated authority) is not just a formal extension of informal public opinion.
The formal institution is by its nature committed to some principles of the kibbutz, both in adherence to ideological tenets and
to organizational procedures, whereas informal public opinion
represents the more fluid currents of ideas and interests of the
people whose opinions comprise it. There is a great variety among
these persons, ideas, outlooks and interests; and their combined
judgments are far less committed to such adherence. So, it is
not simply a matter of a continuum on which effectiveness of control is marked (in response to the varying seriousness of the
breach). The agencies themselves vary from one another not only
in relation to their respective measures of effectiveness but also
in relation to what they represent. And what they represent is
not necessarily the same 'opinion.'

The presence of people in the official institution of the
Assembly, i.e., the democratic voluntary association of the
kibbutz, and the fact that the latter is 'General,' constitutes
a guarantee that this institution will not be an arena in which
current affairs are discussed and interpreted solely according to
their relevance to abstract tenets of kibbutz ideology. Informal
public opinion thus influences the more formalized institutions
for making decisions. Undercurrents of feelings, evaluations and
opinions which take no such commitments as, say, the primacy of
the collective interests or the meshek's efficiency, arise in the
situation of the Assembly simultaneously with arguments which
advocate the meshek's (and its officers') interests. If the
issue at hand is not of the broad nature which would rally 'public
opinion' but rather give rise to 'opinions,' then the outcome of
the Assembly may become even less predictable.

If we overlook for a moment the mobilization, use, and even
possible exploitation of personal ties and social groupings and
networks in the Assembly, by a member; if we do not enter the
discussion of norms, let these be informal as they may; and if
we concentrate on the residual components of informal public
opinion in the formal occasion of the Assembly, a further dimension will be revealed. This can help in better understanding the
advantages a member like Olya or Ohad may derive from the organization of democratic institutions of the kibbutz. In other
words, one can see how this distinction, subtle as it may be,
between informal public opinion (and what it represents) and the

113

formalized institution which is presumed to be the authoritative
public opinion, helps in understanding the resources of deterrent
power associated with permanence in work.

I have emphasized, almost to the point of excess, that the
labor officers cannot automatically and invariably count on the
Assembly to help them in exerting pressure on individual members.
I have also stated that public opinion as present in the situation
of the Assembly, is not uniform and indeed is unstable.  One of the
reasons for this state of affairs lies in the recognition, shared
virtually by all, that permanence in work should normally be sought
and, not less important, retained, by every member.  This in itself
has already been stated.  Underlying this recognition, and, furthermore, the support which goes beyond recognition, is the weighting
by members of the community of the alternative to this approach.
If the individual's permanence in work, conceived as the individual's right to permanence in work, is not reasonably protected and
is not sanctioned positively by the community (and consequently
left to the efforts, devices and means of the individual), then
almost everyone could find himself in an insecure position.  Members would not invariably identify themselves with any caprice or
any obnoxious person in any situation, but what is regarded as
the right to permanence in work cannot be conceived as unequally
distributed amongst members of the commune.  It is not essentially a matter of the abstract value of egalitarianism applied to
a specific issue which determines the conception that this right
should be equally distributed amongst the membership.  Equality
in permanence in work is not a value in itself, recognized as an
ideological tenet of the kibbutz.  The public argument in the
issue of the young man of Hardoof shows  that.  One could almost
argue to the contrary if the discussion was on purely theoretical
grounds:  in principle all the members of the kibbutz alike
stand in an equal position in relation to the kibbutz's right to
shift each of them from one job to another according to the needs
of the meshek.  It is not only even a theoretical, or logical,
extension of the positive sanction that public opinion has
applied to the individual's search for permanence, although, as
stated previously, public opinion does sanction this search.  But
also viewing this approach to the problem of the right to permanence from the 'extension' angle would leave us in the realm of
values and the structure of its logic.  It is the realization
that one's position of permanence is reasonably secure when it
is so recognized by others, which is, to a large extent, at the
bottom of the informal public's sanction; and this position is
recognized by others if it is conceived as a right and not only
as a de-facto achievement; and it can be conceived as a right
only if other members of the fundamentally egalitarian society
share - and have the opportunity to exercise - the same right.
It is a matter of estimation and evaluation of the situation

114

rather than a matter of 'pure' values. The interest of the individual member in achieving and retaining a permanent position in
work, when abstracted from an actual event of a particular member
in a particular branch (and members, after all, do change branches
yet seek permanence in any branch they choose to join), must be
viewed as a phenomenon in itself. It coincides with the same
interest of his fellow-members in this field. To be sure,
individuals' actual interests in branches may clash; they do not
always agree as individuals, but the search for permanence in
work as such is virtually common to all. The phenomenon of the
search of the individual per se coincides with other such phenomena. A threat to the position of permanence held by one member
arouses caution and even concern in others; and these others are
aroused to be prepared to defend this right.

This state of affairs constitutes a system of bonds whose
essential nature is that of a mutual guarantee to reduce such
threats to a minimum. In the informal situations, when information spreads about an issue of permanence in work (or a threat
to it), the people who are present are not free, in viewing and
judging the case, from this kind of consideration. They are
aware of the implications of a threat to permanence itself, not
to mention other considerations which they may have and which
result from what I would term "redundant knowledge" (in the
cybernetic sense) of the case and the person in question. Unless
they are to be personally adversely affected by the success of
the member in question in retaining his permanent position, they
would tend to view the other member's attempt to cling to his
position as they would view their own, i.e., as a right vis-a-vis
the community. A threat to the other member's permanence is
indirectly a possible threat to my own. This, in effect, is a
significant asset for the individual member when struggling for
the retention of permanence in work.

This asset does not altogether fade away in the more formal
situation of an open meeting. The commitment of the kibbutz
institutions to promote what is conceived as the kibbutz's interests over that of the individual weakens, of course, this kind of
bond among people who are present at the meeting (whether the
latter be an official committee meeting or the Assembly), but it
does not eliminate this asset. These underlying considerations,
obviously not infrequently anti-economic in nature, may not coincide with the recognized 'interests of the meshek' and they may
even run counter to the latter. These informal considerations,
crystallized as 'public opinion,' are present in the formal
situation of the open meeting and weaken, in their turn, the commitment of the official institution to the collective's primacy.
Such so-called (in kibbutz terminology) "social" considerations
have had a significant impact on the economic policy (and labor

policy) of Hofra. (See, in this connection, Kanovsky, 1966:
134-137.) Small branches on the decline were not liquidated for
years so as to let members working in them retain their permanence
in work as long as it was regarded as possible by both the meshek
and the individuals concerned.

Note, incidentally, the context in which the term 'social'
is applied. 'Social' is used to refer to the community while in
fact the so-termed 'social considerations' apply to the individual.
It is a tacit recognition that, in the commune, problems in which
the individual is enmeshed are, or become, essentially interpersonal
and relevant to the community as a whole. In the present context,
'social considerations' imply considerations on the part of the
community of individuals and their problems within it.

## Expectations from a permanent branch-man

For the individual, a permanent position in work may have
an intrinsic value. It may meet personal striving for 'self-
realization' in the realm of labor which might be inhibited or
blocked if not achieved through stable and continuous work in the
same field. A person immersed in his work may find many gratifying
and satisfying experiences in facing, daily, the expected and
unexpected challenges which confront him. Such feelings can be
satisfied through persistence and stability in one's work. Alternatively, one may perhaps derive satisfaction from sheer routine in
the field of work. Yet another member may find permanent work
intrinsically dull. Whatever meaning this position in work may
have for the individual, gratifying in its variations and nuances
or dullness in its routine, it is the importance for and the effect
on the individual vis-a-vis his counterparts in the community and
vis-a-vis the collective itself that interests us here. The
social position of permanence in work is viewed, then, from this
angle. Each member seeks permanence; and if a member in a permanent
job wishes to retain this position, he faces demands, or rather
informal expectations, on the part of his fellow-members and evolv-
ing public opinion. Fellow-members and public opinion may support
him in his quest, whether actively or passively. But, as said
before, support cannot invariably be expected. Permanence in
work requires compliance with a few expectations. Failure to
comply with these expectations undermines the goodwill and the
potential, let alone the active, support a member may hope to
enjoy. It is not sufficient, then, to know what the social resources are which the member may employ in his search for permanence, the claims on others which he may activate, or the agents
he confronts. The employment of these, as well as of others
which have been mentioned in the present discussion, whether in
an active or in a deterring way, whether consciously by mobilizing

116

some of them or by letting them run without being aware of it, is related to the measure to which the member fulfils those expectations. As these expectations, by their very nature, are those of others, it is their fulfillment which determines to a large extent the approval or the support of those others, individually as well as collectively.

In discussing the case of Olya, I stated that her position was undermined because she had not complied with the rules of conduct expected of a member who has won permanence. In discussing the twin cases of Yamin and Yonah, I mentioned that the two young men did not win permanence in a branch from the outset because, so it was said by members of Hofra, they "are not yet ripe for it." In other words, they were not regarded as members who could abide by rules of conduct expected from permanent members of a branch. Members had those rules of conduct, or norms, in mind when discussing their position in work, though they did not refer to the rules as such and probably did not think of them consciously.

Members work together in branches. Furthermore, Hofra is small enough to consider the work in the entire meshek as one big task which is done jointly by its members. There is widely spread knowledge about the meshek and redundant knowledge of the members about one another. Working together in the same meshek and working for the same meshek for the professed common interest of all, give rise to expectations shared by all the members concerning the conduct in work of those who have claims to the primary position which the field of work contributes to a social position in the community. Branches differ, of course, from each other in particulars of work as well as in other aspects, but there prevails the common denominator of work and, in the present context, the member's search for permanence in it. Therefore, while keeping in mind that there are differences between branches, in the work required in each of them, and consequently expectations regarding this work, one can abstract the residual common expectations of members in all the branches. These expectations crystallize for the entire working collective as rules of conduct. They evolve as norms, that is to say, as instruments of social control. They become important components of public opinion. Through these norms members in the branch-team and in the kibbutz as a whole, exercise control over fellow-members in the field of labor. In general, members accept these norms and internalize them, or, at least, abide by them. In the event of failure to realize these norms in practice, knowledge of the failure spreads throughout the community. Fundamentally, failure to abide by these norms is treated as failure to conform to the accepted normative system in other fields of behavior in a social context.

One who does not conform to norms of permanence in work is not likely to enjoy permanence of work. He either does not acquire it or risks losing it.

Accepting the rules of conduct in work which prove to be associated with permanence is for the individual a commitment vis-a-vis his fellow-members individually, his branch team and the meshek. Practice of the rules in conformity with the expectations of fellow-members confers on the member the position of a co-sharer of those expectations and norms. In other words, in fulfilling in practice his fellow-members' expectations he acquires the right to expect the same practice from others. One's position of permanence in work is likely to be safe as long as there is no variable arising from a situation external to these considerations. The position of permanence is thus retained when the member takes upon himself the commitment (informal as it may be) to fulfil the requisites (informal as well) implied in the position he has acquired. He has acquired a position not only in the technological and economic aspects of work but in the social aspect as well, vis-a-vis his fellow-members. This social position can be retained if the requisites which stem from the social context are met.

The requisites of permanence in work appear to people as obvious. Indeed, so obvious do they seem to be, that it is doubtful whether the people of the community would stop to discuss them or to define them systematically. They would, however, do this if expectations concerning behavior in work are not met. Response to violation of norms would normally crop up in relation to a specific event or to a particular person and would be expressed - verbally or otherwise - in relation to them and to an abstract formula in a set of rules. Again, it is mainly through "deviation" from the rule and the response to this that light is shed on the requisites in question.

The first requisite is continuity in work. This seemingly obvious requisite has two aspects: (a) continuity in practice, and (b) demonstration of goodwill to continue working in the same unit or branch. The two aspects do not always come together as can be seen in the following instance.

Neil joined the kibbutz (Hardoof) in his early thirties. Until joining the kibbutz, he had been self-employed as a skilled technician. His clientele consisted largely of kibbutzim throughout the country. He thus visited many kibbutzim. When he made up his mind to join the kibbutz he had already accumulated knowledge of kibbutz life in general, and of the occupational structure of the kibbutzim with which he had contacts. When he applied for membership in Hardoof, he knew that his skill would not be in great demand, though the kibbutz could do with a limited use of his professional skill. He expressed his willingness to work "wherever necessary." Nevertheless it was informally agreed that when his skill would be in demand (knowing that that would occur infrequently), he would be employed accordingly. He was assigned to an agricultural branch. Ostensibly, he showed goodwill. His continuity in work was, however, frequently disrupted, in the main not owing to calls to practice his previous skill. Various events of misfortune in work succeeded one another. He frequently had to visit the district physician; he was involved in a considerable number of accidents at work and often injured. All this resulted in frequent absences from work. He was, in addition, very active in the Committee of Cultural Affairs ("The Cultural Committee"), activities which claimed part of his work-time; he also showed interest in meeting visitors to the kibbutz, temporary volunteers as well as official foreign guests and tourists, and he spent much of his leisure time entertaining them and in describing and explaining the kibbutz, an interest which eventually claimed part of his work-time as well; and, lastly, he was on rare occasions asked to employ his previous skill within the meshek. Yet, he was considered "permanent" in the agricultural branch. That was "his" branch. All these events disrupted Neil's continuity and gradually affected his position of permanence in the branch. The members of the branch-team did not, to my knowledge, doubt Neil's goodwill to remain in the branch, but they were increasingly annoyed with his absence which affected, in turn, the course of work in the branch. The trust they had in his wish to remain in the branch, coupled with the tolerance with which a new member is treated in his initial period of adjustment to manual, and in particular to agricultural, labor (if he shows goodwill), and their adherence to the norm of the member's "right" to permanence, all combined to prevent Neil from leaving the branch. Goodwill he showed indeed, but in practice he proved not to have followed the first rule of behavior in work associated with the position of permanence, namely, continuity in work. As soon as an alternative employment, not in agriculture, became available, Neil was assigned there by mutual consent. Neil's difficulties may have stemmed essentially from a personal lack of interest in agricultural work; they may have arisen from poor adjustment to heavy manual labor; or they may have been accidental. He may have had an unexpressed preference for non-agricultural as against agricultural work. All the above may have contributed to his failure to work continuously in the branch despite his apparent wish to retain his permanence in it. The fact remains that his work proved to be far from continuous. As his work was not stable in the branch, he eventually lost his position in it and dropped out of the branch altogether.

The second requisite is to work with a fair measure of
responsibility, by showing, vis-a-vis the other workers, some
care for the work done.  The spectrum of apparent responsible
behavior in work is fairly wide.  One is not required to work
zealously "to the limits of exhaustion of one's strength," as
the Hebrew expression goes.  There is no expectation to follow
the "legend of Degania" where "There seemed to be no limit to
the work we could get through; what the body couldn't do the
spirit made up for" (Baratz, 1960: 54).  Nor is it expected
that one devote oneself excessively, and almost totally, to
work to the extent of seeking self-redemption through (first and
foremost) labor, as implied in the Religion of Labor.  At the
other end of the spectrum, a totally irresponsible attitude
towards work would not be accepted.  Measure of interest in the
work varies, of course, from one member to another and this
variety is certainly reflected in their difference in practice,
but what will not be tolerated is sheer negligence in work.
Responsibility and negligence in work are difficult to measure
and are, in themselves, beyond the limits of this discussion,
but I prefer to use these terms as they express the features of
behavior they stand for, namely, the measures of accomplishment
in work as judged in relation to the ability of the people
concerned.  I shall clarify this statement.

Firstly, responsibility can be a feature of conscience if
it is internalized.  It may, if it contains an intrinsic value,
emerge in different degrees of intensity in different persons.
As such, the problem of responsibility cannot be discussed here
as it is beyond the scope of social-anthropological analysis.
But responsibility is also liable to be called to account;
accountability stretches to cover one's acts.  As such it
becomes a social feature and does fall within the scope of this
discussion.  Therefore, in saying that a "requisite [for per-
manence] is to work with a fair measure of responsibility,"
while not denying that this commitment may be widely internalized by the people concerned and, in having an intrinsic value,
plays a significant role in their behavior, I feel that it is the
action on the part of the person concerned that can be discussed.
The action is, in most events, observable and can be weighed
against the actions of other persons.  Therefore, in a social
context, "to work with a fair measure of responsibility" means,
if reduced to a minimal common denominator, "to show, vis-a-vis
other workers, some care for the work done."  A member of the
kibbutz has obviously a plurality of motivations to work as he
does: adherence to values of the Religion of Labor and searching
for personal Redemption or self-realization through labor may
comprise some of them.  There are others.  This discussion is
concerned with the show of responsibility in work in association
with the position of permanence in work.

Secondly, if it is actions and behavior which are weighed, many of them are measurable in principle. They can best be weighed against a quantifiable accomplishment. It is possible then to measure one's accomplishment in work against a norm required by the meshek institutions, whether formal or informal, and to draw conclusions about the member's behavior in this field. This need evokes not the employment of the notion of responsibility, but the employment of notions of personal accomplishment or output. As the economic activities of the members of the kibbutz are not based on wage earnings, there are various forms of social control to bring home to the member his duty to follow the quantified norm of accomplishment of work and to back it by negative sanctions if this duty is not fulfilled. Why, then, employ the notion of responsibility rather than that of accomplishment?

Indeed, some measure of expected accomplishment does present itself in people's estimation of a man's work. Accumulated experience of people working in different assignments and in various economic units, coupled with knowledge of norms prevalent throughout the country (and not necessarily in the kibbutzim alone), are, indeed, present at the basis of the criteria employed by the members in their estimation. But this measure of accomplishment is quite vague when applied to the individual's output. It is present, vaguely, in the background when one's work accomplishment is weighed, but it is far from constituting a formal norm which applies to all and to every individual. At the bottom, there also prevails the recognition of differences between members in relation to ability at work. This recognition is associated with the 'redundant knowledge' throughout the community. Many aspects of the member's ability, talent, competence, physical health and disposition to adjustments are observable in his daily behavior. As one is exposed to constant, though not necessarily structured, observations by one's fellow-members, one's behavior is constantly weighed and even judged. One's accomplishment in work is admittedly weighed and measured in accordance with the informal criteria present in the background, which have been mentioned above, but the 'redundant knowledge' is employed in the process of the estimation. Redundant knowledge thus coincides with, or rather provides, an informal social guarantee to the application of the kibbutz tenet of "from each according to his ability." Expectation of an absolutely equal accomplishment in the field of work would be unrealistic, exceedingly rigid and impracticable. Consequently, accomplishment in labor is weighed and judged, to a considerable extent, in relation to the individual's merits in this field. It is not an absolute, detached, notion of accomplishment, then, which determines the assessment of one's responsibility in work, but that accomplishment which is expected of the particular individual. This assessment is based on both the general knowledge of norms of accomplishment in the field of work and on knowledge about the individual concerned. In reference to the "spectrum of apparent responsible behavior," it is neither a perfectionist performance nor a total ineffectiveness which is expected from any individual within the range of his "ability." In the social context of labor the expectation is that his care for what he does in work should be evident. If he thus shows care, he has fulfilled the second requisite. His chance to acquire, and particularly to retain, a permanent position in work, improves.

The combination of these two requisites constitutes, of course, the minimum which is expected of one's conduct in work. The community and any branch-team may hope for more. The ideal may be that the member shows devotion to the task, a good performance in work, creditworthy achievements, and unlimited responsibility. But this ideal cannot be regarded as a requisite or an expectation for permanence in the branch. It is an ideal and should be treated so. Ideally, members may hope that a colleague of theirs shows all these merits. In practice, however, there is room for doubt whether a member who fulfils all these hopes would indeed be accepted with unequivocal appreciation and not, also, be 'put in his place' - the ideal may be extolled, but the expectation is humbler.

A member may lose his position of permanence despite his conformity with these rules. This can happen either, (a) because he wishes to discontinue his present work for reasons irrelevant to these rules or to the problem of permanence altogether, or (b) because a major economic change has taken place. The branch in which he works may be decreased in size or its demand for labor force may decrease owing to technological innovations; it may cease production altogether or a new branch may be established instead. In such cases, even with the utmost conformity to these unofficial rules of behavior in work, one can lose one's permanence in one's branch. But if the discussion concentrates on existing branches, and on factors associated with the behavior of the member, discussion of the rules affecting the member's behavior in this situation is in order. In order to gain, and particularly to retain, the position of permanence, (a) the individual should be aware of these expectations of him which emerge as rules of work, and (b) he should act accordingly. That the norms are informal does not decrease their effectiveness in guiding both the behavior of the individual and the response - for better or for worse - of the group and of the community.

122

## Conclusions

The permanent attachment of the member to an economic branch has been viewed from two main angles: (a) the gap between demand for and supply of labor, and (b) the common interest of all the members of the community as individuals in maintaining permanence. The former is an outcome of the economic growth of the kibbutz and, in turn, it gives rise to a process of decreasing the dependence of the individual on the authorities of the kibbutz. It is a necessary condition for the increasing independence of the individual in this field. The latter is itself an effect of the former: permanent position in work being acquired, it is in the interest of the member to maintain it. In maintaining his permanent position in a branch he is equal to his fellow-members. He is equal to them, in the sphere of labor, in that he does not depend on the communal authorities (manned by his fellow-members of the community) more than others do. Like them, his interests, wishes and even whims have to be considered. He can maintain his position if other members co-operate with him. They will co-operate if they share, in principle, access to a similar position of permanence. Having an equal access to a permanent position in work (and retaining it) is thus conceived as a right.

Following this line of analysis has led me to refer to the set of values of the kibbutz, which conceptualizes rights, obligations, expectations and norms or rules. Of course, there prevails no sole, rigid consistency of normative expectations. In different situations different people may refer to different norms or values, presented by their own logic of relating norms to each other. But "... both individuals and publics do not act unrestrainedly. Their choices and their manipulation of these choices are set within certain limits, controlled by established rules and procedures" (Gluckman, 1972: xxvi). These are expressed in terms of values. To ignore them in the analysis when they are relevant would have been remiss.

The position of permanence is significant when it is viewed vis-a-vis others. The extent of co-operation between the individual and the group depends, in various situations, on the underlying interests of both and on their ability to meet each other's expectations. The group concerned may be the branch-team, whose extent of co-operation (in relation to the issue of permanence) is exemplified in the case of Neil, or it may be the kibbutz as a whole. In order to maintain this position the individual must acknowledge and conform to the elementary expectations of the kibbutz. This can be regarded as a primary condition for permanence.

The interest of the member in permanence, and the economic or organizational interests of the kibbutz, may be congruent with or may complement one another. But there are situations in which they do neither. In such situations the individual member confronts the group or its authorities. This confrontation may be open or it may be tacit or potential. In connection with these situations, I have analyzed the position of permanence in work in terms of deterrent power. These are situations to which an analysis of the power of the individual, even in an egalitarian society, is relevant. I have recapitulated the discussion of this deterrent power earlier in this chapter.

I have referred to the role which permanence in work plays in enhancing equality amongst members. Members are not always conscious of this role as mainly conscious of its existence when particular members fail to achieve or to retain it. Nonetheless its presence is crucial for the position of the individual in the field of labor. If it is absent from the elements which comprise this position, the position is adversely affected. When it is present, additional elements will tend to cluster around it. Some of these elements will be discussed in succeeding chapters.

NOTES

1. 'Return-yielding' is the term used to denote a branch of the kibbutz's economy whose products are sold directly to the market and comprise income. This term applies to labor in these branches ('return-yielding labor') as well as to any form of labor for which the kibbutz (representing its working members) is remunerated. This term was introduced by the Audit Union for the Labor Agricultural Co-operation, a body which was established by the Histadrut.

2. The point of departure for Spiro's analysis of the kibbutz (Kiryat Yedidim) is the 'moral postulates of kibbutz culture.' Ideological tenets of the kibbutz have thus become analytical tools for interpreting its social realities. In discussing 'the kibbutz as a political community' and 'the crisis in the kibbutz' in his Epilogue, Spiro employs ideas suggested by Troeltsch (1931).

3. The term Labor Distributor is borrowed from an American commune of the Society of Brothers which I visited in 1957.

4. This is not to argue that prestige is the only determinant of status. Control of resources, such as membership in a work group, is another variable. Membership in the work group is discussed below.

5. For an elaboration of the idea of sideways move, particularly in various forms of promotion, cf Peter and Hull (1969: 45-51 and especially 32-35).

6. The discussion touches another problem: a member may wish to retain, if not to extend, her areas of competence at a time when an increasing work-load leads to specialization. I have no space here to discuss this problem.

7. It is her personality as a whole which people have begun to refer to. For a further discussion of the treatment of 'total identities' see Garfinkel (1956: 420-4).

8. Frankenberg seeks an analogue for his analysis of role relationships and studies them in relation to a rural-urban continuum. The model for studying role relationships on any point of this continuum is adapted from theories of communication, notably from Cherry (1957). 'Redundancy' in this model, refers to the number and the patterns of the channels of communication. The more channels there are and the more links there are in the communication network, the more information flows from one actor to another. The same

basic information flows through a number of actors. There is redundancy. I am aware that there is distinction between communication (or any relation, in essence) and knowledge. Redundancy is essentially quantitative and therefore is better applied to studies of relations (or relationships). Nevertheless, what I wish to stress in selecting this term is the accumulation of information, correct as well as distorted, which flows and reaches virtually every member through many, "extra, in one sense, unnecessary additional channels" (Frankenberg, 1966: 281). The alternative term "excessive" knowledge would have implied value judgment.

9. On attributes of the 'total social personality' of an individual and on situations in which the individual appears as such, see Gluckman (1955: 23).

10. Note that this 'knowledge of the person' as a 'total identity' (Garfinkel, 1956: 420) operates not only in situations where "the public identity of an actor is transformed into something looked on as lower in the local scheme of social types" (1956: 420), but - at any rate in the kibbutz - in all situations in which the individual confronts the kibbutz as a whole.

11. This is, of course, true not only in relation to the situation of the formal meeting. It is true in many situations of face-to-face meeting within an established set of relations (Gluckman, 1963: 312-313; also Gluckman, 1968: 32, on the role of gossip and scandal). A breach of the rule not to discuss a person in his presence, applies particularly (a) to his 'total identity,' and (b) when it is done in the formal situation of the Assembly, such a breach entails an adverse effect on the offender. In Gluckman's words (in discussing scandal): "For the battle of scandal has its own rules, and woe to him who breaks these rules. By the act of carrying his scandalizing too far, he himself oversteps the values of the group and his scandal will turn against him..." (Gluckman, 1963: 313).

12. For Dahl (1957: 203), 'negative power' denotes a power relation in a situation where an initiative on one actor's part has the effect of inducing the respondent not to respond as requested, but inevitably to do otherwise. In this situation the initiating actor wields negative power over the respondent.

13. Of course, in relation to other issues and in other contexts, statuses of the members concerned are differently allocated.

14. I have found it necessary to add 'mutual (tacit) assessment' to Schelling's use of 'tacit bargaining' because Schelling presupposes, for the productivity of his discussion, two

126

premises which I do not employ: (a) a rational, and not only intelligent, behavior (1963: 3); and (b) the dependence of bargaining on rational strategy of the participants in the relation. The term 'strategy' denotes "the interdependence of the adversaries' decisions and ... expectations about each other's behavior" (1963: 1). While both may be present in the situation I discuss (the emergence of deterrent power in the sphere of labor in the kibbutz), I have no evidence to support such assumptions a priori. Nevertheless, I find the concept of 'tacit bargaining' illuminating and useful also without recourse to Schelling's own premises. I suggest that assessment is associated with, and logically precedes, bargaining.

15. For a study of members of kibbutzim working for and on behalf of The Movement, see J. Shepher (1966: 39-59).

16. See Chapter II, p. 27.

17. Of course, there is not only one continuum along which types of social control can be arranged. The one mentioned here is arranged in an order according to the degree of force employed. Other orders of continuum may be arranged according to the number of persons involved in a situation, or their relationships with a defaulter, etc. In other words, types of social control can also be arranged in an order based on criteria related to size or properties of the public, congregation or set of social relationships concerned.

CHAPTER IV

THE ONE AND THE TEAM

## The asset of team-support

A member who works in a branch does not work there alone.
He is a member of a team, the branch-team.  There is rarely a
one-man branch in any kibbutz, though the number of workers
varies from one branch to another.  Permanence in work has been
examined so far mainly from the viewpoint of the individual
member vis-a-vis the community as a whole.  The individual, in
short, does not stand in a direct, dyadic, relationship to the
meshek as a whole.  The meshek is diversified in that it is
composed of several economic branches and services.  The individual's position in work, then, is mediated through his membership
of a branch-team.  Some further aspects of the role played by
membership in a work-team in the evolvement of the member's
position in the community will be discussed in this chapter.

The conditions of permanence are:  (a)  the two main
requisites, namely, continuity and observable responsibility;
and (b)  stability in the branch.  If a member fulfills these
conditions, he may expect another element to be added to the
cluster of components of his social position.  He may expect
support from his fellow-workers in the branch.  Thus support is
virtually guaranteed in situations in which the very working
position of the member is considered relevant, or is felt to be
at stake.

When a member becomes involved in a dispute with the
representatives of the kibbutz over work assignments, he would
normally enjoy the cooperation and support of his fellow-workers.
If he disagrees with others, outside the branch, about matters
connected with the branch (such as arguments over economic and
agricultural resources or means of production), he will normally
get support from the branch-team.  The degree of support a person can rally becomes apparent when there is a controversy or a
dispute, and at such times therefore the position of a member
within a branch can be assessed by observing the amount and
type of support he obtains.  However, for most members it is
potential support which is important.  Dispute or controversy
are not necessarily experienced or actively participated in
by all, or even by most, of the members.  Members may work in
their branches for years without getting involved in any disputes; they may cooperate with the communal agents without
raising an issue; or they may avoid confrontations by various
methods of negotiation or settlement.  But potentially, every
member may find himself, at some time, caught up in an issue

in which his own position in work (and therefore his social
position in the community, though the latter is by no means
identical with the former) is tested. Danger, if not there,
is always imminent. If he feels that he should rely on his social
resources, he will consider, to say the least, the potential support he may expect from his fellow team-workers. Conversely, one
may say that when a communal agent, or any member, is engaged in
an action which questions or tests another member's position in
work, this agent cannot overlook the probability that by so doing
he may invoke the defensive support of the respondent's fellow
branch-members.

Elaboration on this subject requires illustration by a few
examples. The first is concerned with the alignment of the
branch team.

Yoel is a young member who recently returned home on com-
pletion of his military service. Like his fellows, he joined a
branch and has since attained a permanent position in it. However, during his own branch's slack season, in the height of the
summer, he was asked to leave his own branch temporarily and
help out in the irrigation in another branch. It was obvious
that the move would only be temporary. Yoel, to put it mildly,
was anything but enthusiastic about the move but, like his age-
mates, he did not strongly object to help out elsewhere occasionally. The general problem was brought to the committee concerned.
Yoel himself was absent, but the urgency of the need overrode the
customary requirement that a member's moves should only be discussed in his presence. Yoel's fellows lined up in an apparent
opposition to the request that Yoel be "drafted" to temporary
work elsewhere, and took an active part in its debate.

Such events are far from being rare. Debates like this
may take place at any time of the year, whensoever demand for
labor arises. Given the shortage of labor in the kibbutz, it
may sometimes be difficult to assess whether the opposition on
the part of the branch-team to a call on one of their members
to an assignment elsewhere is based purely on the economic-labor
needs of the branch, or on other considerations. Obviously,
economic-labor interests of a branch are present and are accepted
as legitimate, and the members of the branch are the ones immediately concerned with these interests. They are expected by the
wider community to protect such interests. What is illuminating
in Yoel's case is the conspicuous absence of these legitimate
grounds, as the meeting was held during the slack season for the
branch. It is noteworthy that Yoel himself appeared to adopt a
somewhat indefinite position. He did not rule out the possibility that he should work temporarily in a branch other than his

own though he gave a clear impression to his fellows that he was
not interested in moving. So his fellows mobilized to offer him
collective support. Certainly, had Yoel continued to work un-
interruptedly in his branch, he would not have been left unemployed
there: in any branch there are always some long-delayed tasks to
perform. But, while labor resources are scarce, the inevitable
problem is to determine priorities. The meshek agencies had
determined that summer irrigation be given priority over the
branch's "routine" work, yet the members of the branch-team
showed a clear preference for their particular interest. As one
can hardly accept that it was the 'pure' economic-labor interest
which motivated their collective stand, one may look elsewhere
for the explanation.

This consideration, then, fundamentally is not economic in
nature, but political. The individual may find himself in situations in which his wishes are congruent with the interests of
the collective, but he also may confront situations in which his
wishes and the interests of the collective cannot be reconciled.
The position of the individual should be so designed as to tackle
both. When his wishes match the interest of the collective, his
main consideration would be to remain equal with others in respect
of the basic elements of his position. If it is a situation where
interests clash, he wishes to be equipped with assets which contribute to his deterrent power and strengthen his bargaining
position. The support of one's fellows, even if only partial, is
such an asset. As such, it is political in essence. Access to
this asset is attained by virtue of belonging to a branch. This
access being attained, he is one of a team, regardless of his
personal characteristics. In other words, membership in a branch
in itself provides some degree of access to this asset irrespective of the personal characteristics of the individual. He gains
access to an asset to which all members of a branch team have a
claim, namely the expectation of support. A system of mutual
guarantee thus emerges within the branch-team. The significance
of support for everybody in the team - whether actively in the
event of dispute or potentially - imbues it with its mutual
nature. Everybody may need it. The mutual nature of the
guarantee of support strengthens the position of the individual
member, but at the same time it lays duties on him. As a permanent worker in the branch he is expected to support other
branch-members should they become involved in a dispute. Although
there are no stated rules regulating the behavior of the branch-
worker in this connection, he can hardly ignore a claim of support
from his fellow worker. The claim on him by others implies a
commitment by him.

The member does not always call for support. Nevertheless,
assuming that normally a member would prefer to stay in the branch

rather than move out, the very mention of the news that a worker has been requested to move out of the branch would cause the members of the team to align in his support. Their argument would normally be stated in economic terms, such as the needs of the branch. Yoel's case shows clearly that it may be applied in situations far beyond the realm of purely economic-labor considerations. The mutual guarantee which is at the base of this alignment is, then, essentially political and as such interferes with economic considerations and sometimes runs counter to them. Yoel's case also shows that commitment to support the individual in resisting pressure to move out of the branch does not necessarily depend on the respondent's expressed reaction. If he does not explicitly accept the request to move out, this is commonly interpreted as a refusal to do so. On this assumption the team can be called into action. I was not present when Yoel himself broke the news that he had been approached to move out of the branch, but I can recall numerous similar occasions.

The suggestion that the team's alignment is basically political in nature requires some qualification. In the present work I have on a number of occasions referred to Kibbutz Hardoof. Hardoof is larger than Hofra in population (approximately 800 people) and also in size of the meshek (though it is less diversified). Comparison of the two kibbutzim suggests that the smaller the meshek (and the community), the greater the tendency of both the individual and the team to respond positively to requests made on behalf of the whole meshek. Also, the smaller the agricultural branch is and the more it is markedly seasonal, the more readily its workers move out in slack seasons. These propositions suggest that the political considerations which influence a branch-team to support its individual members when the latter are asked to move are not unlimited, but in practice have limits set by the economic features of the branches. If a branch is small and highly seasonal, workers cannot resist being transferred to other, if temporary, work. In the slack season in Hofra the small vineyard branch is temporarily disbanded, and in the small flowers and artichoke branches each only retains a handful of essential maintenance workers. The larger agricultural branches, though also subject to seasonal fluctuations, because of their larger cores, can mobilize more effectively. It is more effective to rely on support obtained from a group than to rely on one's own individual resources. If the meshek is composed of fewer, but larger, branches, seasonal mobility tends to decline. When, in addition, the meshek itself is larger, and by implication so are its main branches, then each of the teams can be more effective in their mobilization of support. I do not suggest that the alignment of branch-workers in resisting a transfer of one of their team-members is the sole, or the main, explanation for the latter clinging to his permanent work in the branch. Or, looking at it from the collective point of view,

131

neither is it the only explanation for the low rate of mobility within the meshek. But it does play a role, and it is this role which is being discussed here. The effectiveness of the team's support, then, when it is not economically plausible, is nevertheless affected, in turn, by economic variables, such as the sheer size of the branch and the seasonal nature of the work it performs. Nonetheless, the support of the team is potentially present; it works; and with the increasing consolidation into fewer and larger branches, it grows more effective.

It should now be obvious that the significance of the alignment for support emerges when there is a dispute. Disputes are not frequent but the ever-present possibility of their occurrence contributes to branch solidarity. Another feature of the mobilization of support is its relevance to two closely related domains in which the team's support can be expected: (a) labor, and (b) the branch. The claim on the team's and its constituent individuals' support in issues which transcend these domains grows weaker, the more members consider an issue to be remote from issues with which the branch itself and the work therein are concerned. Over issues which are considered irrelevant to the branch and to labor, an individual tends to utilize his other social resources. In fact, the public is much more concerned with relationships other than those of the branch-team when a problem of inter-personal solidarity or support is at issue. I cite a few of the connections of which everybody in the kibbutz tends to take cognizance in analyzing a member's behavior when he is utilizing or mobilizing potential support: country or region of origin, past membership in a section of the Youth Movement, common experience in the pre-settlement group-life (see Chapter II), peer- and age-group membership, and ties of kinship and affinity. These relationships tend to show some propensity to be persistent. Talmon-Garber (1956: 153-178) called them "secondary solidary groups." It is these relationships which are regarded as much more relevant and meaningful to the individual than his position in a branch. But for the present these 'secondary solidary groups' are not relevant to my analysis.

When an individual activates the potential asset of support from his fellow branch-men, it follows that his acts should be definable in terms accepted as relevant either to the branch or to the individual's position in its work. The closer the issue is shown to be related to these domains, the more readily can the response be expected.

Given these conditions, a member can use this system of expected support in the opposite direction. Once this system is institutionalized, even if not in a formal way, it can be

used for the two opposite aims: for protection from a possible
call to move out and for an initiative to do just that.  A short
affair involving Haray, a permanent worker for a few years in an
agricultural branch, bears witness to this.

Haray had been considered permanent in his branch.  During
the summer season he was always assigned, with his consent, to
an irrigation job.  As time went on, he decided to leave the
branch for another one.  His decision, as far as I know, had no
connection with the specific assignment to irrigation nor was it
motivated by the nature of the work.  Nonetheless, he did not make
his decision publicly known nor did he discuss his plan to move
out with his fellow branch-men.  One can suggest that the constraints on the individual by the mores that a member should be
interested in retaining his permanence in the branch compelled
him to conceal his intentions until a situation emerged in which
he could lift these constraints with less embarrassment.  Eventually he was summoned to a committee meeting in which it was
suggested - and subsequently decided - that he should take a
certain temporary responsibility for a project outside the branch,
which would involve him leaving his branch for a while.  On the
following morning he announced in the branch that he had decided
to accept the committee's decision and would not return there-
after to the branch.  Nobody, he said, had even bothered to attend
the meeting, though its agenda had been published on the notice-
board in the dining hall, let alone come to argue for his continuing work in the branch.  Therefore, he saw no point in continuing
working with them in the same branch, and he ceased to regard his
obligations to the branch as binding.  As soon as the season was
over, he would leave the branch for good.

Haray thus conceded that he did have obligations to the
branch, but implied that as he had not had 'support' from them at
the meeting, mutual responsibilities ceased and he was free, and
no longer one of the team.  Therefore, once his social and
political position in the branch had been so defined de facto by
the action, or rather inaction, of the members of the team, he saw
no point in persisting in his economic-labor position in it.

When the season was over Haray had not yet left the branch
after all, but this, in my opinion, has no significance for the
present context.  From the outset he wanted to leave for reasons
irrelevant to the team's system of mutual support and when he
found it expedient, he broached the failure of this system to
function as an excuse for his decision.  By so doing he brought
into the open the existence of this system.  Even its inaction
was used by him as a justifying frame of reference.  In any
event, he brought into the open the normative, even if informally
defined, aspect of this system, namely, the expectation of every
member, by virtue of his belonging to the permanent team, to

133

obtain as well as to offer support. Note also that the issue was one directly related to the domains of labor and the branch, and therefore it was clearly relevant for the problem of activating the system of mutual support. But Haray used the mutual expectancies in a manner contrary to their apparent manifest function (which is to help members in resisting pressure to move out).

Another feature of team-support is the arena in which it is activated. The system of team-support itself, as has been emphasized, is not formally defined, yet the arena is. It is the meeting of a communal institutionalized organization, the General Assembly or a committee, in which labor problems may be legitimately discussed. The committee in question may be the Secretariat, or the Labor, the Meshek, or the Education Committee. All these bodies are official organs of the kibbutz, endowed with specific responsibilities to the kibbutz as a whole and, in the case of the committees, their membership is elected according to formal procedures. The features of the arena in which support from the fellow team-members is expected are, then:

(a)  it is an official agency of the kibbutz (distinguished from the notion of the active agent);

(b)  as such the main responsibility of this agency (Assembly, committee, etc.) is to the kibbutz and the meshek as a whole; and

(c)  the situation in which it convenes as well as the procedures and conventions of the debate are usually formal.

It follows that whereas the framework within which the issue is discussed and determined is formal, and the members who take the responsibility for the decision are bound to conform to rules which pertain to both procedure and substance, the support which an individual can mobilize on such an occasion is not through one of the formalized kibbutz institutions. More accurately, the arena is formal both in procedure and in its commitment to the priority of the meshek; the support is not.

The organs concerned are instructed, by their very existence, to discuss issues raised in the realm of labor and branch composition, and relevant to these, while the primacy of what is considered to be the needs of the meshek is in the background. Arguments on the part of both the meshek office-holder and the respondent usually refer to these needs in these domains as conceived by the respective actors, according to their position in the issue as a meshek representative and as a respondent respectively. Usually, the officer-holder, the Labor Distributor, the Labor Organizer, or the Meshek Organizer would present the

134

case, taking a view wider than that of the particular branch from which help is requested. This presentation would be followed by a particular demand, pointing at a particular respondent. The respondent's argument, in objection, would refer to other economic and organizational 'needs.' Usually, he would elaborate on the 'needs' of the branch and his particular assignment in it. On the latter he may consider himself, and be regarded by others, as not less competent than the central office-holder. The intervention of the third party, the members of the respondent's branch-team, does not depart from this pattern. The member of the team tries to show that the support given by him and by his fellow workers is congruent with the 'right' conception of the needs of the meshek. Should he mention variables other than 'labor' or 'branch,' he would try to link them to these domains. By so doing the branch-supporter conforms to the conventions of the formal institutions of the kibbutz: he accepts the primacy of the interests of the collective but views them from the realm in which he is acknowledged to have more knowledge than the central officer, namely, the branch he represents. He appears as defending the elementary interests of the branch, one of which is its smooth running through the availability of labor. The branch and its problems are regarded in the community as first and foremost the responsibility of its permanent workers. And in doing this in the formal situation of the committee (or Assembly) meeting, he (a) acknowledges the authority of the convening body to make the decision; (b) re-affirms the rule that such arguments should be settled in the institutionalized organs of the kibbutz; and (c) accepts the manner in which such arguments should proceed.

It is noteworthy that the support, though not institutionally mobilized, is channelled both in the institutional bodies of the kibbutz and the institutionalized mode and contents of the argument. The subjection of both procedure and selection of arguments in the discussion to the principal elements of the kibbutz system follows, of course, though not solely, from the situation in which the issue is discussed and settled. It is imperative that one should conform to both acceptable procedures and contents of argument. The nature of the situation determines that. And, of course, such a subjection is not unique to the kibbutz. The channelling of support through the formal bodies of the kibbutz is significant when looked at from another, so to speak, negative point of view. It is negative, that is, from the point of view of the individual respondent.

The active part taken by members of the branch-team in the meeting of the institutionalized body reflects the limits to which the members of the team may agree to go in their mobilized support for the individual. Firstly, it is the formal situation to which they ostensively come. By doing so they show their fellow member, vis-a-vis the members of the decision-making body, that they carry out their mutual obligations. Also, in that situation, whatever is said on their behalf has some notion of commitment and it is so accepted. Their very appearance comes as a message both to the fellow-member in question and to the congregation. But, when this support is actively given in this situation, it does not follow that it is given in other, informal, ones. The expectation of, or the extent of control which can be exercised by, the individual over his fellow branch-workers, cannot (effectively) operate outside this situation. Institutional bodies and procedures for the solution of problems arising in the sphere of labor are indispensable, but they do not exhaust the means through which such problems may be discussed, negotiated and settled. The mobilization of support informally strengthens the possibility of effective action in the formal situation. The concentration of the members of the team at the formal arena may carry the message that this is the limit to the display of group solidarity. Whatever can be gained in this arena would be welcomed, but the commitment does not extend to other situations.

Secondly, as the formal situation and procedures limit the area of discussion to labor matters it is made clear to the particular individual that though he has the support of his branch over the issue of labor, that support is restricted to this particular field of problems and cannot be mobilized outside it. The careful emphasis on 'needs' of the branch, as it is usually presented and expressed, makes it difficult to apply this argument to situations or issues irrelevant to the apparent subject of the discussion, namely, the branch and work therein. Consequently, it would be exceedingly difficult for the team-member to apply the same elements of the arguments to issues other than those defined as relevant to this field. By referring to this set of arguments the team-member, by implication, protects himself (in this capacity) from further claims on the part of the respondent beyond the limits of branch and work. Ultimately, it is the branch and the work therein which constitute the basis for the system of mutual guarantee of support. Support can be expected from branch-fellows, individually, only if social relationships other than those marked by working in the same branch evolve between them.

Thirdly, the participation, or even the presence, of a team-member in the conspicuous formal situation, also shows the respondent the extent to which his claim on his fellow-branchman is effective. For the respondent this act on the part of his fellow branch-workers may seem the minimum he would hope for; he may also wish him to take an active part in the argument and contribute some substantive help to his cause. This is

hoped for, but cannot always be expected. The claim imposed
on a fellow is limited to the conventional display of solidarity.
For him it may be the maximum he would "supply" in accordance
with the operative rules of branch-group solidarity.

From the above discussion of the limited extent of efficient
team support, it may be inferred that the support expected from
the branch fellow-workers can in itself be defined as a mere
convention. It can be assumed that the display of verbal support
in a selected situation is essentially a substitute for a more
powerful support which is potentially contained in the team's
collective will. After all, the fate of the branch, which is an
essential element in the running of the meshek, is entrusted to
the members of the team working in it. If they consider it
essential, they do have the ability to take further, effective,
steps in "an industrial action." But such an assumption has
two snags. Firstly, a 'mere convention' is a social fact in
itself. As such it is from the actor's angle a variable to
consider in the assessment of one's social position and one's
links and ties with one's social surrounding and it cannot be
overlooked in any outsider's analysis of the actor's behavior.
The convention is significant for sociological analysis insofar
as it in some measure regulates behavior. Members of branch-
teams, in fact, do follow this convention and display mutual
support, by attending and speaking at the meetings of the relevant institutional bodies. Further, their evident support at the
meeting and the verbal support they give to their fellow-worker
are not merely a substitute for more effective action. They are
in themselves binding actions. The statements they made are
regarded as commitments and are taken into consideration when
the decision is made. Limited in their efficacy as they may be,
their actions comprise an element in the cluster of components
which together underlie the deterrent power of the individual.
Their action is not simply an empty convention but provides an
assessment of the assets potentially available to the individual
in the event of serious dispute over his assignment.

The task of defending an individual who is called to work
somewhere else is first and foremost that of the branch foreman.
Other members of the team are also expected to align with the
respondent, but it is the foreman with whom ultimately this
informal responsibility lies. This pressure on the foreman,
exerted by the individual in the subtle means described above,
derives strength from the general expectation that a branch
foreman should give his branch priority over all the other
interests of the meshek. As one of his main responsibilities
is to accomplish all tasks on time, and as productively and as
efficiently as possible, his concern with labor is conspicuously
apparent. Usually, it would be in the interest of the branch to

keep all its workers, because there is always some job which needs
to be done. But since labor is the most conspicuous resource and
everyone works, the disposition of labor is an issue on which everyone is sensitive. A foreman is expected to protect the interests
and pride in their work of his branch particularly against anything
which disrupts their work. The pressure on the branch foreman, in
the form of expectations, is thus exerted not only by the person in
question within the branch, nor only by the team collectively, but
also by the rest of the community. This is one of the kibbutz's
mores pertaining to the branch foreman. He is not just a foreman
or a manager. In the idiom of the kibbutz, the term is Merakkez.
The same term is applied to the Meshek Organizer, the Labor Organizer and chairmen of committees. Literally it means "centralizer"
and the connotations of 'manager' or 'director' in the extra-
kibbutz sense are stripped from it. He is also the spokesman
for the branch and the team. As such he has to represent the
branch in forums where issues of, or pertaining to, the branch
are discussed. Other members of the team are usually invited when
problems of relevance to their branch are debated and they are
expected to attend, but the request for his presence is emphasized.
It is possible to suggest, then, that the wider and the more
diverse is the responsibility of a member within the branch, the
heavier the pressure upon him to support his fellow workers. As
a recognized spokesman he has to take an active part in the formal
debate. If, for some reason, he cannot attend the meeting, he
usually sees to it that other members do. In all the meetings
known to me, save the one in which Haray's temporary transfer
was discussed, it was the branch foreman who acted as the
spokesman and voiced the expected attitude of the branch-team.
It will be recalled that Haray had not communicated with his
fellow-workers in the team either about the issue itself or his
own response to the request that he be temporarily moved. It may
be assumed, therefore, that had the branch foreman in question been
activated by Haray in the usual way, he would have responded
appropriately. He either did not know of the issue or, examining
Haray's conduct of the affair, judged Haray's intention rightly,
and by appearing to refrain from action, did in fact act. The
convention that the branch foreman speaks for the individual's
staying in the branch is, then, maintained and re-affirmed through
the omnipresent, so to speak, pressure from all sections of the
community, and particularly from within the branch, to do so.
Whether through conviction or convention geared by pressure, the
support given in the formal debate by the foreman is an asset for
the individual respondent.

As in the case of such verbal support given in the meeting
by other members of the team, the effectiveness of the foreman's
support is curbed by its being confined to the formal situation.
Surely, one should look for (a) situations in which support can

138

be given by the same actors beyond this defined situation, and (b) the mode and system of the signalling, made by the same people during a meeting which communicates in its message to the congregation the extent of the branch-members' support.

Let me go back to Yoel's case (p. 129 above). Several members of Yoel's team attended the committee meeting and took an active part in it, repeating, more or less, the same argument: that the tasks left for the team to accomplish after the branch's peak season should not be overlooked by the central authorities and that the fulfilment of these tasks necessitated Yoel's continued work in the branch. The most active member of the team was the foreman, who took the floor several times and went into details. Nevertheless, to the best of my knowledge he confined his action to the meeting only. He did not press the point beyond it. Not so the foreman of the receiving branch. Anticipating the alignment of the other branch's team, their vocal argument in the meeting, and the possible influence of the branch foreman, he had approached both the <u>Meshek</u> Organizer and the Labor Organizer in advance and discussed the issue with them informally. He had not insisted that only Yoel would do, but only that he needed extra help and left the labor officers to suggest that Yoel should be drafted. Yoel's foreman could not make an equivalent case because the tasks before his branch apparently could not be defined quite as urgently necessary as the irrigation in the hot summer. When the committee convened and all the parties concerned were present, the circumstances appeared as follows: on the one hand appeared a branch team proving its urgent and pressing need for help in labor force; and doubling the weight of its argument by having taken the necessary informal steps in advance. The pleading branch-foreman proved in his conduct that his concern was mainly task-orientated; that his claim on Yoel was not personal since he had agreed to accept any other suitable member; and that the task itself was of a paramount importance to both the branch and the <u>meshek</u> as a whole. He was able to do all this without help from his branch-workers. He represented an essentially economic interest of the branch. On the other hand. his counterpart, although taking an active part in the debate, concentrated on two aspects: on the tasks left for his team to perform and on the importance of Yoel's contribution to this performance. As from the outset the former argument could not match the opposite arguments, Yoel's branch-foreman was left with the conspicuous object of 'defending' Yoel from a temporary transfer. Unlike the foreman of the receiving team, he was helped by his own members. The participation of his fellow branch-workers in the discussion, which is significant in itself, could not alter the situation. Indeed by the feebleness of their arguments, the members of Yoel's group proved the essentially political nature of their alignment. This foreman had not taken any informal steps to prevent the pressure on his branch from taking place. In an informal discussion with the Labor - or the Meshek - Organizer he would have had (a) to concede that another branch's tasks were prior to and more urgent than his own, and by this concession he would have undermined the strength of the argument of the cause he found himself compelled to advocate; and (b) to disclose the political nature of his obligation to express his objection to the suggested move. Apparently, Yoel's branch-foreman did not wish to find himself in such a situation, and therefore he avoided it.

This brings us back to the problem of whether it would be right to consider the behavior of the branch foreman (i.e., Yoel's branch-foreman) as only paying lip-service to the cause of an individual within his branch. If the foreman, having realized that he is at a disadvantage in the argument, avoids attempts at using informal contacts to solve the problem in the way he wishes, it can be argued that his verbal activity in the meeting amounts to no more than a political demonstration of loyalty to his fellow-workers vis-a-vis the central organizational institutions of the kibbutz. Essentially, this problem has already been discussed above. I have suggested that though the arena in which the debate takes place is limited, it holds some weight nevertheless because of the formal nature of the convening body and the commitments taken within and by it. In the present connection, however, an additional aspect emerges. Because the foreman may find himself at a disadvantage as regards the issue itself (and not only in the explicit argument), his argument in the meeting may be more effective if he is not impeded by a disadvantageous informal move of his own prior to the meeting. If he refrains from involving himself - and the branch - in informal negotiations in which he may be bound to make a major concession, the field is clearer for his argument, whatever weight and merit it may hold. It seems, then, that certain circumstances may emerge in which the branch foreman is compelled, by the nature of the issue, to select only the formal arena for his active - and apparent - support of his colleague, knowing that his cause is at a disadvantage. I do not believe that this behavior can be defined merely as lip-service.

Another parallel can be drawn to the previous discussion of the 'negative' aspect of the selection of the formal arena for the alignment of the team. When the branch foreman refrains from resorting to informal measures, he signals his assessment of the circumstances and the issue. He also shows in practice what he is not prepared to do, and which arenas he does not utilize and his readiness to take the consequences. But the signalling this time is directed mainly at the central office-holders of the meshek. If the foreman does not intervene informally in the

course of events and does not approach the Labor or the Meshek
Organizer outside the official bodies and the official proceedings,
the Organizers take notice and get the message.  They can then
interpret the foreman's moves: they assess the extent to which,
and the limits within which, he is willing to argue for the cause.
Having recourse to, as well as refraining from, informal arenas
of discussion, argument and negotiation, signals to the central
officers the foreman's definition of the nature of the 'defense'
given to the branch colleague, i.e., whether it is basically
economically orientated or politically orientated.

Several weeks after Yoel moved to the other branch, the
latter's peak season was nearing its end.  Yoel's original branch
had just begun to prepare for its own peak season; its foreman
did not want to wait for Yoel's return to be arranged by the
central officers and demanded that he return to the branch without
delay.  This time he did not confine himself to the formal meeting.
Simultaneously with his request that his demand for Yoel be put on
the agenda of the Meshek Committee, he opened a campaign in informal
arenas.  He approached the Labor Organizer, the Meshek Organizer
and members of the Committee.  Other members of the team joined
him in keeping the issue alive by discussing it throughout the
community.  This time there could be no doubt about the meaning
of the steps taken by the foreman and his colleagues: they meant
business.  It was not mainly their commitment to Yoel that mattered
and geared them to action; it was the imminence of having work for
the branch.  On this basis they could argue in formal as well as
in informal arenas by standing, as it were, on a common ground with
their counterparts in the other branch.  Whether essentially
economic (as indeed it was) or political in nature, the two branch-
teams' arguments were fundamentally the same and so were the steps
their foremen took.  Even an insensitive observer of the course
of action, and of the argument and its nuances, by the people
involved, could have predicted that this time Yoel's own team
would win their cause.  Although Yoel's irrigation work was still
important, urgency of irrigation work was lessening whereas prep-
arations for a new season had already got underway in Yoel's
branch.  But these considerations, were not the only ones present.
Balancing them, there were still (a) the need for irrigation and
(b) the mere fact that Yoel was working at the time in his
temporary job.  So, on the relevant level of economic and labor
aspects of the argument, there was still room for debate and both
foremen had taken informal steps in advance.  But the branch in
which Yoel was temporarily working was short of at least one
asset held by the other branch: the team had no personal claim
on Yoel.  He was not part of their system of mutual political
support.  He was part of the other team as a permanent worker.
In addition to the economic arguments considered and used by
both teams, one team could and indeed did activate its political

141

commitment to and in its individual member. Obviously, the other team did not have, as indeed it could not have, such a commitment to and in Yoel. This commitment to support constituted a variable which added, when employed, decisive weight to Yoel's team's conduct both before, and in, the second debate. Thus, whereas this consideration, when divorced from the sound economic one, had lacked the power to affect the decision in the first instance, it proved to have a considerable weight, and was perhaps the determining consideration when other factors remained equal. The support for the colleague, then, whether given gladly or reluctantly, proves more effective in one situation than in another. It is its relation to other variables (from which I have abstracted it for the purpose of the present analysis) that affects its significance and effectiveness. Yoel's case shows that it does have weight even when the argument, as can be judged from both formal and informal proceedings, is regarded as essentially non-political.

The channels of informal communication between the branch foreman and the <u>Meshek</u> and Labor Organizers, as well as those with other branch foremen and other members, provide almost innumerable opportunities for any of them to deal with the problems and issues with which they are concerned. As stated above, they can avoid these channels and restrict themselves to formal contacts, or they can use these channels when it is deemed desirable or necessary, or they can avoid any act of communication, whether formal or informal. The choice of each of these kinds of contact is affected by the setting of the variables concerned, and itself affects, in turn, the outcome of the encounter. It also signals the limits within which the issue is wanted to be, and in practice is, handled by the participants, and areas into which they do not wish to enter. If the branch foreman does make use of the informal channel, one of the choices open to him is to find a device which would enable him to conduct the issue so as perhaps to satisfy all the different parties concerned.

The branch foreman has duties and powers, but he always performs his task under certain constraints. He is responsible, of course, for the running of a branch in its organizational, scientific, technological and economic aspects. He co-ordinates the various work tasks and therefore takes responsibility for priorities which he, principally, determines. He makes plans and changes these plans, and he allocates tasks among the members of the team and assigns them to various undertakings, and works with them. And, of course, he is their spokesman. All these constitute the duties and powers of the foreman. But he is also a member of the corporate <u>meshek</u>. Firstly, the interests and the needs of the <u>meshek</u> are not alien to his interests. He may be open to persuasion if these are presented to him for consider-

ation. Secondly, beyond the understanding he may have (and show)
of the wider problems of the collective enterprise in which he is
a co-sharer, he works and acts under the constraints of his office
as a foreman. Being a foreman implies an ability to reciprocate
in dealing with other branches and with the central authorities.
The efficient running of the meshek (and its two leading Organizers in the field of labor) depends on his co-operation to a considerable extent, but so does his own performance. The branch
receives, so to speak, from the meshek the input in the form of an
inflow of investment and operating capital, its allocation of
land, water and other resources, and its quota of labor, both of
permanent and impermanent members. In exchange, the meshek
expects, of course, the end product, and - in the field of labor -
productivity and efficiency. But it also expects from the team
a large measure of co-operation with the central authorities, and
this expectation is focussed mainly on the foreman. He must be
able to reciprocate and co-operate with these authorities in
order to achieve his - and his branch's - undertakings. Thus
the foreman finds himself under constraints which are not always
manifest but which are always potentially present, and these
constraints come from outside the branch proper. One of the
requests occasionally made to him is obviously the one which is
being discussed in this chapter, the request "to free" (to use
the kibbutz' idiom) a member of his branch-team, so the latter
can be "mobilized" temporarily ("mobilization" is always associated with temporary assignment) to another branch. The situation,
then, from the foreman's point of view, when a branch foreman is
called on "to defend" or to support his fellow branchman against
a transfer, is that he is under constraints stemming both from
the branch and from the public weal.

It does not follow of course, that any approach to the
branch foreman by any agent outside the branch, whether by a
central officer, another branch foreman or by any member, automatically raises the question of consequences for, or doubts
about future co-operation with him, if he refuses to respond
positively. But his failure to co-operate is taken into account
and it tends to be cumulative. It may affect both his branch
and his personal career.

In such a situation, the obligation to the fellow-member
of the foreman's team can be adversely affected, if it is not
supported by a publicly recognized need of the branch. Indeed,
the obligation may, in certain events, diminish into a mere
lip-service. This is the feeblest form of support which the
commitment of the foreman may force him to wield. If a member
does not really want the team or the foreman to refrain from

"speaking for" him (as happened in Haray's case), then there is always some form of support.  I do not know of a case in which not even the feeblest verbal support has been shown.  Just as a genuine effort on the part of the foreman necessitates that he make informal approaches to the central officers, so does the lip-service to the cause.  Two similar steps, seemingly contrasting with each other in their meanings, are, then, taken by the foreman in his ostensible support of the individual member of his team: the genuine effort and the display of lip-service.[1] This statement should be clarified.  I have suggested that the foreman, under the commitments he has mainly, but not solely, to the members of his team, can choose between three basic choices of action: he can establish no contact at all with the communal officers; he can restrict his contact to the formal arena (an instance of which has been discussed above); and he can use channels of informal contact.  I have suggested that restriction of activity to the formal arena only, does not in itself prove that only lip-service is being paid by foreman. It mainly reflects the foreman's assessment of the circumstances and his chances of success.  But I should state that I have, of course, no proof that the selection of formal arena as the only stage for support is never used only with the aim of paying lip-service.  Logically it is possible, though it is exceedingly difficult, to establish evidence on this matter.  I do suggest, however, that if the branch foreman really wishes (or finds himself in a situation in which he prefers) to pay only lip-service to the cause of his fellow worker, he will communicate with the central officers informally and discuss the issue with them.

The second stage of Yoel's case has shown how the branch foreman did employ informal communications with the Meshek and the Labor Organizers in his genuine attempt to ensure Yoel's speedy return to the branch.  The first stage has shown how the foreman, knowing the limits within which he could align the team's support for Yoel, contented himself with the formal arena. The employment of lip-service as an acknowledgement of obligation by the foreman entwined with full co-operation in action with the Meshek Organizer, thereby contradicting the contents of the verbal support, will be exhibited in the following case.

A branch foreman, Miron (G7), was absent from Hofra when the Secretary and the Labor Organizer were looking for a candidate for a temporary job.  The temporary job involved an absence from work for some two to three weeks.  It had to do with helping organize some activities for a youth group staying at the time at Hofra and accompanying the group on a tour of the country.

144

As the job involved young people and direct personal communication with them, the officers looked for a young person. Following a consultation with the Meshek Organizer, they approached a young man, Yarimi (GlO). He had had experience in youth work and in educational and cultural activities and was regarded as a suitable candidate. Yarimi worked in the citrus grove. His response was far from enthusiastic. Apparently, the suggestion did not attract him, although his objection was expressed mildly. The members of the team as well as the central officers acknowledged his refusal, but they also noted the mildness of his expression of it. They were unanimous in their assessment that whatever argument between the branch and the representatives of the meshek would follow and whatever the outcome of the argument would be, he would accept the decision of the authorized bodies of the kibbutz. There was no great cause to defend this time. The harvesting season was over, and considering the internal division of labor in the grove, the branch could do without him for the period required. If he had had to remain in the branch, he would not have been unemployed there, to be sure, but there was no state of emergency in the grove. Assessing the circumstances and Yarimi's own position, the officers decided to bring the issue to a formal meeting of a relevant committee. After Yarimi had been approached personally and before the meeting of the committee, Miron returned to Hofra. He contacted the Meshek Organizer and discussed the issue with him. He told me later that he had agreed in that discussion that Yarimi was the best candidate for the job; he further agreed that Yarimi's acceptance of the job would result in a necessary absence from work in the branch; and he agreed that Yarimi should take the job and the branch should take the consequences. He acknowledged his obligation as Yarimi's foreman by agreeing with the Meshek Organizer that in the formal meeting he would voice some feeble objection to Yarimi's temporary removal from work.

I do not know whether Miron informed the members of the team of his agreement with the Meshek Organizer, but my impression at the meeting was that the members of the committee either knew of the agreement in advance (the Meshek Organizer may have tipped them off) or gathered that that was the case. They listened patiently to the Labor Organizer presenting the cause of Yarimi's "mobilization" to the organizational-educational job; and they listened to Yarimi's objection and to Miron's unconvincing statement on the needs of the branch which allegedly ran counter to the contents of the Organizers' motion. It is noteworthy that no one raised any question, any objection or any point whatsoever. (One can always make an attempt, at least, at halting the proceedings by suggesting that the issue be referred to another committee, arguing that the other commit-

tee was either the true relevant one or more authorized to take
the decision. I have seen no equivalent to the insistence in
Hofra on a clear allocation of responsibility and authority
among the various committees in other kibbutzim known to me.
In Yarimi's case the issue could have been referred to the Meshek
Committee, the Secretariat, the Labor Committee, or the Absorption of Immigrants Committee which is responsible for providing
for all physical needs of temporary residents. With some effort,
other committees could be involved as well.) Unlike situations
in which the members of the committee are aware of the genuine
argument, whether restricted to the formal debate or not, and
show interest in the debate and take a decision at the conclusion of the debate, in this situation they let the issue pass as
a matter of formal routine. Everyone could sense that the
argument, as far as the Meshek Organizer and the foreman were
concerned, was a matter of formal ceremony. Members of the
committee admitted later that they had regarded the situation
as such. They understood, accepted and respected the foreman's
acknowledgement of his obligation to Yarimi. It was expected
of him that he act accordingly. Some of them told me that they
were convinced that some informal deal had been made between the
two prior to the meeting. Yarimi's mild objection may have
contributed to the members' apparent indifference, but had
Miron insisted on his cause and had he declined to admit the
Organizers' premises, by elaborating on his own branch's 'grave
situation,' the members of the committee would have got a different message and they may have adopted a different mode of
behavior and a different resolution. Yarimi was expected to
act in the manner in which he conducted the issue. His position
in the branch and in the community at large committed him to
that. (This aspect of the issue falls, however, outside the
scope of the present discussion, which focuses mainly on the
foreman.) So, the proceedings in the committee and - to an
extent, at least - the outcome of the meeting were affected
by the behavior of the branch foreman. Everyone knew that the
meaning of his behavior was merely lip-service to the cause of
the individual concerned; everyone understood the circumstances
and accepted Miron's behavior; and everyone knew that beyond the
lip-service there was an informal agreement between the central
authorities and the branch foreman in that particular situation,
whereas under different circumstances the 'service' to the
individual's cause would be genuine and affect the foreman's
behavior accordingly. So, the committee unanimously adopted
the Meshek Organizer's motion and Yarimi accepted the decision.

As soon as the meeting was adjourned, Miron, while walking
with a few members of the committee, commented, "Fools [referring
to the promoters of the motion]. Why did they choose Yarimi?

146

Of course he is the best candidate when the merits of the job are taken into consideration, but this cannot always constitute the major, conclusive, consideration. There are others. Besides, Yarimi is not interested. Here, in our branch, we have Yahli [Gil]. They are almost the same age. But whereas Yarimi is active in the community, has accumulated a lot of experience in communal affairs, is always given public tasks, knows his way around and, most important, has established contacts and relationships in various circles, factors which he can utilize and enjoy in social as well as in personal affairs, Yahli has none of these. Why did they not pick him for the job? He might be interested, though he lacks these qualities which we attribute to Yarimi. He is in a need of a helpful push in his interpersonal relationships... Of course I would have voiced objection. This is my obligation. Did I not do it tonight? You know that there are ways and means of dealing with such situations. They should have waited and consulted me before approaching Yarimi, then we might have made some deal; they could have nominated Yahli to the job; Yarimi would have been pleased, and I would have played my part ...."

This statement, of which only the relevant excerpts are cited here, was made to an audience of at least four persons, following, as indicated above, the adjournment of the formal situation. It was made, it should be noted, to the same persons who had been present, and were supposed to take an active part, in the previous discussion.

The payment of lip-service in this case to Yarimi's cause was accompanied by a statement not only admitting it (to the Meshek Organizer, to me and to members of the committee) but also by the suggestion of alternative which would have involved another performance of lip-service. Furthermore, there was a hint in this statement that the foreman himself, had he been informally "consulted," would have made a suggestion which would result in a gap between his expected behavior as a foreman and his assessment of needs and situation. He would have acted accordingly on both stages, as it were.

I have placed the various tactics used by the foreman in an imaginary continuum (footnote 1, p. 189), each related to the situation in which the foreman may find himself expected to act in both his roles as manager of the branch and as spokesman for the members of the team. But the selection of the arena is not always up to him. He cannot always control the course of events, even in its procedural aspects. Yet at all events, if the individual member is not willing to co-operate with the central authorities without first attempting to settle the issue in his favor in the formal arena, or at least without a formal debate in that arena, the foreman is obliged to speak in his cause. So, in addition to the selection of the mode of contact, the foreman almost invariably finds himself engaged in talk. The members who are present at the meeting can - and do - get the message by listening to his argument. It is difficult to establish a general act of arguments used by the foremen, a set which is applicable to all branches and to all possible events. The art of presentation and representation is not equally mastered by all foremen. Ideally, one would expect a set of a maximal number of arguments considered as relevant to such a debate, arguments which can also be placed in order of weight. Then, the art of the spokesman would be to convey to the people present in the meeting his real appreciation of the situation by selecting both a particular set of arguments and by assessing the latter's relative importance. The model of the content of arguments considered as relevant at the meeting of the Labor or the Meshek Committees would emerge, then, also as a continuum. This continuum would cover possible statements ordered according to both quantity (number of possible relevant arguments applicable to a certain type of situation) and quality (relative weight of different arguments), and it would stand in a certain relation to the continuum of possible tactics used by the foreman. In other words, one could expect a pattern of argument which would strengthen, by matching other acts selected by the foreman, the latter's case. Alternatively, this pattern of statements (selecting the number and the weight of arguments) could substitute for those other acts. However, in my attempts to make content analyses, I have found no such consistent pattern. The always-present argument is that of 'the needs of the branch.' Other than that, it is the mode of the foreman's argument rather than the number of admissible subjects which conveys the message. If the people attending the meeting (whether it is a committee meeting or the General Assembly itself) have no previous detailed information on the issue or choose to ignore that information, they learn to receive the message by listening to the 'supporting' speech of the foreman. The perception of the meaning the foreman himself attributes to his speech may require experience and lengthy residence in the community, but I know of no failure in communicating the desired message. That is not to say that the foreman is always successful in such debates even if he uses this art of conveying his genuine meaning skillfully, but it is important that his (or the team's representative's) view be fully understood.

I feel it significant to note that I have never heard any expression of resentment in relation to the foreman's conduct of affairs in situations in which a member of his team was, without his consent, required to move from the branch. Although people do sometimes tend to overlook differences between situations in their assessment of issues and appreciation of behavior, I have heard no critical comments on foremen acting in their roles as supporters of their fellow workers, nor have I heard such comments on matters such as the selection of tactics, the choosing of arenas, or the contents and style of their statements. In Haray's case, his criticism was pointing at the foreman's (or the team's representative's) <u>failure</u> to fulfil that role. And that comment was used as a means of facilitating his pre-meditated plan to leave the branch.

## Moving from a branch

The situations thus far analyzed exhibit that all members, in their own interest, assume that fellow branch-members wish, initially at least, to express their right and have support, in resisting the request to move. Even the case of Haray shows how this assumption affected Haray's own behavior vis-a-vis his fellow workers, when he avoided telling them of his plans. It was then assumed to be obvious that he would not want a move.

But members do sometimes want to change branches and take appropriate steps to do so, even if no-one wants to revert to being a 'cork.' After changing his branch, a member will take the necessary steps to secure a permanent position in his new work. I now analyze not the change itself, but the response of the other members of the team to a move by one of their group. I have suggested that by securing a permanent position in the branch the member establishes a claim on his fellow workers and can activate, if this is necessary, the system of mutual support. But when a member leaves his branch, or expresses a wish to do so, how is this asset of his team's support affected?

Arguing that support is a constituent element of permanent work, and even of a measure of power, is one thing. One must also analyze situations when this element functions adversely. In both cases we have to disentangle the variety of forms of support, as well as the varying circumstances and weighting of different arguments.

Table 3.4 shows that about two-thirds (65.1 per cent) of the members who have worked in the 'return-yielding' branches for over five years have changed their branches, at least once, since 1952 (i.e., over a period of 18 years). In opening my analysis of this important fact, I note that the team's response to a wish to move usually contains ingredients both of negative

reaction and of acceptance. It is obvious that the individual
will want to have the weight of the overall response expressed
in a way that should help, or at least not handicap, his cause.
The negative reaction of the team should not overcome its acceptance. This is important for him while he is still in the branch,
as Haray showed in his attempts to avoid pressure, criticism and
annoyance coming from his fellow branch-men; and it is important
on his way out, while his incorporation in a new team is still
in its anticipatory stage. It even remains important after he
has successfully accomplished his move, since he remains a member
of the same commune, as do his former colleagues.

The practical reaction of the team may take different
courses, which in a logical order, are: an apparent attempt to
persuade the member to stay; an attempt, through the communal
authorities, to delay his leaving the branch; refraining from
taking an apparently active step; or giving him the farewell
blessing with full co-operation. The significance of each of
these courses as well as their subsequent implications for the
individual's position can be shown best by presenting the
evidence itself.

## Attempt to persuade the member to stay

Nahari (011) is a new member of the kibbutz. As a temporary resident he had worked in most of the agricultural branches
(usually during their respective harvesting seasons), and he has
established himself in the orchard. He was not particularly
interested in agricultural work, but in choosing to settle in
Hofra he realized that he had to adjust to the local conditions.
The scope of occupational alternatives for selection by the
members of the kibbutz is limited, so long as they work within
the kibbutz and, as seen, identity of membership in commune and
in meshek-corporation, and residence in Hofra, implies attachment to a relatively small unit. Looking at this unit from an
occupational angle, it is conspicuous that variables such as
size (of the meshek) and composition (the meshek being based on
agriculture) affect the scope of selection. So when Nahari,
although not interested in agricultural work, decided to join
the kibbutz, he looked for a branch which he has been quoted as
considering 'the least evil.' The reasons for his choice of
the orchard and the personal reasons for his thought later that
he might leave it need not be discussed here. Suffice it to
say, that he reached a stage when he considered the possibility
of leaving the branch. He did not conceal his doubts and hesitations; and people in as well as outside the team were aware of
the situation. For some time he was left alone. Apparently,

there was no definite suggestion that he join another branch, so he did not raise the issue of leaving the orchard nor was he approached by the members of his own team. It is, of course, possible that various and other considerations were involved in his being left to work out his hesitations. But whatsoever those considerations were, the mechanism of approaching a candidate for a move, in an attempt to influence his decision, was set into motion as soon as an alternative did become possible and known. I do not know whether it was the Labor Organizer or the Meshek Organizer who presented Nahari with the definite alternative, i.e., another branch, but it was a central authority. Nahari considered the matter; the new suggestion was not concealed. Now it was the fellow branch-men's turn to consider the new situation. Nahari's contribution to the branch had not been great: he was somewhat detached, and he did not belong to the "in-group" of the team; and he was new, unskilled and seemingly unambitious. But eventually he could be absorbed into the internal system of division of labor and given some responsibility in the branch. He could, in due time, take some responsibility also vis-a-vis the transient laborers and the hired workers. Also the prospects for absorbing other candidates into the branch for quite a long time to come were gloomy: there are very few immigrants who come to Hofra with the aim of joining the kibbutz as candidates for membership; there is virtually no flow of candidates from the Israeli towns to Hofra; people who do come from the outside do so mainly within the framework of the Ulpan, i.e., they come only for a short period. Young members who do work in the branch are planning to go to higher education centers and there is an acute competition by all the branches to attract the future candidates for work in the meshek. These considerations must have had some weight. Nahari was approached by members of the team who at the same time discussed the matter with the two central Organizers. The Organizers did not insist on their suggestion, although Nahari showed signs inclining to accept it. He talked about it favorably. Whatever his personal considerations were, by his discussing the issue in public, and particularly by the favorable manner in which he discussed it, he gambled on the move materializing and he must have understood it. Perhaps Nahari's performance in work was not considered an exceedingly valuable asset. Perhaps they wanted Nahari himself to determine the issue; or perhaps their suggestion was essentially an exploratory move. It was left to Nahari and the orchard team to discuss and settle the issue. Members of the team took the initiative and persuaded Nahari to stay in the orchard. I was not present at the discussions, which were informal and therefore I cannot say whether any promises were given to Nahari, but it seems highly unlikely. The only possible, practical "promise" could be the eventual incorporation of Nahari into the system of allocation of responsibilities within the branch, a step which was expected anyway if Nahari was to go on working in the orchard. They could not have promised any change in the present allocation of responsibilities, as such a move would have affected the personal tasks and positions of the other members. A verbal promise may be given, even with the utmost sincerity, without it being subsequently followed by concrete steps; and a member may fall for such a promise, either because he tends to trust the promise or those who make it, or because he merely derives satisfaction from being approached and begged to say or join, or because he may consider that the promise made to him can be used as an asset by him, an asset whose content can constitute his claim on those who have made the promise. But from all I know, such a promise was not given. Neither of the parties, particularly Nahari himself, has referred to any agreement based on a promise of accelerating the pace of Nahari's incorporation into the branch's system of allocation of responsibilities. I repeat, Nahari probably knew, or could have known, that for practical purposes he needed no such promise: he would have been incorporated anyway. Perhaps the significant factor for him was the goodwill expressed by his team. It may have been that he was satisfied by the very act of his fellow branch-men in approaching him, because this indicated their support.

The step taken by members of the team was, in a sense, a test case. It proved that Nahari, even though he was not rated, at the time, particularly highly as a workman, would be regarded henceforward as one of the team. The system of mutual support would be set into motion once he was identified as such, and the present issue provided the opportunity for this act of identification. The approach itself was significant, not any promise which could have been made.

Although his performance in the branch had not (or had not yet) been outstanding, nevertheless he had shown some promise as a worker and as a cooperative colleague. His relationships within the team had not yet been thoroughly established. The orchard was a large branch, so Nahari's somewhat weak attachment to the team could be - and indeed was - attributed, in addition to his apparent indifference to agricultural work, to the size of the team: with the division of labor within the team he was said to have been inhibited in developing his attachment to the group. It is possible that had Nahari had a longer seniority in the branch team, there would have been no such attempt. That is not to say that the team, or members thereof, would not have taken any steps at all to meet the situation (this is the subject of the following case), but it seems highly unlikely that they would have

152

attempted personal persuasion. When a senior member makes his decision to leave his branch, he may be assumed to have considered all the consequences. Once it is a decision, not a state of hesitation, of fidgeting, there is hardly any room for informal persuasion on the part of old colleagues. They are faced with various alternative responses. The first, according to my hypothetical order, is the attempt to decelerate the course of events, if not to reverse the decision.

## Attempt to delay departure and refraining from action

The central figure of the following case is Yardeni (V4). Upon returning from military service and another year in Service to the Movement, he established himself in the vineyard. The vineyard is a small branch in Hofra. It is planted on a few adjoining plots in the central hilly area of the Valley, in all totalling some 130 dunam. When Yardeni joined the vineyard-team it consisted of six members, four of whom had returned from military service a short time earlier and at approximately the same time. These four men belonged to 'the young generation,' in the sense that (a) they had all been brought up in the kibbutz educational system in Hofra; (b) they had spent their earlier years in the relatively small, close-knit peer-group called "Society of Children"; (c) they had experienced army life, and particularly so at the same period, a short time before or immediately after the 1967 war. They shared basically similar problems and interests in returning to the kibbutz, selecting occupations and establishing themselves in work, and planning their personal lives. The vineyard is alleged to have been a focus of attraction to young men. When asked about the nature of the attraction, the common reply was, "We could - and did - develop a group-spirit, an essence of esprit-de-corps, in our own terms. We used 'our' cultural idioms and had a good time."

The team may have had 'a good time' indeed, but the attractive esprit-de-corps did not resist other foci of attraction, evidently stronger. Of the four 'young' men, one who was the foreman at the period of Yardeni's arrival, left the kibbutz. Another, his successor, accepted a mission for the Movement abroad. And the other two left for university education (with the kibbutz's approval and financing). Another returnee from military service joined the branch, but one of the old-timers was forced to leave it (and agricultural work altogether) due to illness. Thus the relative importance of Yardeni's work in the branch increased, as the team now only comprised three men. Yardeni was the only one who had driving-

153

license for a lorry, a qualification of considerable importance
in the harvesting season, when quite a few workers had to be
brought to and from the vineyard. Groups of youngsters, from
the local school as well as from various schools in Israel, and
groups of Ulpan people and youth groups from abroad, all of whom
were engaged in part-time work at different times in the day,
depended, to a considerable extent, on his driving. In addition,
there was always the need to load transport and unload goods and
equipment for the branch. When transportation was not provided
for all these tasks by the Transport Organizer of the kibbutz,
it was Yardeni's task to do it. Yardeni, like his other two
colleagues, was familiar with all the essential work of the vineyard: irrigating, spraying, ploughing and cultivating, picking
grapes, loading boxes both on the carriage (between the vine
lines) and on the lorries, and the like. Taking into account
that some of this work, particularly during the summer harvesting
season, had to be done at night, thereby putting more pressure on
the remaining small team, all the members of which, in practice,
became managers; and the position of each individual in the team,
Yardeni included, grew even more important. So Yardeni's work
in the vineyard was not only important; it was very essential.

Yardeni spent a few years working in the vineyard. He
worked with the remaining two members of the small team, with
temporary workers of all the transient groups in Hofra, with
hired workers, and occasionally with the students, his former
colleagues in the branch when the latter spent their vacations
in Hofra. Working together with the latter gave rise to a
remarkable awakening of the old esprit-de-corps and high spirits.
It looked as though this kind of reunion, not only during leisure
after work, when peers and what Talmon-Garber (1956: 153-178) calls
'secondary solidary groups' tended to spend time together, but in
the situation of work, made other possible jobs seem more attractive. To be sure, these attractive alternatives to the vineyard
and to agricultural work in general, had always been present,
mostly, of course, outside the meshek (see comments on Nahari's
scope of occupational choice). These attractive alternatives
became reminiscent in leisure time, when the relatively few
young members, returned from military service, missed their
peers as well as the company of other people whose social
properties they could share. They were revived whenever students,
or even defectors from the kibbutz, left for their respective
destinations after spending time in Hofra. But these reunions
in work, pleasant in themselves, kept the problem of occupational
and other alternatives alive.

Eventually, Yardeni decided to change his occupation and
to specialize in special youth education. This conclusion

154

implied, in the context of his links with the branch, three
practical consequences: Yardeni would leave the vineyard, he
would leave Hofra temporarily for his higher education, he would
not return to the branch afterwards.

Yardeni's colleagues at work did not challenge his decision
in principle. They voiced no objection to his making this step.
As far as I know, they made no attempt to persuade him to give up
his personal plans for the benefit of the branch. There is no
question that his staying in the branch would have contributed
to its benefit. Nor is there a question that the team would
have preferred Yardeni to stay, on grounds of both the branch's
and each member's interest. They did, however, demand that he
continue working in the vineyard until the harvest was in. This
demand was expressed in a direct personal approach to him and was
followed by a similar request made to the central authorities.
The other members of the small team wanted Yardeni's promise
that he would not abandon his responsibilities to the branch
(and therefore to them) in the following year and particularly
during the forthcoming season. They also wanted the central
authorities' commitment that the kibbutz, while not necessarily
preventing Yardeni from fulfilling his long-term personal aims,
would do its best to reconcile its own decision on Yardeni's personal request, with the urgent interests of the branch. It was
not very difficult to obtain such a commitment from the central
authorities. Yardeni's plans involved training in an institution
of higher education, probably in a university. The kibbutz, in
accepting that all its second-generation members are entitled to
post-secondary education at the kibbutz's expense, has established
a general scheme to regulate the demand of candidates and adjust
it as far as possible to the kibbutz's own means, its expectations of members, and its code of behavior. The relevant conditions for acceptance into the scheme, in this context, are:
that the young man should fulfil the year of Service-to-the-
Movement, either following or preceding National Service, and
work in Hofra for at least a year. Once a member is eligible
to enter the scheme, he expects to be included in the annual
quota of students supported by the kibbutz, a quota whose size
is determined by the kibbutz. A large number of considerations
set the quota: personal, financial, the scheme's impact on work,
future employment, the relevance of the proposed course of study
to the kibbutz and its economy, and yet others. It normally
takes at least a year for the candidate to move through the
various stages of discussion in committees and the Assembly
until he can leave for his studies. Yardeni had fulfilled both
his Service to the Movement and his obligatory minimal period
of working in Hofra. He now had to wait for his inclusion in
the following year's quota, while taking preliminary courses

in higher education.  Thus it was not too difficult for the central
authorities to consent to the vineyard team's request.  Yardeni
himself agreed to meet the request.  He may have had reasons of
his own for accepting it: he was a permanent worker in the branch
and therefore he may have had no particular wish to leave it anyway before his departure for his studies; he was still working
on preliminary studies in his spare time and working in his branch
may have been considered more feasible than studying while working
at another task; and, of course, he very likely felt responsibility towards the kibbutz in general, the kibbutz which had brought
him up and supported him and which would support his future studies, the kibbutz which he had not decided to leave.  In other
words, Yardeni may have had reasons of his own for complying with
the team's request other than those which motivated the team.
Whatever Yardeni's own reasoning may have been, his conduct in
the situation, i.e., his promise, may be viewed in the following
context.

    Yardeni has a responsibility to the kibbutz as a whole;
but within the realm of work it is the branch which mediates
between the individual and the meshek.  For a permanent member
there is no work in the meshek at large.  The member works in a
branch and any display of responsibility takes place there,
whether vis-a-vis the team or the entire membership in general.
As long as the member works in a branch, and certainly as long
as he works in the branch he is attached to, it is there where
his responsibility, as displayed in his work, is tested and
judged by the community.  Responsibility towards the kibbutz,
in the realm of work, can only be demonstrated through the
branch, and through the team with whom one finds oneself working
in the branch.  True, it is not only the permanent members of
the team who observe a member's performance in work and perpetu-
ally assess and judge it; other kibbutz members do so too,
particularly those associated with economic and labor problems,
but it is first and foremost the members who are nearest to him
who judge him.  Their reference and opinion is highly valued
when public opinion about a member is being formed.  And, it is
always being formed.  But in the present context, it is not so
much the observation on the individual by the team which is crucial.
It is the observation of the community at large on the individual's
performance in his particular branch.  The branch not only
'mediates' between the individual member and the kibbutz in the
former's practice within the general sphere of work, it also constitutes the field where the show of responsibility to the latter
as a whole can take place.  If one's conviction, 'hakkara,'
(Spiro, 1956: 88; 97), or assessment of the situation one is in,
leads one to behave responsibly in the work situation, responsibility to the branch does not cease abruptly and automatically

with one's decision to leave the branch. One measure of judging one's sense of responsibility to the kibbutz as a whole is the manner in which a member behaves in the branch after he has made public his decision. If he responds to needs arising in the branch while he is still there, his behavior is appreciated throughout the community.

What emerges is that not only does the branch, any branch, mediate between individual and community in the practice of work and in providing an arena where a sense of responsibility to the community can thus be shown, but also action here has a role in affecting the individual's position in the community even beyond this sphere. Responsible behavior (or what is so conceived) is rewarding. Positively, it is rewarding if the individual has accepted the values and norms of the community: he is gratified by his very realization of the values he has adopted. It is also rewarding when colleagues and members[2] express some appreciation of one's conduct. Such appreciation, in turn, may in due time and in suitable situations ripen into forms other than esteem, when other variables enter the scene. Negatively, it is significant in what it prevents. If the member in question does not meet the demands, or expectations, of the kibbutz that he respond to needs and even contingencies of the branch before his final departure (and sometimes even afterwards, as will be shown), he is at risk of being regarded as an irresponsible person. Whatever his intentions and motives may be, it is his behavior - or in this context misbehavior - which counts and which is added accumulatively to his social liability, as it were. If responsible behavior brings esteem, irresponsible behavior brings disrepute. The account of a member's deeds accumulates through his life-time. Informally, the communal memory keeps this account alive and usable in various situations. This communal memory is invoked if the member in question is involved in disputes or in controversial issues, whether directly or indirectly, personally or through a mere voicing of his opinion. It can be invoked in the forms of a joke or of gossip, criticism or direct accusation, whether relevant to the issue at stake or not. In other words, a member's misbehavior (judged against the moral code of the community)[3] not only can be sanctioned negatively when it occurs, or immediately follow-ing it, but it also creates a bad reputation which in future situations may be held against him. This is true in general, not only in connection with the issue of the process of leaving a branch, and furthermore, it is not restricted to behavior in the sphere of labor only, but it comes to the fore conspicuously when the situation under discussion occurs.

157

It is not very frequently that any one member moves, let alone demands publicly to move, from one branch to another or from a branch to an altogether different occupation. Most of the members who have changed branches did not do so more than once (see Table 3.4). It follows that the sequence of acts of the individual - as well as the steps taken by the team - are particularly conspicuous against the background of the daily 'routine' of his work hitherto and his relationships with his branch colleagues. Although the event is 'normal' in the context of the member's occupational life history (most of the members had changed branches in their work career in Hofra; see again Table 3.4), it is not frequent in the context of the present distribution of permanent workers in Hofra. Very few members (three altogether) left their branches for another one in Hofra throughout the whole of 1970. Little wonder that such an event becomes a focus of attention and interest. The event, in addition to its being significant to the individual concerned and to the branch he leaves, takes place in a wider social context. It changes his definable position in the community as a worker, as a member of a particular team, as an authority on a particular topic or skill, as a person involved in partic-ular networks, - all variables which (together with other social properties) define his position in the community. The event is thus closely watched by members of the community. The members, conscious of it or not, are coerced by his move to re-define their relations to him. It is, directly or indirectly, significant to them.

Thus each such action provides an element for prediction of his behavior in subsequent events. Those who are going to absorb the member into the new branch (and not only those whom he leaves behind), as well as all those who are affected by his change of occupation, are involved, in turn, in the informal observation and testing of his behavior.

The community does not necessarily define responsibility in this context by reference to a formally sanctioned code. It does so rather in the form of expectations. For the individ-ual to behave responsibly, as Yardeni did when he promised to continue in the vineyard, means to live up to expectations. Whether the member seeks it or not, the communal sanction is positive. In Yardeni's case, to behave up to expectations meant to continue to work in the branch, to co-operate fully with fellow workers in all tasks, and not to leave the branch before the harvest was in. Yardeni did his best to keep his promise. It is therefore reasonable to assume that the col-lective memory has added an approving positive element to his accumulated social assets. Yardeni, like others, may have

153

made no such calculations; he may have acted simply according to norms he accepted as self-evident, but his 'responsible' behavior has set in motion one mechanism of social response rather than another, which is relevant to his future position in the kibbutz.

Thus the individual's response to the demand of the branch team has to be set in the context of the constraints which emerge from his attachment to the wider community. He is recognized as a reliable and responsible member and he has acquired this asset through a reciprocal interplay between himself and the community.

In discussing the response of the member to the team's request as an asset for his social position, the problem of the response of the branch team to the individual's act of taking steps to leave the branch arises again. It is through his consent to the team's demand (or expectation) that the departing individual is furnished with the asset of esteem. It is through the response of the individual to the team's claim that the community at large confers on him the status of a responsible member. I shall try now to account for the behavior of the team.

It will be recalled that the team demanded that Yardeni should continue to work in the vineyard until the end of the season, but expressed no objection to Yardeni's decision to leave the branch altogether. It is necessary to explain why the team refrained from objecting to his complete departure. Relationships with Yardeni within the team were certainly not strained, hence I can rule out a search for intra-team relationships as a possible explanation for the behavior of his colleagues. I assume that if members of the team had felt that they could have induced Yardeni to stay with them, they would have done everything within their power to achieve this. They certainly would have preferred Yardeni to remain in the team and work in the branch. Therefore, the problem is to discover the factors which affected the team's conviction that a direct challenge to Yardeni's plan was bound to fail, and that the most they could win was a delay. I have stated that during my stay in Hofra only three members left their permanent branches. In no case did the team raise objection to the move itself. In all cases the teams tried to decelerate the proceedings and defer the act of departure.

The first factor involved in explaining the behavior of the team lies in the sphere of labor itself. I have already called attention to the growing autonomy of the individual in

choosing his vocation and branch. I have linked this process
to the concomitant growing gap between the demand for and the supply
of labor, within the kibbutz. If a member wishes to change one
place of work for another, he will often find that there is room
available for the 'supply' he offers. There are exceptions of a
very few occupations in which the voluntary supply of candidates
exceeds the economic limits on the demand for workers, particularly of mechanics. None of the three cases concerns these
occupations. In other words, the growing measure of autonomy
in selecting a permanent branch also applies to the context of
changing from one branch to another. Because of this growing
gap an individual can increase not only his autonomy in choosing
a place of work but also in resisting pressure exerted on him
not to move. This situation cannot but affect the branch team
to which the individual in question has been attached. The
more the individual's measure of autonomy in attaching himself
to and detaching himself from a branch increases, the less
effective is the branch team's control over his freedom of
action. If his fellow-branch-workers realize their weakness in
controlling his permanent attachment to the branch, they can
still attempt to achieve the 'least evil': they can attempt to
prolong his stay with them.

Everyone agrees that one agricultural season is a reasonable period of continuation of work, so that all immediate tasks
can be completed. During this period attempts may be made to
look for a replacement, to make adjustment for the forthcoming
cycle, and sometimes to persuade the individual to change his
mind.

The second cluster of variables suggests the extension
of the scope of the argument beyond the limits of the economic
and labor backgrounds. While trying to concentrate, as far as
possible, on variables which operate within, and are relevant
to, the context of labor, I shall discuss the following suggestions as briefly as the subject permits. My aim is to offer some
insight into the variables, other than labor, which are relevant
to the present problem.

(a) Public opinion as a constraint on the team

Public opinion appreciates the agreement of the individual
to work for a 'reasonable' period in the branch he intends to
leave. As the definition of the 'reasonable' period is usually
agreed upon among the three parties concerned; and as the meshek
central authorities become spokesmen for the communal public
opinion on the matter (through mechanisms I cannot discuss here),
the members of the team face enormous difficulties if they try

160

to extend their demand beyond the limit which the community's public opinion is prepared to accept. The office-holders may be as happy as the members of the team if the latter are successful because it reduces the difficulties of the meshek and their own difficulties. But the officers can function only within the limits of the 'present-day' norms of 'public opinion' which reflect social relationships in the community. Public opinion as the normative expression of the community of individuals, and their relationships and interests, cannot side unequivocally against an individual member, let alone a member who conforms with the accepted degree of responsibility towards, and co-operation with, the team he intends to leave. It cannot do so as many members who constitute the collective community (and take part in the 'public opinion') may sometimes find themselves, their children, relatives or friends - to whom they have personal commitments of support - in a similar situation. Although the kibbutz has the supreme authority to compel a member to work wheresoever it deems necessary (and, by implication, not to leave a branch), it would be hampered in attempting to exercise this authority by the 'community-of-individuals.' (See discussion on the distinction between the two in relation to Olya's case above.) The officers of the community can, therefore, support the team (if they consider the claim of the team admissible) only to the extent that they act with the approval of public opinion. A positive public opinion about a responsive, co-operative, member - who has proved his sense of responsibility to the meshek - not only sets limits on the expectations from the individual himself and on the would-be behavior of the central officers, but also imposes constraints on the team. In other words, it is through the interplay between the individual and the community, conducted by the careful, co-operative and 'responsible' behavior of the former towards the latter that the team finds itself under constraints which compel it to co-operate with the individual. Like the central officers, the members of the branch-team can only function, in matters of significance to the community, within the limits of public opinion. In other events and in different contexts they would be, like their counterparts and the central office-holders, an integral part of the 'public' themselves. Public opinion has accepted (or 'determined') that the norm required from a member who leaves his branch is to continue to work in the branch for a certain period of time. By doing this Yardeni proved that he accepted the norm and his allegiance to the collective. The community approved and appreciated his conduct; and this approval and appreciation became 'social facts' with which the team had to conform.

## (b)  Institutionalization of the Precedent

The pattern of behavior of the member, the team, and the
central authorities when a member leaves a branch, has developed
over time.  Although changing one branch for another falls within
the jurisdiction of the Labor Committee and, in the case of
return-yielding branches, of the Meshek Committee, they do not
(nowadays, at any rate) exercise the formal authority bestowed
on them beyond the limits approved by public opinion.  The
limits themselves have crystallized through a series of events in
which various members of different branches with different
personal goals took part.  I do not know whether in the early
period of the meshek, before the discrepancy between the economic
needs of the meshek and the kibbutz's ability to supply labor
wheresoever and whensoever necessary became apparent, the central
bodies exercised their authority over all those events.  I do not
know (a)  whether a member could leave a branch without the
relevant committee always being directly and actively involved
in the move; and (b)  what the various stages of change were which
public opinion underwent until it crystallized into the present
communal approach and (c)  what the pattern of behavior was of
the members of branch teams in such events in the past.  But at
the present time such an issue is seldom determined in the committees, although committees are active and the distinctions
between authorities of the different committees are zealously
stressed.  To be sure, in Yardeni's case, it was the Committee
of Further Education which made the decision to include Yardeni
in the list of prospective students for 1971, it was the General
Assembly which approved the decision, and it was the Meshek
Committee which acknowledged it even before the recommendation
of the Committee of Further Education was brought to the Assembly.
Similar proceedings take place in similar cases.  But it would
hardly have been possible for any one of the committees to have
acted differently.  Thus although the communal bodies usually
do function, once a determined member has fulfilled the requirements accepted by public opinion, the organs of the kibbutz are
hardly able to resist him.  It would be exceedingly difficult
for them to challenge a member who is in good standing, since
he can point to a prevalent pattern of behavior already approved
by the community, or at a precedent, here that other members
of the second generation had been allowed to get higher education.  Since all members are equal, all in particular categories
have to be treated similarly.

Precedents are frequently talked about, and serve as
references in many arguments.  There develops an art of selecting precedents as arguments in debates.  Almost any step,

162

whether brought about from outside or taken under pressures
from within, involves the whole community. Any move, therefore, does not concern the immediate parties to the issue only
but also has an effect on the community, and quite often on
the meshek corporation which underlies the community. A step
taken by one person or group of persons in a given situation
may be picked from the collective memory and selected for an
argument by a different set of persons in an entirely different
situation.

Every act done by man in a social context, one may argue,
may be regarded as a step in a process of change. It contributes something to the new, to the hitherto non-existent, or
somewhat different, structure of relations. Therefore, as
there is no identical repetition of the same step in the same
situation under the same conditions, even when the pattern of
behavior in the relevant context does extend over time, one
may argue that the unique, the different, the special, which is
inherent in the act of a man, contains the essence of precedent.
Obviously, there are elements in every human act which are not
unprecedented. Those elements may follow patterns set up long
before the 'unique' act. An act is a precedent insofar as it
precedes others of its kind. It does have some essence of the
new, of the innovation (this is its first condition), but its
other twin aspect is its relation to a pattern of behavior
which emerges subsequently and is explained by reference to it.
In other words, it becomes a precedent if a subsequent pattern
of behavior can be explained by reference to it. If I may
borrow an analogy from horticulture, it cannot be a mutation
without a following. A third condition for an act to become
a precedent is that it be selected on a later occasion by a
person or a group applying its 'innovating' elements to a new
situation. The relevance of the previous situation to the one
in which the attempt to apply its 'message' is made, must of
course be admitted by the people who constitute the congregation or set the scene. Precedence is therefore relative: it
is a precedent if a certain act is conceived as such and is
selected by people to be applied to an issue which has at
least certain elements that are similar. The degree of similarity can always be debatable. The problem of precedent
arises therefore in the context of argument or justification.

Although theoretically every event in the social context
may be referred to as a precedent in a debate or an argument,
only events pregnant with some apparent significance for the
community are selected for this purpose. The event in which
a person is involved should, if it is to be selected as a
precedent, represent a conspicuous change in that person's

position in the community and compel the members of the community to be conscious of the change and to reconsider the state of their relationships with him. The significance of the event for both the individual and the community, its conspicuousness, ensures that it becomes part of the 'collective memory.' If a parent takes his child from the communal children's home to spend the nights at his own home for a considerable period of time, it is regarded as precedent; or if a member disobeys the kibbutz's regulations of labor and sets, so to speak, rules for himself and gets away with it, it is considered a precedent. And once the kibbutz has approved higher education with no specific instructions for future occupation, this move becomes a precedent. Such moves affect the community in that (a) they confront the members with the necessity to consider their response to the move; (b) they compel them to reconsider their relations with the 'innovator'; and (c) they urge the members to consider the possibility of subsequently applying the 'innovation' to themselves. The effect in itself, regardless of the specific contents of the event, becomes significant. These are the elements which help an issue to become an outstanding event, subsequently available for use in a different issue. The member who raises the argument of precedent in order to justify his own or his fellow member's move, or to forward an interest, may do so under circumstances entirely different from those which prevailed in the previous event. Nevertheless, once the relevant precedent has been set, and once the previous event can be enforced on the congregation's memory, the latter cannot avoid it in making its decision.[4]

When Yardeni decided to change occupations and to go on to advanced education, the significance of the decision for himself was obvious. When he made this decision known, it became significant to the entire community as well as to the vineyard team. But Yardeni was not the first member to leave a branch nor was he the first member to go on to advanced education. When he applied formally, the mechanism of the precedent was set into motion. The kibbutz could not, in fact, challenge his plan and refuse him permission. The point I am making here precedes the issue of favorable judgment on Yardeni's behavior both logically and temporally. It is after Yardeni's long-term plan had been publicized and approved that his short-term move became significant. Yardeni's long-term plan was accepted nominally on its own merits, but members, when pressed, referred to the precedent in relevant situations; once the kibbutz has begun to send its young members to attain higher education (i.e., approved of and even supported demands for higher education), the course of events could not be reversed.

The kibbutz is fully aware of the role of the precedent in its making of decisions. In a conscious attempt to avoid possible pressures to surrender to every personal demand, the kibbutz has even tried to legislate against it. The Assembly, or committees, have on several occasions decided to treat issues brought to them as 'bearing no precedent for future' events, or as "exceptions" inapplicable to other issues. Usually these attempts have been deemed to failure from the outset. Furthermore, public recognition of the new course is often given in the form of a generalized rule applicable to all, in principle. Higher education for the 'young generation' became everybody's 'right,' established by the kibbutz, after several 'precedents' had occurred. The rule that higher education is a right does not overrule, however, the authority of the kibbutz to refuse an individual member's request on its own merits or on any other 'reasonable' ground. But, with the precedent taken into account, it is highly improbable that the kibbutz would exercise this authority.

The vineyard team could, presumably, have objected to Yardeni's departure. Knowing his tasks in the branch, the objection would have had considerable weight had it been assessed against the importance of Yardeni's work in the vineyard. The kibbutz's central authorities could have challenged Yardeni's plan. But the rule of the precedent waved aside any possible opposition once Yardeni had conformed to the minimum requisites expected from the applicant.

Beyond the above, what is important is what is achieved through the use of the inherent properties of precedent. This is the subject of the following section.

### (c) Involvement

Whether he is trying to forward his interest or supporting another's cause, a member does more than justify his request by appeal to precedent. He takes steps to neutralize prospective opposition by reference to identifiable persons who have been involved in previous events and whose possible opposition he aims to prevent. If the person concerned cannot mobilize active support (and he will tend to try to mobilize some support), he can still hint at potential sources of pressure which would involve many people. It will concern the persons directly involved in these previous affairs, it will concern those who co-operated with them and supported their requests, and it will concern all the members by virtue of their membership in the community which has admitted and absorbed the 'precedent.' While trying to activate commitments of support from various

sets of relationships the person in question uses the precedent
to disarm potential objectors.

Precedent compels people to respond to a move taken by a
member, to reconsider their relations with him and - not less
important - to consider the relevance of the move to prospective
moves of their own, when they may be confronted with essentially
the same problems. Thus they find themselves involved.

Involvement, of course, exceeds the realm of debate in
which precedent is mobilized. Members of the kibbutz must
continue to live together, to share membership in the same
economic corporation, to practice a communal pattern of consumption, to remain neighbors and to bring up their children in the
same educational framework, so that a move in one sphere will
inevitably bring about response in another. The members will
continue to meet in the various contexts of communal life and
in different situations. Talent, gift, personal ability in
various subjects, position in the economic corporation, influence
and the like may be unevenly distributed in the population, but
ultimately the members are equal in their membership of the
kibbutz. This equality adds a dimension to the involvement and
sets further constraints on any hypothetical deviation from the
rule of the precedent as applied to all.

I do not know how the vineyard team overcame the crisis
which was caused by, and must have occurred in the wake of,
Yardeni's departure, for I had left Hofra before these problems
were solved. The community, in implicitly accepting Yardeni's
long-term plan by its approval of his responsibilities, curbed
any effective, hypothetical opposition on the part of the team.
The members of the team were aware of the situation: they could
assess the prospects of opposition in the light of the nature
of the issue. They were only too familiar with the role of
precedent in the kibbutz and its significance for the kibbutz
as a whole and for its constituent members. They had no chance
of winning an argument which would run counter to a cause of a
considerable importance to the community and counter to the
alignments in which people of the community found themselves.
Their membership in the wider community and in various networks
in itself checked their actions to serve the branch. Here, as
in the reaction to the short-term work of Yardeni in the vineyard prior to his departure, forces operating in the wider
context of the community determined the behavior of the team
vis-a-vis the individual.

Thus, in a dialectical way, the team comes to accept the
will of the individual. It is then not only through work in the

166

branch and attachment to a team that the individual attains
and retains a position in the community.  It is also through
mechanisms operating in the wider community, seemingly irrelevant to the branch, that the individual adds - or at any rate is
potentially able to add - another element to his position in
his place of work.  This is another dimension in which the
position of the member of the kibbutz in work has to be understood.  This element of power is built up and is developed
in the community and chanelled into the branch's relationships.
In the present context, it is the effect of the wider set of
relationships in which the member is enmeshed on the smaller set
within the branch, as these focus on the individual, that paves
the way to co-operation on the part of the team.  The acquiescence of the team is another asset for the position of the individual.

## Active support

The next stage on the continuum of a team's reaction to
a member's defection from the branch is when the team ostenꞏ
sibly adjures any opposition to the individual's initiative to
leave the branch by acceding to his wish at once, and giving
their active blessing to him in an official public arena, at
some meeting.  This gesture does not preclude complaints on
the part of the members of the team that they are insufficient
to cope with the tasks imposed on them because the branch has
suffered the loss of a permanent member.  They often do complain.

Theoretically, two suggestions, not mutually exclusive,
come to the fore:  (a)  The members of the branch team may be
indifferent to the defection of the particular colleague or,
at any rate, may not be particularly concerned about it; and
(b)  while they assess both the occupational future of the
leaving member and assess the problems they will encounter in
the branch following his departure, they would like to leave
options open for future co-operation with him within the branch.
This last suggestion will be clarified presently.

Hevyon (C3), who worked in an agricultural branch in
1969, expressed his wish to work as a driver in the regional
transport co-operative.  The co-operative is a joint organization of all the kibbutz settlements in the Valley; its tasks
are to transport all products of the meshakim to the market
centers throughout the country and to the sea and air ports,
and to deliver purchased goods and equipment back to its member
settlements.  In addition, it is involved in a nationwide commercial transport business.  Each kibbutz assigns a certain

167

number of members to work in the co-operative according to an
agreed quota.  As the total number of kibbutz members has
proved insufficient, the co-operative employs hired drivers,
and garage and maintenance workers.  Driving work in the co-
operative is known in the kibbutz to be a highly demanding and
sometimes strenuous job.  The driver frequently works at unusual
times, early at dawn and late at night, and he is often required
to work extra hours, though the job does offer several compensations, particularly a cinsiderable degree of freedom of movement, job satisfaction, and recognized pecuniary compensations
by the co-operative.  Although he has to strictly obey instructions given by the co-operative's Labor Distributor, and the
labor regulations of the co-operative, social controls exerted
on him as a member of the kibbutz are loosened considerably once
his activity in the realm of labor takes place outside the meshek
proper and outside the residential settlement.

Hofra's quota of drivers in the co-operative was full in
1968/9.  Nevertheless, there was room for a kibbutz member to
get a driver's job since not all the member-kibbutzim provided
their own quotas.  The same situation prevailed in 1970, when
Hevyon repeated his request.  Unlike the case of moving from
one branch to another within the meshek, when the person usually
approaches members of the team of his chosen branch before the
subject is discussed with the central authorities, getting a job
in an enterprise or an organization outside the meshek, an
organization of which the meshek itself is a constituent member,
or in which it has a share, cannot follow this pattern.  The
interested person has to depend on the Meshek Organizer (usually,
the kibbutz's representative in such organizations) to manage
negotiations there, as well as on him to manage the issue within
the kibbutz.  The co-operation of the Meshek Organizer is essential.
The present (1969, 1970) Organizer had been successively the
Labor Distributor and Labor Organizer of the co-operative itself
prior to his election to the post of Meshek Organizer and was,
while acting as the Meshek Organizer, the representative of Hofra
on the Secretarial Board (similar to the office of Board of
Directors) of the co-operative.  Hevyon had to discuss his plan
with him.  When Hevyon first applied, he was turned down.  Instead,
he was asked to join the relatively new cotton-growing branch.
Cotton is a highly mechanized branch, efficiently run, and is
considered highly productive.  In the slack season the members
of the team are sometimes "mobilized" to help other branches
whose busy season coincides with the cotton's slack period.
They usually work as lorry or tractor drivers then, work which
is regarded as an extension of what they do in their own mechanized branch.  Hevyon agreed.  At the same time he applied to the

168

Secretariat of the kibbutz to let him attend an Army Officers'
course. This would entail a long period of voluntary military
service and hence absence from the kibbutz. The Secretariat
discussed it but did not make a definite decision as his acceptance for such a course did not seem to be likely immediately.
But they did not reject the request outright and the "impression"
was that they tended to accept it. So, everybody in Hofra knew
of Hevyon's two plans, of attending an officers' course and of
eventually joining the co-operative as a driver. Meanwhile
Hevyon worked in the cotton branch. In the early winter at the
end of 1970 he was assigned to the citrus grove to help in transport during the citrus' high season. Successive events occurred
which cast doubts on his 'responsible behavior' as a worker. He
was involved in events in which cargoes of fruits were neglected
and not transported according to plan and in which work plans
were messed up because of his alleged failure to accomplish his
work as expected. Naturally, such a failure affected not only
plans in the branch but also people, who had to depend on his
efficient services. So, he aroused public antagonism, within
and beyond the grove.[5] People within and outside the branch
demanded that Hevyon be brought to a "clarifying discussion" of
his conduct. A "clarifying discussion" is an official enquiry
to which a member alleged to have committed a breach of an accepted
norm is summoned to explain his conduct. It is held in a meeting
of a committee considered relevant to the sphere in which the
breach has allegedly taken place. No decision on the issue, let
alone verdict, on the person involved can be made unless this
"clarifying discussion" is first held, in which the alleged
offender participates.[6] However, the very summoning of a person
to a "clarifying discussion" confers upon him the uneasy element
of a defendant's position while on members of the committee it
confers an element of the role of a judge, embarrassing in itself
in the involved social relationships of the kibbutz. The relevant
committee to discuss the issue with Hevyon was the Labor Committee.
At approximately the same time Hevyon raised again the issue of his
wish to work in the co-operative. It seemed as though everything
accumulated together: the alleged misbehavior in the grove, the
repeating of Hevyon's demand to work in the co-operative, and
the unclear plan of his absence from work while on military
service. It was agreed among the central office-holders that
the whole complex should be discussed at one and the same time.
Following below are excerpts from minutes which I took in the
meetings of the Meshek Committee, on December 13th and on December
20th, 1970.

## 1. The meeting on December 13th

Present:    the Meshek Organizer (M.O.) (Chairman), the External Treasurer (E.T.), the Purchase Organizer, the cotton branch foreman (B.F.) (member ot the Committee).

Absent:    the Labor Organizer (attending another meeting), another member (elected personally and not by virtue of office), the previous Meshek Organizer (who was invited for that particular item on the agenda).

Hevyon was present at this meeting.

Chairman (M.O.):    We are moving to the next subject on the agenda now, a clarifying discussion with Hevyon. We have felt that we cannot discuss his request to work in the co-operative before we clarify problems which have arisen in his [conduct in] work...

B.F.(C):    The clarifying discussion were better dispensed with.

M.O.:    We can dispense with the clarifying discussion in relation to the past. Hevyon should, however, hereby announce in public that he is prepared to accept the conditions of work as demanded by the co-operative before he commences to work there and not after he has begun. He should make clear that he is going to abide by the regulations of work in the co-operative.

Hevyon:    (nods).

M.O.:    The Labor Organizer has announced the resignation of the Labor Committee. I am therefore bringing this subject to this Committee and not to the relevant one. Two clarifications must be made.
Firstly, Hevyon asked a year ago, when he had ended his work in his previous job, to move to the co-operative. I said, "Let us see you joining a branch. After you have proven a year or so of competent branch work, you may raise again the issue, if you still wish to work in the co-operative. Then we will consider [your request]." In the meantime [during the course of the year], it has emerged, the Secretariat discussed another request laid by Hevyon, that he should take leave from work to attend an officers' course. The Secretariat tends to accept this request if it proves practical. However, let it be clear: it is impossible to assign a member to a new place of work and at the

same time to let him attend a lengthy course outside the kibbutz.  It should be clear to us outright if the plan of the officers' course has been, under the circumstances, cancelled.

Hevyon:     It has (for me), since there is no date known [for a beginning of a course into which I will be accepted].

M.O.:     Secondly, the co-operative is a special place of work. Working in the co-operative is done under special conditions.  It is better that one knows about the special [physical] efforts and the special conditions before one enters it.  These conditions imply that: (a) the driver is at the command of the [co-operative's] labor Distributor twenty-four hours a day; and (b) there are many duties based on rotation, sometimes they fall on every Saturday [Sabbath] and again, on all these occasions the driver is at the Distributor's command. One must follow the regulations to the point.  It all leads to the conclusion that "punctures" [disturbances] in work must never occur, while they do happen at home ... [referring to Hevyon's alleged failures in this field].  If they do occur, the man is sent back home. There is no need to emphasize that it is embarrassing when it happens.  I, as an ex-Distributor, have already seen it from three angles: (1)  from the meshek's angle;  (2)  from the co-operative's angle; and (3)  as one who has dismissed a driver and sent him back to his kibbutz...

B.F.:     I would like to voice support for the plan [that Hevyon should join the co-operative] because Hevyon wants it. [I support it] although we have benefited by his work. And we have benefited by his work even if misunderstandings have occurred.  People of a 'higher respectability' than Hevyon's have caused 'problems' as well. I only hope that Hevyon manages to follow the regulations [of work in the co-operative].  Within the meshek it [the following of norms of work] is based on conscience; in the co-operative, more on regulations. If we need Hevyon's help in the harvesting season, he is prepared to come.

E.T.:     Yes, ... like HX [another driver working in the co-operative] who willingly left [the co-operative] for the season this year.  If drivers really wish, they can leave the co-operative for a while and help in the meshek.

171

Hevyon:     No objection whatever.  Work in the cotton is pleasure.

M.O.:       I will write then a letter to the co-operative and I
            will expect a reply.  They will have to appoint an
            experienced driver to train Hevyon.

B.F.:       I take this opportunity to state that I will not carry
            out the instalment of the remaining area [destined for
            cotton in the Eastern Spout] with the newly arrived
            irrigation pipes because HY (C2) [another permanent
            member of the small cotton team who shares, to an extent,
            the foremanship with B.F., and whose own part-time
            absence from work in the branch for studying purpose
            was approved by the kibbutz] already studies in the
            regional college for his matriculation.  When he gets
            his matriculation he will certainly go to further
            education.  (No comment.)

2.  The meeting on December 20th.  On the agenda: The cotton
    branch, planning for the year 1971.

Present:    M.O. (Chairman), previous Meshek Organizer, External
            Treasurer, Purchase Organizer, Cotton branch foreman,
            a member personally elected to the Committee.

Absent:     Labor Organizer.

Invited:    The cotton team (HY, Hevyon, Z - another young member).

Item three:  Labor force.  (Excerpt)

HY:         Two more men are necessary in the cotton branch.
            Hevyon is going soon to the co-operative and I will
            be available only part-time during the season.

M.O.:       Hevyon will come back in the summer.

HY:         Don't be casuistical.  Hevyon?  He will come back?...

Everybody
(laughing): He will come back as A went to the co-operative for
            one year only [he has been working there three years];
            as B went there for three years [he has been working
            there six years]; as half a job is kept for the
            Internal Treasurer in the banana branch because "half
            a day is enough for me in the office to accomplish
            my duties" [the Internal Treasurer has a full-time
            job and the bananas branch has been extinct for the
            last six years].  He will come back...

| HY (to M.O.): | Yours is not a [satisfactory] answer. |
|---|---|

| B.F.: | I have talked with Y. I have talked him into joining the cotton branch. [Y, a young member, works in the orchard.] You all know that he is dissatisfied with the orchard. He grumbles. He considers changing his branch. If he does join, and if HY continues to give a third of his time to the branch, it will work. Z [the youngest member of the team], though apparently uninterested [he was present], should be the foreman as I "grow in age" [B.F. is 35]. We will not be in Y's way when he goes to higher education. HY will probably return by that time. |
|---|---|

| Previous M.O.: | The matter should be transferred to the Labor Committee. |
|---|---|

| H.Y.: | The Meshek Committee should discuss it, because it is this Committee which ultimately determines the priority of one branch over another. It was done so [it was the Meshek Committee who made the decision] when W was assigned to the vineyard and Z was assigned to the cotton branch. |
|---|---|

(No conclusion was arrived at at the meeting.)

Several points which emerge from this account of the two meetings deserve attention. Firstly, the committee which discussed the Hevyon affair was the Meshek Committee, not the Labor Committee. The Labor Committee had indeed resigned, but no one suggested that the issues included in the "Discussion with Hevyon" should be postponed until the Committee withdrew its resignation or a new one was elected. It seems that the Meshek Organizer made the statement on the resignation of the Labor Committee during the first meeting of the Meshek Committee so as to waive any possible attempt at the meeting to prevent it from being involved in the "clarifying discussion" with Hevyon on formal grounds. The Labor Committee did not withdraw its resignation between the two meetings of the Meshek Committee nor was another committee elected. Nevertheless, the previous Meshek Organizer did try during the second meeting to refer the subject to that committee. This attempt was objected to since it was "this Committee which ultimately determines the priority of one branch over another." It was this Committee which had previously assumed power to assign members to branches and to intervene in problems of labor in the branches. The objection on the part of

173

the branch men did not refer at all to the resignation of the
Labor Committee. It pointed at the well-known process of the
growing power of the Meshek Committee vis-a-vis the Labor Committee, and emphasized the branch-workers' willingness that the
interests of the branch be discussed in the organizational institution considered to be more competent to deal with the problem.
They did not interest themselves in the formalistic aspect; they
weighed the relative competence of the two bodies and wanted
their issue to be taken care of by the more competent one.

Secondly, the meeting of a central committee is a significant occasion for public censure of a member's misbehavior.
Rumors, gossip, and grumbling go on in the community through
various channels of communication. Some people go as far as
taking the liberty to comment on alleged misbehavior in the
presence of the accused. Some may take him personally to task.
Such events, significant as they may be, are not marked by a
communal recognition. But if a member is summoned to offer an
explanation of his alleged misbehavior to an official communal
agency, the affair becomes a legitimized public concern. This
is a situation every member tries to avoid. I have witnessed
numerous cases of members trying to ignore, or even defying,
rebukes, comments and jokes made by comrades about their alleged
breach of conduct. When a possible summons to a committee's
discussion was mentioned, in those conversations, some became
very indignant. Two members in particular, one accused of having
misused the lorry under his responsibility and the other accused
of having misused another vehicle, tried to ignore all comments
on their conduct. With their close friends they tried to make
a joke of the whole affair and ridicule the person in charge of
the kibbutz's vehicles. These members went as far as saying that
they would like to be summoned to a "clarifying discussion"
before an authorized committee. If they were summoned, they said,
they would take the offensive; they would "expose the truth behind
the office-holder's complaint" by showing that it was he, the
office-holder, who plotted the issue so as to develop it to "an
affair"; they would even tell the members of the committee present
in the meeting of their personal offenses in the past; they would
show that the committee meeting itself was an unimportant event
which should not be taken seriously. In other words, they, as
individuals: (a) would take the offensive rather than be on the
defensive; (b) would neutralize the individuals who comprised
the committee in exposing the latter's offence; and (c) would
challenge the efficacy, if not the formal authority, of the
elected central body itself. They would... but they did not!
These "hawkish" young men, when present in the meeting, to which
they were summoned, proved to be perfect "doves." It was they
who had to take the role of the defendant, to make the explanation,

174

to wait for the decision (if not for a verdict) of the committee; and it was in a very apologetic manner that they played their role in the meeting. Whatever the decision of the committee might have been, being summoned to a "hearing" proved to be a very unpleasant experience indeed. To be summoned, while virtually every member of the community knows of the summons; then to be confronted by a group of members authorized to make a decision, not to mention the social position of these members in the community, with or without regard to their membership in the particular committee; to give account of one's own conduct; to be questioned and possibly to be rebuked; and then to know that the decision of the committee will be made public, both officially and otherwise, is sufficient to turn a hawk into a dove.

I have reported above what was said in the two meetings of Hevyon's work and conduct. Indeed, the discussion was short. One of the reasons for its being short lay in the fact that most of its contents had been widely expressed in the community prior to the meeting. All the members of the Committee knew about the allegation. Although no official rebuke was made in the presentation of the subject by the Meshek Organizer, it did contain the rebuking message. Although a "clarifying discussion" on past aspects of Hevyon's misbehavior in the meshek was avoided in the meeting, the emphasis on labor regulations, discipline and possible dismissal from the future job in the co-operative conveyed this message. The warning in reference to the future employment contained the censure on Hevyon's career in the past. That was obvious to all the people present in the meeting. More important than the wording was, of course, the situation of the meeting itself. When censure is voiced, or a fortiori when a motion of censure is adopted as a resolution, this situation can be very distressing. So, it is the situation, not less than the contents of the discussion, which is significant to the individual. It contains the elements of both the formal framework of the kibbutz and interpersonal relationships within the community. The contrast between the angry and threatening statements made by the two drivers prior to the meeting as against their actual behavior in it shows the significance of this situation in both these terms. Since it is distressing in itself for the individual, the representatives of the community can take up issues with him on their own initiative.

Thirdly, it is noteworthy that the team asked that the 'clarifying discussion' be altogether dispensed with. Indirectly, the cotton-branch foreman did what the two drivers mentioned above had boasted of doing before they were summoned to a meeting, and what Hevyon presumably may have wished to do: he stated that "people of a 'higher respectability' than Hevyon's have caused

175

problems as well." The branch foreman personally was not in the position of defending himself or explaining his conduct. Nor was he a foreman of the branch to which damage had been caused by Hevyon, a member of his team. He could not, on available evidence, justify Hevyon. Hevyon's conduct was not excusable on its own merits, but the foreman could ask to dispense with a formal hearing, the certain contents of which must have been known to all those present in the meeting. By giving no explanation for his motion of order (to dispense with the hearing) he made clear the fact that the issue was actually known to everyone. Secondly, by reminding those present that people of a presumably higher status could themselves be dragged into an uncomfortable position if similar events were unveiled and talked about in the course of the 'clarifying discussion,' he took the wind out of the sails of a possible criticism of Hevyon. If members did want, however, to go on with the discussion, they would risk the opening of a Pandora's Box, that is, the invocation of affairs contained in the collective memory of Hofra. The use of such affairs, as the use of any memory in a different situation, would not have to be precise, undistorted, fair or relevant to Hevyon's case in the present. It could be otherwise. Would it not be better to avoid it altogether? The opening of a Pandora's Box in the course of a meeting may be promptly ruled by the Chairman as out of order and irrelevant, but channels of gossip from the meeting, added to by comments made outside it, would not abide by this rule. The foreman's message was, then, that it was better to restrict the affair: Hevyon was informally censured by members of the community anyway, reference to his misbehavior in the past would be made in relation to his future employment, and no official hearing would take place.

Fourthly, I would like to draw attention to the argument the team gave in their active support of Hevyon's request. "I would like to voice support for the plan because Hevyon wants it," the branch foreman said. I have already discussed the growing autonomy of the individual in choosing his permanent branch. I have also drawn attention to the normative "superstructure" which has evolved within this process, so as to give rise to the conception of 'right' in the individual's choice of a branch. Here the team makes a public announcement of support for such a move away from the branch "although we have benefited by his work." It recognizes the right of the member, of a member of the team, to leave the branch at will. Once it is a right, it should be respected. In previous cases I have shown how members of the team tried to persuade their colleagues not to leave. I have no evidence on such an attempt in relation to Hevyon. Whatever the members of the team had in mind, they gave a public unqualified verbal support to the 'right' once Hevyon raised anew the issue of his occupation. And the verbal support was based on the argument that "Hevyon wants it."

Fifthly, the public announcement, made by the branch foreman, that Hevyon was prepared to leave the co-operative to give temporary help to the branch during the harvesting seasons, and the confirmation given by Hevyon in his superlative definition of the work in the cotton branch, show the nature of the agreement, presumably (I did not personally hear it) reached in advance of the meeting. Hevyon undertook a commitment to help the branch in the demanding peak season and obtained a fair support for his personal plan from his fellow branch-men. Not only did they express support for his plan in the meeting: they averted the unpleasant experience of a public 'clarifying discussion.' They did not display any act of relief, imaginary or genuine, at his leaving them; they did not participate in the general censure - steps which they well could have taken once Hevyon was going to leave them; they did not even display indifference, let alone objection, to his moving away. They acknowledged his wish and gave active support to it. They did not justify his alleged misconduct, but the only critical remark on his work with them ("even if misunderstandings have occurred") was qualified by the allusion to the persons of 'higher respectability' who, they claimed, 'caused problems' as well. The nature of the agreement was, then, one which enabled both parties: (a) not to sever links; and (b) to keep options open for future developments.

In the peak season nearly every team requires extra help, which is more valuable if it is experienced. Very few members have worked in the relatively new cotton branch, and furthermore, very few are at the Labor Organizer's disposal when help to the cotton-growing-branch is needed. Thus the chances of getting people who have had experience in cotton work are slim. If Hevyon were available, the team was assured of overcoming possible difficulties in the crucial season. Other members could have helped in the branch even without belonging to it, but they would be inexperienced help. Hevyon could be assigned to jobs other than mere driving and transport; he could be instructed to go to various plots without much confusion about their location; he could use tools with which he had obtained familiarity, and so on. By promising to <u>volunteer</u> to join the team in the harvest period of the annual cycle he put himself under a commitment to do more than the formal share which is expected from every worker. During the peak season extra work is often demanded and responsibility is shown not only in terms of the common denominator discussed in the previous chapter, but also by shouldering extra undertakings involving greater physical efforts and lengthier hours of work.

177

A volunteer is expected to take all these with a clear appreciation of the situation and its requirements and with an outstanding measure of devotion.

Work in the co-operative may, furthermore, prove to be
temporary. If Hevyon left the co-operative and returned to work
in the meshek, he might consider rejoining the cotton branch.
Did he not declare it to be a pleasure? So, in maintaining some
association with him, first through the public statements made
at the meeting and secondly through his seasonal 'mobilization'
into the branch every summer, the branch might eventually bring
him back to it as a permanent worker. I am not arguing here that
the team was, in fact, determined to do everything in their power
to ensure the eventual return of Hevyon into the branch as a
permanent worker. I am arguing that by maintaining this kind of
association with him, by their conduct in the whole affair,
including their move to avert the public censure, they left open
options for future use. They did secure the temporary help from
an experienced worker and they did give a chance both for Hevyon
and for themselves to consider such a long-term move should
another change in Hevyon's occupation be imminent. And Hevyon
on his side, with the team's support, avoided the possibility of
degrading public censure.7

Also, and this seems to be more important, the agreement enabled Hevyon to return to the branch eventually. The
Meshek Organizer, it will be recalled, mentioned indirectly that
Hevyon's initial period of working in the co-operative would be
probationary. He implied this in saying that an experienced
driver [not necessarily from Hofra] would have to train Hevyon
when the latter would join the co-operative. The experienced
driver's report on and his estimate of Hevyon's performance,
coupled with the close observation of others on Hevyon's adaptation to the new conditions and regulations of work, were to be
crucial. There are members of kibbutzim in the Valley who have
not been admitted to an independent driving job in the co-
operative when their performance in the probationary period
proved unsatisfactory, and the Meshek Organizer mentioned that
he had himself sent home, i.e., dismissed unsatisfactory drivers.
Those drivers may have been in their training period; they may
have been experienced men who failed to abide by regulations or
obey instructions; they may have committed offenses of various
kinds. It was therefore important for Hevyon to leave the
option of returning to the branch open.

Sixthly, and incidentally only, I would like to draw
attention to the jocular manner in which the people present in
the second meeting reacted to the Meshek Organizer's statement

in reply to the team's request for help for the season. He mentioned that Hevyon would come back to the branch to help. He said, that Hevyon himself had promised this and the team had declared it. But the people attending the meeting, the cotton workers apparently included, were skeptical. They met the Organizer's statement with skepticism, not because they were certain of Hevyon's permanence or indispensability in the co-operative, nor, it seems, because they doubted Hevyon's sincerity in making his commitment. They were skeptical because they had witnessed members leaving agricultural work but proclaiming, and probably assuming, that that move of leaving agriculture was only temporary when in fact it would prove not to be. Theirs was a skeptical reaction, clothed in a good-humor, a reaction of people whose main concern was the maintenance and the running of the meshek in general and of the agricultural section in particular, and of people who were agricultural workers themselves.

In conclusion, the discussion of the case of Hevyon, the last on the continuum of the team's reaction to a member leaving the branch, illuminates a few elements of the latter's position in the sphere of labor.

Firstly, regardless of his personal standing in the community at large and of a possible not-too-successful performance at the branch itself, the individual need not worry that his fellow branch-men will act to humiliate him when he leaves the branch. The grounds for such a worry may lie in the individual's fear that the team might do this because it will be left short of labor, as well as because its internal tensions may find an outlet in a display of relief at his 'defection.' Such a display need not necessarily reflect a genuine reaction, but it can serve its function: the 'defector' can presumably become a scapegoat for failures of the branch and for interpersonal strain. A public situation in which the scene of formal departure takes place could become an ideal occasion for an unpleasant experience for the individual. Potentially it probably is. I do not argue that members of a branch team never express such a reaction in private or in small, close, circles. Nevertheless, I have not witnessed a public scene of this kind, in which a public denunciation of the member, upon his departure, is made. Even if we assume that, in close circles, members of the team may make critical, and even denunciatory, comments about colleagues, it is significant that they refrain from doing so in the public meeting. They appreciate the difference between the two situations and are aware of the consequences of making such comments in both.[8] However, a situation may arise in which this distinction will not seem worthwhile for the team, either because of the manner in which the candidate for 'defection' conducts his course of departure or because of his conduct in work while in the branch. Hostility felt by the team may find its way into the formal occasion. It is this situation to which I have referred in stating that it can be ideal for public denunciation of the individual by the team. Since the emergence of such a situation seems, at least theoretically plausible, I refer to it as being potential. But as I have stated above, I have not witnessed a public scene in which a member, upon leaving the branch, is denounced by his colleagues. Therefore, in saying that a member need not worry about hostile action by the team once the issue is brought to a public arena, I am merely making an empirical generalization about past action. And therefore this statement does not contain the predictive property of a law.

I have argued why the cotton men had good reasons for refraining from criticizing Hevyon, and even from joining in other people's criticisms, to the extent of supporting him. I further showed that not only did they refrain from taking a critical approach towards him, but they supported him in the formal meeting. This was not only because they wanted to ensure his help in the future. This, and similar behavior in other circumstances, has to be seen in a wider context, and analyzed in the case of Yardeni: The ever-present constraints of living together in the wider community, not to mention relationships and networks within the community with which both the individual and members of the team are associated, help to restrain everyone's behavior.

Secondly, the unstated but implicit, mutually understood, agreement between the permanent member of the branch and the team, that the team should show interest in keeping the member in the branch, comes into the open again. It reappears in a subtle way. The branch foreman, on behalf of the team, voiced "support for the plan because Hevyon wants it." Had Hevyon not publicly expressed his wish to change occupations, the team would have been bound to 'defend' him, whether or not the members were interested in doing so. The 'defense' may not be genuine, but it is necessary. The foreman's announcement of the team's support for Hevyon's departure contained the apologetic explanation intimating that it was the latter's proclaimed wish that that role-of-defense should not be played by the team. It seems to me that the active verbal support by the team contained, in its presentation, the allusion to the team's responsibilities. Had Hevyon, presumably, wanted the team's 'defense' (to remain in the branch), its spokesmen would have voiced objection to a plan for his transfer to another branch. By failing to do this, they would have provided him with either: (a) an opportunity to re-assess his position amongst them in the branch; or (b) an excuse for a request to leave the branch (as was shown in the case of Haray). The extent of objection to a colleague's leaving is an index to his position in the branch. Should the member wish to leave, and should the team's spokesman support him (for such reasons as mentioned in the case of Hevyon), the support should be formulated in a manner which will contain the allusion to this commitment of the team. The objection of the team to a transfer of a colleague to another branch, or even the allusion to it as contained in the formulation of the team's support for the individual's plans, is an asset for the individual. He is not dispensable.

Thirdly, in a similar manner, the blessings, or the good wishes, given by the members of one's former team are important for one in two contexts: (a) in the context of the new job; and (b) in the context of maintaining relationships with the former place of work.

Gossip and other channels of communication spread the informal appreciation of the newly joining member and the assessment of his work before he approaches the new team himself. When he does approach the new team, the information pertaining to his ability, responsibility and devotion to work will have already reached the people concerned. Nevertheless, if members of the former team are careful in their comments in public, and particularly if they express their support and good wishes on formal occasions, the member stands a chance of achieving his transfer without losing face. The move itself is not interpreted, when discussed publicly, in terms of failure in the former job or maladjustment to certain kinds of work nor is it related to failure in developing good personal relationships with his fellow workers. It is usually discussed in terms of the member's preference for, and interest in, work other than his former one. The active support and the expression of good wishes are explained by the former team in terms of respect for the individual's interests. Thus, even though informal information may differ sometimes from the public versions, and even though practically everybody may be aware of this discrepancy, the fact that a member can lean on the public version does help him in his new quest for permanent, satisfactory, work. I would like to stress again that although informal information may hinder his chances as these are opened by the public version, the very possibility that an individual can refer to the public manifestation of the team's goodwill is not a negligible asset for him. People usually observe the convention that in discussing a member's change of branch they begin with the public version given at the time. This in itself is important. Someone unfamiliar with the informal versions of the reasons given for a member's occupational change needs time to learn that factors other than those specified in the public version may have operated. Those factors are defined idiomatically as "various kinds of reasons." Those "various kinds of reasons" are not always discussed even in an informal gathering of people. That such a situation is to the advantage of the member concerned when he develops a new position is obvious. It helps to impede, if not to prevent, a possible objection to the transfer on the part of the receiving team, or of some of its individual members. Similarly, it helps to pave the way for the central labor authorities to accept, to acquiesce in, and even to take an active role in the transfer.

More significant for the present analysis is the context of the member's relationships with his former team. Admittedly, good relationships with former colleagues can be maintained even without the public blessing such as was manifested by the cotton men in the case of Hevyon. At any instance on the continuum of team reaction to the individual's departure, a member can keep good relationships with his former team. But the 'friendlier' (i.e., the closer to his interests - the term "interests" being used in the broadest sense) the expression of the members of the team to his plan is, the greater the chance for a future voluntary co-operation between them grows.

I draw attention here not so much to such temporary help as promised by Hevyon, as to the other probability I have mentioned above, the probability of permanent return to the branch, a return which is more probable if the move is to another agricultural branch, or another place of work within the meshek. Three members work with national organizations; seven members are employed in the transport co-operative; five are employed in the regional kibbutz economic enterprises; and seven work for the Movement away from Hofra. The last two are by definition categories of temporary employment. Both the Movement and the kibbutz regional economic enterprises set rules against the permanent manning of jobs in their organizations. The members who work there, whether as 'activists,' officials, managers, manual workers or drivers etc., can do so as they are officially 'sent' there or 'mobilized' by their kibbutzim to do the work, and upon the termination of the 'mobilization' call they are supposed to return to work in their respective meshakim. In the case of the transport cooperative, there is no such rule, but driving for the co-operative is commonly regarded as initially temporary. While in the initial period of work as a driver in the co-operative the member makes up his mind whether he wishes to remain in this job (itself given to sub-categorization according to type of vehicle, cargo, distance of ride etc., within which a driver may presumably move from one type to another), and the

182

co-operative, on its own part, makes its own decision on retaining him.  The fact that the final decision lies with the co-
operative and not with the constituent kibbutz from which the
member comes and within which he can mobilize support, adds another
element to the recognition of this work as impermanent.  Add to
this the insistence of the kibbutzim that they may call the
members 'home' to work in the meshek, any time, and this recognition gains even more weight.  Sometimes it does seem more desirable to call members from these 'outside' jobs to take responsibilities and to disrupt the course of the running of branches and
members' stakes in them.  The reader will recall the case of Ohad
discussed above in Chapter III.  Since the main perspective of
labor in the kibbutz lies with its independent economy, employment in the so-called 'outside work' does not bear the same
essence of permanence that work in the meshek does.  The overall
perspective is that some time the member will come back 'home'
and be employed in the meshek.  Although 'outside work' has its
own advantages for the individual member,[9] it lacks the advantages vested in work in the meshek discussed in this book.

   Not all 'outside workers' have moved to their present jobs
from agricultural branches or related services.  It is most
likely that not all of them will rejoin the branches, when they
return to the meshek.  Those, however, who have moved to their
present employment from the branches of the meshek, and furthermore, those who consider their occupational future in the meshek,
are more closely involved in this problem of relationships with
a branch and a group of members working in one.  Or, as one
driver employed by the co-operative has defined it:  "After three
or four years of driving for the co-operative one must question
oneself whether one resigns oneself to an occupational future
as a co-operative lorry driver or prefers to establish oneself
in the meshek.  And, if so [if the latter is preferred], where."

   So, although good relationships can be maintained by the
member and his colleagues of the former team even without the
active support of the latter in his cause, leaving their branch,
their support is pregnant with the chance of his rejoining them,
when - and if - he returns to work in the meshek pending his
resignation from his 'outside work.'  He has maintained some
link with the branch.  Through this link he keeps a stake in
the meshek proper: he is linked to an economic branch within
the economic corporation.  He may return to this branch, he may
not.  But the existing link, developed through work in the branch
and enduring, despite moving out of it, through the promise to
help and, more particularly, through occasional help in the
harvesting season, prevails.  I cannot argue that members who
take some of their working time in 'outside work' off so as to

help branches in the _meshek_ always do it with this aim in mind, nor do I argue that they are always conscious of this effect on their future occupational career. They may act with the conviction that their help is needed and appreciated; they may even seek this appreciation, which might give them acclaim for helping the _meshek_ and their former team; or they may act simply in response to a call by the kibbutz's authorities. But in doing so they establish a personal stake in the _meshek_ and in a branch, they prove their association with the course of its running economy, and they gain prestige in the community for showing their concern with the affairs of the _meshek_ in spite of their employment outside it. These are important assets for the individual. He can best achieve them through giving his share to the interplay between "the one and the team."

Conclusions

Permanent attachment to a branch has emerged as an asset in the establishment of the position of a member of the kibbutz in the sphere of labor. Indeed, from the point of view of the individual, it has emerged as the primary condition for establishing a meaningful positive position. Because nearly every member has achieved permanence it is mainly the 'negative' and defensive aspects of permanence which have emerged during the discussion. The defensive aspect of which I speak is the ability of the member to resist possible threats to significant social assets contained in, and dependent upon, the position of permanence. Once a member has achieved permanence in an agricultural branch he is provided with another asset: support from the branch team. The significance of permanence in work for the member's social position lies initially in its defensive function, i.e., in its power of resistance, though it is also a 'positive' condition for advancement in fields of specialization and professionalization (the subject of the next chapter). Furthermore, the significance of the support from the team, is that it helps the individual to retain his permanent attachment to the branch and to resist pressures to move.

A team composes a system of mutual support which is an important asset if one needs to deter or resist any threat, or possibility of threat to his work position. When he acquires permanent attachment to a branch team a member can expect his colleagues to align with him and to help him stay in that branch. The alignment of the team is activated almost automatically when stability in work of any of the permanent members is threatened and in that respect the team has a corporate aspect. Mutual support is conceived as an obligation irrespective of personalities. Support, in whatever form, or withdrawal of support, can thus serve as an index of a member's inclusion in the permanent corporate team. The individual himself can test the degree of his incorporation by creating a situation in which the alignment of his fellow branchmen is tested.

Once a member is part of the team he undertakes the obligation to support other branchmen. The support he expects from colleagues is equally expected from him. But support can be expected only when the issue is relevant to the raison d'etre of the corporate bonds of the team, namely, in the branch and in the sphere of work. In spheres other than these, individual members of a team can be counted on for support only if bonds other than those which emerge from the branch and work are present.

The members of the team can choose among a variety of methods of support. The choice is determined by the degree of importance they consider the issue to have for the branch. Roughly, there are two main methods: (a) adherence to formal procedures of settlement of controversies, i.e., meetings of the relevant organs of the kibbutz; and (b) employment of additional methods, such as lobbying. Recourse to the former is inevitable, and it is the skill with which the representatives of the team communicate their verbal support in the debate which signals to the people who are present the degree of support they are giving. But the branchmen can also employ informal channels of communication outside the arena of the formal debate to convey to the central authorities the practical degree of their support to their colleague. Recourse to both methods usually means that the corporate action of support is to be taken seriously, and that the economic, productive, and organizational interests of the branch are involved. A formal debate, if all efforts are made to convince the authorities of the merits of the cause, can communicate the same message, but it can also reveal that the aligned support is not based only on economic and labor considerations, but also on political ones. It can, if the appropriate skill is employed, convey the message that it is the corporate obligation to the individual concerned which aligns the team-members irrespective of economic considerations, whether relevant to the branch or to the kibbutz as a whole.

The choice of method of support by the team and their conduct of the affair in the formal arena also communicates to the individual himself the degree of effective political support he may expect from his branch fellows. Not only is the team support possible only when the issue is relevant to the economic and the branch spheres, but the argumentation can only have some effect if it is directed to these spheres. This is so because

185

(a)   the arena is a meeting of a formal body of the kibbutz
(such as the Labor or the Meshek Committee) whose only authority
is to discuss subjects which fall within its jurisdiction; and
(b)   a formal body of the kibbutz which deals with economic
subjects is committed to give priority to the interests of the
meshek over personal interests.  This situation exerts constraints
on the representatives of the team in the support they can proffer
a colleague.

Finally, the team-support an individual may expect from
branch colleagues is wide-ranging.  But whatever the form of
support, it is a social and political asset to the individual
vis-a-vis the community and its representatives, and in his future
relationships within the team.  Varying degrees of effectiveness
of support affect the degree of power which resides in this asset.

I have also examined the relations between the individual
branchman and the team from another angle:  the possibility of
his eventual departure from the branch.  I have suggested that
the different responses of a team can be seen as lying on a continuum: from (a)   an attempt to persuade the member to remain
in the branch; to (b)   an attempt to postpone the departure of
the member; to (c)   refraining from taking any active step in
the issue; and finally to (d)   official public support for his
departure.

In the background of relationships inside the individual
team is the very complex web of relationships running throughout
the meshek and the whole community.

Within the realm of the branch, the team appears to show
two modes of conduct, seemingly in opposition to one another, in
response to a forthcoming departure of a colleague.  If all the
situations classified above were points on a continuum, they would
show on the one hand interest that the colleague remains in the
branch, and on the other hand that they voice no public opposition to
his plan to leave them.  They would rather have him in the branch,
because of the scarcity of permanent workers.  If they cannot
persuade him to remain, they expect him to share the immediate
tasks of the branch at least until the harvest is in.  But the
extent of his co-operation will be influenced by their response
to his plan of eventually leaving them.  If they show no active
opposition to his long-term plan, they may expect his full co-
operation.  His co-operation may exceed the short-term period of
his work in the branch until his departure: he may periodically
return to the branch to help, (if he is a student away from
home or works outside the meshek (proper)).  If he works outside
the kibbutz he may return to the branch upon resigning his job or

186

post. The individual, in turn, establishes assets of considerable importance: negatively, he is freed from his colleagues'
opposition to his plan and he is free from fear of denouncement
for defecting from the branch. Positively, he retains relationships with a team. He secures an access to his branch which is
important in two respects: (a) if and when he resigns a job
outside the meshek he has a permanent branch to return to; and
(b) while he is away from the meshek, his periodical return to
the branch maintains and renews his connections to and familiarity with the meshek. This is important since the meshek corporation is of a paramount value for the kibbutz itself and its
existence. Periodical returns help to anchor an individual in
his position in the kibbutz.

The presence of the wider community at large introduces a
dialectical quality to the individual-team relations. The team
mediates, so to speak, between the individual and the community
in the sense that the member works in a branch and not in the
meshek 'at large.' Therefore he is under considerable control
of the team vis-a-vis the community: assessment and appreciation
of his performance, devotion, and responsibility in the sphere
of work is initially made in his work-place and then communicated by the team-members to all the members of the community.
An important aspect of kibbutz communal life is thus controlled
by the work team. But if the individual adheres to communal
expectations in the sphere of labor, he can count on support
from the community vis-a-vis his branch fellows. If he wishes
to take a step which is considered to be legitimate in the
kibbutz (such as going to university studies) which involves
his departure from the branch, the acceptance of his wish by the
community, and more important, the certainty of such acceptance,
assures him of co-operation on the part of the branch-team.

In the analysis I have discussed some mechanisms by which
the larger community controls the conduct of the team, such as
the involvement of the team-members in the community in their
roles of members of the kibbutz, the importance of precedent in
making decisions, and public opinion as the expression of interests of a collective of individuals whose interests, real and
anticipated, are involved.

I conclude this part of the discussion with one comment:
in an egalitarian society, i.e., in a society in which resources
are allocated consciously on an equal basis, public opinion is
an important factor. If public opinion, particularly when it
is supported by rules of the kibbutz (such as those regulating
higher education and change of occupation), supports the

187

individual, this is another important asset for him. His position, not only in the community at large, but even within the sphere of labor and the branch, is enriched by this asset of communal support. This dialectical set of relationships between the individual, the team and the community sheds light on resources from which the individual derives elements which constitute his social position in the field of labor.

# N O T E S

1. "Seemingly in contrast." There is a contrast if the focus is on the aim of the foreman, i.e., if the aim is to win support for his fellow-worker or if it is not. The contrast is only apparent, however, if the focus is on the action of the foreman itself. There is no contrast in the action of establishing informal contact, only in the aim of the foreman and, most likely, in the contents of the verbal encounter. If we accept these two different objectives as extremes, they may be put on a circular continuum, as it were. Both extremes require resorting to informal negotiation whereas objectives which fall in between, for some reason, in the foreman's estimate, do not.

2. Haverim, or Chaverim (singular: Haver or Chaver). For the diverse meanings of the Hebrew term, see Spiro (1956: 8; 30-31).

3. See Gluckman (1963: 312-315 and 1968: 28-37).

4. For an analysis of some aspects of precedent, in particular its being selectively cited according to moralistic view, see Gluckman (1955: 173, 234, 256).

5. In discussing this case, I am tempted to bring in, as in other cases, variables from the wider context of the community which are relevant to Hevyon's story, but are not essential to the discussion of the subject as outlined above. I will, therefore, restrict the discussion to the sphere of labor.

6. I cannot go into the discussion of the subject of this institution of "clarifying discussion" here. Nor can I go into discussion of the internal judicial system of the kibbutz and its relation to other forms of internal social control, and to the wider legal and judicial systems of the State, and their derivatives which regulate membership in relation to voluntary associations.

7. For a discussion of a degrading experience in public, see Garfinkel (1956).

8. See, in this connection, Chapter III above, which discusses the case of the young man of Hardoof.

9. Labor of members of the kibbutz outside the _meshek_ requires an anlysis of its own. I regret I cannot get into this matter in this book. I touch upon this subject only in the aspect relevant to the present discussion. But see Talmon Garber (1956: 153-178) and J. Shepher (1966).

# CHAPTER V

## DIVISION OF LABOR WITHIN A BRANCH AND THE POSITION
## OF THE INDIVIDUAL

The division of labor within the team adds another asset to the individual's permanent position in it. It does so by encouraging the development of personal skill in the specific tasks which are allocated to him. Having a specific role within the branch's division of labor and allocation of responsibility constitutes a resource through which the member can establish a social position. The personal role may be related to skill, expertise, scientific or technological knowledge and its practice, management, or personal competence in specific jobs. One or more of them can become elements of the individual's position which emerge in situations when division of labor takes place within the branch, and can influence relationships of the individual both in the team and also vis-a-vis the meshek and its representatives.

### Size of branch teams and choice of branch by the individual

Usually, the greater the demand for labor in any given branch, the larger is the team. I say 'demand for labor' rather than 'the larger the branch is,' because there is no unqualified and direct correlation between the size of an agricultural branch, whether in terms of land, general input or income, and the size of its team. Different crops require different technological methods and tools. These, in turn, affect the amount, as well as the quality, of labor required to implement the economic goals of the given branch. Table 5.1 shows the relation between various components of the 'size' of branches in Hofra and the number of permanent members of the respective branches.

It is evident that different crops require different amounts of labor per unit, whether this unit is land (as has been shown in Table 5.2) or weight of yield (tons), or a unit of exchange such as financial income. When various crops are grouped together in one branch (Table 5.2 and p.274, footnote 5), the situation appears more complex. The difference between the amount of labor required for the new cotton branch (1.25 labor-days per dunam) and that required for the orchard (10.75) is conspicuous. The differences within the latter between, say, plums (17), apples (12-13) and avocado (6) are not less important. A diversified range of crops are grown partly because of the view held about the value of mixed farming (Kanovsky, 1966: 105-106)

191

Table 5.1: Size of Branch[1] and Number of Permanent Members, Hofra, 1970[2]

| Branch[3] | (in dunam) | Input (including labor) (in IL) | Output (in IL) | Labor days (1969) (total) | Permanent members[4] |
|---|---|---|---|---|---|
| Chickens | - | 764,000 | 785,000 | 4,845 | 16 (including hatchery) |
| Citrus | 560 | 391,500 | 534,800 | 6,853 | 12 |
| Orchard | 525 | 430,200 | 492,500 | 5,645 | 10 |
| Cotton | 980 | 275,400 | 350,000 | 1,226 | 4 |
| Artichokes | 35 | 37,100 | 40,000 | 600 (1970) | 3 |
| Vineyard | 142 | 120,100 | 122,000 | 2,745 | 2 |
| Fish Ponds | 292 | 144,600 | 170,700 | 856 | 2 |

Source: Economic Plan for 2970, Hofra.

Labor Records, Hofra, 1969.

192

Table 5.2: Labor-days per Dunam Invested in Different Crops in 1968/9 and Estimated for 1969/70, Hofra

| Branch/Crop | 1968/9, Figures According to Table 5.1[5] | 1970, Estimates by Meshek Organizer |
|---|---|---|
| Citrus | 12.24 | 12 |
| Shamouti | | 11.5 |
| Valencia | | 12-13 |
| Clementines | | 15 |
| Blood Orange | | 10 |
| Densi | | 17 |
| Grapefruit | | 10 |
| Orchard | 10.75 | |
| Apples | | 12-13 |
| Plums | | 17 |
| Pecan | | 6-10 |
| Avocado | | 6 |
| Mango | | 12-15 |
| Persimmon | | 20 |
| Cotton | 1.25 | 1.5 |
| Artichoke | 6.32[6] | 12 |
| Vineyard | 19.33 | 22 |
| Fish | 2.93 | 2.9-3 |

Source: Table 5.1

Communication by the Meshek Organizer, 1970.

193

and diversification (Cohen, 1963) and partly to exploit the variable ecological conditions. The different crops require different inputs of labor. Various crops, usually related, may be cultivated by one branch. The branch, and not a particular crop, has become the organizational unit of labor. The different labor demands of different crops have brought about differences in the size of labor forces in branch units. Therefore, in conclusion, it is the size of branch in terms of labor which determines the size of the team, more than the other components of 'size,' such as land, input, or income - though the latter have a non-negligible influence.

But the suggestion that a higher demand for labor is readily met by the kibbutz's labor force where it is needed economically does not, in itself, lead to a concentration of permanent workers in the demanding branch. Since it is the permanent members who comprise the branch team, it means that a given size of a branch (in terms of labor required and even supplied) does not in itself entail a team of proportional size. Demand for labor as such is not sufficient to attract members to a branch, large as it may be. Members tend to seek permanence in a branch, the crops of which require labor throughout most of the year, rather than in branches from which they will have to move out during the slack season.

Some figures will clarify this statement. The kibbutz assumes, for its economical calculations, 25 labor-days a month per member. Table 5.1 gives information on total number of labor days invested in branches in 1968/9 (i.e., labor-days of all categories of workers in Hofra). If all the permanent members of the team of any given branch are occupied in their branch, then by dividing the amount of labor-days in a branch in a given month by the number of those permanent members, we should get at a number not smaller than 25, the higher figures representing labor of other categories of workers. Assuming that in a slack season workers who are not members are assigned to other branches and some members may take leave, the resulting number may be somewhat lower than 25. I should make the qualification that since not all the members take their leave at the same time, however, the figure should not be too remote from 25. Table 5.3 shows the difference, in this respect, between the various agricultural branches. I have selected for each branch the records of labor for the three months of lowest employment. By dividing the absolute numbers of labor-days by the number of members of the team we can realize how close, or remote, these branches are from the full-time employment figure (of 25); in other words, how close or far they are from being

194

able to offer permanence throughout the year. Obviously, if the figure (in column d/b in the Table) is much lower than 25, it means that the members of the team, or some of them, are employed elsewhere. Part-time employment in another branch when the latter is in need of help, would not in itself raise questions as to the position of permanence of a member in his own branch. But, if a member is forced, by the seasonality of a branch's crops, to look for alternative employment for a considerable period every year, the attraction of his branch would diminish. Three months a year, every year, working in a branch other than one's own (while other branches do not require their members to search for employment elsewhere) does raise questions as to the nature of one's permanence and the desirability of working in that branch.

Table 5.3 shows that the citrus grove and the orchard offer full year-round employment for the permanent members of their respective teams, thereby facilitating the latter's achievement of permanence. The figures of 21.2, 20.5 and 21.5 for the three months of low employment in the chicken branch do not fall far below the figure of 25. Indeed this is the branch least affected by the seasons, and even its foreman agreed that this branch suffers from redundancy rather than scarcity of workers.[7] The reader may keep in mind that this Table aims to show the effect of seasonal low demands for labor in the various branches on the permanence of members in them. It does not query productivity or efficiency within the branch, nor does it, nor indeed can it, study the pattern of recruitment of particular individuals to particular branches. The figures for cotton, artichoke, vineyard and fish show that these branches cannot offer employment for their own permanent workers for at least one quarter of the year. In terms of seeking permanence, these branches cannot be too attractive.

In conclusion, the size of the team of a branch is affected by two major variables: (a) the size of the branch in terms of demand for labor as determined by the composition of crops and the suitability of the latter to advanced technology, and (b) the ability of the branch to offer employment throughout most, if not all, of the year, rather than compelling the member to seek work in the labor assignment of the entire meshek.

Various crops within one branch in Hofra are usually related: the orchard includes deciduous crops; the grove is composed of citrus of various kinds and varieties; different varieties of grapes are grown in the vineyard; different varieties of cotton are grown within the same branch; and different

Table 5.3: Labor in Agricultural Branches per Permanent Member of Team, Hofra, 1968/9*

| Branch | Permanent members | Month I | | | Month II | | | Month III | | |
| a | b | Calendar month c | Labor days d | d/b | Calendar month c | Labor days d | d/b | Calendar month c | Labor days d | d/b |
|---|---|---|---|---|---|---|---|---|---|---|
| Chickens | 16 | November | 339 | 21.2 | August | 327 | 20.5 | September | 345 | 21.5 |
| Citrus | 12 | July | 367 | 30.5 | August | 383 | 31.9 | September | 357 | 29.7 |
| Orchard | 10 | February | 308 | 30.8 | April | 229 | 22.9 | May | 349 | 34.9 |
| Cotton | 4 | December | 2 | 0.5 | January | 3 | 0.75 | February | 4 | 1 |
| Artichoke | 3 | April | 42 | 14 | June | 16 | 5.3 | September | 35 | 11.7 |
| Vineyard | 2 | October | 32 | 16 | November | 8 | 4 | December | 3 | 1.5 |
| Fish Ponds | 2 | January | 45 | 22.5 | February | 17 | 8.5 | March | 28 | 14 |
| Flowers | 2 | December | 83 | 41.5 | January | 54 | 27 | February | 35 | 17.5 |

Source: Labor Records 1968/9, Hofra.

*See Tables 3.1 and 3.2.

196

groups of stock are raised respectively in the chicken-run and in the fish ponds. Exceptions to the rule are sub-tropical crops grown both in the orchard and in the grove for reasons to be explained below. These branches are not, therefore, what Cohen (Cohen, 1963: 385) calls 'roof branches', i.e., "the grouping of several independent branches into a new complex unit." They are still the same organizational units which were established when the crops were introduced to Hofra. If the term 'roof' is applicable here, the branch is 'a roof' for a variety of related crops, and all the team members work on the full range of crops.

Another implication in the above suggestion is that there is an objective limit on the number of members in a branch. The figures presented in Table 5.3, in particular those related to the smaller teams, show that the smaller branches only offer a very relative permanence, to a very few members. Whereas these branches - the vineyard (most notably), the fish ponds, the cotton (and even the vanishing gladioli and artichoke branches) - can offer employment to members during their peak seasons, their teams do try to get help from other member-workers, but they cannot meet the basic interests of the individual member. They cannot offer him stability in work in the branch. Very little labor is needed for, at least, the three slack months. A member who would like, for whatever reason, to attach himself to one of these branches must be prepared to be a transient worker for a considerable part of the agricultural year. The meshek may need this partly-transient labor force, but this is a situation in which the interest of the individual does not necessarily coincide with that of the meshek. Very few members, particularly those who are at the initial stage of their adult work, would tend to choose the role of a branch-man who must look for employment elsewhere for a considerable part of every year. The idea of forming a 'roof branch,' by combining the two different vineyard and fish pond branches, was raised by the Meshek Organizer. Neither of the two factors discussed by Cohen (1963)[8] was at issue. The Meshek Organizer believed that labor could be best used by channelling the slack season labor (see Table 5.3) of each of the branches into the others, i.e. making them 'complementary.' (The two branches neighbor one another.) He further suggested that by merging, or confederating them, new volunteers would choose to join the new branch. It is the interest of the meshek in maintaining branches which yield good income (particularly the fish) and the recognition of the interest of any individual member in permanence, without which no team can be organized to keep and develop a branch, that led to this suggestion. He apparently hoped that the merger would meet individual interests in maintaining the cyclical mobility of the workers within the same branch, and also that this merger would reverse the individual's disinclination to join the two branches in their present state. But, the suggestion had not been generally discussed, let alone implemented, by the time I left Hofra.

The agricultural branch-teams can be roughly categorized into the large teams (ten and more members) and small teams (four members or less). These figures by no means apply to meshakim other than Hofra, and their application to Hofra is possible because of its specific economic structure (i.e., the selection of crops, the allocation of land, water and other resources, preferences and priorities in selecting these crops, and the absence of other crops and animals which have either never been introduced or have vanished from the meshek, such as bananas, flower-bulbs, vegetables, wheat and cereal crops, bees and cows). Figures of different magnitudes would probably prove relevant to situations other than those prevailing in Hofra. But I hope to show that this division into rough categories of teams is relevant to the forthcoming analysis. The analysis will focus on the elements of the position of the individual member which emerge from the division of labor within the team. In this respect, the difference between the two categories of branch-team is qualitatively significant.

## Division of labor within a branch

The larger the team, the more developed is the division of labor within it. Conversely, the smaller the team, the more the occupational roles of its members tend to overlap because division of labor is not sufficient to offer - or enforce - distinct spheres of specialization, responsibility and authority for the individuals comprising the team. But I am only arguing here that this suggestion applies to the meshek of Hofra, and more specifically to its agricultural branches, and to its present level of technological skill.

The 'large' teams, like the whole of the meshek, are relatively small. Hence the division of labor cannot have developed much within the teams. The magnitude and the complexity of the agricultural economy of Hofra are not comparable, in these terms, to modern industries where both magnitude and complexity leave Hofra far behind. They are also different in quality because agricultural production in Hofra, entails a seasonal cycle of labor which calls, in turn, for various kinds of knowledge. Nevertheless, there has been differentiation between various branches and within the teams of the branches from Hofra's early settlement.

198

The system of the division of labor within the branch is a complex one. There is a division according to: (a) different plots of land and responsibility for them; (b) specialization and professionalization - scientific knowledge of the crops; (c) technological skill; (d) assignments; (e) physical efforts required for a job; and (f) involvement in managerial tasks.

In practice, however, there is no clear-cut distinction between these variables when labor is divided. They tend to cluster together and therefore to make analysis difficult. But these variables, used as analytical criteria in discussing division of labor in a branch, are indispensable, however mixed and interpenetrating they may be in practice. They constitute assets for the individual and components of his position in the sphere of labor. The very diversity of the economic structure of the meshek, the plurality of branches and crops, the variations in size of branch and team, and the emerging division of labor and allocation of responsibilities, point to the presence of differentiation. The prevalence and growth of the division of labor introduces differentiation amongst the members. Cohen applies to this the term 'role differentiation' (Cohen, 1962: 76). Although the various forms of division of labor in a branch function as mechanisms of further differentiation, and although they are different in content from one another, their common denominator is their amenability to analytical reduction to one theoretical framework. They form constituent elements of the position of the member and his social assets.

## Allocation of plots

### (a) Spatial division of labor - the chicken branch

One form of differentiation within the team is the 'horizontal' allocation of responsibility over different plots of land or buildings amongst members of the branch team. This form of allocation is most conspicuous in the poultry sheds and the citrus grove.

The poultry (or: chickens) branch is the largest of all in Hofra, both in terms of output (gross income) and of number of permanent members. The Economic Plan for 1969/70 estimated its expected income to total IL 785,000.-. The commercial enterprise comes next (IL 767,600.-). Of the agricultural branches, on which the present analysis is focused, it is the citrus grove which comes next with an output estimated at IL 534,800.-. However, the same plan estimated expenditures

for the poultry branch to total IL 764,000.-, leaving only
IL 21,000 for depreciation and profit. Assessment of the former
leaves the branch with practically no profit. Two main factors
account for this low profitability: (1) diseases at the time
(1969/70) and (2) a low level of productivity.[9] The latter
stems from the disproportionate number of workers to the size of
the branch. Hence the low level of output per labor day which
was affected also by the damage caused to the branch by fowl
diseases.

A team of 16 people work permanently in the branch, 4 of
whom work in the hatchery which constitutes a separate unit.
As for the remaining 12, the branch foreman estimated that for
the routine jobs to be carried out satisfactorily, 7 people
would suffice. Five workers are thus actually redundant, though
working full time in the branch, thereby lowering the rate of
productivity of the branch. Nevertheless, most of these 12
members have joined the team since the present (1970) foreman took
charge of the branch 17 years ago. They have all done so with
his approval, and even encouragement.

I cannot discuss the development of the branch and the team
in retrospect. But members of Hofra agree that the foreman was
"a person of imagination and of daring," using the former term
to denote both the positively-considered combination of far-
sightedness, inventiveness and vision and an unrealistic approach
to financial considerations. This combination of appreciation
and criticism ascribes to him the development of the branch as
well as its commercial and economic failures in the level of
productivity and to some extent the failure in the birds' health
conditions, all of which led to a decline in profitability.[10]
The foreman's field of interest is said to have included considerations which were not only limited to the economic profitability
of his branch. He also took an active interest in domains other
than economics and was involved, at times, in cultural, political
and other social activities. These other interests, it is said,
caused him to argue that the chicken-run could employ people
who were handicapped by age, health, or physical disabilities.
Furthermore, he maintained that although the role of productivity
of the branch might fall when people of limited ability worked
in it, their very work in a 'return-yielding' branch would
raise the productive output of the meshek as a whole to some, even
though a marginal, extent whereas no such effect would take place
were these members assigned to "services-to-man." The decline
of the rate of productivity of a branch was thus considered by
him against an expected marginal rise in income for the meshek
as a whole and against the distribution of labor force of the
membership between 'return-yielding labor' and the 'non-return

200

yielding labor.' He argued that a branch such as his was under
obligation to absorb individuals who could work in it while they
could not (or would not) work in another branch. The foreman,
whose main responsibility was supposed to involve productivity,
efficiency, competence of branch workers and skill, acted as a
protagonist of the whole kibbutz's interests even when these
diverged from those of his branch. Furthermore, the considerations to which he gave priority were not wholly economic even
though he used some economic arguments. Whatever his considerations, the outcome of this policy has been an increase in the
number of the members of the team. For this increase he has
been widely criticized in the community. As a branch foreman
he was expected to give priority to the economic considerations
and the development of the branch. This was his primary role.
It has been so regarded, of course, in situations in which the
economic aspects of the poultry branch have been discussed, and
mainly by those concerned with economic affairs. Again, although
I cannot discuss the subject in retrospect, it seems improbable
that the movement of individuals from other branches into the
poultry branch could take place without the knowledge and acquiescence of, if not active approval by, the very central labor authorities of the meshek, by whom critical comments have been expressed.
In a sense, the central officers of the meshek, whether by silent
approval or by an active encouragement, have shared the foreman's
responsibility. They do acknowledge the so-called 'social' aspect
of the problem (as distinct from, and in this case counter to,
the economic one) for the individuals, the meshek and the branch
by saying more than once "The foreman has indeed solved 'problems'
[referring to individuals] for The Kvutza." He would have
probably been criticized had he not offered employment for some
of the present workers of the branch. Expression of appreciation
and gratitude is usually rarer than the expression of their
opposites and when it is made, it is often accompanied by critical
comments. Nonetheless, in situations in which economic considerations do not take priority, appreciation has been. expressed.

The fact remains that twelve members who have joined
the branch at different stages of its development work in it
permanently. The relative larger number of workers has given
rise to a system of division of labor, of which the 'geographic'
allocation of tasks constitutes one form.

There are five buildings housing chickens, two batteries,
an egg store and a group of brooding homes, all clustered in
one large area. Roughly, each one of them is the responsibility
of one member. In addition, there is a group of old buildings
in another part of the 'camp-site' which used to house the branch.
This section serves as a regulatory agency and is used to

201

accommodate birds when necessary.  The routine work of the members
responsible for the different buildings consists of collecting
eggs four times a day.  (The more times and the more often eggs
are collected the higher the rate of eggs suitable for breeding.
A soiled egg becomes contaminated and is considered unfit for
breeding.)  The routine work also consists of cleaning water-
troughs, changing water, feeding, collecting dead birds, cleaning
the buildings and helping the team of seasonal workers who may
temporarily join the particular section the member concerned is
responsible for.  No work is done in a section of a branch,
usually co-terminous with a separate building, without the person
in charge of this section taking an active role in it.  He is consulted in advance and any expert work, if it be performed by
others, is co-ordinated with him.  It is 'his' section, so to
speak.

Two members work together in the egg store.  They steam,
clean and grade the eggs.  Another member takes charge of the
brooding homes into which chicklings are transferred from the
hatchery.  The egg store and the brooding homes are considered
as separate sections with the branch.  Thus within the branch
differentiation has developed between workers who are given
individual responsibility over particular sections defined spatially (though not exclusively so).  Other members of the branch
team may have other positions in the branch but not that of a
person in charge of a separate chicken-run.  There is a team
involved with the 'selection' section of the branch and a
seasonal insemination team, and there are some individuals who
have not been given charge over particular buildings.  This
division of labor within the branch, giving rise to individual
allocation of responsibility according to building-section,
also gives rise to differentiation between these individuals
as a category and the other workers.  The relation of this
division to the problem of refining elements in the constitution
of the position of the member in the sphere of labor can be
shown in the following events.

A special team is recruited for the insemination season.
In addition to the foreman and one other (who are considered
'permanent' in this team), three more people should be recruited.
Members in charge of chicken-run sections are often asked to
join the insemination team and move with it from one building to
another until the round is completed.  Recruitment of members to
carry out other forms of injection is also sought within the
branch team.  When a member is asked to join the injection team,
someone else must be requested to substitute for him in his own
section.  It has often happened that members in charge of

202

chicken-runs have refused to move from their particular sections. The usual argument is that as the member is substituted by another person, "Why should the person who is asked to substitute not be recruited to the temporary injection team in the first place?"

By clinging to 'his' section, even though the request is only to move within the branch for a short period, the member becomes further 'entrenched' in his section. He is not to be substituted for or by another. One may well keep in mind that in a large team almost everyone can be substituted. When a member falls ill, there is always someone within the branch team to substitute for him and likewise there is always someone to take over when he leaves for holidays, particularly when in the virtual state of redundancy not all the members of the branch team have particular sections under their personal responsibility. By pointing at those other members, and arguing that they should be recruited to the injection team, the individual who has a section under his personal responsibility reinforces his position of permanence in his 'own' section to the exclusion of others. He acts so as to solidify differentiation within the branch. This, taken collectively, is of course a by-product of the individual's effort to maintain his position in the branch. He is concerned with his own position, in his own section, and with his refusal to be substituted. He may indeed not be concerned at all with (or even conscious of) the outcome, namely the emergence of differentiation between categories of workers in the branch and the consolidation of the position of the individual who takes charge of a particular section.

The counterpart of this situation is the behavior of those who have been left without sections of their 'own' to run. Those of them who have no particular responsibility according to other forms of the branch's division of labor and whose assignment is to work in the chicken-branch 'at large,' keep asking the foreman for work to do. They are apparently concerned with the problem of daily output of labor, an output which is affected by the prevailing redundancy of workers in the various tasks within the branch.

They have no specialized asset to hold to in the branch division of labor, and hence hope to strengthen their personal position in the branch as a whole. Work itself is their asset in the sphere of work. In other words, while other members of the branch team derive elements of power, deterrent and otherwise, from the role allocated to them in the branch, a role which contains resources of a social position in work other than 'mere' work, these members, having no such roles, depend exclusively on their performance of work in maintaining their

203

position in the sphere of work. When their position in the sphere of work is assessed by others, sharing of management tasks, technological skill, scientific knowledge, and stake in a particular section cannot be taken into consideration. Only work itself, and permanence in and responsibility for, work can. This is, of course, an asset in a community which attaches a paramount value to work (Spiro, 1956: 10-19). But when a member enjoys other assets, such as the one derived from the 'horizontal' division of labor, his position is more powerful and requires more consideration on the part of the other people concerned.[11] These people, then, who have no access to resources other than work itself, keep asking the foreman for more work to do.

In Hofra people refer to this phenomenon in terms of the age idiom. One of the central functionaries of the kibbutz said to me, "The poultry branch represents the old-age appearance of an old kibbutz. The older member sticks strongly to work, unlike his younger counterpart. He is afraid of losing his place of work." The foreman, when discussing the phenomenon of members in the branch asking for more work and for additional assignments, has also classified them as the "aging members": "Look who keeps running and asking for work," he pointed out. "These are the older members. By so doing they combat aging." The interpretation in the community goes that while every member seeks permanence in work, if one's permanence in one's work is disrupted, one would look for permanence in another job or branch. Whereas a younger member would tend to select his future employment carefully, seeing to it that the nature of the new job would satisfy his interests in acquiring and retaining not only permanence in a branch, but some sort of expertise in, or control over, the new job, the aging person would be content with just securing a permanent employment in a branch so as to remain productive. It is much more difficult for an aging worker who has lost his job (either because the branch has ceased to exist or his particular job has become redundant or if he has decided himself to leave his occupation because of physical, personal or inter-personal reasons) to be selective than for his younger counterpart. He will accept occupations and jobs which he would not have accepted in his younger years. His wish to be productive overcomes misgivings he may feel in accepting employment which lacks the opportunities of getting some kind of control over his work, whether this control stems from knowledge, specialization, a managerial role or even responsibility over a section within the branch.

This interpretation by members of the behavior of people in the sphere of labor has its merits. It is well grounded in a society which places labor as a central tenet in its set of

values; which instigates mechanisms to control the behavior of
its members in this field; whose most ostensible resource of
economic existence and development is its members' work; which
passes judgments on individuals according to the latter's devotion
to, and to an extent performance of, work, so that an individual
member would tend to secure a position in this sphere for as
long as he is able to carry on in his work. If his position in
this sphere can no longer be enriched by assets related to 'mere'
labor, the member would tend to rely in his quest on the residual
component of this position, work itself.

This problem applies first and foremost to older members.
Members who have moved from permanent positions in branches into
other occupations, but have not accepted roles of responsibility
yet, and acquire a position of permanence in the new branch, are
mostly old-timers. Their devotion to work, as exemplified in
their consistent request for more work to do, is often stressed.
People appreciate it and praise their behavior. Some members
go as far as associating this behavior not only with age but with
the identity of their generation as well. This, they say, is the
generation of pioneers, of foundation layers, of those who have
put into practice the ideas of their youth movement, of the
kibbutz. These are people who simply cannot lead a full life
without being tied to work. In other words, there are members
who tend to interpret the behavior of these people in terms of
the latter's age and/or historical role in The Movement and the
kibbutz. (See also Levithan, 1976, particularly p. 53).

This interpretation is particularly significant when the
point of departure is the occupational fate of members who have
lost their jobs after having held them for many years. A long
attachment to a job or an occupation may entail difficulties in
finding a new job which will meet the personal requirements of,
and have advantages for, the individual concerned. A long
attachment to a branch or to an occupation may understandably
be linked to age. A cluster of variables such as health and
physical conditions, adaptability to new physical, technological
and scientific requirements of the new job, as well as communal
appreciation (or lack of it) and assessment of his skill - all
contained in the idiom of age - may affect the occupational
perspective of the individual who joins a new branch.

Most, but not all, of the members who have joined the
poultry branch in the last few years and who have no particular
responsibilities may indeed be old-timers, but that is not to
say that those who have those responsibilities are 'young.'
Some of them are of the same age, roughly, as the old-timers.

205

Age does constitute a factor in members' moving from one job to
another, in other branches as well as the chicken branch, but this
is one factor only (itself containing a variety of variables).  A
significant element in the approach of these members to labor lies
in their position in the branch itself.  Diligence and devotion may
be personal properties, sometimes regardless of the position in a
group, but in general they are not detached from the latter.  The
fact that those who are 'entrenched' in their sections, including
old-timers, do not sometimes try to extend responsibilities to
other sections within the branch, even when this seems necessary
and feasible to the branch foreman, while others seek more employment, can be explained in terms of the differential distribution
of responsibilities within the branch.  Some members are able to
consolidate their positions only through work wherever necessary
whereas others have access to other additional assets.  As stated,
one of these assets is personal control of a section.

The co-operation of the member in charge of a section with
his branch colleagues is essential for the branch.  Any action
taken in relation to his section must first be co-ordinated with
him.  The small example above, in which several members of the
poultry branch expressed complaint and dismay, shows that the
person who is in charge of a section not only can offer help,
encouragement and goodwill, but also can cause difficulties and
set obstacles.  The possibility of withdrawal of co-operation,
even to a limited and infrequent extent, lies at the base of his
position in the branch, as does his expected willingness to work
for the development and advancement of the branch.  In an analysis
of his position, this 'negative' aspect should not be overlooked.
His ideas as well as his behavior, and sometimes even his whims,
are taken into consideration by other members of the team, by the
branch foreman, and by the meshek officers.  One should not
exaggerate the power which lies in this individual's asset in the
functioning of the kibbutz, but it is present.

The story of the poultry branch shows that not only scarcity
of members contributes to the consolidation of the position of
the individual member in the sphere of labor, but even redundancy
may bring its share.  The difference, however, is that while
scarcity gives rise to differentiation between members of the
kibbutz and other categories of workers in terms of permanence
and its implications, redundancy of members in a given branch
introduces this kind of differentiation into the team of members
itself.  While some jobs in the branch proliferate so as to
engage more members in them, some members remain 'general workers,'
'help,' etc.  It is not only vis-a-vis the branch foreman and the
team as such that the individual in charge of a section consolidates his position; he does so vis-a-vis the 'help' as well.

## (b) Spatial division of labor - the citrus grove

Four plots, separated spatially from one another, comprise
the branch of the citrus grove. One, the old "Home Grove"
(planted on an area adjoining the 'camp-site' - hence its name)
covers 35 dunam; another, covering 68 dunam, is planted in the
Wadi Kubani Area; the third plot is detached from the main land
of Hofra. Various deciduous crops as well as sub-tropical
fruits were planted on this plot together with citrus. The
fourth grove was planted in Gderoth Area which was allotted to
Hofra after the 1948/49 war, and faces the Eastern Spout. Some
201 dunam are planted there with citrus. Altogether there are
approximately 500 dunam of citrus.[12] (See Map 1.)

The branch team consists of twelve members. The 'horizontal'
division of labor, i.e., the allocation of responsibility for
plots to individuals, is far from rigid. Most of the members of
the team move from one plot to another when necessary, following
labor requirements entailed by seasonal fluctuations. A single
branch foreman co-ordinates the activities of the team in all
the plots. But elements of spatial, or territorial, division of
labor can be discerned in this branch as well. The Wadi Plot is
not under the specific authority of any one of the team. All
work done there is co-ordinated and planned by the branch foreman
and the members come and work there whenever it is deemed necessary. The Gderoth Area is considered as being under the personal
supervision of Oreg (G2), an old-time member of the team. When
Oreg, a veteran citrus worker in the citrus groves of the Jewish
'colonies' joined Hofra, he was already experienced in this field.
His 'managerial' role seems to consist mainly of giving expert
instructions and of having intimate knowledge of the area. His
advice is often taken by the team. He does work in other plots,
together with other members of the team, but his main concern
lies in the Gderoth Area. He has been involved, comparatively
more than others, with the history of the grove in this area,
and with its development, cultivation and care. It is inconceivable
that any move concerning the area would be taken without first
consulting Oreg. Most of the work to be done in this area is
carried out under his supervision.

The 'Home Grove' situation is different. One member, Olami
(G4), works there permanently, usually with a hired worker, himself
considered permanent in the branch and to an extent in the plot.
Olami's attachment to the 'Home Grove' seems to be unbreakable.
His management of the plot shows that he regards the citrus branch
as a loose confederation. He notifies the branch foreman of his
demands concerning equipment, transport of fruit, labor, and tools.
He expects the branch foreman to provide his plot with all the

services it requires.  He considers the foreman as an agent who
should see to it that necessities are met.  But within the plot
it is he who organizes work, who allocates tools and equipment
(he keeps a store in a hut within the plot apart from the branch
store in Gderoth), who supervises all the work done, particularly
that of the temporary workers, transients and hired laborers.  In
addition to these jobs, he checks twice a day the presence of all
workers, whose assignment to the plot is reported to him in
advance - to the amusement and (critical) grinning of his colleagues, who find it an absolutely unnecessary waste of time and
a showy pretence.  One of the old-timers in the branch has commented, "I have been wondering for years why Olami behaves in
this strange way.  It is childish, is it not, to walk around with
the notebook open so as to prove to everybody that you are the
boss.  Then I have realized that childish as it may be, this is
exactly the point: he must be a boss.  He must prove it ostensively to everybody.  Management should not only be practiced,
he thinks, it should be seen.  Whether the responsibility for
this plot is actually management to begin with, is a different
matter..."  Members tend to accept his behavior.  Because they
know him personally in communal contexts other than the grove,
they regard his manners in the grove as an extension of his
otherwise naive, good-hearted, but stubborn, total personality.
The tendency to judge the individual as a total personality, as
revealed in the total social context of the community, and to
define it in terms of his 'mental' qualities, may be seen quite
clearly in this case.  This helps members to dismiss his behavior while in fact accepting the essence of his conduct.  At the
same time it helps him to build up his seemingly curious position
in the meshek as an 'organizer' ("merakkez") on his own.  It is
not my intention to discuss, nor to question, the psychologically-
defined assessment of Olami shared by members of Hofra, let alone
to suggest an alternative explanation, in these terms, of his
conduct of affairs.  What I am stressing is the systematic build-
up of Olami's position in the branch (and, indirectly, in the
meshek) as a person who maintains control over a particular plot
within the grove which is a branch owned by the meshek and
managed by the branch foreman.  He pays the price, just as Olya
pays hers in the way she conducts, or misconducts, her management
of her job in the office, but he has maintained his position.
'Funny' he may appear, but the control, at least partly, is his.
Unlike Olya, his conduct has not been considered as causing harm
or damage to anybody personally or to the meshek's interests, nor
has he hurt anybody.  This control can therefore be tolerated.

The degree to which he controls the plot can be observed
not only in the daily routine of work in it.  Some people may
accept ceremonial displays of authority on the assumption that

they represent no significant authority. By accepting or toler-
ating these displays of daily demonstration of supervision from
Olami, they may free themselves from the need to respond to
appearance rather than to substance. In a sense they respond,
"Let the 'elderly child' now arise and play before us" (following
II Samuel, 2, 14) - as long as Olami's display creates no particular difficulties and as long as his devotion, responsibility and
diligence are helpful and to the advantage of the branch. Co-
operation on the part of the team with a ceremonial authority,
particularly with a self-assumed authority, may benefit both
parties as well as the branch itself. And if the individual in
question does hold a degree of control, it entails no necessary
adverse effect for others. Yet the degree of Olami's control can
be seen in the following event.

The 'Home Grove' is the oldest citrus plantation. It was
planted in the mid-1930s and has passed its peak of profitability.
The members of the grove's team argue that it should have been
uprooted and the plot replanted long ago. Yet, the old grove
has survived these threats, even though they came from 'within'
the team, and routine work goes on in it as usual: oranges are
picked; the trees are pruned and watered, the area ploughed, and
spraying etc. goes on. Members of the team argue that although
the grove should have been replaced, they cannot carry out this
economically sound idea because Olami is in the way. He would
not listen to reason. He would not let them do it. The grove is
still fruitful, he claims, and as long as it goes on yielding
fruits it will continue living. He agrees that his grove has
passed its peak period, but insists that it is still worthy of
care as long as it yields fruits. Other members of the team
Oreg in particular, argue that the data on the fruitfulness of
the plot are confused and even misleading. The citrus grove
is fruitful as a whole, but it is the large quantities of citrus
fruits grown in Gderoth which cover up the virtual decline of
the 'Home Grove.' And, they all agree, when asked, that if not
for Olami, the area would be replanted. The extent of Olami's
control thus seems to exceed by far the ceremonial daily routine
of management ascribed to him. One may go as far as to say that
it is the fate of the plot that is controlled by him. He is not
the only one in control of this fate: there are the members of
the team, the foreman, and the meshek authorities, but the
controversy over 'his' plot shows that he has control. The plot
has survived because of his control.

In discussing this issue one cannot escape the doubt that
the case is not quite so simple as it appears. Firstly, were
the old grove uprooted, it is unlikely that another person would
have taken over Olami's charge. If that is so, he struggles not

only to secure his control over the 'Home Grove,' because it is
almost certain that he would have been called to take charge of
the replanted plot, but he must also be motivated by considerations irrelevant to the economic interests of the branch or even
the future management of the plot. Whatever his motivations are,
and these are beyond the scope of this analysis, some of the considerations he does express are based on emotional arguments which
are regarded by his fellows as irrational. The 'Home Grove' is
said to have been planted and cared for by his close relative who
died years ago. Olami is said to regard the grove as the 'life
project' of his late relative to the memory of whom he seems to
devote emotional energy, respect and loyalty. These considerations
are regarded as irrational in the economic context, yet in the
complex set of social relationships in the kibbutz, the collective,
in its rational response, cannot ignore such considerations simply
by dismissing them as 'irrational.' They may be considered to be
irrational on the part of Olami, but in considering the situation in the branch and considering the persons involved in making
so important a decision as uprooting the trees and replanting the
plot, the collective must assess the situation rationally. The
collective may be the team, the kibbutz, or any authorized body
within the kibbutz.

What emerges is that irrational behavior by one of the
partners to a controversy, or what is considered to be irrational
argument in the course of a public controversy, becomes a variable
to be considered by other partners in a rational assessment of the
situation and of the issue. Since Olami's views are well known;
and since he is persistent in expressing them, though not necessarily in formal situations; and since his views are consistent
with his behavior in the branch, his reaction to a major decision
in relation to the future of the grove can well be taken into a
rational consideration. So far no decision adverse to his interest
(as he conceives it) has been taken. In fact, no decision has been
taken at all. Members explain this state of virtual non-decision
by employing the argument that it is exceedingly difficult to
confront rationally an essentially irrational argument which is
coupled with an emotional attachment to the plot. By so doing
they, in fact, help to strengthen Olami's position of control over
the plot.

I am convinced that the team, as well as the meshek as a
whole, could have made a decision had either considered this to
be of major importance. Personal, social and even sociological-
type, considerations do interfere with economic ones,[13] but the
scope of this interference is limited. Within the sphere of the
'return-yielding' section of the economy of the kibbutz, weight is
laid on considerations of economy and efficiency. Whole branches

210

have vanished from Hofra's economy, as well as from other kibbutzim, with or without the approving agreement of the members most directly engaged in their work. Their disappearance from the meshek did not take place without a decision to that effect being taken by the kibbutz. The organizational institutions of Hofra could, then, make a decision even against Olami's wishes despite the stir, the uneasiness and the strain that such a decision might arouse. It seems, therefore, that in addition to the consideration mentioned earlier and indicated here, namely, the wish to avoid inevitable strain on direct personal relationships and on complex sets of relationships in the kibbutz, another variable has played a role in restraining people from coming to a decision. By alluding to Olami's 'idiosyncracies' and position, members can shrug off responsibility and make an excuse for not making a decision. Olami, in turn, is only too anxious to take this responsibility, at least morally. The state of indecision has again helped, in turn, to consolidate his position in the branch at least in the short run: for his prospects of taking charge of the new grove which eventually will have to be planted unless the whole grove is abandoned, cannot increase in the course of his aging. His opinion has been accepted without a formal debate and the state of indecision, in the continuation of which he is interested, is attributed to his personal attitude. Thus the interplay between the team and Olami, whether looked at from the viewpoint of the team or otherwise, has led to his position being strengthened.

Discussion of the third plot introduced another dimension of the 'horizontal' allocation of responsibility within the branch. In a way, this discussion resembles that in the previous chapter of the case of Yardeni, in that it explains this mode of division of labor in an economic branch in terms of the wider context of the kibbutz community. The relevance of a person's position in the community at large for the treatment he gets from his branch colleagues has been partly touched upon in discussing Olami's role in the branch. It comes more to the fore in the following case.

For many years Ozer (GI), one of the founders of The Kvutza and of Hofra, has worked in the citrus grove. His familiarity with and knowledge of citrus preceded the settlement of The Kvutza in the Valley and the planting of Hofra's independent grove. He acquired his knowledge of and skill in citrus growing while working in The Colony (See Chapter II). The historical records of Hofra provide evidence that he can justifiably be considered as the founder of the citrus branch. In the course of time he has acquired expertise in this field and has become a central figure in the branch. At the same time he has been active in a wide range of spheres in the kibbutz: in economics, labor and education

in particular. He has acquired general respect and is considered
to measure up to the highest communal moral standards. Members
point out that despite his advanced age he is still active in
work in the branch as well as in communal public life.

In the 1950s he lost his son. The young man was Hofra's
second casualty in the Arab-Israeli war (the first was killed in
a battle during the 1948 War of Independence). Ozer's son was
the second, but the first child born in Hofra to die in the
hostilities.

Ozer came up with a request: he asked the kibbutz to let him
launch a new project to commemorate his son. He wanted, according
to the records, to set up a memorial which would be named after
the deceased but which would 'live' in the meshek, not just a
monument, a garden corner or a building which would be, in a sense,
all 'dead' objects. Ozer wanted a project which would be a living
and ostensible contribution to the development of Hofra. Along
with the well-established Zionist (and hityashvut)[14] cultural idiom,
the nature of the project was meant to be 'The Appropriate Response'
to killing and destruction - further development. Furthermore, he
wanted the project to be such that he himself would be able to take
part in it, probably the leading part. A new grove was to be
planted in an area hitherto only extensively cultivated. Ozer
asked the kibbutz to name the new grove after his dead son. Understandably, Ozer decided to devote his time and energy to this new
grove and run it as an independent project.

The kibbutz consented, though not without hesitation. Perhaps the fact that the deceased was included in the almost-sacred
category of Israel's dead warriors was a decisive variable in the
decision; perhaps it was the fact that he was the first casualty
of war (in the Israeli, Bible-based idiom, 'victim' or 'sacrifice')
of the children born in Hofra. This introduced an element of
shock as it was the first personal acquaintance of the members
with death as a real, and not merely imminent, implication of the
national war. Or - another aspect of the same problem - perhaps
it was the public request of the father, the first father in Hofra
to lose his son in the context of a national cause, that forced
the community to overcome its insistence on egalitarian treatment
of its people, in death perhaps as well as in life. Members of
the kibbutz overcame their apprehension that such a move might
introduce differentiation in the treatment of the dead people of
the community; that it might call for subsequent requests, similar
in principle, on the part of relatives in other situations; that
it might set a precedent which Hofra would not be able to follow.
They had to overcome the fear that future initiative to commemorate members, particularly of the second generation, would be

recognized, by the public consent to Ozer's request, as first and foremost the personal task of the closest relatives. It was not only the abdication of responsibility on the part of the kibbutz as a whole which worried the members; but they were also conscious of the fact that the members of the kibbutz, while enjoying a very high degree of equality in the kibbutz, cannot individually offer equal contributions to the commemoration of the people dearest to them: children, parents, relatives, close friends, etc. Obviously, there are not always resources available for introducing a new branch or establishing a new building or monument; not always is there an Ozer to take such initiative and not always can one draw the line between categories of the dead. Nevertheless, their consent was given. Perhaps considerations pertaining to the living, and not only to the dead, operated in the process of making the decision; perhaps the promising prospects of economic growth, boosted by an enthusiastic initiative, played their part; and perhaps social and kinship relationships were also at the background. And one should not overlook the 'simple' explanation, that people were convinced by the merits of the cause itself. The fact remains: the kibbutz consented and the third plot was planted. Ozer has taken charge of the plot and the grove is officially named after his son.

Thus considerations which are mainly relevant to the community at large and to the position of individuals in it have brought about an important enterprise in the economic field. They overcome worries in the community as well as apprehension amongst the branch team. They have affected the internal division of labor within the branch as a prominent member of the team has concentrated his efforts, knowledge, expertise and other assets on the new project. And it has contributed to further 'horizontal' division.

The planting of the new plot has boosted the process of this division by yet another step. Crops such as sub-tropical varieties and pecan nuts, usually planted and cared for within the framework of the orchard branch, were introduced in this plot. Undoubtedly suitability of soil in, and climatic factors affecting, the parcels of land within the plot on which these crops were planted were taken into consideration. Yet, the planted plot as a whole, with the exclusion of unplanted areas within it, is a branch framework, autonomous in relation to both the citrus grove and the orchard branches. The plot is considered to be a part of the citrus-grove branch. Harvesting, transport, cultivation, spraying and so forth, jobs which cannot all be done by Ozer and his one associate, are co-ordinated and regulated by the branch foreman and team; but when it comes to the crops which are conceived as belonging to the orchard branch (and they do grow in the orchard), the orchard-team steps in. The orchard-team mans the jobs on demand and when

213

necessary supplies the equipment. The supervision over all work
in the plot, planning of details, initiatives which result in
large-scale co-ordination by the branch foreman, remain with Ozer.
The need for inter-branch co-ordination and the work of members
of two different teams in the same plot though on different crops
inevitably enhances the autonomy of the workers of this plot,
particularly Ozer's, in their relationships with the rest of the
team.

The history of Hofra and of the citrus grove is not,
relatively speaking, very long. Ozer is one of the founders of
The Kvutza and Olami and Oreg, old-timers themselves, are the
members who are personally involved in the process of the growing
autonomy within the branch. People in Hofra, and certainly within
the branch team, have a living memory of events associated with
this process and they tend to interpret this process in terms of
the personalities involved. But the process, if all the events
discussed here are linked to a process, as I suggest, surpasses
the persons with whom its inception was associated. At present,
two young members of the team, Yahli (G11) and Yarimi (G10),[15]
are attached respectively to Oreg and Ozer and to the plots under
their respective responsibility. They share work and some of
these responsibilities with their seniors and are regarded as
permanent in these plots. There is every intention, so I was
told by the branch foreman, that they will go on sharing their
responsibilities in the future and remain permanent in their
respective plots. Not only do they work within this framework
of division of labor, but they are also expected to carry it
through in the future.

I have no space to give more illustrations or to elaborate
the issue further. I have chosen to discuss the incidents in
relation to the spatial division of labor. I have shown that
this form of division can be related to scarcity as well as
redundancy of permanent workers, to personal positions in the
community in general, and to specific events in the branch.
Whatever it is related to, there are two general features discernible in it in Hofra: (a) it emerges in large branches (large in
terms of labor invested in them); and (b) it emerges in branches
where the contiguity of the various constituent plots or buildings
is broken. The buildings of the chicken branch are separate from
one another; the plots of the citrus grove are distant from one
another. The whole large branch of the orchard (525 dunam), on
the other hand, is planted on a contiguous area in the Gderoth Area.
There is a division of labor within the branch team, but a clear
spatial pattern of division is absent.

214

I have shown further how this form of division of labor strengthens the position of the member who takes responsibility over a specific unit within the framework of the branch. It does so by providing that member with a measure of control over that unit as defined spatially. In other words, the division itself provides open access to resources of control. The spatial division opens access to the pattern of control described and discussed in previous chapters, and other types of division and their effect on the position of individuals will be discussed below.

### Assignments to different jobs

Other types of division of labor are encapsulated in the simplest form of division, other than the spatial: the assignment of members to different tasks according to the requirements of the crops. More accurately, they take these tasks. Their performances complement one another in relation to the overall work of the branch, which is divided so that in effect the division secures a maximum of permanence for an individual in a particular task.

But some clarifications are necessary here. I do not refer to occasional assignments to different tasks. Contingencies always have a considerable weight in planning of work in the branch and in agricultural work in general. They can only be met if people move from their previously assigned jobs to more urgent tasks. Rain, hail, wind, sharav, a docks strike, difficulties in transport, damaged equipment and the like, constantly force members, no matter how permanent they are in their jobs, to participate in a concerted effort to cope with the difficulties by leaving their own assignments for others. Frequently a member will do so on his own without being involved in a group effort. But notwithstanding the frequent occurrence of such events, they are occasional.

For, I repeat, the allocation of different jobs within the branch has a tendency to be permanent, running for years, as it has in irrigation or spraying against insects in the citrus-grove. Therefore permanence in a job within the branch is highly relative. The member who irrigates every year is permanent in irrigation - during the summer; the member who sprays against insects does so, perhaps, throughout the year, but at various intervals. The same remark applies to those engaged in pruning, or sorting fruits, or sowing, or the like. But in other seasons they are engaged in other tasks. This pattern of permanence is, then, a pattern of returning to the same jobs in successive seasons or at regular periods one year after another within the branch.

215

In the small branches, where division of labor is not developed, the roles of workers obviously overlap. In the larger branches different jobs are allocated to different workers (subject to the classifications set out above). But that is not to say that every individual is given a unique job, a job from which everyone else is excluded. Some members may share the same job. A few members may be engaged together in picking fruits while other members may be irrigating and yet others may be driving or doing some other work. Nonetheless, the fact is that not all the members of the team perform the same job. They do not all share the same job at the same time and in tending to keep doing their own jobs in successive seasons they virtually exclude themselves from the jobs performed by their other colleagues. Thus, the division of labor within the branch is not, and cannot be, as rigid as the division of labor between branches. Hence a pattern of division of tasks emerges within the team which gives rise to mutual exclusion of members from various jobs. It is not a total exclusion, but the pattern is there.

In the orchard at the peak season the members of the team reach the sharpest division of labor. They must cope with different demands at the same time (See Table 3.1, Chapter III). Different members are engaged respectively in picking apples; picking first sub-tropical fruits, such as persimmon and pecan; irrigating; spraying; transporting the fruits within the orchard into the packing shed; transporting the fruits to regional packing-posts and to the market and to refrigeration-stores, and so on. Every member tends to take the same jobs every year. This, in principle, applies in the citrus grove. If in the small branch members of the team tend to share the same tasks and perform the same jobs, in the larger branches the tendency is to specialization.

Viewing the branch as a whole, it is possible to suggest that the roles of the team members complement one another in a concerted service to the branch. To borrow Durkheim's terminology (Durkheim, [1893] 1964), the overlapping tasks taken by workers of small branches give rise to a 'mechanical' organization of the branch whereas the more elaborate division of labor in bigger teams give rise to an 'organic' type of branch organization. The co-operation among the team members in a small branch, without necessarily presupposing amity between any two or more co-operating actors, is 'mechanical' because it is based on the similitude of the tasks they take and the jobs they do. The tasks which members of a larger branch take and the jobs which they perform complement one another while the tasks themselves are different from one another, hence their cooperation itself is 'organic.'

216

Viewing, again, the team as a whole, I suggest that both patterns, the 'mechanical' and the 'organic', contribute to a degree of equality amongst the members of the team. But the equality within each pattern is of a different nature. In the small branch virtually every member of the team has access to the resources of the branch. I refer thus to those elements which can be used as resources for establishing a social position in the sphere of labor. Work as such, performance in the field of work, is such a resource. (See the discussion above of the workers in the chicken branch.) Knowledge of the different aspects of the branch's work (the crops themselves, and service to and use of the crops) is another. Use of equipment and technological skill is yet another, and so is sharing in the management and running of the branch. In a small branch, though - to be sure - access to all these resources is not <u>totally</u> equal, every member has a chance of gaining access to them. The branch cannot survive for long if the few members who work in it cannot, for lack of access to most if not all of these resources, work together or substitute for one another. The small size of the branch does not give rise to a highly elaborate specialization and to a variety of jobs. It is essential for the running of the branch that each permanent worker know the different tasks. It is essential that the members of the small team are able to meet contingencies by substituting for one another. Members may be unequal in ability, in talent, in ambition or in willingness to make use of the access to the various resources available to all permanent workers. They may prefer interests in fields other than the branch or the sphere of labor altogether. Some members may attempt to control some of the resources so as to block access to them by others. Nevertheless, if the branch is to endure and to develop, access to these resources must be open, and this contributes to equality amongst members.

The role of the 'organic' pattern is different. The organic pattern by its nature enhances differentiation (Cohen, 1962: 76). Each member of the team gains access to <u>different</u> resources in the branch. Work itself is different in different tasks. Skill in irrigating in the orchard or in the grove is different from the skill required for picking fruits or driving a vehicle. In acquiring knowledge of one job the member leaves his colleague to acquire detailed knowledge of another job. The more jobs are in demand and the more they are done by different people, the further advanced the 'role differentiation' (Cohen: 1962 ) within the team. But this differentiation itself, which introduces elements of inequality, contributes at the same time a degree of equality in a different sense. It is not an equality which stems from access to similar resources but an equality which stems from access to different resources. Access to resources which is available to one with the relative exclusion of others from these resources is,

217

in principle, available to any one, to the exclusion of some others. Only the resources are different. Thus, it is not the resources which are shared more or less equally by the members of the team which are crucial in analyzing the present problem but the availability, in principle, of access to resources which themselves are different from each other.

Perhaps viewing this problem from another angle will clarify the position taken in relation to the present problem. I have stated more than once that I do not regard all the members of the team as equal in all respects. The very discussion of the term of 'equality,' which connotes a variety of meanings and interpretations, sometimes conflicting with one another, may lead this discussion to problems well beyond my subject. But the problem remains: in what sense are members of a branch team equal, in relation to the branch division of labor?

They are equal in being members of one group on whom authority is bestowed, and indeed duty is imposed, by the kibbutz as a whole, which owns the meshek, including the branch. They have to "come together occasionally to carry out some collective action" (Radcliffe-Brown, 1950: 41). This is an aspect of a corporate group. The members of a branch team to "come together... to carry out some collective action." Other elements of corporate behavior in the branch team were, in fact, shown in the previous chapter, when the team's actions in relation to the individual vis-a-vis the community were discussed. Another aspect of a group endowed with corporate properties is the equality of its members qua members. They need not be equal in terms other than their equal access to membership. Within the group and in other contexts they may differ. Their status of membership in the group modifies, or affects, differences and differentiation in relevant situations.

The team "controls [though it does not own as a group] property which is collective" (Radcliffe-Brown: 1950:41), another respect of corporateness. But in controlling the branch as a group the team makes the second step: it makes available access to the different resources to those who are its members. Being a member of a large team promotes the chance that access to some resources, the control of which is not equally shared by all, will be open. In short, equality of members of a team, besides being derived from membership in the kibbutz, which is its premise, is equality in the sense of membership in a corporate body; and once this dual nesting membership is established, it also entails equal access to resources not individually controlled by other members of the team. I hope that in the course of the discussion the argument will become clearer since these theoretical points are as yet only premises.

218

First, I must emphasize that when I discuss both the
'organic' and the 'mechanical' patterns of branch organization,
it is not my intention to discuss branch cohesion, a problem
which is tempting to tackle, even if only for its association
with the terms borrowed from Durkheim. This problem is discussed
by Cohen (fully in Cohen 1962 and 1963a and partly 1963b) and
touched upon by Rosner (1964). I cannot do it in the space I
have for the discussion of my central problem, the position of
the individual.

The analysis of the position of the individual in the
'organic' pattern thus adopts a dialectical course: at the bottom
there is the fact of differentiation caused by an elaborate
division of labor. Thus, when one searches for features in the
'organic'-type of organization of labor which are relevant to the
role of the individual member of the team, within differentiation,
one's observation is focused on the common denominator. But one
of the properties of the common denominator itself is the availability of different resources to different members within the
single framework of the branch in successive seasons. It is
generally in the interest of the individual member to secure a
position in this division of labor which is independent of, and
different from, positions of other members. This position, in
turn, seemingly centrifugal in nature, bears significance only
in the social context of the group itself. In other words, it
is against the background of one branch that differentiation
emerges and often sought by members. And it is against the background of 'role differentiation' (Cohen, 1962: 76) that we can
look for the features shared in common by the members who take
different assignments.

The repercussions of the difference between the two types
of division of labor on the individual can best be discussed if
observation is made on branches which give rise to either type.
Although the main attention of the present discussion is concentrated on the more elaborate type of division of labor, this
pattern itself can be better understood if contrasted with its
counterpart.

## The 'One-man' Branch

There are a few one-man branches: an equipment and
incoming-cargo store, intra-meshek transport (whose task is to
deliver goods within the meshek), landscaping, and a children's
farm. The latter is attached to the local school and children
work in it together with the member in charge. There are two
other branches,[16] the carpentry and the shoemaker's store, in
each of which only one member works, but both employ hired workers

219

permanently and cannot therefore be regarded as one-man branches. The local electrician used to follow this pattern, but a new member has joined him, thus eliminating this branch from the present list. Essentially, these branches can reasonably be regarded as services to the meshek or services to the kibbutz, although the shoemaker, and to an extent the carpenter, do render services to the individual. A purely service-to-man branch is the local store in which members get their personal goods (such as toilet and home requisites, sweets, cigarettes, etc.) according to choice within a fixed individual budget.

In a one-man branch the member controls all the controllable resources. I say "controllable" because he (or she) cannot control all aspects of the branch. Quotas for shoes, for example, are decided upon in the elected bodies of the entire community and not by the shoemaker; the limits within which an individual may acquire goods are decided annually by the Assembly and not by the store-keeper; the goods and equipment for the agricultural branches are initially ordered by the relevant branch and purchased by the kibbutz's Purchase Organizer who directs them to the central store for further delivery. It is indeed the duty of the member in charge of such a service to deliver the ordered goods to the branch or to meet applicants' requests, if the latter do not violate regulations of the kibbutz. In this sense he is under control of his clients. Nonetheless, the range of resources under his control is large. To mention some of them which have already been mentioned: performance in work is determined solely by himself; knowledge of particulars remains with him; routine determination of priorities; the manner in which the service is rendered; the method in which it is carried out; and so forth, are all controlled by him. This is indeed a wide range of control, though, as I will show presently, it has its drawbacks as well. But taking responsibility for all the tasks which one person is expected to accomplish means that this one person must perform different jobs in one office.

To avoid devoting unwarranted space to this problem I give only one illustration. The landscaping man is responsible for all the gardening in Hofra, i.e. for both the central, communal, lawns and landscaping sites and for the other gardens which adjoin public agencies (such as children's homes, the cultural center and other buildings). In addition, he supplies plants for the private gardens around members' homes. Needless to say, he is supposed to combine knowledge, skill, ability, organizational competence, and the art of public relations. He must co-ordinate the different daily and seasonal tasks so as to be able to cope with all his responsibilities. Daily he mows the lawns, irrigates (a task which requires

constant shifting of pipes), prunes, rakes, weeds and removes
rubbish.  In a sense, the combination of his jobs is the division
of labor in an embryonic form.  Indeed, when he does get help,
usually from a transient assigned to his 'branch' by the Labor
Distributor, the emergence of division of labor is immediately
discerned.  Some of the jobs are assigned to the temporary worker
whereas others he retains for himself.

Obviously, it is not only the competence to deal with
different undertakings combined in his single branch up to which
he must live, and therefore it is not only his responsibility for
his different tasks which counts.  He also exerts control over
the performance of work; he determines the priorities in the order
of accomplishing the different jobs, an order of performance that
may often determine the very fate of the task; he can establish
the desirability of introducing a particular variety of flowers
or plants because he controls (or is authorized to control) knowledge of the problem; by co-ordinating periods of irrigation he
controls the use of the lawns during people's leisure; he distributes plants to private gardens, and so on and so forth.  So,
although he is under constant pressure to meet all requirements
of the branch, he has a considerable control over the resources
of the branch.

Perhaps an index of the extent of his control can be discerned in the constant grumbling about him, and sometimes the
open complaining against him, throughout the community.  When
pressed, they give the impression that it is his control with
which they are dissatisfied.  In fact, the more the control over
the branch is concentrated in one person, the more liable he is
to be criticized and complained about.  That is, the greater the
control by an individual, the greater the uneasiness which spreads
and is expressed amongst people.

This applies to others besides the gardener.  It applies,
though in different manners, to the electrician, the carpenter,
the store-keeper and their like.  The forms of grumbling and
criticism are different as the persons concerned are different
from one another in their individual as well as their social traits.
I cannot get involved in the whole variety of factors which operate
to modify the forms in relation to the different persons involved.
But none of these people is free from being criticized and complained against.  And the extent of grumbling and complaining seems
to stand in direct proportion to the extent of the branchman's
control over his branch.  Members are reluctant to be dependent
as clients, on the management and the manners of one person.  The
ultimate dependence of the branchman on the community and on the
collectivity of all its members is not immediately realized, but

the dependence of the individual member and of an individual branch, both as clients, on the branchman is direct and immediate, and fully realized. The grumbling, although usually expressed in reference to personal traits[17] (such as industriousness or its absence, general responsibility or irresponsibility, generosity and its opposite, honesty, goodwill and the like), reflects the reluctance of people to stand permanently in client-type relationships with the same person who, in other contexts, is a fellow member. Moreover, it reflects reluctance to grant the wide range of control he has on resources they value (Schelling, 1963: 3-4, 6-7). His permanence in this position adds intensity to this state of uneasiness. An incumbent of such a position can reduce resentment if he (a) is aware of the situation; (b) is capable of handling public relations; and (c) acts according to his awareness and renders his services as industriously and efficiently as he can. But reducing resentment and reluctance does not eliminate the problem.

It should be noted that the 'right to permanence' is relevant here as it is relevant to other branches. A carpenter, an electrician, a driver or a store-keeper of equipment is not different, in this sense, from an orchard man, a tractor driver or a fisherman. This 'right,' in turn, modifies and eases the criticism expressed of them. Again, in turn, the channelling of resentment and uneasiness mostly in a controlled form of criticism, such as gossip, in addition to its function in facilitating the maintenance of interpersonal relationships with the criticized, indirectly controls the incumbent (Gluckman, 1968: 31). Although he may not always be present when criticized, there are methods of bringing home to him his fellow-members' resentment and criticism; while sometimes he is informed by members about what they think of his conduct.[18] But at the same time this restrained type of resentment is, in a sense, an advantage for the incumbent. He is not under the imminent danger of direct confrontation and the possible loss of his job.

A possible means by which the public can further ease the control of one individual over resources of value to members or to branches is by introducing into the relationships of control and dependence an element which will change the relationship. This can be done if the element referred to is one which unmistakenly introduces, in turn, dependence of the incumbent on his client (Emerson, 1962: 31-37). As I have said, it does not alter the relationship radically: it does not strip the incumbent of a large measure of control, but it does ease the extent of this control. One such means is the institutionalization of some of these positions as elected posts. The public office, as this post is recognized to be once it is decided that the incumbent be elected, is not

permanent and no member can have a claim to permanence in it.
The incumbent has to be elected by a popular vote for a limited
period after which he is replaced or re-elected, again by popular
vote (sometimes in secret ballot).  Some kibbutzim have practiced
this institutional pattern.  In Kibbutz Hardoof the keepers of the
members' clothing-store, the children's clothing-store, and the
small-supply store, are elected every three years.[19]  Services
to the branches or to the meshek are usually regarded as permanent
places of work.  But in Hofra where the system of annual elections
(in secret ballot) is zealously maintained, none of these posts
- as far as I know - are manned through elections.  The one-man
branch, then, is indeed under the influence of critical public
opinion and gossip, but is free of the control exerted by the
institutionalization of the elected post.  But where this system
does operate, it is effective in introducing an element of dependence and control on both sides of the relationship.

People in the egalitarian kibbutz are reluctant to let
control over resources of value be concentrated under a single
person.  As stated, the amount of complaining and grumbling can
serve as an index of this.  Another possible means to cope with
the situation is to diffuse the power of control by dividing the
control itself among a number of people.  This can be done
(a)  by assigning another member to the branch (in which the
division of labor would not be highly developed and the new
member would share some control); or (b) by institutionalizing a
form of public control or supervision over the branch or the service,
or by both means.

Any worker who joins the one-man-branch dilutes the extent of
monopoly held by the one-person-team.  This applies to a transient
or a hired worker as well as to a member.  True, if the joining
worker is not a kibbutz member, the member in charge ostensibly
controls to a large extent the former's work.  If it is a service-
branch to which individuals and branches make requests, these
should be, and are, transferred to the member in charge.  All
matters which require planning, co-ordination or investment fall
within the areas of his authority.  But in daily, casual, matters,
considered to be of a minor importance or of the utmost urgency,
members do approach the 'help' directly.  In so doing they get a
direct service from the 'help.'  In time they develop relationships of mutual agreement with him.  The very access of members
to the 'help,' limited as it may seem, dilutes the amount of control
the incumbent possesses.  This process is possible because a
potential, incipient, division of labor begins to evolve in the
branch, and, even if very rudimentary, it paves the way for diffusion of one-man control.  It does so by enabling the public, the
clientele, and every individual or branch, to exploit the division.

223

Casual approaches to the other worker, and requests for favors or for services and the like, once met and fulfilled, prove that the extent of monopoly is weakened. The control of the sole incumbent is diffused. A mechanism which intensifies this process is the spread of 'information' about the talents, goodwill, competence and efficiency of the 'help.' Such 'information' cannot but be discussed in association with members' assessment of the incumbent's own merits. If it is a kibbutz member who joins the branch, the branch ceases, of course, to be a one-man branch. The essence of the change (in relevance to the present discussion) is that a member, by virtue of his membership, gains access to a greater number of resources in the branch than the transient and this gain is to resources of a greater value in the context of the total relationship of control and dependence. The more this gradual process develops, the more the new member shares control with the previously sole incumbent. It is inevitably gradual, because, as discussed above, a member usually consolidates his position in his place of work over a long time during which he establishes growing permanence in the branch. Insofar as the community as clientele is concerned, he shares more and more responsibilities, a process which helps, in turn, also to dilute the resentment.

The institutionalization of public control over service-branches is another means of public control. It is carried out through the machinery of committees of elected members. The tasks of the committees are to draw plans for specific actions within the annual plan of the meshek, to discuss and determine routine problems within their respective areas of authority, to supervise the relevant officers' management of their responsibilities, and to function as courts of appeal in cases of disagreement between officers and individual members. Amongst the committees which are elected annually there are: a Landscaping Committee; a Services Committee; a Building Committee amongst whose functions is the allocation of basic furniture. Some kibbutzim also elect a Small-Supply Committee. And of course there are always the Meshek Committee, the Finance Committee, and the Secretariat, who have a direct control over financial resources. In viewing carefully the tasks of the committees in relation to the one-man branches and services, these committees emerge as instruments for exerting control on the part of the clientele over the person upon whose performance they are largely dependent in daily routine. In conclusion, assignment of workers to the one-man branch, itself associated with economic and organizational considerations, and the working of public committees, manifestly designed to deal with many aspects of the communal life, both function as instruments to dilute the concentrated control by one person over the branch.[20]

This discussion of the one-man branch has been incomplete and far from exhaustive. It shows in short, that a concentration of different jobs and tasks in one person's work tends to be divided among a whole team, if the branch grows.

## Small-team branches

I turn now to what I have above described, analogously from Durkheim, as the 'mechanical' co-operation in small teams. Cohen (1963: 380) has stated that although there is some division inside it,"it is the branch... [which sets] the limit for specialization and differentiation. All the jobs within the branch are accomplished by all the workers with no permanent, defined, internal division of labor prevailing amongst them." But Cohen (1957; 1962; 1963), following Talmon-Garber (1970: 146-170), is interested in classifying kibbutzim, once defined as 'communities' (as against 'Bunds') into different categories. He further establishes relations between some of these categories and different types of meshek organization (1963). He takes a further step to associate the different types of meshek organization with different structures of the branch (1963 ). Thus, 'undifferential meshek' structure is associated with 'unindependent' branch structure; 'federalistic' structure of the meshek is associated with 'crystallized' (or 'cohesive') branch structure; and 'centralistic' meshek structure is associated with 'nuclear' branch structure. The quotation from Cohen, if applied to all the branches, would classify Hofra as a 'federalistic' meshek within which the branch team functions 'cohesively.' However, studying other branches such as the grove or the orchard, would place Hofra in a different category. Therefore it seems that there is no necessary association between the category of the entire meshek, let alone the category of the community, and the internal division of labor within the branch team. Variables such as the size of the branch itself (branches of various sizes are to be found in the different meshakim), the nature of the crop, and the requirements of work enter this scene. As for the classification itself, Cohen himself (1963: 368) indeed states that the 'structural types' are rather ideal types, should possibly be present in reality within one meshek, and the same would apply to the presence of different types of branches. My own argument focuses on a somewhat different problem, namely, that although access to all the resources in the branch is not necessarily equally open, it is nevertheless available to all. Since all members accomplish the same jobs and have access to the same resources, they share control over the branch and its resources, so that as members of the team have a stake in a similitude of resources in the branch, this gives rise to their sharing a similitude of control. Unlike control of different resources in the large branch where labor is highly divided with a tendency for the division to establish a

permanent pattern, the control in (and on) the small branch is in
sharing the same jobs and therefore access to the same resources.
This is the 'mechanical' pattern of the branch organization and
the team cohesion.

In the fish-ponds branch, two permanent members comprise
the team. They do get help in seasonal work, particularly for
tasks of fishing and sorting the fish, but they share whatever
job they do. Of course, one man may be engaged in fishing while
the other is engaged in sorting, or one man may be sorting fish
while the other washes and cleans them before shipping. But
there is no single job which either one of them would not do. In
most tasks they work together. They may alternate their tasks
according to a variety of considerations, but I have no evidence
to suggest that they ever consciously alternate their jobs for the
sake of alternation itself, or in order to secure access for
either of them to all the jobs. The running of the branch compels
them to share all tasks. A small team would be incapacitated in
carrying out its tasks if one person could not substitute for
another at any point of time. Most of the time they must and do
work together, consult one another, plan daily and seasonal work
together, and co-ordinate their work. In a word, they are both
involved in the branch's affairs so that their contributions to
the branch in terms of daily work, knowledge, management, planning
and use of equipment overlap extensively. When transient workers
are assigned to help them, either one of them works with these,
instructs and supervises them. Usually both do this together.
The bond between them, in the context of the branch, is that of
'mechanical solidarity.'

The respect they get in the community (aspects of which
will be discussed later in the chapter) for their performance in,
and management of, the branch is shared by both. They are both
approached by the kitchen store-keeper and by individual members
for fish. The advice of both and of each one of them is sought
on matters pertaining to fish or to the branch. Handling of
machines and technical equipment is shared by both. In other
words, their overlapping areas of work in the branch result in
overlapping areas of control over elements valued by themselves
and by others in the community, elements which, if analyzed in
social (and not only purely economical or organizational) contexts,
constitute resources for social position.

In principle, the same observations apply to the vineyard
with its permanent members. Although daily work in this branch
gives rise to a somewhat more elaborate division of labor (in
some seasons a larger number of tasks must be accomplished simultaneously), all the members of the small team do the same jobs.

226

Every member of the team at some time irrigates, prunes, thins
the branches, sprays, ploughs, drives, picks grapes or supervises
a group of pickers.  True, the variety of tasks facilitates personal choice, but the few members invariably share all the tasks.
Considerations external to the running of the branch, and to
securing a footing for each of the team members in each job, are
also involved.  People sometimes fall ill; sometimes they take
unexpected leave, or go on holidays; or they fulfil their service
duties in the dining hall and on night-guard; or they leave for
their National Service in the reserve military units.  For the
branch to be run appropriately each member must be available for
any work, if and when the need arises.  But whatever the considerations may be, the fact is that, like the pattern of work in the
fishponds, all the members of the small team share the same work
and essentially the control over resources of the branch.  Again,
I stress that sharing control by the members does not mean that all
the resources are equally distributed or, indeed, that access to
all the resources is equally open.  A branch, as an economic and
organizational unit of the meshek, has a recognized foreman, an
office normally held by one person.  Another person may be physically more fit for particular jobs than others.  Another (or the
same) person may possess a particular talent which may prove
relevant to particular situations, and so on.  A fuller analysis
of this problem of collective work, responsibilities and authority
in the small-scale branch and its relation to its division of
labor and control would indeed be profitable.  But it must, for
purposes of my central problem, suffice for me to say here that
a member of a small team, by virtue of his permanence in the
branch over time, and his investment which induces him to remain
in it, establishes a stake in control similar to others.  Therefore, the elements of his position in the sphere of work which
are derived from the branch's rudimentary, impermanent and overlapping division of labor and by the nature of its correlate, the
allocation and sharing of control over the resources available in
the branch, are essentially similar to those of his colleagues.

I have already analyzed how, in contrast, in the large teams
of Hofra, which number ten or more members, although the members
do derive elements which are components of their individual social
position from the common sharing of work in the branch, the division of labor allows them to get access to resources not shared
by all of them.

## Professional knowledge

Professionalization provides a special division of labor
in a branch.  Professionalization in the branches of the kibbutz-
economy is usually discussed, both by members and analysts, against

227

the background of growing specialization within the branch. Indeed, it is defined by some sociologists as 'professionalization of work roles,' roles being themselves discussed in respect of their growing differentiation (e.g. Cohen, 1962: 76-77). In other words, professionalization is associated with the branch's division of labor. In the following discussion I shall try to elaborate on this suggestion. For the time being, however, I shall treat 'professionalization' as applying to knowledge of the branch as a whole, as well as to knowledge of a single role within it.

It is in the interests of the meshek to have specialization and professionalization in branches (Cohen, 1962: 76-77). Whereas in the small branch, team members must share knowledge of the various aspects of crops they grow, the large team provides the possibility of a more differential distribution of knowledge. Some members of the large teams endeavor to specialize and professionalize and others tend to remain in the branch without pursuing further professionalization. Both tendencies are in operation at the same time. Some knowledge is shared by all, but its equal distribution is not essential in order for the large branch to survive and for the members to cooperate in the branch work. Nor is it essential, from the individual's standpoint, for the member to retain his position of permanence in the branch. He can tolerate a differential distribution, either because he is resigned to it or because that is the limit of his interests.

Large though it may be, the branch is after all relatively small. It is a part of a meshek which is itself not very large (altogether 2661 dunam of tilled land). The demands of agriculture compel the team members to change assignments, work together, and substitute for one another. Beyond the common knowledge which develops out of this situation, interests vary. Two processes evolve, then: (a) members show a differential amount of interest in further knowledge; and (b) members develop individual interests in different aspects of the branch. These two processes are related, but they are not identical. A member may combine an interest in general knowledge of the branch with a particular interest in one aspect within it; he may, alternatively, be interested in that particular aspect only, or vice versa or in neither. The distinction is important because it means that possession of professional knowledge is not necessarily linked to differentiation of specific roles. It may be relevant to the branch as a whole, or the crop as a whole rather than to a specific task within it. A member may derive influence from his differential access to knowledge of general aspects of the branch. He may derive influence from his control of knowledge of a specific aspect or a specific issue.

Defined in a positive way, my suggestion is that possession
of professional knowledge is a source of influence. It affects
one's own and others' considerations as well as planning and
performance of work. In other words, it affects the branch, and
other people, by virtue of the authority vested in knowledge.
Defined in a negative way, the possession of knowledge which, at
least partly, excludes others from it, compels the others at least
not to ignore the possessor. This is essential, of course, when
the knowledge held by the possessor is in demand. It is, in turn,
in aggravated demand when the possessor shares joint interests
with 'the others.' His knowledge is as important for them. He
cannot be ignored, he must be taken into consideration, when the
resource he controls, knowledge, is relevant to the issue at hand.
In the branch context, the joint interests are evident on three
levels. On the individual level, the member collaborates with
colleagues. His performance, let alone success, depends to a
large extent on them. It is in his interest, as well as the interest of all the members of the team, to accommodate one another
in the framework of the branch. He must recognize that knowledge
provides the authority to tell others, himself included, to do or
to refrain from doing, things to which this knowledge is relevant.
Furthermore he must accommodate the possessor of the knowledge
who is another member of the team. Hence the interests of the
branch itself, and its welfare and development, must be given
considerable weight.

On the branch level itself, the joint interests are evident
in the joint responsibility of the team as a whole for the running
and the development of the branch. Difficulties or even animosities
may indeed be present but the common regard of the members for their
joint enterprise overrides these. The team as a whole is entrusted
to take responsibility for the branch and knowledge of any of its
members is an asset for the collective and the branch.

Thirdly, the members have joint interests in the branch as
members of the meshek, the economic corporation. The development
and success of the branch is in their interest, now as members of
the kibbutz (see Spiro, 1956: 82-36). If goodwill and immediate
realization of this premise are for some reason absent or fail to
function, the independently-functioning mechanisms of gossip and
public opinion with their power of feedback are at hand to remind
members of their obligations to the meshek's prosperity and its
supremacy. The meshek explicitly expects members of branch teams
to do their utmost for the development of the branch through the
use of whatever resource they control, particularly resources
which are vested in their persons. Gossip and public opinion can
function as mechanisms to bring home to the team-members these
obligations because as members of the kibbutz they are united

229

with the other members in the "pursuit of common objectives"
(Gluckman, 1963: 314). Incidentally, by so functioning, not only
do these mechanisms maintain 'group values' implicitly (Gluckman,
1968: 33) by being the standard against which defaulters' behavior
is assessed, but they tend to emerge into the open and thus make
these values publicly reminiscent.

Thus, the 'common objectives' of the group, on different
levels, make the use of a member's professional knowledge function-
ally desirable. Once accepted as functional to the interests of
the branch and the meshek, professional knowledge becomes an asset
to the individual who possesses it. It further strengthens his
position in the sphere of labor.

The greatest part of professional knowledge derives from
experience in work itself. I will substantiate this statement
later when I discuss professional training. In working in the
same branch, and possibly in most of the jobs within the branch,
in successive seasons the permanent member accumulates technical
skill. But he accumulates professional knowledge as well. A
member who works in the orchard gradually learns the laws of plant
growth; structure and suitability of soil for various crops;
relations of water, its quantities, frequency of irrigation,
methods of irrigation and the like, to the functioning of the
soil and to the growth of the tree and the development of fruits;
the significance of pruning and its various applications to different crops; and so on and so forth. Likewise, a vineyard worker
learns the difference between varieties of vines; their differential
fruitfulness; their suitability to different markets and industry;
control of percentage rates of sugar in each variety; timing of
harvesting; composition of anti-insect poison in each round of
spraying and its particular end; and the like. He acquires all this
knowledge either by working with others, by changing assignments with
them, or by substituting for them.

Therefore for the worker in the grove or in the orchard who
has acquired experience in irrigation, part of the work has become
routine, whereas for a substituting worker some jobs in irrigating
present extremely difficult problems. The specialist knows the
timing of irrigation; quantities for different crops; regulating
and co-ordinating the different sources of water; moving pipes;
repairs; location of valves; and a variety of details which would
mean practically nothing to another person until the latter involves
himself in this job.

Even picking of citrus fruits, a job regarded as a 'mass work'
which requires no skill, in fact requires specialized knowledge. It

does require skill to tell one variety from another; to perceive various degrees of ripeness in each variety of citrus; to make the right decision as to the exact time of picking; to know how to pick each variety of fruits and whether to use picking scissors, and if so, for which variety; how to lay the fruits in the bag and in the box; where to spread the boxes and in which order; how to set the ladder in a stable position, how to reach tall branches - and even how to pick grapefruit and other varieties without getting scratched. And just because it is 'mass work,' performed mainly by unskilled transients, workers must know how to run and organize a group or groups of unskilled workers to carry out a job of which they have no knowledge, and in which they have much less interest, according to standards which do require knowledge. This knowledge, as well as the knowledge required for irrigation and for a host of other jobs in the various branches, is accumulated through personal experience. Specialization for most of the members and in most of the jobs is still acquired by this method.

The process of specialization can be viewed from two angles: (a) the individual's accumulation of knowledge of one particular aspect, at least to the partial exclusion of other aspects; and (b) the growing division within the team in relation to knowledge. Both angles reflect aspects of essentially the same process.

The choosing by the individual of a particular aspect, or a number of aspects of the branch's work in which to specialize is, of course, affected by many factors. These include, among others: conditions within the branch, areas of interest and jobs not held by other members, position of other workers, defection of other members, and interpersonal relationships. I would like to draw attention to one other factor. The member may be simply interested in a particular aspect with no apparent purpose in mind. He may be initially attracted to a particular problem such as combatting pests or grafting or the adaptation of a new plant to the regional environment or conditions of birds' fertility. Of course, once this interest is followed by a repeated devotion of time and energy, it becomes an asset to the individual in his intra-branch relationships. Moreover, it fits into a system of branch division of labor; and this counts even more. But what I want to suggest is that the initial choice of area in the branch in which to specialize is not necessarily motivated by considerations of this kind. The sociological properties of the role the member adopts while seeking knowledge of the problem to which he is attracted may emerge only in the course of time.

This comment leads me to another suggestion. Whatever may be the considerations of the individual in concentrating his knowledge on an aspect or aspects of the branch-work, the ones I have mentioned are all associated with resources within the branch itself. As my problem is to isolate some of the elements which comprise the individual's position in the branch, these are, of course, relevant factors. But the very interest of the individual in expanding his knowledge is affected by his interest in other roles he plays in the community and his personal areas of interest. His interests in subjects other than the branch may be more attractive to him; he may be willing to forego advantages he may derive in the branch from expanding his professional knowledge in his other interests. He may value his interest in literature or music or sports or hiking more than his occupation; and once he is established in his work, he may be unwilling to devote more energy to acquiring further knowledge.

What I am stressing here is that not only is there differential knowledge of the branch work within the team, but there is also differential interest in knowledge. This differential interest is related to both clusters of factors, those within the branch(control of others on particular areas of interest, established allocation of responsibilities, the nature and the attraction of the job), and those outside the branch (other fields of personal interest, demands of other roles). I repeat my earlier statement: mastering of knowledge and professionalization are important for the social position of the individual in the field of labor, but it is not absolutely essential for the individual in order to retain his permanence or his acceptable reputation at large. Therefore, it is not necessary to search for political motivation in the individual who shows interest in knowledge. The political asset may emerge over time.

In addition to practice, training and theoretical courses in which elements of the relevant sciences are taught, are available. Members may attend these courses which help them to professionalize. Professionalization contributes to the development of the meshek and the branch and at the same time validates the position of the individual.

The main interest of the meshek in raising the standard of professional knowledge lies mainly in its considerations of productivity, efficiency, profitability, and economic development. These, in turn, are affected by processes of economic development and change on a national scale (see Cohen, 1963) which press the kibbutz to become more and more aware of the crucial importance of these considerations. Further systematic specialization does raise the probability of higher standards of efficiency and productivity, and therefore the level of profitability, a crucial factor in the constantly changing conditions of the Israeli agricultural economy. Members, some authoritative officers of the kibbutz amongst them, add that another argument should be considered,

232

leading to the same conclusion: the satisfaction of the individual.
The idea in brief is that the more knowledge a worker acquires,
the more satisfied he will probably be in work. The more satisfied
in the sphere of labor he is, the more he stands a good chance to
be satisfied in other contexts, thus easing tensions in his social
environment. Within the branch the acquisition of further knowledge should give rise, through satisfaction and easing of tensions,
to (a) a growing interest in work and its detailed processes,
thus contributing to common objectives; and (b) a growing cohesiveness within the team by providing common scientific interests and
curiosity.[21]

These are the essentially collective considerations. The
extent to which these economically based interests in professionalization, and the ideological stress on the welfare and satisfaction of the individual derived from further knowledge, are met, can
be assessed by examining the participation of members in the training and the professional courses. The data are offered in Table
5.4. Table 5.4 is based on Table 3.3, as my intention is to show
attendance of the present members of agricultural teams in these
courses and not the attendance of the entire population of Hofra.

Some comments on the Table should be made: (a) the Table
does not show attendance of courses other than professional (or
'vocational' as these are defined in Israel) relevant to the meshek
work. It does not show, then, courses such as those of general
interest, as on the Bible, literature, kibbutz ideology, painting,
music, and the like; (b) nor does it show involvement in higher
education, such as university studies if these are irrelevant to
meshek work; (c) it does not include members who have left the
agricultural branches and who have established themselves in
services or other occupations; (d) the column of 'other courses'
refers to courses relevant to the meshek work, but not to the
specific branch in which the member works. For example, a member
who works at present in the orchard and has attended two courses,
one on apple-growing and the other on banana-growing, would appear
in the Table as having attended a 'course relevant to the present
branch' and 'other courses'; (e) I felt it necessary to show
length of attendance at the courses as it must have some relation
to the amount of knowledge the student is offered in the course; and
(f) finally, the information is based mainly on questionnaires
distributed by The Movement and filled in by local members appointed
specifically for the job. I was not present at the time in Hofra.
The accuracy of the information relies on the individuals who were
prepared to give it, but all in all, it cannot be too remote from
the real situation.

Most of the courses in which members have participated
involve a general knowledge of the branch concerned or of crops
thereof.  Very few courses in which members participated were
aimed at specialization in a particular task within the branch
organization of work.  Some of the members have pointed out that
the courses they attended took place years ago.  A very few members
attended more than one course.  It all leads to the conclusion
that whatever the value of the participation in these courses has
had for the branch, taken as a whole it has hardly contributed to
further specialization in tasks within the branch.  Indeed if a
worker attends a general course, the knowledge he acquires may be
important, but it is not necessarily instrumental for further
specialization.

Some members evidently take part in these courses.  But the
main problem is to explain the relatively poor participation of
members in a scheme designed to help them to acquire more knowledge, manifestly for the benefit of the branch, but also for their
own interest, whether this interest is conceived in terms of the
ideology of satisfaction or in terms of strengthening each member's
personal position.  The kibbutz movement encourages professionalization; the kibbutz publicly endorses this policy; the teams are
associated with national professional organizations (such as the
Orchard Workers' Association, Flower Growers' Organization and
others) which urge people to participate in training schemes.
And to facilitate this participation for Hofraites, an institute
in which many of those courses are held, is located in the Valley.
There seems to be, then, no apparent reason for the fact which by
immediate considerations seems odd, that many members do not take
advantage of these opportunities and that those who do, tend to be
content with participation in one course.

The attempt to explain this fact leads me back to my previous
suggestions.  I suggest that:

(a)  members largely share the conviction that the essence of
     knowledge derives from work itself and experience in work;

(b)  specialization does not depend on systematic professional
     knowledge, i.e., the knowledge required can also be obtained
     through practice and interest in the job; and

(c)  professional knowledge, beyond the standard knowledge shared
     by the members of the team, is not an absolute condition for
     retention of permanence and belonging to the branch.

Thus the incentive to acquire systematic professional knowledge is differentially distributed.  Not everybody is equally

234

Table 5.4:  Attendance of Vocational Courses
(Length of Attendance by Months) by 1969
(Based on Table 3.3)

| Member | Course relevant to the branch | Other courses |
|--------|-------------------------------|---------------|
| G1 | 1 | - |
| G2 | No information | No information |
| G3 | - | - |
| G4 | 6 | - |
| G5 | - | - |
| G6 | - | - |
| G7* | 1 | - |
| G8 | 1 | - |
| G9 | - | - |
| G10 | - | - |
| G11 | - | - |
| G12 | - | - |
| G13 | - | - |
| G14 | - | - |
| O1 | 2 | - |
| O2 | 1 | - |
| O3 | - | 7 |
| O4 | 1 | - |
| O5 | 1 | 9 |
| O6 | - | - |
| O7 | - | - |
| O8 | 3 | - |
| O9 | $\frac{1}{2}$ | - |
| O10 | - | - |
| O11 | - | - |
| V1 | - | - |
| V2 | - | $1\frac{1}{2}$ |
| V3 | 3 | - |
| V4 | - | - |
| V5* | - | - |
| C1* | - | - |
| C2 | 2 | - |
| C3 | - | 3 |

(continued on page 235a)

Table 5.4 continued...

| Member | Course relevant to the branch | Other courses |
|---|---|---|
| A1* | | 12 |
| A2 | No information | No information |
| A3 | No information | ** |
| F1 | - | 2 |
| F2* | - | - |
| P1 | 2 | - |
| P2 | - | - |
| R1 | 2 | 2 |
| R2 | 1 | - |
| R3 | 2 | - |
| R4* | 3 | - |
| R5 | $\frac{1}{2}$ | - |
| R6 | 1 | - |
| R7 | 1 | 1 |
| R8 | - | - |
| R9 | - | - |
| R10 | - | - |
| R11 | - | ** |
| R12 | - | 2 |
| R13 | - | 1 |
| R14 | - | 1 |
| R15 | - | 2 |
| R16 | - | - |
| R17 | - | - |

Index:  * Present foreman.
        ** Sent by the Kibbutz for higher education relevant to agriculture.

Source:  Questionnaires by Department of Statistics, The Movement.

interested in a branch career and in gaining control of the resources this career offers. In relation to the present problem, not everyone is equally interested either in professional knowledge as such or in the rewards potentially contained in it. The chances of further knowledge, further professionalization and further specialization attract some members more than they attract others. I would like to draw attention to another suggestion made above: in the complex meshek-village-commune, interest may be diffused among various fields, roles and objectives. Although I discuss a subject which pertains to the meshek and within it particularly to labor, I cannot ignore the importance and the significance of other aspects of the kibbutz complex for the individual. I cannot discuss them here but I take note of their relevance. As stated above, a branchman may be less motivated to extend his knowledge in the field of labor because he thinks also in terms of his other roles. He may be aware of the repercussions of his failure to extend his knowledge on his branch career and yet value other resources in other fields more.

Interest in subjects other than work-role and awareness of the repercussions of their preference to possible advantages in the field of work aside, professional knowledge does operate as a differentiating force within the team. Members may be ignorant of it; they may choose to ignore it; they may be personally uninterested in its advantages; they may prefer other resources in the kibbutz. But the member who possesses such knowledge adds an important element to his power. He does enjoy advantages. The member who is not interested in, or does not enjoy, professional knowledge cannot disengage himself from the meshek system which values it. Uninterested he may be, but the advantages contained in professional knowledge do exist, and they are enjoyed by others. A case taken from life may enliven this discussion.

Hadari, in kibbutz Hardoof, joined the grove-branch upon returning from an agricultural school. His interest in the grove preceded his schooldays, for he showed a particular interest in citrus while in school. When he returned to the kibbutz, the grove was being expanded. New plots were planted with different varieties of citrus, pipe-line networks were laid down, internal roads and paths were paved or trodden, and new methods of work sought. Yet Hadari started his career as an adult branchman like a newcomer: older members of the team who had accumulated knowledge and practical experience in the branch did not show any particular confidence in the theoretical knowledge Hadari had brought home from school, nor did they show any particular enthusiasm to share their specialized jobs with him at the outset. To start with, he was given jobs which required no particular knowledge, jobs which in principle any newcomer could share. I cannot say that they showed hostility: they invited him to join the branch, they co-operated with him as well as with other

younger (in respect of time of work in the branch) members in
team-work, and they accepted him as a member of the team. But
he was left to demonstrate his interest in the branch, his re -
sponsibility in work and his preparedness to take tasks other
than professional ones before he was allowed to specialize more.
In other words, acceptance into the branch by the team, while
bearing relevance to his interest and prior knowledge, which
could affect the meshek's economic interest in economic advantage,
productivity and efficiency, demanded that he undergo the process
of initiation irrespective of the assets he possessed already,
even though these were acknowledged. His anticipatory professionalization had to manifest itself first through jobs shared by
others. The team would accept a worker who is professionally
qualified for a special job but they would not agree that he immediately practice only his special skill. Permanent work in the
branch (equivalent to membership in the team) is unconditional.
Hadari was expected to demonstrate in practice that he understood
this premise. In subsequent successive seasons he met these
expectations and at the same time he accumulated practical experience which integrated his theoretical training. Unlike some of
his colleagues who joined the branch at approximately the same
time, he persisted in showing interest in various aspects of the
grove, particularly in professional problems. Access to professional jobs became more and more available to him and he was
invited to join in skilled jobs such as pruning young trees,
grafting and notching. The longer he practiced, the more
valuable his attachment to the branch became. People in the branch,
as well as the central economic and labor officers of the meshek,
could not imagine anyone carrying out a professional task in the
grove without his also taking a leading role in the instruction
and supervision of other workers. Hadari never showed any interest
in managerial roles. Interests in the organization of labor within
the branch, the foreman's functions, and representation of branch
interests in the central meshek, were all alien to him. He came to
be regarded as the expert professional worker of the citrus branch.
The defection of a few skilled workers from the branch strengthened
his position. To be accurate, although he accumulated a vast
amount of knowledge and experience, he did not spread his interest
to all aspects of the grove. Although he was intimately familiar
with the theoretical aspects of the relation of water (its
quantities, composition, timing of irrigation, relation to other
components of plant nourishment, impact on organic activity in soil,
etc.), to plants and of effects of application of particular chemical
elements (through spraying) on the plants, he would not usually
interfere with irrigating or with spraying. He concentrated on
areas in which he was interested: grafting, pruning, close checking
of growth, and the general welfare of the trees. To sum up his
position: he took no part in management yet he had a grip on the

237

essential resources for a social position - namely, expertise in important aspects of branch work. At the same time he acknowledged the division of labor within the branch by not trying to extend his control over other jobs, the responsibility for which constituted resources for other social positions. In his own field, the dependence of others (including the branch foreman) on him out-weighed his dependence on them.

Having become established in the branch, he began to take steps which annoyed other members of the team. Unlike some expert workers in other branches who are considered to be indispensable for their branch's work even in slack seasons, and are therefore slow in giving their share in services based on rotation (kitchen, nightguard, dining-hall), Hadari volunteered every year to work in the kitchen. This in itself would not have annoyed the other members of the team since most of them did the same. But he used to extend his service period far beyond his quota of thirty labor-days. His performance was appreciated in the kitchen, so he had no difficulty in extending the period of his work there. Meanwhile tasks in the grove awaited his return. Members of the team, knowing that he would eventually return, would not take his job, nor, in many cases, did they possess the professional knowledge to do so. They demanded that he return to the grove but he only used to respond that it was for him to decide when to return and to choose his job. Hadari would usually return to the branch a few weeks later than expected. Whatever his personal considerations were (he used to say that he had to alternate work in the grove and in services so as "to breathe fresh air" every once in awhile, and that he would not be able to resume his responsibilities in the branch before he had accomplished that), he accomplished two ends though without necessarily being conscious of them: (a) he tested his position in the team vis-a-vis the whole community every year; and (b) he manifested his control over his work.

Hadari was well aware of his colleagues' annoyance with his conduct. When approached by them, or by the foreman, or by the Labor Organizer (at the request of the branch foreman), he acknowledged their opinions, but dismissed the request to return with the usual answer that it was for him, not for them, to decide on the right time to return. He thus tested anew his position amongst them by the most extreme method: by acknowledgement and yet a clearly flat refusal to co-operate. This aroused negligible effective opposition from the other members of his team. The members of the team, when pressed by others to explain their acquiescence in this apparently uncomradely show of disregard, did not conceal their dismay, but agreed that that was indeed an "extreme case." It would not take a large step further to explain such conduct in terms of the 'total personality,' that is, in psychologistic terms. By so doing, the members, as in the case of Olya (Chapter III) or the case of Olami (this chapter), give recognition to behavior of individuals which does not conform to prevalent standards in the relevant sphere. By so doing they also justify their own inaction in not taking steps to counter misconduct which, if it succeeds, encroaches on their own standing. And finally, in accepting the 'exception,' they in fact help the person concerned, here Hadari, to strengthen his control over particular resources.

This is, admittedly, an 'extreme' case, just as the case of Olya is 'extreme.' Such cases do not occur regularly. But an occurrence of an 'extreme' case reveals elements which otherwise would be more difficult to analyze. Many workers are skilled in their respective branches through the gradual acquisition of knowledge and therefore control some factors which are usable as resources of a social position. Most of them do not go as far as Hadari in testing the measure of their control and manifesting it. Therefore it is more difficult to discuss their relation to the problem. But when a publicly visible 'social drama' (Turner, 1957) occurs, its elements become more exposed and more accessible for discussion.

While members of Hadari's team tended to refer to Hadari's 'total personality,' although they were well aware of his professional resources, the realization of the extent of his control was brought home to them through agencies which were far less concerned than they with the interpersonal encounter with Hadari. These agencies, acting through their agents, the Meshek Organizer and the Labor Organizer, were ostensibly concerned with the degree of control Hadari possessed over resources valuable for the whole meshek. For example, when Hadari worked in the kitchen and refused to return to the grove, the branch foreman was absent and another member substituted for him. The latter was under pressure from both the objective demands of the branch and the demands of the members of the team to act so as to make Hadari change his mind. Obviously the demands of the team were also loaded with resentment. The acting foreman approached Hadari, but Hadari remained adamant. When the acting foreman mentioned that the members of the team would not tolerate uncooperative behavior for long, Hadari retorted, "They would not tolerate? Who are 'they'? What say do they have? They cannot tell me what I should do and when. What can they do?" The acting foreman replied that "they can do one thing": the foreman could call a meeting of the team in which "they may suggest that, inexpert as they are, they may nevertheless take over all your responsibilities and ask the labor authorities to ask you to settle in another branch." Hadari, angry as he seemed to be, nevertheless showed no concern about such a remote possibility. Hadari said that he did not believe that the members of the team would go as far as that. He did not consider corporate action by the team over an issue of division of

239

labor in the branch to be likely. The acting foreman approached the Labor Organizer and the _Meshek_ Organizer. The foreman asked them to intervene and persuade Hadari to return. But he did more than that: he told them of the angry exchanges and the threat he had made to Hadari. Both officers exerted whatever persuading pressure they had to avert this move. The point of interest is that the central officers, unlike members of the team, did not refer to his 'personality' but rather pressed hard the prospective damage to the branch. They urged members of the team to forego their resentment in the interests of the branch; though they conceded that interests of the branch and those of the team were not identical, they stressed the supremacy of the interests of the branch. They were less involved in daily interaction with Hadari; the pattern of their relationships with him had a lesser tendency to permanence and were less affected by the tensions with which the interaction in the branch was loaded, and therefore they were freer to locate the crux of the problem as distinct from Hadari's personal traits and were able therefore to bring this point home to the team. I do not know whether the officers discussed the matter with Hadari. Perhaps he sensed that in the absence of the permanent foreman the established order might change; perhaps he was aware that the degree of control he enjoyed in the branch was not unlimited. A few days later Hadari returned to the grove. Whatever other lessons can be drawn from this case, my main objective has been to show how professional knowledge can become a resource used in the strengthening of a social position in the field of work. The incumbent of this position may not be aware of all the intricacies and implications of his behavior; he may not be consciously interested in it; he may conceive his own behavior in the same psychologistic terms as those employed by others; or alternatively he may consciously pursue the strengthening of his position in labor as an objective. The effect is that control over resources of professional knowledge confers a very important element of power and influence on the individual.

This generalization applies also to less extreme cases. The person who takes charge of spraying is always called into consultation if he does not take the initiative in his own field, and so is the person in charge of irrigation in his, and so on. They may not take as much interest in their respective jobs, or may be less professional than Hadari, and they may not act so extremely, but, to reduce it to the minimal common denominator, none of them can be ignored. The knowledge they have, which is expressed in their work, compels the others to take them into account when considering their own moves or those of the _meshek_.

Another function of professional knowledge can be brought to light in a discussion of the following cases. A visitor to one of

the main offices in Hofra will see a glazed and framed official
document hanging on the wall. It announces that its original
holder, Orgad, is hereby bestowed with the national Labor Prize
for his contribution to the development of orchard crops in Israel.
Orgad (O1) is the founder of the orchard in Hofra and is said
to have introduced sub-tropical crops into the Valley. He planted
avocado, mango, guava (lately uprooted) and persimmon, as well as
pecan nuts, plums, quince and varieties of apples in an area
originally considered to be unsuitable for these crops. Deciduous
crops in the Valley are, admittedly, less successful than they are
in the inland and more elevated regions, but they have not failed.
On the contrary, they have contributed a substantial proportion
of Hofra's income. Nor have the sub-tropical crops failed. Orgad
worked in close association with scientists of the Agricultural
Research Institute and the Faculty of Agriculture of the Hebrew
University as well as with experienced and active members of the
Fruit Growers' Organization. He established working and personal
relationships with a vast number of experts and other activists
in the field. Foreign visitors and students of horticulture are
still sent to Hofra for visits and training. When the branch
expanded, following the allocation of Gderoth Area to Hofra after
the 1948/49 war, Orgad concentrated mainly on the scientific
aspects of the branch, in particular on sub-tropical crops. Other
aspects of branch work were left to other members. He no longer took a
detailed interest in other tasks, important as they were for the
maintenance of the branch. This concentration on particular
aspects has understandably contributed to the growing division
of labor within the team and to the further specialization of
other members in particular jobs. Both his achievements in the
orchard in Hofra and his close connections with national authorities on horticulture have won him national acclaim. His concentration on specific professional subjects helped to win him more
acclaim outside Hofra. In 1961 he was asked to join the Fruit
Growers Organization as an active officer. With the approval of
the kibbutz, he accepted the invitation. Through this office he
established further connections with the Fruit (Horticultural)
Board (which deals mainly with marketing problems on the national
level). He became an employee of the Ministry of Agriculture and
has since divided his working-time between the orchard of Hofra
and the National office.

I have spared the reader the details of Orgad's history in
the field, the details of his relinquishment of his managerial
duties in the branch, his position in the community outside the
sphere of horticulture, and the other considerations which affected
his acceptance of office away from home. These issues certainly
bear some relevance to the course of events, but for the purpose of
elucidating the main point they may be left on one side. The main

241

point is that an industrious acquisition of professional knowledge, application of this knowledge to practice in the field, preparedness to consult qualified scientific authorities and to co-operate with them, and as a result of all these, further specialization in specific aspects of the branch's work, yielded their reward.

The reward to which I refer is not the office in the Growers' Organization or in the Ministry, but the implication which the holding of this office has for the position of the member in the kibbutz. But I must immediately explain why I do not choose to discuss the 'reward' itself, namely the appointment to office which is relevant to Orgad's field of interest, which endows him with prestige, and which gives him some advantages over other members of the kibbutz. A discussion of employment of members outside the meshek proper (which I have called 'outside work,' the term used in the kibbutz itself) is a problem worthy of separate discussion. I touched upon it in brief when I mentioned a problem relevant to Ohad's office (Chapter III) with a national organization. But a discussion of this subject here would distort the present perspective of my argument.

But I must make one comment. Just as there are strong interests to consolidate a position in the kibbutz within the sphere of labor, there may emerge, in certain situations, an interest in relinquishing a position in favor of an attractive job outside the meshek. Individual motivations may vary. They may include material advantages (see Talmon Garber, 1956), access to transport (an official may get a car), physical mobility, enlargement of personal connections, prestige, or, as J. Shepher (1966) suggests, among other motives, job-satisfaction or confidence in the job's value for the kibbutz or for The Movement. But in the present context it seems to me that negative motives may be more relevant: a post outside the meshek, although it inevitably places the member under the control, which may be very strict, of his new place of work and of his colleagues and superordinates as well as of bureaucratic regulations, relieves a man of claims from within the meshek. He remains subject to many mechanisms of control within the kibbutz, but those which operate to control a member in his capacity of a meshek worker can hardly apply to his work. In a sphere as important as labor in the kibbutz, he eases the control by being less dependent.

Orgad has achieved something comparatively rare in the way of 'outside work' in that he has managed to extend further into his special field of interest and not have to plunge into a new occupation. He has eased the branch controls over himself while retaining access (and possibly a more efficient one) to his own interests.

242

But the reward to which I have referred above lies within the kibbutz, in the consciousness of the community of the wider recognition of that member's professional reputation. This recognition serves to limit possible pressures on him. The community shows pride in his knowledge, his office, his connections, which can be of use in and for the kibbutz, and in the fact that he is identified nationally by horticulturists with Hofra. So although his position in the community in other contexts may not be particularly helpful to him, the members are conscious of the elements which are implicit in his professional position. If these factors in themselves are not sufficient to make him more popular or influential in the community, (and I do not discuss this aspect), they at least may have a defensive capacity. From a positive point of view, a professional who works away from the meshek can be of a great value to the kibbutz, regardless of the person's standing within both the professional group and the community, if both are willing to co-operate. Mutual goodwill is necessary. This interdependence also contributes its own share to the position of such an individual.

## Technological skill

Technological skill is in a way a variant of knowledge, the subject which I have just discussed. Engagement of a worker in a job of a technological nature, an engagement which shows some tendency to permanence, is implicitly contained in the above general discussion of branch division of labor. However, I hope to show that in the context of the meshek it is significant on its own merits. Its significance becomes potent when its relation to two factors is discussed: (a) its relation to permanence in a branch; and (b) its distribution in terms of categories of members.

Technological skills are mainly mechanical because Hofra is not an 'industrial' kibbutz, and such skills are therefore applied mainly in work concerned with: (a) agricultural mechanics; (b) driving; (c) services-to-the-meshek (garage); and (d) other services (carpentry, smithy, electricity, etc.). It is mainly the one-man branches which are relevant in the context of the present discussion and they were analyzed earlier. There remain agricultural mechanics and the main agency which services the meshek, the garage.

For lack of space, and because it may lead me away from the main line of the discussion, I refrain from a detailed analysis of the garage. Also, the garage, by virtue of the nature of work in it, is clearly a mechanical and technological plant. Mechanical work is not just one of various jobs in the branch, it is a distinct

243

and total task. However, the garage serves the branches, and
therefore has an aspect which is directly relevant to the subject
under discussion: it can exercise considerable control over the
accomplishment of other jobs. It is this aspect which I shall
briefly review.

The garage 'branch' has encroached on services which
involve mechanical skill other than services to agricultural
branches, and this affects these services. In performing services
to branches the garage workers have accumulated a considerable
weight of control. They assess a prospective job in terms of the
time, the number of workers, the expenditure it will involve,
the problem set, and the desirability, mechanically and economically, of doing it. Furthermore, they express opinions about the
cause of the damage, if damage it happens to be, as well as the
personal responsibility of anyone who has done the damage, and the
means they think are efficient to take him to task. They pass
judgments on people and do not make only technical assessments.
Gossip spreads this judgment through the branches and the community.
But it is, of course, not only the assessments or judgments which
function so as to control the users of the agricultural machines,
tractors and lorries; nor is it only the indirect effect of the
flow of these assessments and judgments through the effective
channels of communication which are relevant. The men who serve
the interests of the branch in the mechanical field also have a
direct control over their clients, insofar as they determine the
pace and quality of repairs, issue warnings and instructions
about the future use of machines, and have a professional say in
the initial purchase of machines and equipment. In short, the
degree of their instrumental control is considerable. Service to
the branch which stems from technological expertise, through
establishing a personal stake in the service-agency, thus becomes
a resource of power and influence in the community and its economy.
This control extends over individual members of the branch team
through the same mechanisms. The individual member is aware that
any failure or imperfect management of mechanical equipment by him
may become known to his team colleagues. Also, of course, he knows
that successful and careful management of equipment evokes appreciation, though this may be less vocal. He knows that his interaction with the service agency will inevitably affect the branch
and his standing within it. In other words, the team-member of the
agricultural branch who handles mechanical equipment is under their
constant and considerable control.

An initial brief comment is necessary here. The standing
of the 'service-to-the-meshek' vis-a-vis the agricultural branches,
as exemplified in the relationship of garage and branch, questions
the validity of the widespread suggestion that "of the various

244

categories of physical labor, agricultural labor is valued most"
(Spiro, 1956: 16), particularly its validity as applied to all
situations of work and all contexts in which ideas on the subject
are expressed by observers. The meaning of the term 'valued' is
of course crucial. I argue that the 'value' given to different
kinds of work varies situationally and contextually. No single
hierarchical scale by which work is valued is employed in the
kibbutz. When gross income is the criterion (see Table 5.1), the
poultry branch stands above the others, but when profit (plus
depreciation) is the criterion, then the citrus-grove comes first.
Similarly, if the number of labor-days per dunam are tested
(Table 5.2), it is the cotton branch; but if 'return-yielding'
sector of the meshek is used, then the agricultural branches as
a whole appear to be highest. But if the criterion is the degree
of the affinity of an occupation with the visionary ideals of the
Youth Movement, agriculture qua agriculture tops the list.

If we accept the close relationship between the ideals of
the Youth Movement (see Chapter II) and the ideology of the Kibbutz Movement and follow Spiro's suggestion that the kibbutz is
"a fellowship of those who share a common faith" (1956: 10), and
we then evaluate work by "the moral postulates of kibbutz culture"
(1956:10), certainly agricultural work is that most highly valued.
But this judgment is valid only in this context and not necessarily in others. Indeed while Spiro himself states that the hierarchical order of value ascribed to different jobs is explained
in terms of the differential scale of the one variable of hard
physical labor, he also suggests that income can also be used as
another criterion (1956: 17).

If another criterion is added, namely dependence on service
and co-operation, then the role of service-to-the-meshek will
reverse that 'ideal' order in which agriculture comes first.
Members are aware of the dependence of the agriculture branches on
these services and of the control that the latter exerts over the
former. The fact that it is the former which 'yield returns'
imposes, of course, constraints on the latter, so though they
share common objectives and are mutually dependent, nevertheless the dependency of the former on the latter is obviously felt
more immediately. If members - and they rarely do this - happen
to voice opinions which assert the supremacy of agricultural
labor, they do so only in specific situations: agricultural
branch members may raise this point when further investments are
required for their branches or, perhaps, when an outlet for
personal or group assertion is sought; while non-agriculturists
may refer to this presumed higher value when they complain about
priorities given to investments in the 'return-yielding' sector
of the meshek, or when they are disgruntled with the conditions

245

under which they work. Also, if they are questioned about the established ideological values of The Kvutza in relation to the degree of their realization in the sphere of labor in the abstract they may find themselves compelled to refer to the postulates as if these were omnipresent in all situations of kibbutz life. In conclusion, then, a permanent job in the mechanical field does not place a member in a disadvantageous position, even in the evaluation of work in terms of prestige, because such evaluation does not depend on a single criterion (see Kressel's discussion; 1974: 106-110).

While the man in the garage (and related services) has some control over the branchman with whom he enters into a working relationship, the latter's access to the mechanical equipment and vehicles and his own degree of mechanical experience and skill contribute to his position in the branch. As with control over any job within the branch and of control which emanates from professional knowledge, having a greater degree of access to mechanical equipment than others helps an individual to consolidate his position. If a member drives the same vehicles repeatedly, if he works the same machine in successive seasons, and if he specializes in use of mechanical equipment, then he establishes his access to the jobs associated with them to the partial exclusion of others. This is, of course, a matter of degree. Members are not excluded from jobs considered necessary in a branch, but expertise in assignments of a mechanical nature is important because it saves time and energy. The seasonal nature of agricultural tasks requires efficient management of the mechanical tools and equipment. The mechanics of the meshek intensify this pressure towards specialization in the use of these tools, vehicles and equipment by demanding that those objects should not change hands too frequently. And, as suggested above, these mechanics possess efficient means to bring this message home to whosoever is involved in this field. Thus a considerable degree of permanent access to, and use of, mechanical objects tends to be associated with particular members within the branch-team. Their responsibility is considerable, and so is the pressure upon them; but in turn, the degree of their control over these objects is great.

A worker in the grove whose 'permanent' job in the season is to drive the tractor may be relatively ignorant about the varieties of crops and fruits, but the driving job and other tasks are his. If, for example, he is assigned to load the fruit boxes and deliver them to the packing store, the efficiency with which he carries out his job determines the work and the pace of work of others and the fate of the fruits in the market. Or, and closer to the point, if a worker uses the mechanical citrus-

picker permanently while others are virtually tied to their ladders
and shoulder bags, the difference becomes apparent. The more complicated a mechanical object seems to be, the more valued is work
with it. The high evaluation of work with this object stems from
the obvious premises that, (a) the more expertise and training are
involved, and (b) the greater the tendency of people who have no
knowledge of the job to ascribe to it the quality of the unknown
which requires more skill, skill which they themselves do not
possess, the more people tend to regard it as important and exclusive. In other words, the partial ignorance or inexperience
of people with a particular machine and its operations, helps
the mechanically-skilled worker further to consolidate his position
in his occupation: he trains more and more in his work, his expertise increases, and in turn he is more in demand for the jobs concerned. Increasing mechanization of agriculture gives rise to a
dual process: more and more people acquire knowledge of and experience in the use of some mechanical objects and at the same time
specialization within this field takes place. The lorry driver
in the grove, the tractor driver with his cultivating plough,
the sprayer with his different kind of tractor and his own equipment, the operator of the mechanical picker, the member who works
the sorting machine, the tractor-driver who distributes empty boxes
and collects the full ones from within the tree lines, all work at
the same time, with others, in the branch. Although their jobs are
not totally mutually exclusive as far as access to them is concerned,
they do show a tendency to permanence. Each one is important in his
assignment, and thus he affects the organization and the success of
the work of other people and the branch as a whole.

Mechanical skill, particularly if related to mobile machinery,
contains a quality which other types of job or professional knowledge do not possess: the quality of retaining permanence in an
agricultural branch while enabling the member to face the possibility of branch or occupational change. Firstly, within the branch,
mechanical skill affects the selection of jobs to which a worker
may be assigned in the changing seasons, and I have shown that
permanence in a job within a branch is relative and is mainly
determined by seasonal changes. If a worker possesses mechanical
skill and experience, he is likely to follow a job cycle in the
mechanical field. It also gives him some degree of daily physical
mobility, which is apparently sought particularly by young people.
Seasonal jobs other than those involving this skill will be taken
by the mechanically orientated agriculturist only as a residual
choice. He moves from cultivating to driving and then to ploughing,
loading and unloading fruits and equipment and so on. In the grove
(and the orchard) he will compete for access to the newly introduced mechanical picker, or in the cotton, to another new machine.
He clings to his permanent branch, but within it he seeks access

247

to machines the use of which is, in principle, relevant to other branches.

Secondly, following on the last point, the skilled agricultural mechanic within the agricultural branch (the degree of whose skill is of course relative to that of other mechanics outside the agricultural branch), by the acquisition and experience of his skill, is potentially mobile. He can be useful in other branches with what are basically the same skills. Tractor driving, ploughing, spraying and the like are equally useful in the orchard and in the vineyard, in the grove and in the cotton field, and are needed in branches as small as the flowers or artichoke. The particulars of these basically similar jobs vary from one branch to another, but they sometimes vary from one crop to another in the same branch. A skilled mechanic can adapt to the different requirements in the different branches if he is moved from one branch to another. Thus, when members are called to help in branches other than their own, the driver and the mechanic are likely to be employed in jobs closely related to the ones they practice in their own branch. Indeed, the unfortunate affair of Hevyon (Chapter IV) occurred when Hevyon, then a permanent worker in the cotton branch, was called on to carry out a driving task in the grove (transporting fruits and people at different times).

The occupation emerges then as one that cuts across branch boundaries. As it shares similarities, it brings about similar effects on the incumbents' positions in the various branches. A member who possesses this skill and practices it is permanent in his branch, is mostly employed in his skill within the branch, and is helpful, in his own skill, in branches other than his own. He can afford to be less resentful, or even more enthusiastic, about moving temporarily from his own branch to help other branches.

Thirdly, a change of permanent branch for the skilled agricultural mechanic is not as painful as for the unskilled. This assumption I deduce from the preceding analysis. In fact, during my work in Hofra, no one with skills as an agricultural mechanic made a change which appeared to be permanent. Hevyon and Yardeni were going to leave their branches altogether. With this qualification in mind I suggest that this skill endows the member with another advantage vis-a-vis his branch colleagues: he can move to another branch relatively easily as his skill is likely to be needed by all the branches.

Fourthly, this potential for easy mobility is also relevant to spheres beyond the boundaries of the meshek. Mechanical skill and experience is in general demand in Israel. Drivers of tractors (particularly heavy tractors) and lorries obtain contracts which prove to be extremely profitable even if they are exhausting and tiring. A person who leaves the kibbutz and who is trained in agricultural mechanics, and particularly in driving a heavy tractor, enjoys an immense advantage during his first steps away from the kibbutz because he has a good chance of establishing himself in his new environment, particularly if he is a young man who can work hard for a long time. A few young members who left Hofra and Hardoof have followed this occupation.

More important for the present analysis, is the impact of this situation on the position of the member who remains in the kibbutz and in the branch. Such a skilled worker is in a position to be attracted by the alternative way of life and use of his skill outside the kibbutz. And the other members know this. Hence the member's position in the field vis-a-vis his colleagues is indirectly strengthened. He is in a bargaining position, even if it may be one of 'tacit bargaining' (Schelling, 1963: 9). A member does not always consciously bargain, nor do his colleagues. If he were conscious of the problem, to begin with, he would in all probability deny that he was in a bargaining situation. Moral postulates and existing social bonds cannot let people who co-operate constantly and who practically share a common lot, in work as well as in many other aspects of life, take conscious cognizance of forces not accepted by these postulates. For a member to realize that such a situation prevails and to realize that he is a partner to it requires either a great measure of detachment or a specific issue to arise, which can occur in the form of a 'social drama' (Turner, 1957) which unveils the situation and the problem at hand. Nonetheless, I suggest that this situation exists. Again, to be sure, a member may wish to leave the kibbutz regardless of immediate opportunities for jobs and for reasons irrelevant to his skill in the meshek or the applicability of his skill outside the meshek; and equally he may wish to remain in the kibbutz regardless of the occupational and other attractions outside it. But the problem at hand is the effect of the use, and potential use, of mechanical skill on the position of the individual incum-bent in the meshek, and I suggest that the demand for such skill, together with its benefits, outside the kibbutz, is a variable which should not be ignored even within the meshek.

Some young members of old kibbutzim, 'children of the kibbutz' as they are usually called, who have such skills, have established a custom under which they take a leave from the kibbutz for a period of six to twelve months, during which their stated intention is to return to the kibbutz. While away they exploit their skills to earn their livelihood and usually to save up money to make a trip abroad to 'the world.' Some of them return, some do not. Some ask to be regarded during this period as members on leave, while some leave formally, confident that they will be accepted back once they return. This skill, then, is very instrumental in young men's considerations. I suggest that this practice, coupled with the attraction which this skill promises outside the kibbutz, accounts, at least partly, for the leniency with which 'veteran' members accept that "the young as such are interested in mechanical and technological labor." This aspect brings me back to that aspect of technological, especially mechanical, skill.

I do not intend to discuss in this connection the subject of the 'young generation' or the 'second generation' of Hofra. In Chapter III, some aspects of these subjects were touched upon in connection with the composition and the functioning of the Labor Committee and its acting officers, and in connection with variations in the degree of permanence in work. If the problem of the 'young generation' as conceived in Hofra is one problem and not a set of sociologically distinct problems, then this is hardly the place to discuss it. But I touch upon this notion here because the effect of possessing mechanical skill on young people is different in some aspects from its effect on others.

People stereotype 'the young' as "crazy about machines." One member summed it up thus: "If you want a young man to work in the laundry, assign a tractor to it and you will have no problem in finding a volunteer." The usual interpretation by members of this alleged proclivity is:

(a)    that a young man is driven to seek 'action' and physical mobility by his very youthful temperament;

(b)    that he seeks a complex and elaborate job rather than simple, repetitive and sometimes dull agricultural work;

(c)    that in following the first two inclinations he follows a trend which is universal outside the kibbutz but practices it within the kibbutz.

These generalizations, significantly, refer to 'the young' as a category; they attribute the mechanical proclivity to a quality of youth; they ascribe to mechanical occupations a property which attracts youth; and they say it by reference to a universal trend. Members do not refer to the implication of mechanical skill for the position in work within the kibbutz.

Most of the members of the second generation are, in fact, engaged in the use of vehicles and mechanical equipment. I will return later to this phenomenon. But other members do not refrain from this engagement. 'Veterans' work in the regional transport co-operative and have acquired virtual permanence in it; and the garage, carpentry, smithy and the electrical services are mostly manned by 'veterans.' Furthermore, all the permanent workers of the agricultural branches at least have driving licenses and use vehicles and other tools in varying frequencies. Therefore the reference to 'the young' as a category can be misleading unless the observation is focused on these people only, regardless of behavior, tendencies and interests of the others. And although most of the members of the second generation _are_ involved in the use of vehicles and mechanical tools, some exceptions to the rule are to be found. There is no evidence, then, to support a distinction between generations in relation to mechanical skill. If people do make this distinction and add their stereotypical interpretation, they can do so because they are in a position to apply an observation on a selective field to a broader field. It is a fact that the 'young' members are engaged more than others in jobs which involve this skill. This, it seems to me, is the sole ground for the generalization.

I suggest that the following factors are associated with this 'social fact,' that is, with "regularities between facts in a social system" (Gluckman, 1968: 29 following Durkheim), although other factors are operative in this field as well. It is possible that as the process of mechanization of kibbutz agriculture (see Cohen, 1963: 382-384) occurred, as it did, in time, newer members concentrated their efforts on getting access to the relatively new and developing jobs within the branch division of labor while other members tended to continue in their previously acquired permanent jobs. This is a possible explanation, but the relation of a newer worker to a newer job is not entirely necessary. If the professional knowledge of a new member has no direct relation to a professional assignment (as in the early stage of Hadari's work in the grove), there is no direct necessary relation between a new member and a newly created job. An older member with a longer tenure in the branch may have a claim on the new job which is entailed by the introduction of mechanization. If a young member has succeeded in establishing access to this skill, additional factors should operate. These factors have been discussed above in other contexts: they reappear here in direct relation to the position of the younger worker in the branch.

First amongst them is the relative inter-branch mobility of the younger members, analyzed in Chapter III. These members are called to help agricultural branches other than their own more frequently than are other members. If these workers possess mechanical skill and consequently, as suggested above, they are likely to practice this skill in another branch, they are also

251

likely to be more willing to move temporarily to another branch. A move may even help them to develop their skill. This aspect of possession of mechanical skill sheds an additional light on the somewhat higher mobility between branches (or the lower percentage of permanence) of the younger members, as shown in Table 3.3. Mechanical skill is, then, instrumental for the younger member of the branch and functional to the interests of the meshek when peak seasons demand some mobility between branches.

The second is the possibility of outward mobility, which I discuss here in connection with the involvement of the younger members, in particular, in mechanical agricultural skills. The reliance of the kibbutz on recruitment of its own second-generation members for its endurance and development, in the virtual absence of other candidates for permanent membership, leads members to make far-reaching concessions to the prospective members of the kibbutz. The recognition of the right to higher education of every 'second-generation' member, as exemplified in the case of Yardeni (Chapter IV), is such a concession, the effects of which on the occupational structure of the kibbutz will probably emerge in the near future. The acceptance of an orientation to mechanical skill as being a 'quality of the young,' which implies access to mechanically skilled jobs to younger members, can be viewed as another concession, on a different scale, within the meshek. The effect of a concentration of young members on these occupations on the occupational structure of the kibbutz and the selective introduction and development of particular branches will most likely emerge side by side with the former process.

In conclusion, technological and mechanical skills in the agricultural branches, contain essentially the same elements which are functional to the position of the individual in the field of work as those which professional knowledge provide. But, unlike the latter, it facilitates a partial mobility between branches, which can be advantageous for the individual and which equips the individual with skill which is exploitable in contexts other than the meshek. This potential mobility further strengthens the position of the individual in the inner context of the branch and the team: it places him in a tacit bargaining position (of which he may even be unconscious) vis-a-vis other colleagues.

I make one last comment: my analysis of power inherent in technological skill should not give an exaggerated importance to the problem. Members are not constantly at loggerheads nor are they constantly absorbed with the problem of establishing individual deterrent power or an advantageous position. They work and co-operate together and are aware of their common objectives and responsibilities to the kibbutz and to one another. But in the context of the present discussion, which is concerned with the elements of the position of the individual vis-a-vis <u>others,</u> elements which contain potential use 'against' others are the objects of my observation and analysis, and can be assessed if they are discussed in relation to the effect they have on the others. I must therefore consider possible incongruences or even conflicts of interest.

## Physical effort

Physical effort required for a job is another criterion by which the division of labor, and its categories of workers, can be assessed, stereotyped and judged. Physical effort affects both differentiation of jobs within, and to some extent between branches. It also determines the nature of reward. The reward for successfully doing jobs which require physical effort is transmuted to a social asset, within the variety of elements which comprise the position in work. The following discussion attempts to elucidate this.

Physical effort can become an asset for a social position if it is related (a) to an agricultural branch; and (b) to team work. Arduous, manual labor in contexts other than these is not appreciated noticeably. Strenuous work in some construction jobs, or in digging ditches, yields no social assets for the individual who performs them, and I am only concerned here with physical effort which is relevant to creating a social position of the member. Jobs associated with physical effort which do not confer high appreciation on the worker and do not yield the reward mentioned above are not performed by members, and will be considered separately below.

Physical effort only becomes a social asset when it both is associated with work done in an agricultural branch, and is a part of a team project. This last seems to be the more important, perhaps because in team work the physical effort of the individual is more conspicuous than in other situations. Also, it is tested against the standards of the whole group which is involved in the project. In this intimate situation, the group and all its members assess the effort made by the individual, test his achievements and physical competence, and control his performance in a concerted action. Two kinds of work are involved in the 'mobilization call' of members for team work. These are: (1) <u>ad-hoc</u> jobs such as loading and unloading of products, goods and <u>equip</u>ment in the agricultural branches at the peak of the branch's season; and (2) mobilization of workers to help branches, notably in the fish ponds, when they have a pressing need for seasonal help. A common denominator of these jobs is the requirement of physical strain which demands the collective efforts of all the participants.

There are three requisites for a worker to participate in a concerted group-project which requires physical effort: physical strength, training in the efficient employment of this strength, and the ability and wish to persist in the arduous work. They also function to distinguish between those of the labor force who meet these requirements and those who do not or cannot. These requisites become, then, distinctive criteria according to which a worker is accepted into hard team-work.

(a) The requisite of physical strength leaves out those incapable of hard work, and tends to call for the mobilization of young men. Hofraites say that the young are the 'natural' candidates to be mobilized for team projects. 'The young' are all members in their 20s and early 30s. Only very rarely would an older member or a teenager be assigned to such jobs. In Hofra, where there prevails a gap between 'veterans' and 'the young' (i.e. second generation and their spouses),[22] 'mobilization' for hard team-work is expressed in terms of 'mobilization of the young.' It would hardly occur to the organizers of these projects that other people might still be physically competent to take part in such concerted efforts, and these are exclusively assigned to 'the young.'

(b) Experience in the employment of physical strength is another requisite. A physically strong man may nevertheless prove to be inefficient because he is not trained in hard, strenuous, work. In the kibbutz literature there are ample descriptions of difficulties experienced in adapting to hard work because of inexperience and lack of training.[23] Strength, in short, is not enough; systematic application of physical ability in little details of work is as important. In practical terms this require-ment leaves out most of the volunteers from abroad, transients and Ulpanites, some of whom may even be eager to join these 'ad hoc' projects in order to demonstrate their inclusion in the exclusive club of able men. In my experience few such men were able to cope with the harsh demands of these projects.

(c) Persistence in these jobs, brief as they are, is the third requisite. The work is arduous and is generally performed in hard conditions - under a hot sun, under the attacks of flies and insects, at inconvenient hours of the day when other people are enjoying their leisure. Persistence in responding to the 'mobilization' call, particularly for a period of consecutive days, or even weeks, becomes a condition if participation in these projects is to produce a social asset for the individual.

Temporary residents and transient workers do not have the same interests as members may have in responding to the call.

The residual group consists, then, of young men, mostly members, and some temporaries for whom the inclusion in the 'club' is important either in terms of personal achievement or in terms of demonstration to the significant others (in their own group or in the kibbutz), or both. As these calls tend to be necessary in specific periods in relation to agricultural needs, and as they tend to occur repeatedly throughout the annual cycle, the same member is likely to be called. He retains his permanent attachment to his own branch, but at the same time he finds himself attached to a certain group, consisting mainly of his peers, in the sphere of labor. He meets them in the situation of group effort, where both the competence of the group and his own physical competence are tested.

When fish ponds must be cleared and fish shipped to the market or, in other seasons, sorted (according to variety, sex and weight), a group of young men is mobilized to help with the job. The work involves getting into the pond. In the late winter the water is cold and all the work is done in uncomfortable water-proof suits. In the summer time it is considered easier and more comfortable to work half naked. Easier it is, but clouds of flies and insects attracted by the dead fish swarm around and on the pond. The nets are spread on the pond and the men drag the nets on their shoulders, towards a bank where the fish are trapped. Mechanical tools <u>are</u> used, but hard work cannot be avoided. The work requires physical co-ordination, strength and sufficient stamina to be able to repeat the work for several hours at intervals throughout the day. It is, then, an exercise in co-operation, co-ordination, physical strength and persistence. When I was doing this work myself, I watched some Ulpanites collapse breathlessly despite the detailed instructions given to them not to overexert themselves. Others, of course, did well.

'Mobilization' for shorter periods is sometimes, though regularly, required in loading and unloading in the horticultural branches. Again, it is physically competent men who are asked to come, so the same men meet both in the fish ponds and on the lorry platform.

These confrontations generate and demonstrate ésprit de corps. While combatting the uncomfortable conditions and the arduous work, the 'mobilized' men develop a cheerful united mood and a show of comradeship,[24] which appears as a mechanism of mutual support in the working situation. Their team spirit also induces in the participants the showing of pride in belonging to the exclusive, physically able, group when they meet in situations other than work. Exchange of impressions, discussion of shared experiences, jokes about experiences at work, occur in situations of leisure, or during meetings in the communal dining-hall, in the cultural-centre and in any public place. The ésprit de corps extends, as it were, to these situations, thus contributing to the exclusiveness of the group, vis-a-vis others. In the situation of work itself, the team-spirit emerges when the group is physically separated from other groups and individual workers in the meshek, but I suggest that the presence of the others in the background is of a considerable importance for its emergence. In the background there exists attachments to work-mates and to others who are not, and indeed cannot be, mobilized. These attachments are significant. The significance of the ésprit de corps is fuller if the presence of those who are not mobilized, as a contrasting category, is considered.

Whereas ésprit de corps animates the group itself, the people in the background, who cannot, or believe that they cannot, perform the same job, are those who give the reward of appreciation and prestige.

Sharing the same job, the same difficulties and the same efforts yields the same prestige: the prestige of the physically fit. The reward of prestige as a component of a member's standing in the group is thus bestowed on some workers to the exclusion of others. Access to the physically demanding jobs and inclusion in the ad-hoc teams incorporate the participant into a group of workers who share the same resource of prestige. The similitude of resources which contribute to a further consolidation of the position of the worker, which has been discussed above, operates here. Leading, dragging heavy nets, carrying heavy equipment, working under hard conditions, are shared by all the participants. The reward bestowed on them in singling them out for prestige is the same for all of them, and all have an equal stake in it.

At the same time it introduces a distinction within their permanent teams since only some workers can participate in loading etc. while others cannot. This distinction also exists across branches, as the same workers are selected for 'mobilization.'

By virtue of his inclusion in this group the individual enjoys the prestige conferred on it. I have suggested earlier that Spiro's statement that the kibbutz culture places high value on agricultural labor, as a category of physical labor (Spiro, 1956: 16), can be accepted if the situation in which it is done and the context in which it is expressed are assessed as well. In relation to the present phenomenon, his statement that "physical labor enjoys the greatest prestige" (1956: 16), has to

256

be reformulated. Ability to perform specific tasks requiring outstanding strength, confers a specific kind of prestige, and this prestige is considerable.

## The effects of an individual's control of different resources: restatement

The principal aim of the foregoing discussion has been to analyze and to demonstrate the coexistence of various criteria according to which division of labor in a branch operates. If the size of the branch and the team are taken into consideration, and neither is very large in Hofra, it follows that it is possible, in principle, for every individual member of a branch team to specialize in some job or task. Specialization in a job or in a skill, whatever its classification according to these criteria, contains the chance of increasing the individual's power (deterrent or otherwise) and influence within the team. The chance that practically everyone has to secure access to one of these resources of influence and to acquire (and retain) some control over it characterizes the 'organic pattern' of the larger branch organization. Skills, job, and tasks as determined by the nature of the branch may vary, but once access to one (or more) of them is within the reach of every member of the team, it introduces a measure of equality amongst them qua members of the branch team. It further elucidates the 'organic' nature of the branch division of labor, namely the interdependence of all workers. The division of labor emerges as a division among members each of whom controls, or can have access to the control of, some resource of importance to the branch. The variety of criteria shows that a member may use various means or resources in different situations in order to assert his position, whether in competition or in co-operation, and whether the position is under threat or not.

The degree of permanence in one of the jobs or the skills within the branch is relative and it is affected by seasonal fluctuations. A member in the agricultural branch must do different jobs in different seasons and in different situations. Whereas in one situation professional knowledge of a particular item is required, in another physical ability may be in demand. In different situations, different allocation of labor are employed to meet the immediate demand. This enables individual members of the team to appear on the scene on different occasions and situations, and thus to assert their importance for the branch and the meshek. The power of control on the branch is thus diffused amongst the members of the team by virtue of their roles in the branch's complex division of labor.

In the large branch power is diffused amongst members through their jobs. But the latter change according to seasonal demands. To be sure, a member tends to return to the same job every season, but this is not always possible and, in the meanwhile he has had to move from one job to another. Changes of jobs (and hence of roles) throughout the annual cycle, the constant emergence of situations in which demand arises for different types of work, and therefore the emergence of a branch organization of varying and sometimes simultaneous jobs, all hinder the permanent concentration of power in the hands of individuals. These factors also hinder the differential distribution of power within a permanent, rigid, hierarchical order of jobs in the branch, and, to a large extent, prevent the emergence of such a permanent order. The jobs, and the skills they require, and therefore the work roles in the branch can be viewed, in their relation to power, as standing one alongside another rather than in a permanent hierarchical order of one above others.[25] This last statement does not suggest a premise that there is equal weighting for all jobs or skills nor does it suggest a necessary detachment of these jobs and skills from one another. It only suggests that there is no permanent hierarchical structure of power.

## Patterns of mutually restraining elements

The relation between the different types of resources involved in social position in work is an object of study. I propose to discuss some of its aspects in the last part of this chapter. I suggest that when these resources are employed and become assets in the position of the individual worker in the field of labor, these assets, in turn, tend to form patterns with seemingly opposed characteristics. In one pattern, they balance and check one another. Thus they function not only to prevent the crystallization of a rigid hierarchical structure of power but also to hinder accumulation of various resources of power by a single worker. This patterning further operates to weaken the degree of monopoly an individual worker possesses over the resources available to him. In the other pattern there is a clustering of some of these elements together in one person. Thus they support one another and strengthen a member's personal position in the branch and in the meshek.

Interrelations between resources from which the branch-worker derives elements for his social position, in labor alone, appear to function as mechanisms to give impetus to the diffusion of power and hence control in the team. They are helped in this function by prevailing conditions in the branch, in the meshek and also in the relation of these two to relevant factors outside the meshek.  These conditions enable these elements to check one another in the context of control over the resources available in the branch.

The underlying condition for this pattern is the presence of a team.  Aside from the obvious fact that division of labor amongst people can only emerge if at least several people are present, the existence of a team is a reminder that in the kibbutz there is no person who cannot be replaced.  An illustration of this was the threat to Hadari by the acting foreman of the grove that, important for the branch as Hadari might be, if he did not comply with the demands of the team and serve its interests, the team would ask him to leave.  Such a threat could be made on the assumption that as long as there was a team, a group of branchmen, someone would be able to take over the vacated job, though possibly not without difficulties for the branch.

The presence of a branch team sets limits on the degree of Olami's control over his plot.  Firstly, of course, the team members are his colleagues and not just subordinates, even when they work in 'his' plot; they are his equals in the kibbutz, not to mention their personal positions as individuals in the kibbutz in contexts other than the branch or labor in general.  Secondly, and this is more relevant to the present argument, one of them can always substitute for Olami, if any major event occurs.  A major event does not necessarily have to be a misfortune or defection from the kibbutz; it can be an unfortunate conflict in the branch resulting in his departure from the branch.  Perhaps, being familiar with Olami's position in the branch and in Hofra in general, I cannot envisage the latter event occurring, but in principle it is potentially possible.  Misunderstandings, controversies or open quarrels have occurred in the kibbutz, leading to the departure of members from their branches.  The vacancy has always been taken up by another member, whether by the reorganization of the work of the remaining members of the team or through the recruiting of a new branchman.  If a branch shrinks or disappears from the meshek, it is not because of a defection of a single member of a larger team.  The history of the meshek has proved that an individual member in a team is replaceable, though not without cost to the meshek.  Furthermore, the kibbutz has experienced defections from the community as a whole as well as from a particular branch.  In some events such defections entailed changes in branches, but the affected branch endured.

Another condition, related to the former, is the size of the branch.  Hofra is not a very large meshek.  As has already been stated, its relatively large branches are not so very large. Permanent workers, therefore, obtain knowledge of and experience in various jobs within their branch.  They may have no specialized knowledge on some aspects, but through working continuously in the branch, they are far from being ignorant. To this I add the factor I discussed in relation to the absence of a rigid hierarchical structure of power, namely, the seasonal fluctuations in the agricultural branch. These fluctuations familiarize each member of a team with various jobs and plots of his branch. When I discussed the division of labor in the grove-branch, I stressed in effect that there was no rigid, distinctive allocation of jobs. Oreg does not work in Gderoth Area only. He works in the Home Grove, the plot under Olami's management, when this is necessary. The sprayer takes other jobs when he does not spray. The poultry worker who has no responsibility for a particular section, substitutes for any one of those who have when they are absent or ill. Through this practice he acquires knowledge of both the job and the section so that he is a potential replacement, beyond being a substitute in emergencies. His presence in the branch controls the behavior of his permanent counterpart in it and restrains the latter's actions.

The principal point is that the one set of implications of the division of labor are checked by other implications. Since division of labor in the branch is not on a single basis (i.e., according to knowledge or to area or to physical ability, etc. alone), a member who specializes in one sphere and gets a considerable control over it faces the fact that in other spheres in the branch others enjoy control. Thus Hadari is very efficient in terms of his professional knowledge and he is also a good scientific adviser to others. But when organizational tasks should be done or when the fruits should be picked or sorted and classified, or when the plots are to be irrigated, let alone sprayed, he is no more of an asset to the branch than others. Other members in these jobs, whose power lies not in professional knowledge but in mechanical skill or in physical competence, check, by virtue of their own position in the branch, the power of his position in it.

Again, Olami is a devoted and diligent worker. He shows a considerable degree of responsibility in his management of his plot. But he cannot accomplish all the tasks alone. He depends on the co-operation of his colleagues: on all when oranges are picked; on the sprayer for combatting insects and diseases; on others for loading the orange boxes or for unloading heavy bags of chemical fertilizer and other equipment; on the tractor driver for seasonal cultivation. Since his control is limited to one sphere of the branch's division of labor it is thus kept in bounds by control of other colleagues over spheres other than his, even within his own plot.

260

Similarly, social exploitation of technological skill is checked by the availability of mechanically oriented men both in the branch and in the meshek in general, use of machines, tools and vehicles. When I discussed technological skill as a resource of power in the branch, unlike the discussions of other spheres of control determined by the various types of division of labor in a branch, I began with the main factor which restrains the possessor of this skill, in the garage and its attached services. The restraint is centered in a specialized agency whose staff's job is to check, supervise and control the users of vehicles, tools and mechanical equipment. They exert at least latent pressure on their staffs.

In the sphere of professional knowledge two mechanisms for curbing control held by individuals (or, in line with Emerson's model (Emerson, 1962: 32-34)[26], mechanisms which are set to control resources held by the possessor of power and his use of them thereby changing the one-way direction of the power-dependence relation) are discerned. The first has to do with the branch and the kibbutz; the second with a relation of these two to a relevant agency outside the meshek.

A means by which professional knowledge is diffused in the team is the participation of members of the team in study-days and in courses. As in the case of other resources, share of professional knowledge by a growing number of members of the team diffuses power which is contained in the control of this resource for a social position. Study-days are organized region-ally and nationally by the professional associations with which the branchmen, by virtue of their attachment to a given branch, are affiliated, and/or by the relevant agencies of the Ministry of Agriculture,[27] or the agricultural Boards.[28] Many of these study-days are held in slack seasons or before and after the harvesting seasons, thus enabling a large number of members to attend. The subjects of the lectures and the discussions vary, and this variety gives opportunities for all the participants to obtain access to some knowledge of aspects with which they may be unfamiliar in their routine work in the branch.

I have discussed agricultural courses above. A member of the team who attends a course concerning the crops of his branch secures access to a resource of social position, but at the same time he establishes this position vis-a-vis another member who has already acquired this knowledge through systematic as well as unsystematic training. In doing so, he limits the possible scope within which the former would be able to exercise his control. He can demonstrate his newly acquired professional knowledge both in the work situation where members witness his

261

performance or in team meetings where he can assert his knowledge vis-a-vis the older possessors of knowledge. It is not uncommon in meetings of branch-teams for a member who has returned from a course to take an active part in the discussion in matters on which he has specialized in the course. There is always the probability that he has brought back the most recent scientific finding or method. The man who has done an agricultural course does add an asset to his position in doing so, but this step also is a means of checking others' positions in the field.

Perhaps the relatively poor attendance of Hofraites at agricultural courses contributes, in a negative way, to the sharing of most members in the same level of basic knowledge. People who do not participate in this programme do not take part in limiting the degree of control held by others, but neither do they hold such positions of control (derived from attendance of these courses) themselves.

An important means by which a sign of an individual's monopoly over professional knowledge is kept in place is the role played by the agricultural instructors of the Agricultural Instruction Administration. If in the realm of technological skill, the garage-men in daily practice, and the eager would-be mechanics, by virtue of their latent availability, intervene in the distribution of power by checking the control held by the skilled branchman, in the realm of professional knowledge this role is played by the agricultural instructor. Firstly, he is available whenever he is needed. He inspects the crops or animals, or birds in which he specializes every so often. He meets branchmen, chiefly the specialists in the branch and the foreman. He advises the meshek authorities. His authority in the field checks the control over professional knowledge held by the local expert. Secondly, he is potentially present, so to speak. Even when he is not in the branch and his advice is not sought, everybody in the branch and the meshek is aware of his possible availability. In the event of disagreement over an issue which requires expertise, he can be called, so that he is within reach of the branchman, the foreman, and the meshek officer. The task of the instructor is to advise and help and an important feature of his job lies in his being independent of local personal and interpersonal considerations. To be sure, he may be involved in interpersonal relationships, but he is not dependent on them. His obligation is the professional care of the crops or animals, and these belong to the meshek, not to individuals, whatever their position in the branch may be. Furthermore, he helps the meshek to overcome difficulties in the realm of professional knowledge in cases of change of personnel or absence of the local expert. When the foreman of the poultry branch (who was also the chief expert) was seriously ill and could not return to work for a long time, and nobody else within the team could take the responsibility for professional control of the branch, the situation was aggravated by an outbreak of fowl disease. Another member took over the managerial tasks, but the agricultural instructor was also called in to deal with the diseases.

The kibbutz, in short, is in a position to use these agents to check both the professional knowledge of its local experts and, if necessary, the latter's social power. The potential availability of these agents is sufficient to make actual recourse to them very rare.

In conclusion, two closely related patterns emerge. I will now summarize them in different order. First, resources in the various spheres of work which are defined by division of labor in a branch and which can be employed in buttressing the position of the individual vis-a-vis others, can also be used to restrain it. Access to professional knowledge, technological skill or responsibility for a branch-section, when shared by others, limits the amount of individual's control over them and therefore his position of power in the branch. Second, control over one or more of these resources, in the context of the team, may cut across control by another member over another resource, thus keeping the distribution of power in the team diffused. These two patterns emerge as mechanisms for checking the accumulation of power in particular jobs and therefore in particular work-roles, which could lead to crystallization of a hierarchical structure of power.

These mechanisms, particularly the second, also check possible tendencies for different resources to cluster together so as to dominate the distribution of power and influence in the team. However, as I stated in presenting the problem of the relations between assets derived from different types of branch division of labor, there is also a pattern in such relationships which runs counter to the 'diffusive' direction. This is now the subject of further analysis.

## Clustering of elements

I return to the case of Ozer (GI), whom I discussed in relation to division of labor based on spatial separation. I have described him as the virtual founder of the whole citrus-branch and as an active member in the team before his decision to concentrate on his particular plot. I noted the training he had undergone in growing citrus before the first grove in Hofra was planted and the long experience he had accumulated in citrus. The occupational life of Ozer in the grove shows that he has enjoyed access to, and the employment of, various resources of a social position in a branch: he accumulated professional knowledge and expertise, he acquired an indispensable experience in different jobs, he employed various tools and instruments in work, and finally, he developed a particular plot, applying to it all his skill, expertise and resources other than those immediately associated with the branch, such as his position of high prestige in the community.

I suggest that Ozer could not have carried out his plan to plant a new grove had he not possessed some control over some of these resources. It is inconceivable that an inexperienced worker could undertake such a job; it is further inconceivable that he could do it without a considerable amount of professional knowledge and with working in it, physically, himself. Should an individual unrealistically assess his ability to cope with all the problems with which he would inevitably be faced if he proposed to undertake such a task, the kibbutz authorities would be aware of his shortcomings.

Once the new grove was planted, Ozer had access to a considerable control over resources in the shape of responsibility for a spatially distinct section and in the shape of professional knowledge which he had earlier enjoyed and, though perhaps to a lesser extent, in the shape of technological skill relevant to his plot. I believe that Ozer's main motivation in setting out to embark on a new project in the grove was his desire to commemorate his son in a way in which he would be able to take an active part, and not considerations of control over resources as such. But whatever his considerations were and now are, and whatever resources he had under control in the past before planting the new plot, there is no doubt that at least two of the above resources together play an important part in his present position in the field of labor: his responsibility for the plot as a whole and his professional knowledge. Other elements play minor parts. In relation to Ozer, these assets cluster together in one person - by coming together, they give a considerable amount of power. They do not keep one another in balance in the arena of the team relationships by being held by two different branchmen. By clustering together, they provide their holder with a disposition over power in the branch, and this is different from the disposition of his colleagues' power. The diffusion of power in the branch, which is not absolute even when the control of assets in the team is distributed ideally, so as to check the power vested in particular work roles, thus faces a further setback. The pattern of grouping of two or more resources under the control of one worker blocks, to

some extent, the opposing tendency to distribute the resources
contained in the branch amongst all the members of the team.

This pattern seems to emerge in a few cases, and these have
to be explained in an historical perspective. The pattern is
related to the development of the branch. A new member in a large
branch tends to acquire, through practice, a general knowledge of
the branch's work. In addition, he tends to specialize in a
particular job or skill. Thus he establishes his position in the
branch. This practice has been followed by Nahari (011)[29] and by
Neil.[30] The probability is that the member gains some control over a
limited number of resources and his position is checked by others.
A member of a smaller branch, on the other hand, enjoys the chance
to specialize in as many aspects as the branch, as a whole, can
offer. As I suggested in discussing the 'mechanical' type of
branch organization, he enjoys the chance to share control over
a variety of resources in the branch. When this branch develops
and expands, a new pattern of division of labor emerges, but his
experience can still be of use in various fields. The clustering
of various resources in one worker's position in the branch is
particularly feasible in the small branch where they, in fact,
overlap, and this is likely to occur particularly in the earlier
stages of the expansion of a branch. Ozer has established access
to the various resources throughout his long tenure in the branch
and in the successive stages of the development of the branch.
For a new member in the grove it is more doubtful.

I must add here one comment: the size of the branch, its
expansion and growth, and the pace of growth are conditions on
the basis of which, in varying degrees, the individual can
develop interest in various tasks. But he will do it, thereby
maintaining his control over a number of resources, if he has
interest in the field. A member may remain in an expanding branch
without developing or maintaining interest in the variety of its
aspects or the variety of the resources available in it for the
development of his social position.

A new member of a large team, I have suggested, faces more
or less an established division of labor within the branch when
he joins it. When the branch develops further, and specialization
thereby emerges, his chances of establishing a relatively independent position in the branch and of developing assets of power,
increase. Together with these prospects, or as an alternative
prospect, he may aspire to a different type of control in the
branch: he may be interested in an active sharing of branch
management, that is, in organizational tasks. The 'Branch
Organizer,' i.e., the foreman, is the holder of the organizational
role par excellence. A member may be interested in the office of

a foreman or in sharing the tasks involved in this office. Indeed, a process is discernible in large branches in kibbutzim whereby the emergent new foreman is the typical 'organization man' rather than the typical expert (Cohen, 1963: 384-387). A branchman may regard organizational tasks and responsibilities as more interesting, attractive or gratifying, or more accessible than other tasks. He may be interested in the office, but he may also be interested in sharing parts of it.

I do not discuss further the office of the branch foreman as such. This subject requires a separate discussion.[31] I wish, however, to mention that the sharing of management of a branch in varying degrees and in various spheres (such as labor organization, marketing, responsibilities, professional advice and supervision, representation in the kibbutz and in economic and professional agencies outside it) is a chance which is open, in principle, to the member of a team in his own field of interest. Any member who holds control over some resource in the branch may find himself in a situation in which he performs managerial tasks. The permanent plot-worker in the grove, such as Olami, does it ostensively in the harvesting season; the expert on pruning does it less explicitly when he supervises the performance of other workers; the tractor driver instructs the people who pick oranges or grapefruits where and how to arrange the fruit boxes, and so on. Obviously, when resources cluster together under the control of one person, he performs more than one task. When he does this, there are more situations in which not only is the power he has through his individual performance in the spheres he controls exerted more frequently, but also he is likely to take on more managerial tasks. This applies to Ozer as well: he derives power from the combination of expertise, experience and authority over a plot and he also shares managerial tasks.

In the list of criteria for types of division of labor I have included sharing of management. But I have avoided discussing power in the branch in terms of managerial position for two reasons. (a) I maintain that power in the branch resides in the resources which the division of labor helps to activate without the mediation of branch management. I hope that I have demonstrated that the effect of holding various jobs, skills and tasks in the branch on the individual members of the team, and on the team as a whole, is not necessarily mediated by channels of management. Involving the discussion of management in relevance to this problem would have complicated and confused the issue; and (b) In the present analysis, I concentrate on the elementary components of the position of the member in the field of labor. Although many members find themselves in various situations involved in managerial tasks, management is not an elementary component of a social position of any member of a team. By virtue of the branch's division of labor, any member has access to some sphere of specialization and therefore to some source of power. The spheres are different from one another and so are the resources, but assets which are derived from them are elementary components of the individual's position. Management, on the other hand, being an instrument of power par excellence, introduces a different dimension.

The following case encapsulates the whole argument about the pattern of the grouping of various resources under the control of one person.

Malakhi (A1) is one of the founding members of The Kvutza. In the early days of settlement in the Valley he changed branches. In Chapter III where I discussed establishment in permanent branches, I reported members' stories about his past occupations. After a few changes of branch, he settled in the vegetable garden. He introduced the artichoke into the wide range of vegetables in the branch. He is said to have been "the pioneer of artichoke" in the region. Like Orgad in the orchard, he showed immense energy in advancing professional knowledge of the crop he had introduced into the meshek and the Valley, and in developing the branch. He specialized in every possible aspect of caring for the crops; he acquired more and more expertise and also routine experience; he stood up to hard, strenuous, work under harsh conditions; and he developed his mechanical skill in the branch. In terms of the present analysis, he held control over a large variety of resources in the branch. His ensuing power in the branch and influence in the meshek were considerable.

But the vegetable garden as a branch declined: eventually it disappeared. The disappearance of the branch from the meshek is associated with processes which have taken place on a national level.[32] Briefly, vegetable crops have become the field in which the moshav has specialized. The kibbutz has concentrated more and more on branches into which mechanization could be introduced, and for which no threat of frequent surpluses of produce is to be feared (Kanovsky, 1966: 53). The nature of the vegetable branch, particularly its constant and frequent seasonal fluctuations, made the maintenance of labor force to meet all the changing requirements of the seasonal crops impossible. Members did not like and would not agree to shift employment frequently; the kibbutz was reluctant to hire workers on a mass scale (Kanovsky, 1966); and the advancing sexual division of labor in the kibbutz marked the exodus of women from agricultural branches, thus making the maintenance of a permanent labor force in the branch impossible. The national trend under which the kibbutzim gave up vegetable crops was thus accelerated by the internal dynamics of the growing

267

tendencies of men to seek permanence in branches which promised fewer seasonal shifts and of women to leave agricultural labor.

Despite this decline the artichoke was continuously planted and grown. The branch, under the management of Malakhi, has become the artichoke branch. It covered a considerable area. As recently as 1967, 193 dunam were planted with artichoke (according to the audited balance sheet for 1966/67). In the Economic Plan for 1968/69 the Meshek Organizer speaks of 192 dunam. The lion's share of its yield was exported and the branch was profitable.

Notwithstanding these advantages for the meshek, the branch shrank from 192 dunam in 1968/69 to 35 dunam in 1969/70, out of which only 24 dunam were effective. Hofra has gradually followed the pattern of the national kibbutz economy: concentration on large branches, fewer in number than in the earlier days of the meshek. Kanovsky (1966: 51-57; 129-130) and Cohen (1963: 382-388) draw attention to nationally effective factors in the economic and the technological spheres: considerations of efficiency and reduction of investment of labor, adaptability of crops to mechanization, intervention of the central planning authorities, rationalization of labor and rational allocation and use of mechanical equipment, and, of course, considerations of profitability. Some of them are relevant to the decline not only of the vegetable garden in general but also more recently of the artichoke branch. Artichoke is a triennial crop. It requires a new area every three years. When an area for artichoke, which must be installed with networks of irrigation pipes, is to be chosen, one must look for tracts which are not planted with perennial crops (such as citrus, deciduous trees or vines). An increasing share of these tracts has been allotted to the new, profitable branch which grows cotton.

But the dynamics of the decline of the artichoke branch can be viewed against the local background of the branch organization and its effect on the members of Hofra. Unlike the orchard or the grove, the branch can hardly promise full employment to all its workers throughout the year. The smaller it gets, the less the employment, the more members are reluctant to consider permanence in such a branch. Nonetheless, all the persons concerned, from the Meshek Organizer, through one-time members of the branch-team, to other people, agree that these difficulties could, and can, be overcome: the Heavy Soil Area, traditionally allotted to, and ideal for, artichoke, on which cotton now grows, could be re-allotted to artichoke. If the branch expands again, permanent employment in it will increase considerably. No decision to cease production in the branch has been taken by any authorized body of the kibbutz. It is still possible to reverse what appears to be a process of decline. It requires that members who work in

the branch should continue to do so; that members who had worked
in the branch and left it should return to it; or that other
members should join.  But newcomers do not come forward; members
who had worked in the branch and left are openly reluctant to
return; of the remaining three, one is going away to university
studies and Malakhi himself, after devoting so much of his life
to the project, has announced that he can no longer carry the
burden of responsibility for the branch.  He concedes that the
absence of professionals means that artichokes cannot be grown,
unless he agrees, as he has, to remain in the branch and play
the 'secondary role' of an adviser to the new foreman.

On the face of it, there could be promise: the branch could
be revived to the benefit of the meshek; it could become an
attraction for a new team; it could attract an energetic and
ambitious young man who would like to be a foreman.  Yet none of
this has happened.  I argue that this situation is an extension
of the problem of control over a variety of resources in the
branch, centered in one person.  I argue further that this concentration of control in a single person has reached a stage
where it frustrated itself.  More specifically, I suggest that
Malakhi has controlled most, if not all, the resources on which
other members of the team could lean in their quest for a social
position in it and this fact has alienated prospective branchmen.
I suggest that his control, held in a branch which is no longer
large, has made things more difficult for others, because,
as I have argued earlier in this chapter, for a small team to
remain together as a branch and to co-operate, access to all the
resources must be assured in realistic terms to everybody in the
team.

I do not suggest that Malakhi had contrived a scheme by
which he would gain, and retain, unbalanced power.  I tend to
think rather, that he regarded the artichoke branch as his life-
achievement in the spheres of production and labor, and therefore
he devoted all his own personal resources to the development and
success of the branch with which he identified himself.  His
devotion to, and stubborness in, the artichoke work is widely
reputed.  His face-to-face encounters with his associates in
work are reputed to be fair: he is said never to have demanded
from others tasks which he himself would not first do.  Sometimes, under difficult conditions, such as stormy winds and rains,
he would ask his associates to take shelter while he undertook
himself to go on with the task.

But the crucial issue for the present analysis is not
Malakhi's own conception of the problem nor his motives.  Prospective members of the artichoke branch were faced with a state

269

of affairs in which practically every resource in the branch on which they could establish their own personal positions - skill, professional knowledge, experience and authority - was under his control. This situation resulted in growing resentment and criticism. Instead of discussing the problem of concentration of power in the branch and dependence of the prospective workers on Malakhi, these prospective workers criticized his handling of the branch: criticism was expressed, for example, about his alleged refusal to mechanize the method of harvesting. He was accused of impeding mechanical progress because of personal attachment to romantic, outdated methods of agricultural labor which involved hard physical efforts, thus deterring people who are more mechanically oriented. He was criticized for his stubborn behavior at work in ignoring environmental hardships, thus creating conditions, it was alleged, for other people to have reservations about permanence in the branch. The object of these criticisms is his handling of the branch. The explanation for his behavior, as is customary, is attributed to his personality: he behaves as he does because he is stubborn, and because he clings to outdated conceptions of agricultural work so as to preserve the prime of his days as an excellent pioneer, good worker, and agricultural innovator, who turned into a conservative. But underneath this psychologistic criticism it is possible to discern the issue at hand: access to all the resources discussed in this chapter was controlled by Malakhi. Professional knowledge certainly resided with him; so did the technological skill. Access to mechanical skill and at least a partial control of it could still be available if new machines and new methods were introduced into the branch, but if these were to be blocked, no incentive in this sphere could exist and attract people who were interested in this channel of specialization. Management of the branch remained with Malakhi. His outstanding performance in physical work, and what was conceived as stubborn defiance of difficulties in this sphere, questioned the probabilities of excellence of others in it. To be sure, people would not like to be engaged in strenuous work permanently, but the chance to excel in seasonal or ad-hoc jobs does have some attraction. Malakhi has demonstrated, and not in ad-hoc jobs, that this resource of prestige resided in him. People thought that this resource was used excessively. In a word, access to all these resources was to be obtained only through Malakhi.

With the reduction in branch size, the problem became more acute: people do not accept an uneven distribution of power in a small team. Malakhi's eventual resignation would not change the situation radically. For a new man to take over responsibility for the revived branch, a complete dependence on Malakhi is necessary. A new branchman cannot dispense with Malakhi's monopoly on professional knowledge. Planning as well as daily

270

inspection and care must still depend on him. Malakhi's suggestion that he play second fiddle can be accepted with relief by the
meshek authorities but they realize that a prospective branchman
may be deterred. The branch is now (1970/71) considered as doomed.
Malakhi has joined the kitchen staff, his second associate (A2) is
joining the chicken branch, and the third young man is on his way
to university studies in agriculture. A fourth member, who was
expected for a long time to become an active worker in the branch
and a prospective foreman (and who took a critical attitude
towards Malakhi), has left the kibbutz.

In conclusion, I repeat, of course there is a problem of
allotment of scarce land to branches; of course there is a problem
of the rational use of and investment in mechanical equipment; of
course larger branches are easier to handle; and of course it is
exceedingly difficult to maintain and to preserve smaller units
if younger people leave the kibbutz. All these factors obviously
have affected the decline of the artichoke branch. But they
could hardly, in themselves alone, account for the decline of the
branch if allocation of control within the team had not been
impeded by an uneven concentration of power which alienated
prospective branchmen. In the artichoke case, this grouping
has, in the long run, frustrated itself. While production in
the branch was still functioning, however, the clustering of
resources around one worker was, in terms of power, self-supporting.

## Conclusions

My aim in this chapter has been to search for the underlying
common characteristics of the assets which the various individuals
in a branch team possess while the assets themselves are different.
It has been a search for the similar properties of dissimilar
elements. The elements are assets for a social position in the
sphere of labor which the individual derives from resources to
which he secures access and over which he holds some control.
Together (and together with assets discussed in previous chapters)
they constitute the position of the individual. Hence their
presence or absence and their distribution in the team in relation
to the individual affect the latter's position. Access to different resources is determined by the branch division of labor.
Labor in the branch, in turn, is divided in respect of authority
over (and responsibility for) spatial sections within the branch,
professional knowledge and expertise, technological and mechanical
skill, physical competence, and sharing in management. The
complex of criteria for the branch division of labor elucidates
the plurality of spheres in which the individual can specialize
and establish his position in the branch and in the field of
work in general. The plurality of spheres elicits the plurality

271

of resources. The resources are different from one another yet they share a basic property in common: access to and control of a resource in any of these spheres provides the individual with an asset which strengthens his position. With this property inherent in any of the resources, the plurality of the latter invigorates the probability that practically every member of a branch-team will have some control over _some_ resource. It amounts to saying that any team-member will have some power in the branch. Put in another way, every member will have a share in the disposition and distribution of power in a branch since potential power resides in any one of these resources.

The distribution of power which resides in the resources of the branch is patterned by the type of the branch's division of labor. In branches where division of labor is advanced, members of the team tend to attach themselves to particular permanent, if seasonal, jobs or skills, leaving others for colleagues. Thus the individual branchmen derive their strength in the team from dissimilar resources in a similar way. In branches where division of labor is rudimentary, even only embryonic, branchmen derive social power from recourse to the same resources. I have termed the former pattern 'organic' and the latter 'mechanical.' The 'organic' pattern tends to emerge in larger branches where division of labor is advanced, whereas the 'mechanical' pattern tends to appear in smaller branches. In branches where organization of work and distribution of power are 'mechanical,' control of resources is shared and positions in the branch overlap. If access to the branch resources is blocked, the team tends to disintegrate.

In branches where advanced division of labor gives rise to the 'organic' types of labor and branch organization and distribution of power, the positions of individuals do not tend to overlap. When resources become elements of social position in the branch, inter-relations between them tend to pattern in two different directions. There are situations in which, owing to the presence of a variety of resources and a variety of possible uses of one resource, the possession of one or more of these elements tends to check or cut across social power which is contained in the possession of another. There are other situations in which one worker holds control over several resources. There is no overlapping here, but a grouping together of several resources of social power in one position. I would hesitate to suggest that there are universal conditions under which either of these patterns would appear. A detailed study of the situation in which they emerge is required.

272

Finally, in any type of branch division of labor, and particularly when all of the types are in operation, there is a chance for the permanent member of the team to establish access to _some_ resource of social position in the sphere of labor and thus establish a position of _some_ social power and influence.

N O T E S

1. The data aim to show the difference in variables which
   constitute 'size.'

2. Number of labor days is taken from the 1969 records. Since
   the size of the branches (save one) has not changed radically
   in 1970, accurate figures for 1969 are preferable to estimates
   for 1970. The exception is the artichokes branch, which was
   reduced from 192 dunam in 1969 to 35 in 1970. Therefore the
   plan estimates the figure of 600 labor days.

3. The flowers branch is not included in this table because it
   is supposed to close up in 1970. It had already shrunk to
   15 dunam and is the only branch to end up with a deficit (of
   IL 800.-) according to the Economic Plan for 1970. It has
   employed two members.

4. The number of permanent members given in this column reflects
   the real number of members working in the branch in 1970 and
   does not include those who 'belong' but are away from Hofra
   or in the process of moving out of the branch.

5. Labor is recorded according to branches rather than crops.
   Therefore no records can be found of labor invested in different crops within the branches. Relation of work to varieties
   of cotton, grapes, and fish are even harder to calculate.

6. This figure is calculated on the basis of data for 1968/9.
   According to the Meshek Organizer's own estimate for 1970 (600
   labor days, 35 dunam) the figure should be 17.14.

7. The paradox that the figures show a degree of scarcity of
   labor, while people argue that there is redundancy, stems from
   the implicit assumption in Table 5.3 that the amount of labor
   invested in any economic branch is allocated according to an
   objective need. In reality, concentration of people in a
   branch - if it is a large one - above a certain level affects
   its productivity. On the other hand, while numerical records
   of labor treat all labor days as qualitatively equal, differences between the workers in regard to physical strength,
   health, competence, age, etc., do exist. These, in turn,
   affect the number of labor days further required. Thus,
   while the records show a low degree of productivity in this
   branch (the value of one labor day was estimated IL 19.- but
   the Meshek Organizer argued that it could reach the value of
   IL 35.-), the concentration of members (some of whom were

limited in physical ability) in that branch (a) required more rather than less labor to meet contingencies; (b) the frequency of illnesses, age exemptions etc. brought about the paradoxical results of figures lower than 25 in the slack season; and (c) helped the meshek to assign members to this 'return-yielding' ('productive') branch rather than adding some of them to the 'services to man.'

8. "The emergence of 'roof branches' stems from two kinds of factors... on the one hand, an 'external' pressure, such as a change in market conditions and the New Agricultural Policy, which encourage specialization and the introduction of new crops thereby bringing about indirectly the decrease in the number of crops and in the number of branches in which the kibbutz specializes; on the other hand, the processes of planning, efficiency and mechanization of the kibbutz's meshek necessitate the grouping of autonomous branch units, each of which has equipment and a team of its own, into a complex branch in which a central control will be [practiced] over the use of the equipment and over the allocation of the workers to the various tasks... A number of small crystallized branches are thus grouped into one 'nuclear' and large branch."

9. See footnote 7 above.

10. I cannot discuss the problems of this branch in full as it would divert the course of my argument. But a few points should be noted. The local chicken-run is associated with two organ-izations: the National Poultry Breeders Union and a regional organization, which regulate respectively the marketing of chicklings and pullets (and therefore influence the policy of egg-hatching for this purpose) and the hatching of eggs of different stocks of chickens. The larger organization raises a levy on any pullet sold and has accelerated thereby a change in the economic policy of the branch, compelling Hofra to abandon an elaborate system of pullet-raising in a close collaboration with individual moshav farmers throughout the Valley. National and regional considerations determine policies which pertain to the following: the allocation of different stocks to different meshakim; the economic objectives of local chicken-runs (such as the latter's specialization in particular stocks for different use - edible eggs, chicklings, pullets, meat, etc.); the prices of products; and the sanitary requisites, etc., although they leave a fair level of freedom to the local meshek. Under the effect of the roles of these organizations (of which Hofra is a constituent member), 1970 was, to some extent, a period of transition in the structure of the local poultry branch and its economic policies. Never-

theless, these changes have not affected labor in the branch or the roles of the members of the team.

11. That is not to imply that a person who does have access to resources such as management, skill etc. has, by necessity, a smaller interest in the performance of work itself.

12. The addition of the areas and the plots marked on the 1962 map issued by the Water Commission of the Ministry of Agriculture totals 498 dunam; the Economic Plan for 1969/70 states the total area as 510 dunam.

13. On this subject see Kanovsky (1966), particularly Chapter VI and Conclusions. Kressel's (1974) exposition illuminates this.

14. See Chapter II on hityashvut.

15. Mentioned above in Chapter IV.

16. Usually I apply the term 'branch' to the agricultural organizational framework within which labor is co-ordinated and carried out. In other words, to the unit which used to be called 'productive branch.' There is no fixed term for these services. The term mostly used in Hofra is 'place of work.' For the lack of a suitable term and since I do not devote much space to these units, I prefer to call them 'branches.'

17. See discussion on this problem in Chapter III, the cases of Yonah and Yamin and Olya. See Garfinkel (1956).

18. The subject of how social control is exerted on him and the particularly interesting problem of all the forms this control takes, cannot be discussed here.

19. This pattern gives rise to a host of problems in relation to permanence of the incumbents in other branches and in relation to employment of aging members; to repercussions of the elections on the incumbents' employment in general; and to problems of competition for the jobs, itself relevant to various networks of relationships in the community.

20. Many problems are left, to be dealt with elsewhere.

21. This argument is also reflected in Cohen's study of team cohesiveness (Cohen, 1962). Professional training appears

to be one of the major variables affecting satisfaction in the branch and group cohesiveness. Cohen analyzes, among other things, the importance of the involvement of the worker in the ends of the production and its relation to professional knowledge and training.

22. See Appendix II.

23. See, for example, Luz (1962: 351-354).

24. On the team spirit of permanent branch-workers see Cohen (1962: 82 and 1963: 380).

25. I hope that it is clear that I am not discussing here the problem of hierarchies in the kibbutz, whether in relation to ideological postulates, to attitudes towards occupations, or in general. Nor am I discussing stereotypical hierarchies in the field of work, a subject discussed by Spiro (1956: 16-17). I have, however, commented on one of the aspects of this problem above in relation to mechanical skill and physical effort. I have touched here only on the diffusion of power amongst jobs and roles in the branch.

26. See recapitulation of the discussion on deterrent power, Chapter III.

27. The main agency for agricultural instruction is the Agricultural Instruction Administration, under the joint direction of the Ministry of Agriculture and the Settlement Department of the Jewish Agency.

28. Production and Marketing Boards are established for most of the crops in Israel (such as: citrus, deciduous crops, cotton, tobacco) in association with the Ministry of Agriculture. A Board co-ordinates the actions of the growers, producers and market agents in matters of harvesting, marketing, prices, export etc. It is involved in instruction insofar as its interest is to keep its constituent members up to date.

29. See Chapter IV.

30. See Chapter III.

31. For an analysis of this subject see Rosner (1964) and Yuchtman (1972).

32. For a study of changes in the kibbutz agriculture on a national level, see Cohen (1963).

# CONCLUSIONS

As the concluding sections in each chapter recapitulate the essence of the argument, I can now directly re-state the general problem dealt with in this book. I also wish to comment on two subjects I have had no space to discuss fully: the relevance of mixed farming and of the presence of non-members in the labor force to the central problem of this book. These comments should put the discussion in its proper perspective.

## A general view of the problem

My aim in this book was to study the social position of the member of the kibbutz in the sphere of the agricultural productive labor. I therefore focused my observation and most of the discussion on this sphere. I only deviated from this course when I felt it necessary to draw attention to constraints which originated in the wider spheres of communal life, and to their effects on the behavior of members in the sphere of labor. The study is concerned with a particular sphere and hence I could obviously take no additional space to discuss the relevance of other spheres of the kibbutz communal life. I do feel, however, that the individual's social position in the field of work should also be examined from starting points in other spheres of kibbutz life. These could illuminate aspects which are not examined sufficiently in the present study and contribute to a better understanding of the subjects which _were_ discussed.

At the background of the reported events, the regularities of behavior, the conception of the problems by the actors, and the analysis itself there is the kibbutz: the community which encompasses the residential unit (the village), economic corporation and the commune of services, collective consumption, and collective education. Here people share many aspects of life and their relationships tend to be multiplex, so that it is very difficult to isolate relevant factors for meaningful analysis. One is at constant risk of doing injustice to one's own analysis by isolating what seem to be the relevant factors.

With these qualifications, I again elucidate the pivotal problem which I posited. The kibbutz is an egalitarian society. Basic resources are shared or allocated on an egalitarian principle (Leon, 1967: 71-89 and also Rosenfeld, 1951: 767, who analyzes inequality). I refer to resources such as housing, food, the education given to each child, and commodities such as clothing and shoes, services to man, and cash. The egalitarian principle

278

of allocation and sharing is modified only by ascribed traits:
age, sex, seniority in the kibbutz, and health (Talmon-Garber,
1956: 153-178). The resources to which I have referred here are
in the direct control of the kibbutz and its administrative
machinery and it is through this machinery, itself controlled by
public regulations, that all the members acquire access to these
resources. The flow of these resources to the individual is
channelled, so to speak, through the publicly-controlled agencies
of the commune which are committed to egalitarianism. But the
kibbutz is not only an egalitarian commune; it is also a productive meshek. Hofra has a mixed farm and a diversified economy.[1]
Occupations and jobs are by necessity different from one another,
since different crops are grown and branches are therefore different from each other. Members in the productive sphere find themselves in a field which is typified by variety and diversification rather than uniformity and similitude.

I have devoted sometimes implicitly and sometimes explicitly,
a considerable part of my discussion of the history of The Kvutza
and Hofra to the argument that the kibbutz can best be understood
when its economic aspect (or its property as a meshek corporation)
is treated as a fundamental and primary trait. The Israeli
kibbutz has prevailed as long as the commune anchored itself in
an independent meshek. The evidence is that all other communes
in Israel have eventually disbanded. The importance of the
economic aspect is obviously one of the major sources for the
paramountcy of the system of labor in the kibbutz: I state this
without undervaluing the contribution of ideologies, flourishing
mainly in the Youth Movement, which extol physical and agricultural labor as values in themselves. A central problem which emerges
is that while resources at the command of the commune are shared
or allocated fundamentally equally, the sphere in which these
resources are produced or created is full of variations. In
other words, variations in the sphere of labor seem to exceed
variations in spheres of consumption, personal services, or
elementary or secondary education.

I have set out to search for the similar in the different,
i.e., for those elements in the sphere of labor in which all
the members in the agricultural branches tend to share in their
respective social positions despite the variety of occupations,
jobs, crops and branches. I suggest that such elements do exist,
and that despite variety in the sphere of labor it is possible
to unveil a few traits of the social position in this diversified sphere which are shared by nearly all the members. In my
search for a common denominator I have limited myself to discussing only those elements which, I argue, are necessary if a
member's social position is to be essentially equal to that of

279

his comrades. In other words, I have dwelt particularly on those elements which constitute the social position of any member in the sphere of agricultural work, and without which the member would lack a primary condition for initial equality with other members. I will return to this problem presently, but I would like to suggest here that if such elements do exist, i.e., if there are some minimal components of the social position of a member, which are relevant to the positions of all the members and without which he would suffer severe disadvantage in this sphere, then these elements become social assets for him. They are assets in the sense that they are essential to his position; they guarantee a standing of initial equality to others; and their absence entails disadvantageous repercussions for him. It is therefore in the interest of every member in the productive field to be equipped with these elementary assets.

I have been led by my observations in the kibbutz to enquire whether common and minimal, morphological or structural elements are to be found in the social positions of all the members in the diversified field of production. I have also endeavored to go further than that. I suggest that a member must be equipped with these assets so as to be initially equal with others in this field. The equality to which I refer is essentially negative in nature: a member is equal to his fellows when, like them, he is in a position to resist pressures from his own community and its representatives. Once he is in the position to do this, he is equal to his fellows in a positive sense. But to get this position, he must belong to a branch. Then his opinion on matters relevant to his branch and work, his attitudes and his behavior, are taken into consideration; they are recognized as having merit; he is one of a team which shares responsibility and takes decisions together, a team which together enjoys access to whatever resources there are in a branch. He is one of a team which, by carrying out its obligations, responsibilities, and tasks, and which by controlling, to a considerable extent, the resources in the branch, is in a position to demand the attention and the consideration of the community.

All members are dependent on the kibbutz, of course, in many spheres, but one measure of equality is the degree to which one is less dependent than others, on the public and its officers, in relation to goodwill, understanding and enjoyment of access to resources, which are shared with others. A member is one of the team, equal to his fellows, in the positive sense, when he is able to resist, or deter, pressures. He is able to resist pressure if he is equipped with these assets. This solves the apparent paradox that enjoyment of a fair amount of equality in the commune in this field requires a fair amount of independence as against the commune. The ability of almost all the members, within limits, to retain this immediate independence[2] is a basis for a band of equals. Therefore the elements in the sphere of labor which contribute to the individual's share of immediate autonomy (while being, of course, involved in relations of mutual dependence in many spheres), are assets for his social position vis-a-vis his fellow branchmen and the community.

The elements of work roles I have discussed are: (a) permanence in work; (b) specialization in work and division of labor; and (c) the corporate support of the work (branch) team. Usually these elements are conceived as self-evident or "natural." Every member engaged in agriculture and related services is expected to be permanent in his branch; to specialize in some field within it, and to belong to the body of a corporate team by virtue of his permanence in the branch. Indeed, possession of, or control over, these assets is regarded as being so obvious that they do not contribute an explicit subject for reflection. They are taken for granted and considered to be the normal characteristics of the work role. Therefore, for the members to realize the significance of these elements and for the student of the kibbutz to be aware of them, there must occur an event, or a sequence of events, in which a member fails to respond to these expectations and thereby brings the problem into the open. Breaches in these regularities of behavior help to unveil these elements and to show their significance. Paraphrasing Peristiany's observation "A study of law in the breach is a study of beliefs in action," (Peristiany, 1956: 34-49), I suggest that a study of common practice, sanctioned by public opinion, in the breach is a study of the expectations of people in action. This is another reason why I have chosen to analyze the constituent elementary assets of an individual's position in work from a 'negative' angle, i.e., as being 'defensive' in nature. Let me repeat immediately that I do not regard them as having 'defensive' or 'negative' aspects only: they are conditions whose fulfilment permits a branch worker further to assert and strengthen his position in the branch and in the team. If a branch worker fulfils these conditions, he can specialize further, he can acquire experience in various fields within the branch, he may share managerial control, he may satisfy personal professional or scientific curiosity, and so forth. If these elements are present in his work role, they may serve as a springboard for further achievements. But their primary value, at least logically, to the branchman is the power they give him to resist threats to his position in the sphere of work. In this sense they have a 'negative,' 'defensive' role. Hence I discussed the deterrent power of the individual (in Chapter III) and of team-support (in Chapter IV), both in relation to the organized community and to its authorities; hence also the discussion about the individual's power which stems from the branch's division of labor, now in relation to branch fellows (Chapter V).

As I have suggested above, the significance of the elementary assets, particularly their defensive meaning, is most clearly discernible in situations where a member is not in the position to enjoy them equally with others. His position in the branch and in the field of labor in general is tested when it is regarded, by the individual himself or by his team, as threatened. Then the significance of these assets, particularly permanence in, and support from, the team, is taken into cognizance. A branchman is equal to others when he enjoys these assets: he is then one with them. If he does not enjoy elementary assets, his membership in the kibbutz is by no means threatened or even reduced, but his position in the important sphere of labor is weaker than that of others. And, as shown in the case of the young man of Hardoof (Chapter III), a weakened position in this sphere also affects the social position of a member in the community beyond the sphere of labor.

To conclude, then: (a) In order to be an equal in the productive commune, the member must, within the constraints of communal life, be invulnerable to arbitrary pressures which originate in the commune itself; and
(b) This relative, immediate, independence from arbitrary pressures is restricted by considerations of the common interests and common objectives of the actors concerned. The individual himself in his multifarious roles as a worker, as a branchman and a team-member, and as a member of the kibbutz, is constrained by the members of the branch-team, and by other members of the kibbutz, particularly those endowed with central authority and responsibility in the field of labor. In the present analysis I have regarded the latter fact as a given. I have referred to this aspect of the interplay between a member, his fellows and the community only when I deemed it essential to do so.

Inevitably, too, the analysis has reflected more areas of strain or of potential strain than it has areas of co-operation. I stress again that that is not to argue that these areas are more important or more significant in kibbutz life or for the understanding of the kibbutz. It is the selection of the problem which has determined the focus on certain areas rather than on others. A parallel focus on the common objectives would enrich the contents of the analysis would render it more meaningful, and would balance the understanding presented here of the sphere of labor in the kibbutz.

## Mixed farming and the position of the individual

Economically, Hofra is a diversified meshek, mainly a mixed-
farm. It will be recalled that The Kvutza embarked upon a policy
of mixed farming from the time it first settled in the Valley.
Citrus trees, vegetables, cereal crops, and fodder were sown or
planted, to be followed by bananas, deciduous trees, sub-tropical
and nut crops, vines, flowers (mostly gladioli), artichokes, and
cotton. Bees, poultry and a dairy were introduced later. In
adopting this policy Hofra followed a national kibbutz pattern
(Kanovsky, 1966: 104-105). Eventually, fewer though larger
branches became dominant (see Chapter V and Cohen, 1963).
Production of vegetables ceased in the 1950s, of dairy products
and the related fodder in 1950, of honey in 1962, of bananas in
1965, and of the last remnants of the cereal crops, once the
romanticized branch ('falha'), in 1969. The artichoke and the
flower branches have just ceased production (1970/71). But this
trend should not be misunderstood: Hofra has not become, as a
result of the disappearance of a few crops or animals, a monocultural farm. Firstly, the introduction of cotton, of fish, and
of some of the sub-tropical crops is relatively recent. They
fill in part of the gap created by the disappearance of cereal
crops, bananas, and artichokes. Secondly, the meshek keeps developing as a mixed farm: the citrus grove as well as the orchard
and cotton continue to expand. The meshek tends to become a
composite unit of a few larger branches each of which encompasses
a variety of crops. Indeed, its plurality of crops, in principle,
is as significant as the decrease in the number of the branches.

Kanovsky considers the practice of the old policy of mixed
farming to be one of the reasons which curtail the profitability
of the kibbutz (1966 , 104-106; 137).[3] I do not enter a discussion
on the economic merits of this suggestion. I would like, however,
to point at another aspect of mixed farming which is directly
relevant to the present analysis. Mixed farming, even on its
present relatively small scale in Hofra, provides the individual
member with some range of freedom in selecting an agricultural
occupation. A private farmer would tend, in all probability, as
Kanovsky shows, to shift crops according to fluctuations in
profitability. The kibbutz is much slower, according to Kanovsky,
in responding to this incentive. But mixed farming allows the
individual in the kibbutz (as distinct from the meshek organization) to consider, within its plurality of crops, factors other
than profitability. While the kibbutz as such must weigh economic
and financial considerations, the individual may select his
agricultural occupation through following personal inclination,
professional curiosity, availability of technological opportunities or various other considerations. Furthermore, mixed farming

283

allows the individual to change an already-held agricultural
occupation for another by moving from one branch to another
within the same meshek. Most of the members of Hofra have
changed branches (see Table 3.4). Change of branch may solve
interpersonal difficulties as well as gratify one or more of
the motives listed above.

In a word, mixed farming helps the individual to maintain
a degree of autonomy in selecting an occupation and a branch
from a variety of choices; and later in having the potential
ability to change branches. The latter is significant vis-a-vis
his fellow branchmen; the former and the latter are significant
vis-a-vis the meshek authorities and the community. In both
cases the position of the individual is strengthened vis-a-vis
the significant others.

Ultimately, economic considerations outweigh other considerations in determining the fate of a declining branch if it totally
loses economic viability. But had I had space, I could have
recorded here a number of instances in which branchmen fought
(by the institutionalized recognized methods) to save their
doomed branch, thereby attempting to save their own position in
the meshek and in the sphere of work. They fought in the face of
economic evidence of the branch's unprofitability. Whatever else
they were doomed to lose and to miss by the eventual disappearance
of their branch (a subject deserving a full-scale analysis on its
own), initial personal autonomy was one of the major assets.

Whatever the economic merits of mixed farming in the
economy of the kibbutz, its implications for the individual are,
then: (a) a relatively wide range of choice in agricultural
occupations and branches; and (b) the possibility to select a
personal occupation according to considerations other than maximization of profits. These two assets give rise to (c) a degree
of autonomy vis-a-vis the community and its authorities; and
(d) a degree of independence, or a bargaining position, vis-a-
vis one's own fellow branchmen.

The member and the non-member

I have referred time and again to 'assets.' For the
possessor of the assets, the term usually connotes a positive
meaning. Although I have referred to aspects of control under
which the individual works and establishes his position, I have
concentrated mainly on those elements of his social position in
the sphere of work which I regard as assets. I wish to stress
that the discussion has concentrated on the position of the

284

member. However, the members of the kibbutz are not the only workers in the agricultural sector of the meshek. There are also various categories of other workers: transient groups of secondary and agricultural school pupils who come for a few days to earn money for a group project; groups of members of the youth movement (affiliated with The Movement) who stay and work in the meshek for harvesting seasons; the Ulpan group, whose people work for six months half a day and study the other half; individual temporary visitors; and, finally, hired workers. In my analysis I have referred to the presence of these workers who are not members, directly in the introductory part of Chapter III and by implication throughout the discussion. As I have had no space to devote to the division of labor between members and the 'others' (as I called them in Chapter III), relevant as it is to the analysis of the position of the member in the meshek, detailed study of the positions and the roles of these workers falls, regrettably, beyond the scope of my present analysis. But in order to give the appropriate perspective, I report that in the agricultural year 1968/69 the members' share of all labor in the agricultural branches was 61.3 per cent, the share of temporaries and Ulpan members was 12.7, and the hired workers' share 26.3 per cent.[4] The significance of the presence of non-members in the labor force in the present context is that it enables the student to contrast the position of the member with that of the non-member in respect of the main line of the argument. I have argued that growth and development of the mixed farming economy of the kibbutz affected, through social processes and mechanisms, the position of the individual in the meshek, so that the individual is in a position to derive assets from this situation which makes various resources available to him. The member has access to these resources and he can derive assets for his position by virtue of his status of membership. By contrast, the non-member, who works in the same developing meshek, has no access to these assets. In other words, processes of economic growth and change have led to differential access to assets: they open access to assets to members to the exclusion of others. When this is realized, the significance of these assets for the member emerges more clearly.

In very broad terms, permanence in the agricultural branch, which is the primary asset in establishing an autonomous social position in the meshek, is enjoyed only by the member. The two annual cycles of employment mobility (discussed in Chapter III) show clearly that while members tend to move in a cycle of jobs within the framework of the branch, the non-members tend to move in response to seasonal demands for labor from one branch to another. Their 'orbit' is wider on the whole meshek scale. They cannot establish an attachment to the branch similar to that of the members who comprise the residual nucleus of branch workers. They are not an integral part of the branch team.

Permanence is pregnant with potential specialization. A worker who is permanent in the branch, and who very seldom leaves it, enjoys the potential access to jobs the demand for which arises in the branch, while the impermanent worker may be sent to work somewhere else. By remaining in the branch, the permanent worker stands the chance of enhancing his familiarity with multiple aspects of the crops, the work, and the branch in general. Without permanence, chances of specialization, systematic as well as unsystematic, are hindered. This advantage over the impermanent worker extends further into situations in which the impermanent does work in the branch. Professional knowledge and skill are controlled mainly by the permanent workers, namely the members. So is access to vehicles, and complex tools and equipment. The kibbutz sends its members to regional study-days, and to training and theoretical courses, thus advancing their range and depth of knowledge of and experience in the field of work. While growth and development of the meshek and the branch give rise to specialization in a variety of spheres, these processes, by economic and organizational necessity, raise the demand for seasonal mass-labor as well. If specialization brings advantages in job-satisfaction itself and in social power and individual autonomy, mass-labor places the worker in a comparative disadvantage in both respects. Thus the social significance of specialization appears more clearly against the background of the presence of workers in the branch who have no, or hardly any, access to achieving it. To be fair, I should perhaps add that most of the transient worker-residents have no interest either in permanence or, more clearly, in specialization.

As has been shown, the non-member is significantly more mobile than the member. Temporary workers are assigned to jobs away from the branch as soon as the seasonal pressure is over, with the full consent of the remaining permanent team. When demand for labor in other branches is high, hired workers are assigned to those branches as well, leaving the members in their branch. The mechanism of branch support is activated in relation to these categories of workers only when demand for labor is still high and pressing within the branch. The political support, which, I argue, is activated by the team both in situations of economic need and beyond them does not apply to non-members in the latter situations. Branches compete for temporary and hired workers during their respective peak seasons, but their teams would not align to keep these workers in the branch beyond what is recognized by the meshek to be an essential need. The political element of support is applicable mostly when a member is concerned.

Perhaps it is possible to suggest, in conclusion, that the situation in which the non-member functions is complementary to that in which the member functions. The nature of agriculture demands a considerable degree of fluctuation in work and seasonal

286

mobility of workers, the more so as the meshek develops. An individual is in a position to acquire and establish assets of permanence in his work and further specialization when another individual takes over the temporary, seasonal work which mostly requires mass labor. And it is expected that the system of team-support would apply mainly to the permanent, residual workers, who are members of the kibbutz. Pressure on them is eased because there are non-members available to be moved to meet the needs of the meshek.

In the course of the discussion I have referred to the value-judgments prevailing in the community, which enhance conformity of members to expectations. These operate in the field of allocation of labor to different categories of workers. Members offer value-judgments and notions of what is appropriate or inappropriate, right or wrong, in respect of the practice of the division of labor in general and in respect of the rights and duties of the members. It should be noted that in this brief discussion of the assets the member crystallizes in his social position vis-a-vis the non-member, I do not wish to suggest that the non-member has no assets at all vis-a-vis the members of the kibbutz. There is a wealth of material on this subject, some of it in sociological studies, but I cannot devote more space to it here.

The point of my last comments on the work of non-members in the meshek is that observation of the position of the non-member can shed light on the position of the member in the relevant sphere and help us to understand and assess it. And it is the study of the social position of the member of the kibbutz in the sphere of labor on which the analysis has concentrated.

# N O T E S

1. The term 'mixed farm' pertains to the agricultural economy.
   'Diversified economy' designates an economy which encompasses
   both agriculture and industry or manufacture (R. Cohen, 1968).
   Kanovsky (1966) applies the latter term to mixed farming only.

2. 'Immediate,' because in a wider context any member is dependent on the kibbutz for livelihood, social status and social
   security.  The members of the kibbutz share common objectives
   and common interests.

3. "... another factor which might explain the generally poorer
   profitability of the kibbutzim [as compared with moshavim]
   is their adoption of the concept of a diversified economy
   [see footnote 1].  The rationale was the avoidance of wide
   fluctuations in production, income, and labor requirements
   which typify a monocultural economy.  However, the goal of
   a diversified economy often runs counter to the maximization
   of profits, and will frequently bring about lower average net
   incomes than those obtainable through specialization"
   (Kanovsky, 1966: 105).

4. For more detailed data, particularly in relation to seasonal
   shifts, see Table 3.2 (Chapter III).

## AUTHORITY [OF THE KIBBUTZ]

### (Excerpt)

7. The kibbutz shall, for the purpose of performing its objects, be empowered:

(a) To establish and operate projects, whether permanent, temporary or of an isolated nature, in the fields of agriculture, fishing, quarrying industry, craft, building, public works, transport, education, culture, medicine, art and science, tourism, recreation, entertainment and sport.

(b) To carry out business, commercial, financial, insurance and other acts of whatsoever kind connected with the administration and development of the projects of the kibbutz, the supply of raw material and other needs of the agricultural kibbutz, and all other projects thereof, the marketing of their products, the supply of the needs and services in all fields of the members of the kibbutz and their dependents and of any other person other than a member of the kibbutz residing within the confines of the kibbutz settlement in accordance with a special agreement of the kibbutz.

(c) To enter into contracts, to acquire, and lease, moveable and immovable property and rights of any kind whatsoever, including patents, trademarks, production rights and concessions of any kind, to hold and transfer the same in any manner, and to be a party to any negotiations or agreement, or a litigant in any legal proceeding or any other dispute.

(d) To receive from any person or entity without limitation, loans, deposits, guarantees and credit of any kind, and incur liabilities of any kind, and, with respect thereto, to give securities and bonds, including mortgages, pledges, and charges of property whether moveable or immovable, and rights of any kind whatsoever.

(e) To give loans, deposits, guarantees and credit of any kind and with respect thereto, to receive guarantees, securities and obligations, including mortgages, pledges and charges of property whether moveable or immovable and rights of any kind whatsoever.

(f) To sign, draw, receive, endorse, transfer, sell, collect, discount, issue and do any other act with respect to promissory notes, bills of exchange, debentures, shares, other than the issue of shares, bills of lading negotiable or other transferable instruments of any kind.

(g) To insure itself, its members and their dependants, and likewise its workers, and guests, against damage to property and person, and likewise against other risks of whatsoever kind, and to enter into agreements of guarantee and mutual liability with other settlements.

(h) To participate, whether as members or otherwise, in associations, companies, partnerships or other legal entities.

Source:

Regulations of the [Kibbutz] Association, issued by The Movement as a Central Co-operative Association, Ltd.

CHART 1.    APPENDIX II

# DISTRIBUTION OF ADULT POPULATION ACCORDING TO YEAR OF BIRTH AND CATEGORIES OF POPULATION, HOFRA, 1970.

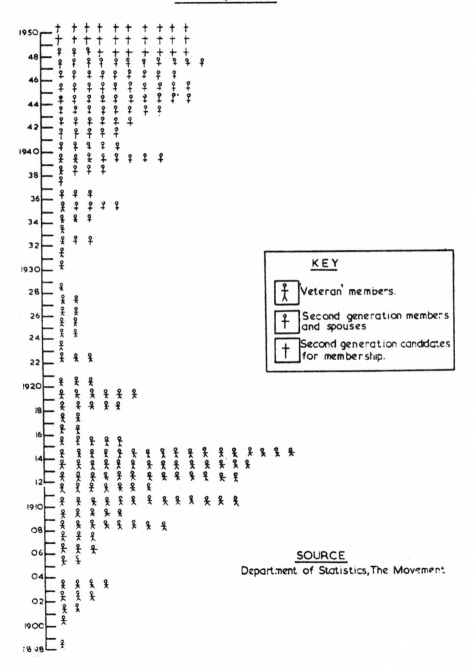

KEY

Veteran members.

Second generation members and spouses

Second generation candidates for membership.

SOURCE
Department of Statistics, The Movement.

291

# REFERENCES

Abarbanel, J.S.
(1974)    The Co-operative farmer and the Welfare State;
          Economic Change in an Israeli Moshav, Manchester:
          Manchester University Press.

Avi-Yonah, M.
(1964)    'The History of the Valley of Hefer', in: Essays
          and Studies in the Lore of the Holy Land, Tel-
          Aviv - Jerusalem: M. Neuman (Hebrew).

Baldwin, E.
(1972)    Differentiation and Co-operation in an Israeli
          Veteran Moshav, Manchester: Manchester
          University Press.

Ben-Avram, B.
(1976)    Hever-Hakvutzoth; Its Social and Ideological
          Development, Tel-Aviv: Am-Oved - Tarbut
          Vechinuch  (Hebrew).

Ben-David, J.
(1964)    'The Kibbutz and the Moshav,' in: J. Ben-David
          (ed.), Agricultural Planning and Village
          Community in Israel,  (Arid Zone Research XXIII),
          Paris: UNESCO.

Bierstedt, R.
(1963)    The Social Order, an Introduction to Sociology,
          New York: McGraw-Hill.

Bowes, A.
(1975)    Ideology and Communal Society: The Israeli
          Kibbutz, Working Papers in Social Anthropology,
          Vol. 1, Durham: University of Durham.

Buber, M.
(1949)    'An Experiment that Did Not Fail,' in: Paths
          in Utopia, Boston: Beacon Press.

Cherry, C.
(1957)    On Human Communication, New York; M.I.T.;
          London: Chapman & Hall.

Chinoy, E.
(1961)    Society, an Introduction to Sociology, New
          York: Random House.

Cohen, E.
  (1957)   'Forms of Institutionalization of Work Organiz-
         ation in the Kibbutz,' <u>Niv Hakvutza</u>, vol. 7,
         no. 2 (Hebrew).

  (1962)   'Integration of the Labor Groups in Hakibbutz-
         HaArtzi,' <u>Hedim</u>, no. 70 (Hebrew).

  (1963a)   'Changes in the Structure of Work Organization
         in the Kibbutz,' <u>Economic Quarterly</u>, vol. 10,
         no. 40 (Hebrew).

  (1963b)   'Meeting of the Branch Workers in the Kibbutz,'
         <u>Hedim,</u> no. 75 (Hebrew).

  (1966)   'Progress and Communality: Value Dilemmas in the
         Collective Movement,' <u>International Review of</u>
         <u>Community Development</u>, vol. 15-16.

Cohen, R.
  (1968)   <u>The Kibbutz Settlement, Principles and Processes,</u>
         Tel-Aviv: Hakibbutz Hameuchad (Hebrew).

Dahl, R.A.
  (1957)   'The Concept of Power,' <u>Behavioral Science</u>,
         Vol. 2.

Daniel, A.
  (1975)   <u>The Co-operative Legislation in Israel</u>, Tel-Aviv:
         Am-Oved - Tarbut Vechinuch (Hebrew).

Dayan, S.
  (1947)   <u>The Moshav Ovdim</u>, Tel-Aviv: Palestine Pioneer
         Press Library, no. 6.

Devons, E. and Gluckman, M.
  (1964)   'Introduction' and 'Conclusion,' in: M. Gluckman
         (ed.), <u>Closed Systems and Open Minds, the Limits</u>
         <u>of Naivety in Social Anthropology</u>, Edinburgh:
         Oliver & Boyd.

Durkheim, E.
  (1964)   <u>The Division Labor in Society</u>, New York: Free
         Press; London: Collier-MacMillan (French
         original, 1893).

Eisenstadt, S.N.
  (1967)   <u>Israeli Society</u>, London: Weidenfeld and Nicolson.

Emerson, R.M.
  (1962)   'Power-Dependence Relations,' <u>American Socio-</u>
         <u>logical Review</u>, vol. 27, no. 1.

Fedida, M.
    (1972)        The Dynamics of Career Patterns among Political
                    Activists in a Kibbutz, M.A. Dissertation,
                    University of Tel-Aviv   (Hebrew).

Frankenberg, R.
    (1966)        Communities in Britain, Harmondsworth, Middle-
                    sex: Penguin Books.

Garfinkel, H.
    (1956)        'Conditions of Successful Degradation
                    Ceremonies,' American Journal of Sociology,
                    vol. 61, no. 5.

Gerth, H.H. and Wright Mills, E. (ed.)
    (1967)        From Max Weber: Essays in Sociology, London:
                    Routledge & Kegan Paul.

Gertz, A.
    (1955)        'The Story of the Settlement,' in: A. Gertz (ed.),
                    Emek Hefer, Facts and History, Emek Hefer:
                    The Regional Council   (Hebrew).

Gluckman, M.
    (1955)        The Judicial Process among the Barotse of
                    Northern Rhodesia, Manchester: Manchester
                    University Press.

    (1963)        'Gossip and Scandal,' Current Anthropology,
                    vol. 4.

    (1968)        'Psychological, Sociological and Anthropological
                    Explanations of Witchcraft and Gossip:
                    Clarification,' Man, vol. 3, no. 1.

    (1972)        'Introduction,' in: M. Gluckman (ed.), The
                    Allocation of Responsibility, Manchester:
                    Manchester University Press.

Gordon, A.D.
    (1962)        The Nation and Labor, Jerusalem: The Zionist
                    Library   (Hebrew).

Hakvutza
    (1924)        Anthology, Tel-Aviv: Cultural Committee,
                    General Federation of Labor (Histadrut)
                    (Hebrew).

Halperin, H.
    (1957)        Changing Patterns in Israeli Agriculture,
                    London: Routledge & Kegan Paul.

Hofra

Balance Sheet for 1966/67; for 1967/68 (Hebrew)

Economic Plan for 1969/70 (Hebrew)

Labor Records, 1952-1970; 1968/69 (Hebrew)

Labor Registration, 1969 (Hebrew)

Local Bulletin (Hebrew)

Ihud Hakvutzoth Vehakibbutzim
(No date) Regulations of the Association (Hebrew)
(Department of Statistics) Population Census.

Kanovsky, E.
(1966) The Economy of the Israeli Kibbutz, Cambridge,
Mass.: Harvard University Press.

Katz, F.
(1968) Autonomy and Organization, the Limits of Social
Control, New York: Random House.

Kressel, G.M.
(1974) "From Each According to His Ability...,"
Stratification vs. Equality in a Kibbutz,
Tel-Aviv: Gome, Czerikower (Hebrew).

Kuhn, M.H.
(1964) 'The Reference Group Reconsidered,' Sociological
Quarterly, no. 5.

Labes, E.
(1962) Handbook of the Moshav, Jerusalem: Haikar Haoved
and the Youth and Hechalutz Department of the
World Zionist Organization.

Leach, E.R.
(1954) Political Systems of Highland Burma, a Study of
Kachin Social Structure, London: G. Bell and
Sons.

Leon, D.
(1964) The Kibbutz, Tel-Aviv: Israel Horizons in
collaboration with World Hashomer-Hatzair.

Levithan, U.
(1976) 'Centrality of Work in the Life of the Elderly
in the Kibbutz,' Gerontologia, vol. 2, no. 2(6)
(Hebrew).

Luz, K.
(1962) Milestones, Tel-Aviv: Mifaley Tarbut Wechinuch
(Hebrew).

Martindale, D.
    (1964)       'Formation and Destruction of Communities,'
                    in: G.K. Zollschan and W. Hirsch (ed.),
                    Explorations in Social Change, Boston: Houghton
                    Mifflin & Co.

Orni, E.
    (1963)       Forms of Settlements, Jerusalem: Youth and
                    Hechalutz Department of World Zionist
                    Organization.

Orni, E. and Efrat, E.
    (1966)       Geography of Israel, Second Revised Edition,
                    Jerusalem: Israel Program for Scientific
                    Translation.

Peristiany, J.G.
    (1956)       'Law,' in:  The Institutions of Primitive
                    Society, Oxford: Blackwell.

Peter, L. and Hull, R.
    (1969)       The Peter Principle, London: Pan Book.

Peters, E.L.
    (1963)       'Aspects of Rank and Status among Muslims in a
                    Lebanese Village,' in: J.H. Pitt-Rivers (ed.),
                    Mediterranean Countrymen, Paris: Mouton.

    (1972)       'Shifts in Power in a Lebanese Village,' in:
                    R. Antoun and I. Harik (ed.), Rural Politics
                    and Social Change in the Middle East,
                    Bloomington: Indiana University Press.

Radcliffe Brown, A.R.
    (1950)       'Introduction,' in: A.R. Radcliffe Brown and
                    C. Daryll Forde (ed.), African Systems of
                    Kinship and Marriage, London: Oxford University
                    Press.

Reshumot          The Official Gazette of Israel, Jerusalem
                    (Hebrew).

Rosenfeld, E.
    (1951)       'Social Stratification in a Classless Society,'
                    American Sociological Review, no. 16.

Rosner, M.
    (1964)       'Difficulty and Reward in the Role of Branch
                    Manager,' Hedim, no. 76-77   (Hebrew).

Saunders, M.
    (1970)       Alternative London, London: Published by the
                    Author.

Schelling, T.C.
    (1963)      The Strategy of Conflict, Cambridge, Mass.:
               Harvard University Press.

Schweid, E.
    (1970)      The World of A.D. Gordon, Tel-Aviv: Am Oved
               (Hebrew).

Shatz, Z.
    (1929)      On the Border of Silence, Tel-Aviv: Davar
               (Hebrew).

Shepher, J.
    (1966)      'The Kibbutz Members as Office Holders in the
               Kibbutz Federation,' Niv Hakvutza, vol. 15,
               no. 1 (Hebrew).

Shepher I.
    (1972)      The Significance of Work-Roles in the Social
               System of a Kibbutz, Unpublished PhD Thesis,
               Manchester: University of Manchester.

Shepher, Z.
    (1960)      Society in its Growth: the Kibbutz, Tel-Aviv:
               Am Oved (Hebrew).

Shibutani, T.
    (1955)      'Reference Groups as Perspectives,' American
               Journal of Sociology, LX.

Simmel, G.
    (1950)      The Sociology of Georg Simmel, edited by K.H.
               Wolff, New York: The Free Press of Glencoe.

Spiro, M.
    (1956)      Kibbutz, Venture in Utopia, Cambridge, Mass.:
               Harvard University Press.

Talmon-Garber, Y.
    (1956)      'Differentiation in Collective Settlements,'
               Scripta Hierosolymitana, no. 3, Jerusalem:
               Magness Press, The Hebrew University.

    (1964)      'Sex-Role Differentiation in an Equalitarian
               Society,' in: T.G. Laswell, L. Burma and
               S. Aronson (ed.), Sociology and Life, Chicago:
               Scott, Foresman & Co.

    (1965)      'The Family in a Revolutionary Movement,' in:
               M. Nimkoff (ed.), Comparative Family Systems,
               Boston: Houghton, Mifflin & Co.

Talmon-Garber, Y.
  (1970)         'Parental Role in Occupational Placement of the
                 Second Generation,' in: The Kibbutz, Sociological
                 Studies, Jerusalem: The Magness Press, The Hebrew
                 University (Hebrew). Originally published in
                 Megamoth, vol. 8, 1957.

Toren, A.
  (1955)         'On the Fauna and Flora,' in: A. Gertz (ed.),
                 Emek Hefer, Facts and History, Emek Hefer; The
                 Regional Council  (Hebrew).

Troeltsch, E.
  (1931)         The Social Teachings of the Christian Churches,
                 New York: MacMillan.

Turner, V.W.
  (1957)         Schism and Continuity in an African Society,
                 Manchester: Manchester University Press.

Veblen, T.B.
  (1922)         The Instinct of Workmanship and the State of
                 Industrial Arts, New York: B.W. Huebsch.

Weber, M.
  (1947)         The Theory of Social and Economic Organization,
                 New York: Free Press.

Weitz, J.
  (1939)         The Sharon, Tel-Aviv: Omanuth   (Hebrew).

Yuchtman, E.
  (1972)         'Reward Distribution and Work-Role Attractive-
                 ness in the Kibbutz, Reflection on Equity Theory,
                 American Sociological Review, vol. 37.

Ziv, J.
  (1960)         The Sharon, Tel-Aviv: Mifaley Tarbut Wechinuch
                 (Hebrew).